CLASSROOM ORIENTED RESEARCH IN SECOND LANGUAGE ACQUISITION

NEWBURY HOUSE PUBLISHERS, INC.
ROWLEY, MASSACHUSETTS 01969
ROWLEY • LONDON • TOKYO

1983

Library of Congress Cataloging in Publication Data

Main entry under title:

Classroom oriented research in second language
    acquisition.

    1. Language and languages--Study and teaching--
Addresses, essays, lectures. 2. Language acquisition--
Addresses, essays, lectures. I. Seliger, Herbert W.,
1937–   . II. Long, Michael H.
P51.C56 1983   418'.001'9   82-22533
ISBN 0-88377-267-1

Cover design by Leslie Bartlett

NEWBURY HOUSE PUBLISHERS, INC.

Language Science
Language Teaching
Language Learning

ROWLEY, MASSACHUSETTS 01969
ROWLEY • LONDON • TOKYO

First printing: October 1983
Printed in the U.S.A.   5   4   3

Contents

Contributors

Kathleen M. Bailey, Monterey Institute for International Studies, Monterey, CA.

Leslie M. Beebe, Teachers College, Columbia University, New York, NY.

Ellen Bialystok, Department of Psychology, York University, Downsview, Ontario, Canada.

Craig Chaudron, Department of English as a Second Language, University of Hawaii at Manoa, Honolulu, HI.

Stephen J. Gaies, Department of English, University of Northern Iowa, Cedar Falls, IA.

Nancy Johnson Nystrom, School of Education, Tulane University, New Orleans, LA.

Diane Larsen-Freeman, School for International Training, Experiment in International Living, Brattleboro, VT.

Patsy M. Lightbown, TESL Centre, Concordia University, Montreal, Quebec, Canada.

Michael H. Long, Department of English as a Second Language, University of Hawaii at Manoa, Honolulu, HI.

Charlene J. Sato, Department of English as a Second Language, University of Hawaii at Manoa, Honolulu, HI.

Linda A. Schinke-Llano, Department of Linguistics, Northwestern University, Evanston, IL.

Herbert W. Seliger, Department of Linguistics, Queens College, City University of New York, NY.

1

Introduction: What Is Classroom Oriented Research?

Herbert W. Seliger and Michael H. Long

A question that inevitably arises at conferences on second language acquisition is concerned with the relationship between research findings in second language acquisition and what takes place in the language classroom. Language teachers sometimes express impatience, bordering on hostility, with researchers and their work. Teachers often fail to see any connection between what they, the practitioners of language teaching, are expected to do on a daily basis in the classroom and what researchers report. How can a discussion of the order of acquisition of certain grammatical structures be relevant to the needs of an inner-city ESL teacher or a teacher of English as a foreign language in a far-off country?

Language teaching, we are told, is a combination of art and science. Research can do little to illuminate that part of language teaching concerned with art. However, research can make a significant contribution to understanding those aspects of language learning in the classroom that are amenable to scientific analysis.

The articles presented in this text are examples of research that has attempted to answer relevant and important questions concerned with language acquisition in the classroom environment. However, while the presentation of such research is not unique—there have been colloquia and conferences devoted to second language acquisition in the classroom—this text attempts to carry the relationship of the language teacher and the researcher a bit further. It attempts, through the provision of questions for discussion and limited research assignments, to get the readers of this text to look at similar phenomena in other classrooms and to begin to carry out research projects on their own. In short, it is hoped that this text will demonstrate that the language classroom provides excellent conditions for the study of second language acquisition.

Good language teachers have always acted like researchers, realizing that language teaching and learning are very complex activities which require constant questioning and the analysis of problematic situations: Why do students have difficulty with certain tenses? What is the relationship between what the textbook presents and what students are able to acquire at a particular stage in their language learning development? Why do some learners progress at a faster rate than others? How does the social context of the language classroom affect language learning qualitatively and quantitatively? Important questions such as these can lead the language teacher to either shrug them off or step back, observe dispassionately, form hypotheses about what has taken place, and then carry out his or her own research in the class.

In short, the language teacher and the researcher share the same goal: understanding what is involved in the process of second language acquisition. For the teacher, such an understanding can lead to better facilitating language acquisition in the classroom. For the researcher, the study of language acquisition in a classroom setting provides a unique opportunity to observe in a more controlled environment, to manipulate variables, and to set up conditions for testing specific hypotheses. At the same time the classroom contains enough elements of reality so that, while it is not artificial to the extreme of verbal behavior experiments in a psycholinquistic laboratory, it is also not chaotic in the way that the study of language acquisition in a naturalistic context would be. In this sense, the classroom may be seen as either quasi-naturalistic or quasi-clinical.

The advantages implicit in such research are that findings may be more easily related or applied to actual classroom teaching on the one hand or, on the other, aspects of findings may be further isolated and investigated under more laboratory-like conditions.

The Organization and Content of This Book

This book is divided into five parts. In this introductory chapter, we introduce our views on the nature and role of classroom centered research and its relevance both for the classroom teacher and for second language acquisition (SLA) research.

Part I, *Methodological issues,* consists of just one paper, previously published in *Language Learning* and the only contribution not written especially for this book. In it, Long discusses the variety of procedures for data collection and data analysis available to the classroom researcher who wishes to study what goes on inside that relatively unknown territory that is the SL classroom, the "black box" of the title. Long first describes each procedure and then points out some of their strengths and limitations. The idea is not to advocate use of one procedure over all others. Rather, it is suggested that *all* will be useful at times, depending on the nature of the research question, and that the options can usefully complement each other in a coherent research effort. Long also notes that most existing systems for coding classroom conversation emphasize *process* over *acquisition* variables, and suggests that the latter, too, should inform future instruments. As we suggest in the Introduction, in other words, the two lines of research on instructed and naturalistic SLA should be recognized as fundamentally related.

Part II, *Learner strategies and learner variables,* brings together three empirical studies which focus on the classroom learner. Beebe first reviews the psychological, linguistic, and ESL literature on risk-taking, and then reports on her cross-sectional study of risk-taking among twenty Puerto Rican elementary school children in New York. Risk-taking and accuracy are found to vary (inversely) with each other and with the ethnicity of the interviewer, and also with the linguistic domain studied (phonology, morpho-syntax, and semantics). Beebe interprets her findings in terms of Giles's Accommodation Theory and draws implications for classroom teaching and testing.

Bailey's study, the second paper in this section, provides intriguing insights into competitiveness and anxiety in adult SLL, and does so through the medium of a diary study which seems to hold great promise for classroom research, especially for the study of affect variables. After forming a hypothesis, based on her own experiences in a college class in French (as a foreign language), as to the relationship between competitiveness and anxiety, Bailey reviews ten other (unpublished) diary studies for further evidence for this relationship. She suggests that language classroom anxiety can be caused and/or aggravated by learners' competitivenes if (a) they perceive themselves as less proficient than their fellow students, and (b) the comparison entails ego involvement. Bailey concludes by addressing the controversial issue of the generalizability of findings from diary studies, and discusses some contributions the diary study methodology can make to our understanding of SLA.

The final paper in this section, by Bialystok, focuses on a cognitive strategy, inferencing, and its role in the SL reading process. After reviewing the literature on various types of inferencing and on reading, Bialystok reports two experiments—an initial study, followed by a replication—conducted in Canada with students of high school French as a SL. Results suggest that readers can be taught inferencing techniques which allow them to better utilize supplementary information, verbal or visual, as an aid to comprehension of SL prose. Supplementary lexical information appears to boost both global and lexical comprehension; additional global information, such as that provided by pictures accompanying a text, aids global comprehension only. Bialystok cautions, however, that further research is needed to determine whether the newly learned inferencing techniques are retained over time or whether these apparently beneficial effects of instruction are ephemeral.

Part III, *Teacher speech,* consists of two papers on different aspects of instructional talk. Chaudron and Schinke-Llano describe empirical studies of the speech modifications made by teachers of non-English speakers. Drawing on data from his previous research on foreigner talk by ESL and content teachers, Chaudron illustrates various types of speech adjustments made for students who are non-native speakers of the language of instruction, and proceeds to question their widely *assumed* role in facilitating comprehension. He suggests that "simplifications" of these kinds by teachers may actually *increase* the cognitive processing load for the SL learner, and that elaborations of classroom language may have the reverse effect.

Schinke-Llano's paper is also an empirical study of foreigner talk, but this time during content instruction in twelve fifth and sixth grade classrooms, each of which contained a small number of limited English proficiency (LEP) students. She reports significant differences in the teachers' treatment of LEP and non-LEP students in both the number and functional type of exchanges in which they were involved. The non-native speakers generally participated in half as many exchanges as their English-speaking classmates with only one-third of these exchanges being instructional and all of them briefer. She suggests that the cumulative effect of such classroom inequality will be detrimental to the LEP students' self-esteem and also to their SLA.

There have been at least a dozen studies of ESL teachers' feedback on learner error. Part IV, *Teacher and learner feedback,* brings together two new studies of feedback of a rather different sort. Nancy Johnson Nystrom's paper uses videotaped data from twenty lessons by four teachers of first grade bilingual classrooms. Sequences of students' errors and teachers' responses to them were analyzed for characteristics relating to "interaction" models of child language development. Three styles of feedback were isolated: overtly corrective, covertly corrective, and non-corrective. Teachers were found to be consistent within these traits, but varied in their method of "correction."

The study by Gaies is, we believe, the first to be conducted of *learner* feedback. The data were derived from audiotaped conversations between ESL teachers and adult learners, in both dyads and triads, when participants were engaged in solving a problem concerning referential communication. In addition to developing an initial taxonomy of learner feedback moves in classroom discourse, Gaies argues for the importance of a subset of the moves, those in the category of unsolicited feedback, in allowing learners to negotiate comprehensible input in the classroom.

The final section, V, contains four papers concerned with describing linguistic properties of teachers' and learners' speech in the classroom, and also with establishing relationships between them. The first paper, by Lightbown, describes a longitudinal study of high school ESL classes for French-Canadians in the Montreal area. A relationship *over time* was sought, but none found, between the relative frequencies of certain grammatical morphemes in the input (texts and teachers' speech) and accuracy orders for the production of those items in the learners' output. Lightbown suggests that factors influencing this result probably include the presence of word-final *s* morphemes (unpronounced in the students' native language) among the items examined, and the fact (supported by the analysis of the language of individual learners) that students were constructing their own interlanguage rules. Lightbown goes on to note that the instruction these students receive emphasizes accuracy over communication, is based on a rigid structural syllabus, and amounts to relatively few hours per week spread over a period of years. It seems to be ineffective in promoting SL development in the students examined.

While the chapter by Seliger does examine two basic types of learners, High and Low Input Generators, it is important for looking at the role of the learner in generating his or her own feedback and learning context. This paper reports on two studies on the effects of different interaction patterns in the language classroom. It was found that learners who create their own opportunities to learn, by initiating and participating in language interaction with fellow students and the teacher, progress more rapidly in terms of overall achievement and produce qualitatively different utterances in the second language.

The study by Long and Sato is, we believe, the first explicit comparison of native speaker/non-native speaker conversation in and out of SL classrooms. Its main focus is a discourse analysis of the role of questions in both types of discourse, with data from recordings of six ESL lessons for adults and thirty-six informal native speaker/non-native speaker conversations. The researchers find that the functions and relative frequencies of questions in the two corpora differ greatly, with related effects both on other features of the linguistic *input* to which classroom learners are exposed, and on the *interactional structure* of conversations in which they participate. Long and Sato outline the role these factors probably play in (un)successful SLA in classroom and naturalistic settings.

In the final paper, Larsen-Freeman reports on her research attempting to construct a developmental index of English as a second language for adult learners. Such an index would be invaluable for sequencing the teaching of grammar as well as for the construction of language materials. In the study reported here, Larsen-Freeman has applied techniques, used previously to study development in writing, to the study of development in spoken second language.

How to Use This Book

The editors hope that this collection of papers will serve two main purposes: (1) to familiarize readers with recent empirical research on classroom language acquisition and use in a variety of settings, and (2) to introduce potential researchers to the major issues in research methodology for carrying out this kind of work. As such, it is anticipated that the book will be used in two ways. First, it can simply be read as a volume of research reports and papers on various technical matters related to classroom research. Alternatively, when it is used as a teaching text, instructors and students may choose to work through the sets of "questions for discussion and activities" which follow each paper. These have been chosen to isolate important issues, both substantive and methodological, raised explicitly or implicitly by each writer. They are also designed to encourage initial research efforts by the reader, often involving limited amounts of data collection, data analysis, design, hypothesis formation and testing, and so on. Some sets of questions will undoubtedly prove too time consuming for certain classes, so it is also expected that instructors and students will exercise their discretion.

PART I
Methodological Issues

2

Inside the "Black Box":
Methodological Issues in Classroom Research
on Language Learning[1]

Michael H. Long

The 1960s witnessed several technological and methodological innovations in language teaching, and attempts by researchers to conduct large scale methodological comparisons which, it was hoped, would evaluate them.[2] With various degrees of success, investigators attempted experimental studies. Where possible, large groups of learners were randomly assigned to experimental and control groups. The treatment consisted of method A, B, or C. After a common period of instruction, sometimes as long as two years, the achievement of all students on the same tests was observed and compared. In most cases it seemed method A, B, or C made little or no difference.

In addition to many of the other problems inherent in methodological comparisons of this kind—history, mortality, the Hawthorne effect, and so on (Williams, 1965)—the studies suffered fundamentally from the investigators' inability to describe, still less control, what went on inside the classroom. There was, after all, no classroom observational component in the data collection for this research, the design for which is shown schematically in Figure 1. In other words, there was no guarantee, once a study was over, that teachers had in fact implemented method A, B, or C as prescribed, or that the methods did not overlap in some respects (e.g., through their shared use of a common subset of classroom procedures). In the research context, this means that it is impossible to ascertain which subjects received the treatment. Therefore, even if different groups were to perform differently on a set of achievement tests, there would be no way of knowing to what to attribute the differential performance.

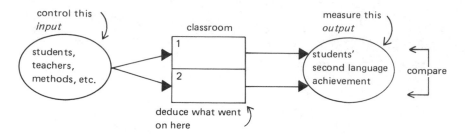

Figure 1.   Schematic representation of design used in the "comparative method" studies

One "solution" to the problem has since been to pre-record the lessons in a study in order to control for—here meaning eliminate—the teacher variable (Levin, 1972; Freedman, 1975). However, this method of increasing internal validity constitutes a rather extreme form of intervention in normal classroom processes, and so considerably reduces external validity, or the generalizability of findings. It is one thing to side-step a problem which is peripheral to the issue at hand, and quite another to set aside a key element in the phenomenon under investigation. In many instances of second language acquisition (SLA) with the aid of formal instruction, including both foreign and second language learning, it is reasonable to assume that what goes on inside classrooms, including the teacher's role in this, is the single most crucial element in determining how students perform (Long, 1979). Hence, the present decade has also witnessed a growing body of research designed to describe natural classroom processes, and in a few cases to relate this to second language achievement.

Students of this approach to the task consider it insufficient to control the input to the classroom language-learning process (students, teachers, methods, materials), measure the output (student achievement), and either ignore or deduce what went on between. They view the classroom not as an impenetrable "black box," but as the setting for a vital field of their inquiries. From this perspective, investigation of classroom language learning may be defined as *research on second language learning and teaching all or part of whose data are derived from the observation or measurement of the classroom performance of teachers and students.*

While "classroom research" may be defined in this way, the methods employed to gather and analyze such data vary greatly. They include the use of behavioral observation systems, discourse analysis, ethnography, constitutive ethnography, and diary studies. These methods fall into two broad categories, those performing some kind of interaction analysis and those describable as forms of anthropological observation. Each has strengths and limitations.

Interaction Analysis

One approach to classroom research as defined above has been the adoption, prior to the period of observation, of some kind of instrument with which to standardize both observers' data-collection procedures and focus. Pioneering work in "content" classrooms (i.e., where history, math, civics, science, etc., not a second language, is the subject of instruction) by Flanders (1970), Bellack, Kliebard, Hyman, and Smith (1966), Wright and Nuthall (1970), and others has encouraged the development of over 200 instruments for describing the classroom behaviors of teachers and students. The field of second language teaching seems to be following this precedent, and there are now at least twenty such systems for coding teacher and student behavior in second language classrooms, whether verbal interaction is classified as discrete linguistic/peda-gogic events or treated as interrelated units of discourse.[3] (See Table 1.) Usually known as "category systems," the instruments consist of lists of (mostly verbal) behaviors which trained observers look for and record (often in the form of tallies or numbers) either while observing lessons as they are taught ("real-time" coding) or later, while working from an audio or video recording and/or a written transcription. The systems differ along several dimensions, apart from the feasibility of their use simultaneous with or subsequent to the initial period of observation and the nature (arbitrary or analytic) of the basic unit of analysis. These differences include (i) the types of recording procedures used, (ii) the kind of items they contain, (iii) their complexity, and (iv) their focus, or the source and range of behaviors they sample.

There are three basic types of instrument as defined by the recording procedure used (Rosenshine and Furst, 1973). When each event is coded each time it occurs we are dealing with a true *category system*. When each event is recorded once only during a fixed time period, however frequently it occurs during that period, we have a *sign system*. When, subsequent to a period of observation, the estimated frequency of a given event is recorded using a scale, usually of from three to seven points, ranging from "high" to "low," "very often" to "never," and so on, we are using a *rating scale.* The procedure used by category systems means that the sequence as well as the frequency of events is preserved, which is important for some kinds of research. However, the use by some sign systems of short time periods lessens this difference between the data they and category systems produce. Several systems employ a three-second coding interval, for example, a period so short that it often does correspond to one (or even part of one) act, such as a question. During rapid drill work, on the other hand, a question and a response often occur within three seconds. Then, following the system's coding conventions, the observer is generally required to alternate between recording, say, teacher question and student response for each three-second period of the drill's duration. The general pattern of this type of interaction is thereby retained, even though individual acts are lost. Such systems, e.g., Moskowitz (1970), are listed as sign systems in Table 1, follow-ing the definitions given above. Systems attempting some kind of discourse analysis of verbal interaction in classrooms, e.g., Allwright (1977), are listed as category systems, as each event in the domain of behavior they handle is coded separately each time it occurs, even if treated as entering a reciprocal relationship with some other "acts" or "moves" elsewhere in the analysis.

Table 1. Classification of Instruments for the Analysis of Interaction in Second Language Classrooms

# Author(s)	Date	Type of recording procedure	Item type 1 Low inf. 2 Hi. inf. 3 Mixed	Number of categories*	Multiple coding	Real time coding*	Source of variables (see Key)
1. Allwright	1977	category	high	16	yes	no	2 4
2. Barkman	1978	category	mixed	61	yes	no	2 3 4
3. Bialystok, Fröhlich, & Howard	1978	category	mixed	47	yes	no	3
4. Capelle, Jarvella, & Revelle	n.d.	category	low	27	no	yes	3 4
5. Capelle, Jarvella, & Revelle	n.d.	category	low	19	no	yes	4
6. Carton	1966	category	mixed	42	yes	no	1 4
7. Fanselow	1977	category	low	73	yes	no	3 4
8. Freudenstein	1976	sign	mixed	53	yes	no	3 4
9. Jarvis	1968	sign	low	24	no	no	2
10. Long, Adams, McLean, & Castaños	1976	category	mixed	45	yes	no	1 3 4
11. McEwan	1976	sign	mixed	36	yes	no	1 2 3 4
12. McFarlane	1975	category	low	17	yes	yes	2 3 4
13. Moskowitz	1970	sign	low	10	no	yes	3
14. Moskowitz	1976	sign	low	34	yes	no	3
15. Naiman, Fröhlich, & Stern	1975	category	mixed	60	yes	no	2 4
16. Nearhoof	1969	sign	low	10	no	yes	3 4
17. Politzer	1977	category	low	16	no	no	2 4
18. Riley	1977	category	mixed	7	yes	no	2 4
19. Rothfarc	1970	sign	low	17	yes	yes	3
20. Seliger	1977	category	low	7	yes	yes	1 4
21. Wesche	1977	category	mixed	20	no	no	4
22. Wragg	1970	sign	low	20	no	yes	3

KEY: *Source of variables:* 1 = *explicit* theoretical or empirical base; 2 = *implicit* theoretical or empirical base; 3 = modification or synthesis of existing system(s); 4 = author-originated categories.#

* Entries based on present author's count or estimation; this sometimes differs from figures and claims made in the references cited.

#This breakdown follows that suggested by Rosenshine and Furst (1973).

There are no entries for rating scales for the simple reason that none seem to have been published for use in second language classrooms. (Many teacher-training institutions use rating forms for evaluating teachers' performances, of course, with scales of "excellent" through "inadequate," etc., but this is not the same operation as describing frequency of events, and is overtly judgmental, not

Table 1 (continued)

# Author(s)	Intended purpose TT/res.*	Unit of analysis (see Key)	Focus: range of behaviors and events sampled (see Key)
1. Allwright	res.	2	1 2 7 8
2. Barkman	res.	2	1 2 3 4 6 8
3. Bialystok, Fröhlich, & Howard	res.	2	1 2 3 6 8
4. Capelle, Jarvella, & Revelle	res./TT	1	1 5 6 7
5. Capelle, Jarvella, & Revelle	res./TT	1	1 7
6. Carton	res./TT	2	1 4 5 6 7 8
7. Fanselow	res./TT	2	1 2 3 6 7
8. Freudenstein	TT	1	1 3 5 6 7
9. Jarvis	res.	1	1 3 6 7
10. Long, Adams, McLean, & Castaños	res.	2	1 4 5 6 8
11. McEwan	res.	1	1 4 5 6 7
12. McFarlane	TT	1	1 2 5 6 7
13. Moskowitz	TT	1	1 5 6
14. Moskowitz	TT/res.	1	1 2 5 6
15. Naiman, Fröhlich, & Stern	res.	2	1 2 3 6 7 8
16. Nearhoof	TT	1	1 6
17. Politzer	res.	2	1 6
18. Riley	res.	2	1 8
19. Rothfarc	TT/res.	1	1 5 6
20. Seliger	res.	2	1
21. Wesche	res.	2	1 2 3 4 5 6
22. Wragg	TT/res.	1	1 5 6

KEY: Unit of analysis: 1 = arbitrary time unit (e.g., 3 secs.); 2 = analytic unit (e.g., move, cycle, episode).
  Focus: 1 = verbal; 2 = paralinguistic; 3 = non-linguistic; 4 = cognitive; 5 = affective; 6 = pedagogic; 7 = content (e.g., grammar); 8 = discourse.
* Teacher training (TT) and/or research (res.) as stated or implied by author(s).
#This breakdown follows part of that suggested by Biddle (1967).

a research activity.) The rating scale benefits from the insights available from holistic, retrospective analyses, although it is also the type of instrument most at risk from the fallibility of observers' memory and the amount of interpretation embodied in the data it produces.

Instruments differ, too, as to the kinds of item they contain, particularly as to the degree of inference they require the observer to make from overt behavior to descriptor in the system. Low-inference items are those refering to specific, local, overt behaviors, like "student responds to teacher's question." High-inference items are those which classify less specific, more global, often covert phenomena, such as "student clarifies." They are "covert" in the sense of not always being explicitly performed and/or taking place over two or more utterances. Thus, classification of the following contribution by a student as "student hypothesizes," "student predicts," involves high inference of the first type:

> S3:   . . . / I don't think the creatures have creativity / because if they would have creativity, they all the they will changing his his way to do the things, / . . . (Long et al., 1976 p. 147)

i.e., where the acts coded are only implicitly realized in the data. Labeling the following moves as examples of structuring, soliciting, responding, and reacting, and the sequence of four as an "exchange," involves (high) inference of both types; i.e., the recognition of acts/moves or some other unit of analysis by the investigator but (probably) not by the participant in the interaction, and use of a superordinate category which includes events at a lower level and which spans series of utterances:

> T: OK. Now. A conductor. (Structuring) Pedro, what's a
>   conductor? (Soliciting)
> S: A conductor is the people who is boss in the in the em   Exchange
>   (inaudible) for example, in music. (Responding)
> T: OK. (Reacting)

Low-inference items are obviously required if a system is going to be used for real-time coding, and tend to be favored for teacher-training purposes, too. Several second language instruments incorporate both low- and high-inference items, and these are listed as "mixed" in Table 1.

The complexity of existing second language systems varies greatly. This is most evident in the number of categories they exhibit—from as few as seven to as many as sixty or seventy. The picture becomes somewhat different, however, if the kind of category employed is also taken into account. Some systems with a large number of categories use mostly low-inference ones (e.g., Fanselow, 1977), and can be far easier to code with than other instruments employing smaller numbers of more abstract categories. Provision is often made for so-called "multiple coding"; i.e., the recording of the same event in more than one category. Thus, when a teacher says

> T: But are dams built by beavers?

he may (at least) simultaneously be evaluating a student's previous utterance and soliciting a further response, as in the following sequence:

> T: Active. Beavers build dams. Passive?
> S: Dams are built by beavers.
> T: But *are* dams built by beavers?
> S: Not *all* dams.
> T: Right. Not the Aswan Dam, for example.

Partly as a function of the number of categories, the (non)availability of multiple coding, the degree of inference required of observers, and the existence of a clear training manual, both the time and training needed to master systems also varies. Some can be operated after a few hours; others take days to learn in their full form. This aspect of complexity needs to be weighed against the amount of time for the analysis of the data different systems require. Some of the superficially simpler ones demand manipulation of raw data—its transfer to matrices, the calculation of ratios of given combinations of behaviors to others, etc.—far more time-consuming than its collection.

Both the source and range of variables incorporated in second language systems tend to reflect those found by others (Rosenshine and Furst, 1973) in instruments for use in content classrooms. Thus, many second language systems record verbal interaction only, with an emphasis on the teacher's public use of language to control the topic of classroom conversation. They tend to analyze his or her behavior in terms of its pedagogic function ("teacher lectures," "teacher summarizes"), and to give considerable prominence to its affective characteristics ("teacher praises," "teacher accepts student's idea"). In one sense, this is to be expected, given that several systems are adaptations—sometimes very close adaptations—of Flanders's Interaction Analysis Categories (FIAC) (Flanders, 1970). On the other hand, it is surprising that so much borrowing should have taken place when one considers that second language classrooms differ from most others in that language is both the vehicle and object of instruction. If for no other reason, one might have expected more second language systems to reflect different levels of language use, along the lines, say, of Paulston's "mechanical—meaningful—communicative" analysis (Paulston, 1970). (Some do, of course; e.g., Jarvis, 1968; Nearhoof, 1969.) The common occurrence in second language classrooms, too, even in the heyday of audiolingualism, of non-public language practice (e.g., students participating in various kinds of dyadic drillwork and other small group activities) might have been expected to produce modifications in the kinds of behaviors sampled. Several systems, especially those developed more recently, do fulfil these expectations. Categories tend to be the authors' own, or to be derived from an (implicit or explicit) theoretical or empirical base. The range of behaviors sampled is broader, often paying as much attention to student language production as to that of the teacher, and sometimes including other dimensions of the interaction. Thus, e.g., Fanselow (1977) deals with non- and paralinguistic as well as linguistic communications; Long et al. (1976), McEwan (1976), and Carton (1966) note the level of cognitive activity engaged in; several systems isolate the content of instruction, e.g., in terms of phonology, syntax, lexicon, and skills being practiced (Naiman, Fröhlich, and Stern, 1975); and some systems attempt to handle verbal interaction from a discourse perspective (e.g., Allwright, 1977; Barkman, 1978). A final characteristic shared by second language instruments and their predecessors in content subjects is that few of the variables represented by their categories have been validated by process-product research—a point to which we return later.

Strengths and Limitations of the Interaction Analysis Approach

There are several obvious attractions of interaction analysis as an approach to describing classroom processes. Two have already been noted; namely, that some of the available second language instruments are relatively easy to learn and simple to use. Another is that, as a result of using mainly low-inference categories, some systems go some way to providing a common terminology for describing classroom life, one that, with a little explanation, can be understood by *both* the observer and the teacher. This is a useful feature at the dissemination stage of research, or if teachers, students, parents, school principals, and others are to have the work explained to them after the study is complete by way of thanks for the access given to classrooms.

The picture may seem rosier than it really is, however. It is no use adopting systems because they are easy to use, or disseminating information that is easy to understand, if the events described are trivial. The value of analytical systems must ultimately depend on the significance for teaching and learning of the categories they contain. For teacher-training purposes it can be useful to "sensitize" trainees to given aspects of their classroom performance only if there is some evidence that those aspects are of pedagogical significance; i.e., that they affect SLA or the conditions that promote it. It is important to recognize, therefore, that with very few exceptions—a tiny fraction of the proliferation of categories in analytical systems—we simply do not know what those aspects are. We have hunches, of course, and sometimes theoretical grounds for believing the hunches to be right, but until data exist to support them, the use to which systems are put may be *non-judgmental* but the systems themselves are no less *subjective* than the impressionistic comments they were designed to replace.

Observational instruments are, in fact, no more (or less) than theoretical claims about second language learning and teaching. Their authors hypothesize that the behaviors recorded by their categories are variables affecting the success of classroom language learning. Very little has been done to test those hypotheses. There is some evidence that indirect teaching behaviors are related to greater student achievement (Nelson, 1964; Rogers, 1972; William, 1973). Indirect teaching has also been related to more positive student attitude (Moskowitz, 1970), and many of the categories in the Flint system (Moskowitz, 1976) have been shown to distinguish teachers judged "outstanding" and "typical" (Moskowitz, 1976) and "best" and "first-year" (Moskowitz and Hayman, 1974). As the researchers note, this does not necessarily mean that the behaviors in the categories concerned relate to student achievement. (They could, for example, reflect the judges' hunches as to what a good teacher is coinciding with those of the investigators.) The hypotheses implicit in observational systems may be a good deal more thoughtfully derived than the beliefs underlying impressionistic judgments, but in most cases we do not know that they are. Their value, therefore, resides in their potential for revealing insights into the relationships between classroom processes and second language learning. Until that potential is tested, one's evaluation must depend on how accurately they reflect existing knowledge about (language) learning and, I suppose, one's own hunches.[4]

There are other problems with interaction analysis as currently practiced, not only for teacher-training but for anyone conducting classroom research on language learning. Among these is the fact that many instruments focus heavily on what the teacher does or says. This is reflected in several ways, including the number and kind of categories they contain for describing teacher and student performance. It is assumed by some that teachers control classroom interaction and can change interaction patterns if made aware of them. In an obvious sense this is true. "Unequal-power" discourse, of which the classroom is one setting, is marked among other ways by the teacher's predetermined ability to control topic and speaker. However, this power is not absolute; Mehan (1974) and Allwright (1977), among others, have shown how standards of correctness, the acquisition of speaking turns, and other factors are also the result of a continuing process of negotiation among teachers and students. To describe student speech in terms of a binary distinction as either "response to a teacher's question" or "initiation" is to say nothing about such issues as *how* particular students get to respond or initiate far more than others, or about the use to which they put conversational turns once they have them. Yet these are two of several related matters of special interest in second language classrooms, given research findings as to the importance of practice as a predictor of second language achievement (Seliger, 1977) and the emphasis on communicative competence as the product of instruction. One important goal of classroom research is, of course, to find out how teachers make a difference, but if teaching is defined as behavior that induces learning, to move directly from observable teacher behaviors to indices of second language achievement is to ignore at least two other possibilities. First, what teachers do may bring about changes in student behavior, and it is certain aspects of the latter which are crucial determinants of achievement. Second, what teachers do may relate to student achievement, but this relationship may be lost because no account is taken of differences in student reactions at the level of individuals. Both these criticisms relate to decisions about research design, which we turn to later in the last section of this chapter. In the present context, however, it is important to stress that no design will be able to rectify the situation if the instruments themselves preclude the possibility of gathering relevant data.

The focus on teacher behaviors in most systems is further restricted to a limited sample of those behaviors, and is then often superficial. Interaction analysis instruments generally ignore nonverbal communication altogether, and anything verbal that is not public, i.e., addressed to the whole class rather than to individual students or to small groups. This, as Boydell (1975) discovered, makes them unusable in informal classrooms unless the observer makes the decision to sample speech; e.g., by moving around the room with the teacher.

Delamont and Hamilton capture the problem succinctly:

> Many of the systems assume the "chalk and talk" paradigm . . .They imply a classroom setting where the teacher stands out front and engages the students in some kind of pedagogical or linguistic ping-pong (teacher asks question / pupil replies / teacher asks question / . . .) (Delamont and Hamilton, 1976, pp. 10–11)

A criticism such as this is even more serious for second language classrooms, where group work and private teacher-student interaction are common. In most systems, furthermore, speech that *is* addressed to individuals, e.g., most praise and many questions, is recorded *as if* directed to the class as a whole, i.e., undifferentiated from it. Thus, "teacher explains" may be used indiscriminately to record both explanations for a class, and those appropriate to, needed by, or heard by some students only. A teacher's "use of students' ideas" may regularly be use of those of one student or a small group only, while his or her ignoring those of others goes unrecorded. Various forms of feedback or evaluating moves may be reactions to individual or whole-class performance and, as Allwright (1975) has observed, need not be heard by some students; if heard, be perceived as correction, or if so perceived, have this effect.

The above limitation is also an example of another characteristic of the interaction analysis approach: such behavior as is recorded is interpreted from the observer's perspective rather than that of the participants in the interaction. As most observers are (a) adults and (b) trained teachers, there is obviously a built-in bias toward making the observer's interpretation coincide with that of one of the participants only. An observing teacher will easily perceive intervention 3 by the teacher in the following extract as constituting an explanation of the use of *conductor* in English to describe one man's job in a train crew, and simultaneously a rejection of the same word to denote the driver of a car.

1. T: OK. What other kind of conductor is there? There's the musical conductors, but what else?
2. S5: The person who drives a car?
3. T: Well, yeah I guess you could say he's a conductor but he's we usually say he's a driver, a car driver. OK? How about on the train? On the train there are conductors on the train, right?
4. S3: Right.

Conductor can be used to mean "car driver" in Spanish, the student's native language, but whether either the observer or the teacher know this, it is questionable whether the student, a non-native speaker, could determine that it is incorrectly used that way in English from what the teacher says.

The same problem arises when there is reason to doubt the cognitive or presuppositional match of teacher and students, as when the latter are children or when teacher and pupils do not share a common cultural background. The work of Barnes (1969) illustrates the first point. He found it is quite common for instruction to be conducted in a register peculiar to a school system or to a particular school subject, and for this to act as a barrier to understanding for students unfamiliar with it. In second language classrooms, explanations of grammar points are sometimes couched in a metalanguage even more impenetrable to some students than the point itself.[5] The potential effect of cultural differences on patterns in classroom discourse, and of the surprises in store for some teachers, is shown by some studies of North American Indian children interacting with adults. Weeks (1976), for example, found Yakima children "evading" her questions, "responding " with personal anecdotes instead. Phillips (1972) found that silences following questions were acceptable to Warm Springs Indian children; "answers," as they are often conceptualized, were not obligatory, since in the cultures concerned it could be assumed that the listener was really listening.

In an effort to overcome the bias in the observer's perspective. Adelman and Walker (1975) have developed a strategy called "triangulation" borrowed from ethnomethodology (Garfinkel, 1967; Cicourel, 1973; Mehan and Wood, 1975). As employed by Adelman and Walker, successive interpretations of classroom interaction are elicited from teachers and students by playing them recordings of the original talk and the other participants' subsequent commentaries. Information gathered in this way is then used to validate or, where necessary, correct disparities between an observer's "commonsense interpretation of action" and that of teacher or students. Techniques such as this constitute one way of avoiding distortions which may result from misclassification of, e.g., a teacher's remark in one of two similar (sometimes vaguely defined) categories, such as "teacher accepts students' feelings" and "teacher uses students' idea," or from gross errors due, e.g., to cultural differences. They are not, of course, part of interaction analysis itself.

In general, interaction analysis systems code surface behavior, and so may miss the communicative value of remarks. This is partly due to their use of low-inference categories. The increase in reliability that these are designed to bring is largely mythical, as Bailey (1975) has shown, and comes at a high price. A focus on overt behavior may, for example, "reliably" preempt the explanatory power of a study by precluding consideration of participants' intentions. An example is when a teacher's use of praise or provision of negative feedback may be designed to (re)establish or protect his or her own authority or status as teacher rather than to reinforce or correct a student's performance in the second language. Consider the following data from an intermediate level vocabulary lesson for young adults. (*Trousers* is a British word for American *pants*.)

1. T: . . . OK? Chemical pollution. OK.
2. S4: (yawning) O o o.
3. T: Trousers! Alright, Carlos [S4], do you wear trousers?
4. S4: Alway . . All my life.
5. SS: (laughter)
6. T: Always. You've worn, I have . . .

 7. S4: Eh wear wear (inaudible).
 8. T: I have . . . well, do you wear trousers?
 9. S5: I wear.
10. SS: I wear, I wear.
11. S4: Yes, I I do.
12. T: Yes, you do. What's how do you say that word?
13. S4: Trousers.
14. T: Trous*ers*.
15. S4: Trous*ers*.
16. T: *Trou*sers.
17. S4: *Trou*sers.
18. S3: Trousers.
19. T: Mm hm. Have you got trousers on?
20. S3: Yes, I have.
21. T: What kind?
22. S3: Jeans.
23. T: Jeans . . . Say the word jeans. Jeans.
24. S3: Jeans.
25. T: Jeans.
26. S2: Jeans.
27. T: Jeans.
28. S1: Jeans.
29. T: OK. OK. Huh! Does anyone need an ashtray?

The teacher's initial choice (line 3) of Carlos (S4) as recipient of his "question" seemed to the observer (myself) to be motivated by his recognition that S4 was bored and thereby indirectly challenging the usefulness of the lesson. To the observer, this seemed a correct interpretation on the teacher's part, the boredom being largely due to the fact that the students were familiar with most of the "new" words already. When Carlos responded to the absurdity of the question with a joke (line 4) which produced amusement in his classmates, the teacher reacted by "correcting" the error (line 6) and "drilling" the students (lines 6–17), thereby reasserting his authority. He was behaving, in other words, not unlike the sergeant-major who, catching sime unruly recruits in an act of disobedience, attempts to break their spirit with a dose of "square-bashing" on the barracks parade ground. Note, incidentally, how an upward shift—from meaningful to communicative interpretation—in the value assigned to utterances in classroom discourse, is a reliable resource for humor often utilized by language teachers:

T: (modeling) I'm a student. Teacher.
S: I'm a teacher.
T: *Are* you?
SS: (laughter)

Carlos seems to have learned this, but not the other apparent rule, i.e., that in this classroom, at least, it is today a resource available to the teacher only. The interpretation so far seems justified when we note that the life (sic) of the drill is artificially extended by the teacher's temporary modelling an incorrect form, having the student repeat this, and promptly correcting the error (lines 14–17). (The *s* on *trousers* is clearly audible in S4's rendition, line 13.) By line 19, the teacher is able to ask his original question with confidence, order having been reestablished, and to elicit obedient performance of the repetition drill of *jeans*.

The above understanding of the extract would not be captured by an instrument designed for interaction analysis. The utterances would instead be coded as something like "T asks question—S responds—T models—S responds," etc., and could conceivably be part of the data for a study which failed to find a correlation between quantity of student participation and second language achievement. One might hypothesize that the same data reanalyzed would, however, shed some light on the relationship between achievement and the ratio of mechanical, meaningful, and communicative language practice by students.

It could easily be argued, of course, that the extract offers no evidence at all for the interpretation I have put on it. We do not *see* the teacher "punishing" S4 or attempting to reestablish his authority; we *see* him modelling the present perfect and correcting the pronunciation of *trousers*. To say anything else is to risk moving smartly backwards into the mire of impressionistic judgments from which interaction analysis was designed to save us. It seems, in other words, that what we *may* gain in insightfulness we will definitely lose in reliability and, hence, validity. Researchers could easily argue about the teacher's intentions (or, had he been interviewed, about his "real" intentions), but it is difficult to argue about the function of "What's how do you say that word?"(line 12) as a question, or of "Trous*ers*" (line 14) as a model for repetition. Nevertheless, as Smith has observed:

> The way a teacher poses his problems, the kinds of goals and sub-goals he is trying to reach, the alternatives he weighs . . . are aspects of teaching which are frequently lost to the behavior oriented empiricist who focuses on what the teacher does, to the exclusion of how he thinks about teaching. (Smith and Geoffrey, 1968, p. 96)

The undoubted reductionist tendency of interaction analysis may also be criticized from a sociolinguistic perspective (Stubbs, 1975,1976; Coulthard, 1977; Hatch and Long, in press). Stubbs (1975), for example, points out that systems like FIAC ignore such dimensions of classroom talk as the fact that a lesson constitutes "a speech event with its own characteristic norms and rules" (ibid., p. 234). Flanders's "two-thirds rule," for instance, which holds that teachers talk for approximately that proportion of time in a typical lesson, only becomes meaningful when viewed in the cultural context in which it was established and as one member of a set of related sociolinguistic conventions. It would signify something quite different in cultures like the Paliyan (Hymes,

1967), for example, with alternative values attached to silence among older members of society. To generalize assumptions built into FIAC and derived systems about indirect teaching, similarly, would be mistaken if applied to Sioux, Cherokee, or Warm Springs Indian classrooms (Dumont, 1972; Phillips, 1972), where "learning" and "talking" are not equated in the same way, or, presumably, to many second language classrooms, too. (The same criticism could also be made of the way FIAC and other instruments ignore individual differences in learning style *within* cultures.) Stubbs observes that most interaction analysis also pays no attention to the intrinsic linguistic organization of classroom talk. Isolated utterances are coded directly as pedagogical acts (T lectures, praises, etc.), and these in turn regarded as clear instances of direct or indirect teacher influence and, by implication, of the teacher's "democratic" or "authoritarian" social role.

Treating classroom talk as discourse rather than verbal behavior means, among other things, that the investigator will seek to ascertain the function of utterances in the interaction instead of coding them directly as indications of teaching method. Their role will depend partly on their position relative to other utterances, i.e., their status as a discourse act such as "frame," "nomination," "elicitation," and "reply." As Stubbs points out, many interaction analysis systems refer to "initiations" and "responses"; they are, however, concerned only with control of topic, not with the structure of the interaction. In fact, description of "sequences" of events in interaction analysis really consists of recording *series* of minimal codable acts. Larger structures, such as Sinclair and Coulthard's (1975) "exchange" or "transaction," are missed altogether. Discourse analysis abstracts from the data, a necessary part of any scientific enterprise, but by definition preserves reference to the context of behavior, to the continuous, dynamic properties of talk. It does not immediately break it down into discrete categories whose basis is an arbitrary time unit, not a more meaningful, "natural," linguistic one. People do not, that is to say, use language to get from 12:10 to 12:10 and three seconds; they use it to structure tasks, to react to others' participation, to allocate speaking turns, and so on.

The final and perhaps most serious criticism of interaction analysis as currently practiced in classroom research on language learning is that it assumes sufficient knowledge of the issues it purports to investigate. It has already been noted that the majority of categories in many systems have been taken over directly from instruments developed for observation in content classrooms. Adoption of such categories assumes that they are relevant ones for the study of second language classrooms, too. If this were really the case, there would be no point in conducting classroom research on language learning at all; one could simply apply the findings of, say, research on geography teaching. While future studies may show such generalizations to be justified, this approach seems to lack face validity at present. It is generally recognized, after all, that second language instruction (and some first language teaching) is distinguished from content subject instruction by such characteristics as the provision of feedback on the formal correctness rather than the truth value of speech, and the relatively insignificant amount of information exchanged, i.e., genuine communication, in the target language. Most systems recognize factors like these via the addition of categories to Flanders's (or somebody else's) original list. The issue of the status of the content classroom categories still remains, nonetheless.

Now the above criticism is really another way of saying that empirical research is needed to validate the choice of categories. This is obviously equally true of any categories, not just those emanating from systems like FIAC, and it is certainly not the purpose of the paper to argue the merits of one set over another. It is also true that all research involving hypothesis-testing—and categories, it has been argued, are but an indirect formulation of hypotheses about what makes (second language) learning tick—necessitates an *a priori* selection of variables considered relevant. The fact is, however, that unlike explicit hypotheses, whose life-span is generally no longer than the experiments they spawn *unless* results do not force their rejection, categories never seem to die. The proof of this is the way they find their way from one system to another over the years, often crossing discipline boundaries in the process, like stateless persons in search of a new home. It is important in this context to note the conclusion of Rosenshine and Furst (1973), based on an extensive review of research where natural behavior in content classrooms was related to student achievement. They found that very few of the variables appearing in observational systems have been validated in that field, either, and that those which had been shown to relate to student achievement were usually more global in nature than the original categories.

Rosenshine and Furst found that nine variables appearing to yield the most statistically significant and consistent results across over fifty studies were: clarity, variability, enthusiasm, task-oriented and/or businesslike behavior, criticism (a negative relationship), indirectness, opportunity to learn criterion material, use of structuring comments, and multiple levels of questioning (e.g., requiring inferential thinking as opposed to fact-stating). These were correlational studies only, i.e., showing relationships, but not causal ones, between the variables listed and success. Experimental work reduced the list. Six studies manipulated the level of cognitive interactions (fact-stating or higher) required by students, and found no statistically significant results in five cases. Six studies had teachers increase the use of praise and other positive behaviors, and decrease criticism and other negative ones. Again, no statistically significant differences were found on measures of student achievement in five cases. No statistically significant results were obtained in two studies which took quantity of student participant as the independent variable. Thus, persisting with some of the categories in second language systems, it seems, is more an act of faith than a rationally, still less empirically justifiable activity. Their (implicit or explicitly) prescriptive use in teacher-training and evaluation requires no comment.

The Anthropological Approach

Partly as a reaction to the limitations of interaction analysis outlined above, partly inspired by its successful use in such fields as anthropology, sociology, and ethology, and partly as a reflection of changing attitudes to nomological science in general, recent years have witnessed the appearance in educational research of various forms of unstructured observation. This takes two basic forms, participant and non-participant, although each is carried out by researchers from a variety of theoretical positions, including their attitudes to "science." "Unstructured" here should not be equated with "unsystematic." The anthropological approach to classroom research is procedurally highly systematic. *What* is observed and, hence, the data gathered using these procedures, however, is free to vary during the course of the observation as a reflection of the observer's developing understanding of what he or she is studying. The difference, then, is that the structuring is done by the researcher (or through him or her by informants) and not by the data-gathering device chosen prior to beginning the observation. Another fundamental difference is that the researcher in the anthropological approach does not set out, in theory, at least, with preconceived notions as to the variables to be studied or with hypotheses to test.

Participant observation

Often known as ethnography, unstructured participant observation describes the classic research methodology used by cultural anthropologists, such as the late Margaret Mead. While originally used in work on primitive societies, it has since been widely applied in modern urban settings, e.g., in studies of junkies, tramps, skid-row inhabitants, fire-fighters, airline stewardesses, and county welfare organizations.

In a participant study, the observer takes a regular part in the activities he or she is studying, e.g., by becoming a member of a street gang or joining a political group. When the researcher further chooses not to reveal his or her true identity and motives, there is the opportunity to observe properly natural behavior. (One imagines the services of skilled ethnographers are sought by the world's intelligence agencies.) Participant observers do not always follow the course of concealment. Some of those that hide their motives attempt to become, at least temporarily, true members of the "culture" they are studying by adopting its values and life-style as much as possible. Mehan and Wood (1975) report one case where this led an American artist to engage in theft, mass murder, and cannibalism. (This was not part of a study of classroom language learning, but while the individual, Schneebaum, 1969, was living with the Akaramas, a stone-age tribe in the Peruvian Amazon.)

Ethnographers do not set out to test particular hypotheses in any formal sense. Instead, they try to describe all aspects of whatever they experience in the greatest possible detail. This they accomplish principally by making extensive written notes, usually recording their observations as soon as possible *after* involvement in the day's activities in order to avoid compromising their own participant role. Note-taking is as systematic and as thorough as the individual ethnographer cares to make it, and much has been written on the subject. Lofland (1971, pp. 104–106), for example, suggests five types of notes: a running description, memories of previously forgotten incidents, ideas for future analysis of the data, personal impressions and reactions, and reminders as to additional information needed.

The amount of data generated by ethnographers is often massive and, like that produced by open-ended questions in survey research, difficult or impossible to quantify. In fact, many ethnographers do not seek to do this, instead building taxonomies of nominal categories, sometimes those used by informants in classifying the phenomena of interest. K. M.Bailey (1978, p. 229) cites an example of this from Spradley's work (Spradley, 1970) on "hoboes." While hoboes are known by several names in common parlance (bums, vagrants, etc.), Spradley found the men to have their own way of classifying themselves and their own terms for doing so:

> The generic term they use for themselves is not hobo, but tramp. There are eight different types of tramps: ding, boxcar tramp, bindle stiff, working stiff, airedale, home guard tramp, mission stiff and rubber tramp. These different types are based on several underlying variables, such as method of travel (boxcar tramp versus bindle stiff) and means of subsistence (working stiff versus mission stiff). There is another level of distinctions or subtypes—harvest tramp, tramp miner, fruit tramp, construction tramp, and sea tramp—while mission stiffs are further divided into subtypes of nose diver versus professional nose diver (K. M. Bailey, 1978, p. 229)

The richness and functional nature of this classification is obvious when compared to "bum" or "vagrant," and is an example of the kind of insights available to an investigator who (a) suspends judgment until *after* the data have been collected, and (b) is prepared to allow participants' orientations to their actions to guide his or her own.

There have been several participant ethnographic studies in educational settings (Burnett, 1974). The best known research of this type on second language learning is the recent series of "diary studies" (e.g., Schumann and Schumann, 1977; Schumann, 1978; Walsleben, 1976; K. M. Bailey, 1978). The participant observers have mostly been students enrolled in foreign or second language classes (although much of the Schumanns' work involves naturalistic SLA), and in one case (Telatnik, 1978) the teacher of an ESL class. An important difference between the diary studies and normal ethnography has been that the diarists' principal object of study has been themselves, introspection thus supplementing observation as a data-gathering device. Bailey's work, however, also focuses considerable attention on the behavior of other members of her French class, as well as its teacher.

Not surprisingly, given the kinds of data involved, the diary studies so far have been particularly interesting in the light they have cast on personal variables in language learning. Schumann (1978) lists ten of these in two subjects' learning and informal acquisition of Farsi and Arabic. They include reactions to dissatisfaction with teaching methods, desire to maintain one's own language-learning agenda, eavesdropping versus speaking as a learning strategy, and motivation for choice of materials.

Non-participant observation

Non-participant observation shares many characteristics with its participant counterpart. It is not a formal hypothesis-testing operation; no preselection is made of variables to be observed which precludes their abandonment in favor of alternative phenomena of interest. The data gathered is not predetermined by the use of an observational schedule of any kind. The period of study is usually long, and N-size small (e.g., one class). Data are mostly in the form of written notes, analyzed subsequently, but this time generally recorded openly, during the events observed, for in non-participant observation, the observer does not take part in the activities being studied or pretend to be a participant in them. As with interaction analysis, there is no question of the observation being covert (in non-laboratory settings, at least) or, as a result, of the researcher witnessing truly natural, i.e., "unobserved," behavior in the way undisclosed participants can. While the principal means of gathering data may again be note-taking, the non-participant observer will have the option of supplementing this through the use of a variety of other techniques. Indeed, Pelto (1970) characterizes anthropological research by its multi-instrument approach. Alternative devices include interviewing informants and compiling bio-data on them, administering questionnaires, the elicitation of ratings and rankings, and various unobtrusive measures, such as handouts, students' homework, and official documents. In this manner, participants' motives for and understandings of their actions may be probed (cf. Adelman and Walker, 1975).

The above and other forms of instrumentation assist the researcher in attaining the ethnographer's goal of a holistic view of the phenomena studied. This is a perspective from which, say, teachers' classroom behaviors are interpreted as influenced by the wider school, community, or even societal context in which they are located, and by the variety of roles played inside and outside the classroom by the individuals whose roles as *teachers* happen to be the focus of the study in hand. Only as detailed and as complex a picture as this can enable an account to meet the criterion for descriptively adequate ethnography, which, to quote Wolcott, is that a reader

> could subsequently behave appropriately as a member of the society or social group about which he has been reading, or, more modestly, whether he can anticipate and interpret what occurs in the group as appropriately as its own members can. (Wolcott, 1975, p. 112)

Notice that this criterion is not satisfied by a description of the occurrence of events:

> To describe a culture . . . is not to recount the events of a society but to specify what one must know to make those events maximally probable. The problem is not to state what someone did but to specify the conditions under which it is culturally appropriate to anticipate that he, or persons occupying his role, will render an equivalent performance . . . (Frake, 1964, p. 112)

Non-participant ethnography has been applied to content classrooms, particularly in the UK, where several such studies have been reported (e.g., Nash, 1973; Delamont, 1976; Stubbs, 1976; Chanan and Delamont, 1975; Stubbs and Delamont, 1976). There appear to have been no non-participant ethnographies of second language classrooms to date.

Constitutive ethnography

Another recent development in educational research has been the advent of constitutive ethnography (Mehan, 1977, 1978). Mehan criticizes conventional ethnography on two grounds. First, while helping to recreate the flavor of the original events, the anecdotal quality of most field studies makes it "difficult to determine [their] representativeness . . . and, therefore, the generality of find-ings derived from them" (Mehan, 1978, p. 35). The reader seldom knows an ethnographer's criteria for selection of the examples he or she uses for illustrative purposes. Second, ethnographies are summaries of the events observed; readers have no access to the original data and therefore no opportunity to arrive at their own interpretations.

With clear ethnomethodological underpinnings, constitutive ethnography seeks to study the "social structuring activities," the "interactional work," that create and sustain such "social facts" as students' intelligence and achievement, and "routine patterns of behavior," like classroom organization (Mehan, ibid., pp. 35–36). It is distinguished methodologically from previous ethnographic work, Mehan claims, in four respects. First, it employs *retrievable* data, using film or videotape for both data gathering and data display when reporting findings. The advantage of this is that researchers (and research consumers) are provided access to repeated viewings —an "external memory"—of the events studied. Second, data are treated *exhaustively,* meaning that all the data, not just the most frequently occurring patterns therein, are analyzed and accounted for both sequentially and hierarchically. This, it is claimed, checks the tendency for research reports to have a "self-validating quality" by their reporting only such evidence as supports investigators' claims or "findings," simultaneously denying readers the opportunity to disconfirm them or to arrive at alternative interpretations of the data on which they are based. Third, constitutive ethnography performs *"interactional analysis"* (not to be confused with interaction analysis), i.e., seeks to discover participants' uses of words or gestures to structure the organization of social events. A study may, for example, focus on the implementation of a turn-allocation procedure, and devices for its repair when needed, through which one aspect of classroom organization is accomplished. Analysis is confined to

> the behavior displayed among participants [so that] unfounded inferences are not made about the mental states of participants, and the researchers avoid both psychological reduction and sociological reification. (Mehan, ibid., p. 37)

Fourth, an attempt is made to ensure a *convergence* between the structure observers see in events and that which orients the participants. Eliciting their comments on an investigator's analysis after the event is one way of doing this, but the researcher's questions can so structure respondents' answers as to provide what Campbell and Fisk (1959) have called "convergent validation" rather than independent verification of the psychological reality of a given model. Constitutive ethnography, therefore, tests the validity of an analysis during the period of observation. Evidence is sought in participants' verbal, paralinguistic or kinesic behavior; e.g., changes in the rhythm or pitch of a teacher's speech accompanying the completion of a given speech act. Do these and other indications that participants give each other of the interactional work they are doing to organize events both sequentially and hierarchically mark structures which correspond to those perceived by the investigator?

The method described by Mehan has been applied in studies of classrooms, testing encounters, and counseling sessions (e.g., Bremme and Erickson, 1977; Shultz, 1976; Mehan, Cazden, Coles, Fisher, and Maroules, 1976). Some work has been done describing the turn-taking systems in content classrooms in terms of the index they provide of the formality of the classroom situation (Mchoul, 1978), and of that in a second language class (Allwright, 1977). Neither of the latter studies, however, were conducted within the theoretical framework advocated by Mehan. Thus, while each concentrated on a system governing the organization of speaking turns in lessons, they did not attempt to discover the means by which the system itself was established and maintained.

Strengths and Limitations of the Anthropological Approach

Ethnographic field work is primarily a hypothesis-generating, not hypothesis-testing, undertaking. When applied to a field such as classroom language learning about which little is already known, it benefits from its eschewal of the "blinkers" (in the form of a pre-specified list of behavioral categories) which restrict the data interaction analysts collect and, hence, the variables their research considers. The field worker in a cross-cultural setting has, Wolcott (1975, p. 115) points out, an advantage anthropologists consider crucial, namely that he or she is studying "people and customs he does not take for granted." The potentially limitless scope of ethnographic enquiry means that, in theory at least, it has the potential for (re)discovering these or other factors which appear to be important rather than simply taking over variables identified in other (albeit related) fields, and to describe their perceived relevance in concrete settings and from the perspective of the participants instead of that of an outsider. (Just how free from preconceptions a *classroom* ethnographer can really be is perhaps open to doubt, given that most researchers will have had at least fifteen years of formal education themselves, often including some experience as teachers, and would probably not be doing an ethnography unless already interested in some aspect(s) of life in classrooms.) In its participant form, unstructured observation has the advantage, too, of dealing with "natural" data. While non-participant observers (using a structured or unstructured approach) usually familiarize participants with their presence (and that of their equipment if any is used), and try to establish a non-threatening relationship before collecting data, there is never the certainty that what they see is exactly what would have occurred if they had not been present. Finally, the results of ethnographic studies are also far more detailed and comprehensive descriptions than those derived from interaction analysis.

The anthropological approach has some serious limitations, too. Ethnography is only as good as the person doing it, and the qualifications needed, according to most anthropologists (e.g., Wolcott, ibid), include cross-cultural experience, a *thorough* training in cultural anthropology, various personal qualities such as sensitivity, perceptiveness, skepticism, objectivity, and curiosity, and (not least) the ability to write well. (Of course, many of these qualities are desirable in researchers working in any tradition, whose research is similarly limited by their own abilities and training. The point is that the attributes listed above are likely to be rarer among those conducting "applied" ethnographic research in education than are, say, a good background in traditional experimental research methods, design, and statistics.) Even for people thus blessed, ethnographies take a long time to complete, including at least as much time in their writing as that spent in the field. Yet despite the investment of time and effort involved, their findings lack generalizability.

The generalizability issue has long been a controversial one in debate about research methods in the social sciences. Controlled experiments "solve" the problem by abstracting away from the complex of interrelated factors which characterize natural social events, manipulating those in which the researcher is interested and assuming the effect of the remainder will be lost through such processes as the random assignment of subjects to groups, or at least have an equal effect in all groups. Because of the use of sampling procedures and large numbers of subjects, it is considered justifiable to generalize findings obtained in such settings to the population of the original more complex ones from which those studied were drawn. Yet, by definition, what has been studied is different from and simpler than the real world. And just how many random samples of classrooms are needed before one can generalize safely? When dealing with human behavior, what level of difference in observed phenomena may be considered due to chance as opposed to the effect of the variables manipulated?

Many researchers are generally unimpressed by the aura of objectivity that surrounds experimental research, and especially so when it is applied to the study of human beings. Ethnographers recognize the bias inherent in one person reporting events, but some feel it is as safe or safer to trust one's own insights as another's alleged objectivity. They, after all, recognize their biases but wonder if the way results are obtained in a standardized fashion in the controlled experiment can neutralize the biases implicit and often *un*recognized in the hypothesis-generating activity that inspired it.

The position taken here is that the lack of generalizability of the results of ethnography is not due primarily to the tiny N-size of most studies. Size is relative, and an N of 1 is not qualitatively different from one of 50, 100, or 1,000; it is just one point on a continuum stretching from 1 to infinity (or the number of members of the population being studied). While one may feel more inclined to trust 50 instances of a phenomenon as revealing a pattern than 1 or 2, there is no reason to believe it justifiable to generalize from a study with 50 subjects but not from one with 49, from one with 20 but not from one with 19, and so on. Rather, the problem lies in the way an ethnographer's observations are related to the particular context in which the events were observed, and to the personal makeup of the actors (including the ethnographer) as individuals. Again, there is a sense in which such relationships are present in experimental studies, too, and a greater danger that they will remain unrecognized there, and almost never be made explicit. However, the advantage accrued at the cost of abstraction from the natural behavior of unique individuals is precisely this: what is idiosyncratic or otherwise unique to a particular setting may be distinguished from patterns in behavior, and it is these patterns that have a greater value for those interested in predicting and understanding behavior in settings other than those studied.

The need to "apply" findings in this way is felt by many ethnographers. Some suggest that results of more general significance can be obtained by comparing similar studies of the same phenomena. Apart from losing some degree of the "understanding" gained by treatment of unique events in their own right, however, this procedure is of limited potential for practical reasons. Many ethnographers also advocate the writing of ethnographies only by those who conducted the field work; since collapsing other people's studies involves even greater risks of misinterpretation, the comparison of studies should, it follows, also be done by the person who carried them out. The time factor will preclude this practice in all but a few instances. In fact, it should probably not even be attempted (or be considered a weakness of the method), as it may be to make ethnography fulfil a function for which it was not designed and is certainly ill-suited; i.e., the testing (as opposed to generating) of hypotheses.

The generalizability issue, along with several of those discussed above in relation to ethnography, is of equal concern when considering the contribution of the diary studies. On the basis of the evidence so far, diary studies look like an extremely promising source of insights into the classroom language-learning process. Nevertheless, caution obviously needs to be applied in interpreting their findings. First, while intuitively plausible, variables such as eavesdropping versus listening as a learning strategy are factors *perceived* by the diarists as affecting their language learning; the form of the diary study cannot show them to have this effect. Second, they are concerned with individuals in unique learning environments, so generalizations of their findings to other learners and environments is precluded on the basis of the studies themselves. They may be relevant to many or even all learners, in other words, or idiosyncratic. Third, "participant" diary studies of this kind involve the researcher in two related but separate tasks, keeping a diary and learning (or teaching) a second language. This is obviousy a plus as far as their potential for revealing insights into language learning is concerned, but the divided attention resulting from the dual activity could constitute a considerable obstacle to the study of classroom processes *per se.* One solution might be for the researcher to enroll in a class operating at a lower level in the language concerned than that at which he or she is already comfortable.

Constitutive ethnography is certainly distinguished from other methods of conducting classroom research by its theoretical foundations in ethnomethodology. Less certain, however, are some of Mehan's claims for its methodological uniqueness. While again extremely promising, it is also arguably limited in some of the same ways noted earlier with regard to conventional ethnography and diary studies.

First, the emphasis on "retrievability" of data seems an ideal rather than a reality. Many researchers in classroom language learning view videotapes and/or transcripts repeatedly during the analysis stage of their studies, and several show these or display extracts from them in their reports. Wolcott says of ethnographic reporting in general that

any ethnographic account should contain a wealth of primary data . . . [and] coupled with the obligation . . . to order and make sense out of his material [the ethnographer] is duty-bound to present sufficient primary data that his readers have an adequate basis for rendering their own judgments concerning the analysis. (Wolcott, 1975, p. 124)

The use of extracts, of course, is just what Mehan objects to. However, anything else is as logistically unfeasible for conventional ethnographers as, one may presume, for constitutive ethnographers, unless the corpus the latter work on is to be very limited. A skeptic can always request access to the complete set of original tapes or transcripts, and in the event of being refused, may discount the research if he or she chooses. As for the opportunity of reaching one's own interpretations, this is usually possible on the basis of what *is* reported, and this is true of research reported in terms of means, standard deviations, and levels of statistical significance, too. Where this is not the case, the same course of action is available. Mehan can presumably only object to the *degree* of abstraction from raw data that is performed prior to its "display"; constitutive ethnography must do what researchers in any other tradition do for the same (logistical) reasons if their work is to reach an audience wider than the investigators themselves.

Mehan's insistence on "exhaustive" data treatment also seems to ignore common scientific practice. It is true that researchers have traditionally focused their attention on frequent or dominant patterns in their data; for the most part they have, after all, been working in the nomothetic tradition, one of whose goals is to seek out such patterns, and one of whose assumptions is that they exist.

There is undeniable force to the ethnomethodologists' claim that this has diverted attention from the processes whereby those patterns or "facts" are created; i.e., in a sense, by the methodology of the scientific tradition that seeks them. A similar charge could, however, be brought against constitutive ethnography's search for social-structuring activities. If the hermeneutic paradigm is correct, one may wonder why *that* term does not appear in inverted commas, too. The fact that the psychological reality of the behaviors which achieve them is validated by members' perceptions is no less true of much conventional ethnographic research, as shown, e.g., by the use of the tramps' classification of their fellows cited earlier. As Wolcott (1975) observes:

> (T)he anthropologist is duty-bound to look for cultural patterns and cultural forms shared by members of a social system or subsystem; it is hardly surprising that he always finds them. (Wolcott, 1975, p. 112)

It is also not the case that the nomothetic tradition has ignored data which do not fit a given generalization. This is evidenced by its frequent explicit treatment of "outliers" or counter-examples to patterns or theories, as in case studies which seek to uncover causes of the lack of fit, and through such concepts as *level* of statistical significance and *strength* of association. Mehan's criticism, it appears, is the same as that of phenomenologists (e.g., Giorgi, 1970; Merleau-Ponty, 1964) and ethnomethodologists (e.g., Garfinkel, 1967; Sacks, 1972), among others, that the goals and assumptions of the nomological scientific tradition are wrong, that "reality"is not out there waiting to be discovered, that human life is not like that; i.e., that the method creates the phenomena it purports to discover. This is a serious and fundamental criticism, and one that has been made forcefully several times in recent years, including by Mehan himself (Mehan and Wood, 1975). It ultimately reflects a philosophical outlook (just as the nomological tradition does), which is probably impossible to refute.[6] It is not, however, a position unique to constitutive ethnography and, hence, a characteristic that distinguishes it from all other research methodologies in the social sciences.

It is in Mehan's third and fourth distinguishing features—interactional analysis and the search for convergence between researchers' and participants' perspectives—that constitutive ethnography looks genuinely innovative and promising. Knowledge derived from the former would show not simply *what* the organization of interaction in a classroom is, but *how* it is achieved and, hence, what children need to learn in order to be able to participate appropriately. Convergence, as has been noted, matches the goal of many researchers, e.g., conventional ethnographers. It differs from their work in the way it seeks to achieve the goal, however. It is likely to produce more valid results than the use of elicitation frames, for the reasons given earlier, and has the advantage over such procedures as Adelman and Walker's use of triangulation in that it is not a *post hoc* analysis but one which allows testing of the predictions it makes against participants' future behaviors.

Some Suggestions for Future Research
on Classroom Language Learning

The review has claimed that two broad approaches, interaction analysis and anthropological observation, embrace a variety of methods available to students of classroom language learning. Each approach has strengths and limitations, and several of these characterize the methods which exemplify them. In this final section, some suggestions will be made for future research on classroom language learning which uses a combined approach, thereby avoiding some of the limitations of each, and taking advantage of the strengths of both. It will be argued that a combination of methods plus some modifications in commonly used research designs is necessary if the field is to achieve its ultimate goal of testing a theory of second language acquisition with the aid of formal instruction.

The literature shows that, while there is a growing interest in the study of classroom processes, the majority of recent studies, supposedly of SLA with the aid of formal instruction, have continued to be of the input-output variety and correlational in nature. Thus, the dominant line of attack is to obtain measures of some aspects of learner characteristics and to correlate these with students' second language achievement, as depicted in Figure 2. Examples of this type of study include Gardner and Lambert (1972), Genesee (1976), Tucker, Hamayan, and Genesee (1976), and Banko and Perkins (1979). Such work is, and will continue to be useful. It has unearthed relationships between second language achievement and variables like attitude, motivation, and IQ. It does not, however, say anything about classroom language learning since, as Figure 2 illustrates, the research bypasses the effect (if any) of the instructional component. What goes on inside the black box has the same status as "exposure" to the target language in studies of naturalistic SLA. Learner characteristics have replaced "method" variables, but the contribution of teaching and learning is not so much studied as controlled for.

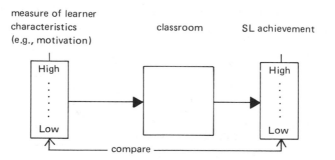

Figure 2. Schematic representation of design for correlational input-output studies with learner characteristics as predictor variable

There are also a few studies, again correlational, which have used classroom data of some kind—teacher or student behaviors substituting for learner characteristics as the independent variable. Examples of this kind of research are Politzer (1977), Naiman, Fröhlich, and Stern (1975), McEwan (1976), and Flahive and Moore (1979). As shown in Figure 3, this type of study looks at some aspects of classroom performance, but ignores learners' characteristics. The work has generally not been able to show clear or consistent relationships, occasionally even finding negative correlations between student achievement and various teacher behaviors which might reasonably be expected to contribute to learning. Possible explanations are not hard to find.

Correlational research of this kind looks for a simple main effect for the learner characteristics or teacher or student classroom behaviors measured, and thereby ignores three issues. First, most people agree, SLA is a multidimensional phenomenon, involving (at least) biological, neurological, social, psychological, affective, and personal variables plus, in this case, it is assumed, the effect of instruction. It seems likely, therefore, that because many factors are involved, no single one of them is sufficiently powerful, in all situations and among all learners, to have a consistent and statistically obvious relationship to success. Evidence of this is perhaps to be found in the often conflicting findings or lack of findings in studies such as those cited, e.g., those concerning attitude and motivation.[7] It may be, in other words, that to *show* the relationships that exist, it is necessary to control for several potential intervening variables, even in cases (such as motivation) where the effect of the variable in which researchers are interested may be expected to operate in the same direction for all learners.

Second, simple correlations of this nature may also produce relationships which are spurious. A striking example of this was recently reported in a study of naturalistic SLA. Oyama (1978) found that scores on a noise test of aural comprehension were positively correlated with lower self-consciousness while learning English, and with greater American orientation and identification, but also (inversely) with age of arrival of her immigrant subjects to the USA.

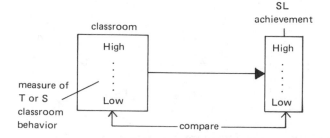

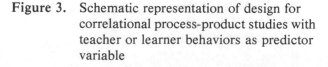

Figure 3.   Schematic representation of design for correlational process-product studies with teacher or learner behaviors as predictor variable

However, these and other socio-affective correlations disappeared, save for a .29 for "present motivation to learn English," when the effect of age of arrival was controlled for. Conversely, when the person and environmental variables were held constant, the strong correlation between age of arrival and comprehension remained.

Third, it is possible for a given teacher behavior to influence different students in different ways, as, e.g., Gardner (1974) has shown in content classrooms. Thus, deductive grammatical presentations may be better suited to learners of a certain age or a particular cognitive style (Krashen, Seliger, and Hartnett, 1974). The same may be true of a particular kind of feedback move (say, identification as opposed to location of error), or the time of introduction of the written mode and its frequency of use while promoting oral-aural skills. In other words, a given teacher behavior may do different things for different learners. The correlation of variables like these with class *means* on the outcome variables may fail to produce statistically significant results, not because a relationship does not exist but because, through an interaction effect, the positive value of such behaviors for some students is cancelled out by its having the opposite effect on others.

There is, of course, nothing new in what is being said in design terms. The fact is, however, that very few studies in the field use factorial designs and the statistical procedures that go with them—designs which would enable relationships such as these to be detected. (See Figure 4.) This may account for the null findings reported in some parts of the research cited on learner or teacher variables. In several of these studies, the investigators had often built theoretically plausible and intuitively appealing rationales for their hypotheses. (See, e.g., Naiman, Fröhlich, and Stern, 1975).

Another possible reason—and here we return to the main theme of the paper—is the choice of variables. This needs to be altered if researchers are ultimately interested in testing a theory of second language acquisition with the aid of formal instruction. The alterations are motivated by the assumed desirability of reflecting what is known about classroom processes in investiga-

$$R_1 \qquad X \qquad Y_1 \qquad O_1$$
$$R_2 \qquad\quad\ \ Y_1 \qquad O_2$$
$$R_3 \qquad X \qquad Y_2 \qquad O_3$$
$$R_4 \qquad\quad\ \ Y_2 \qquad O_4$$

Legend: $R_1-R_4 = 4$ groups of students formed on basis of random assignment within each level of moderator variable. X = treatment (e.g., teaching behavior X), received by groups R_1 and R_3. Y_1 and Y_2 = two levels of moderator variable (e.g., "high" and "low" language learning aptitude). O_1-O_4 = observation, i.e., mean score of groups R_1-R_4 on outcome measure (e.g., test of ESL reading comprehension).

Figure 4.   Schematic representation of simple factorial design with one treatment variable and one moderator variable

tions of SLA in classroom settings. Given modifications in research designs of the kind indicated above, it is here that the potential becomes apparent of an approach to research which uses a combination of methods of data collection and analysis. Specifically, as in the following example, descriptive "anthropological" studies can inform (relatively) large-scale experimental work using interaction analysis.

A correlation might be found between extroversion or risk-taking and SL achievement.[8] Consideration of some characteristic(s) of the turn-taking system(s) used by teachers might show, however, that extroverts or risk-takers are "first bidders," and good at getting turns in this way. (Alternatively, as in the case of Carlos, considered earlier, their extrovert classroom behavior may simply attract language input from teachers who perceive their deportment as a "discipline" problem.) Getting more turns may lead to these students' obtaining more practice in the target language, and *that* factor, as work by Seliger (1977) suggests, may be a predictor of SL achievement.

Allwright's (1977) micro-analysis of the turn-taking system in one ESL lesson at UCLA showed a single learner, Igor, dominating conversation (along with the teacher), and suggested why this was happening in interactional terms. An interaction analysis approach to the description of that lesson would not have captured the unequal distribution of turns, as Igor's portion would have been credited to the ubiquitous "student"; i.e., the nature of individual student participation would have been lost in an approach which typically records all talk as occurring between teacher and "students." It would have shown *what* was happening only in the grossest terms, and not *why* or *how*.

Seliger's (1977) study at Queens College used a simple (seven-category) interaction analysis instrument capable of distinguishing individual speakers in real-time coding. This quantification of talk revealed the importance of the practice variable. Now it should be possible to conduct an experimental study in which measures were obtained on (i) learner characteristics (say, extroversion, cognitive style, or eavesdropping versus speaking preferences), (ii) classroom process variables (e.g., turn-allocation or turn-getting), and (iii) the outcome, or product variable(s), some measure(s) of SL achievement.

Similarly, the descriptive work by Henzl (1973), Gaies (1977), and Chaudron (1979) could usefully be applied in process-product studies motivated by Corder's input-intake distinction. An observational instrument would have to be developed which operationalized some of the "simplifying" features in order to allow data from a sufficient number of classrooms to be handled. Should correlations be found between quantity of "appropriate" input language (cf. Krashen's "i plus 1" level, Krashen, 1978) and achievement, experimental work could be designed which tried to identify interaction effects between this and such learner characteristics as aptitude and attitude.

These and other examples which come to mind have various common features. They assume that there will be no teacher or learner classroom behaviors (or very few of them) that are universally efficient for all students in all environments, and that it was one of the simplistic features of the comparative method studies to expect to find them. They imply the traditional cycle of descriptive, correlational, and experimental research, and simultaneously that the first two alone are as inadequate in this field as any other. They recognize the value of anthropological-type research, but see its real importance as that of informing the interaction analysis approach. They assume the latter to be necessary if researchers are to deal with the N-size and quantification of data that will make any findings generalizable and, hence, interesting. Lastly, they adopt the principle that there needs to be a classroom component in any research whose object of study is classroom second language learning.

Notes

1. Reprinted with permission from Language Learning (Vol. 30, No. 1). I am grateful to Kathi Bailey, Evelyn Hatch, Bob Ochsner and John Schumann for helpful comments on an earlier version of this paper.

2. See, e.g., Keating (1963), Scherer and Wertheimer (1964), Smith (1970), and Oskarsson (1972).

3. This is an important distinction, discussed further in the next section. Systems for both kinds of analysis are included in Table 1, however. Criteria for inclusion were that the instruments had been developed specifically for handling data from second language classrooms, and that their categories attempted classification of all verbal interaction in a lesson (as opposed, say, to teachers' feedback moves).

4. Skeptics might query the value of isolating components of global categories like "direct" and "indirect" behavior if it is the latter that are to be correlated with some dependent variable in research with the instrument. More detailed analyses will be justified, however, if future research is directed at discovering which aspects of, e.g., "direct" teaching behavior have a negative influence on student achievement. It is also easier for teacher trainers to talk about "praise" and "asking questions" than "being indirect."

5. Both teachers and textbooks for ESL students make ever freer use of such terms as "discourse," "contextual reference," "transformations," "notions," and "functions." My personal favorite is a teacher who was overheard telling a student that one of his homework sentences lacked "do-support."

6. See Ochsner (1979 for a critique of the current state of SLA research. He argues for the poetic combination of nomothetic and hermeneutic approaches.

7. "Perhaps," because Oller (1979) and Oller and Perkins (1978) have shown that this is also due to serious instrumentation problems where affective variables are involved.

8. I leave aside for the moment the problems of instrumentation when dealing with variables such as these in populations of second language learners. The OISE group in fact report some validity problems in the use of Eysenck's Extroversion Scale with their subjects.

References

Adelman, C., & Walker, R. Developing pictures for other frames: Action research and case study. In G. Chanan & S. Delamont (Eds.), *Frontiers of Classroom Research*. Slough: National Foundation for Educational Research, 1975, 220–232.

Allwright, R. L. Problems in the study of teachers' treatment of learner error. In M. Burt & H. Dulay (Eds.), *New Directions in Second Language Learning, Teaching and Bilingual Education. On TESOL '75*. Washington, D.C.: Teachers of English to Speakers of Other Languages, 1975, 96–109.

Allwright, R. L. Turns, topics, and tasks: Patterns of participation in language learning and teaching. Paper presented at the eleventh annual TESOL convention, Miami, Fla., April, 1977.

Bailey, K. D. *Methods of Social Research.* New York: The Free Press, 1978.

Bailey, K. M. An introspective analysis of an individual's language learning experience. Paper presented at the second Los Angeles Second Language Research Forum, Los Angeles, Ca., October, 1978.

Bailey, L. G. An observational method in the foreign language classroom: A closer look at interaction analysis. *Foreign Language Annals,* 1975, *8,* 4, 325–344.

Banko, R., & Perkins, K. Predictor variables in relation to attainment in ESL. Paper presented at the thirteenth annual TESOL convention, Boston, Mass., March, 1979.

Barkman, B. Classroom interaction. In P. M. Lightbown & B. Barkman, *Interactions among Learners, Teachers, Texts, and Methods of English as a Second Language. Progress Report 1977–78.* Montreal: Concordia University, 1978, 71–85.

Barnes, D. Language in the secondary classroom. In D. Barnes, J. Britton, & H. Rosen (Eds.), *Language, the Learner and the School.* Harmondsworth: Penguin, 1969, 9–77.

Bellack, A. A., Kliebard, R., Hyman, R., & Smith, F. *The Language of the Classroom.* New York: Teachers College Press, 1966.

Bialystok, E., Fröhlich, M., & Howard, J. *The Teaching and Learning of French as a Second Language in Two Distinct Learning Settings.* Toronto: The Ontario Institute for Studies in Education, November, 1978.

Biddle, B. J. Methods and concepts in classroom research. *Review of Educational Research,* 1967, *37,* 3, 337–357.

Boydell, D. Systematic observation in informal classrooms. In G. Chanan & S. Delamont (Eds.), *Frontiers of Classroom Research.* Slough: National Foundation for Educational Research, 1975, 183–197.

Bremme, D. W., & Erickson, F. Relations among verbal and nonverbal classroom behaviors. *Theory into Practice,* 1977, *16,* 153–161.

Burnett, J. H. *Anthropology and Education: An Annotated Bibliographic Guide.* New Haven, Conn.: HRAF Press, 1974.

Campbell, D. J., & Fiske, D. Convergent and discriminate validation by the multitrait-multimethod matrix. *Psychological Bulletin,* 1959, *56,* 81–105.

Capelle, G. C., Jarvella, R. J., & Revelle, E. Development of computer-assisted observational system for teacher training. Center for Research on Language and Language Behavior, University of Michigan, n.d.

Carton, A. S. *The "Method of Inference" in Foreign Language Study.* The Office of Research and Evaluation, The Division of Teacher Education, The City University of New York, 1966.

Chanan, G., & Delamont, S. (Eds.). *Frontiers of Classroom Research.* Slough: National Foundation for Educational Research, 1975.

Chaudron, C. Complexity of ESL teachers' speech and vocabulary expansion/elaboration. Paper presented at the thirteenth annual TESOL convention, Boston, Mass., March, 1979.

Cicourel, A. V. *Cognitive Sociology.* London: Macmillan, 1973.

Coulthard, M. *An Introduction to Discourse Analysis.* London: Longman, 1977.

Delamont, S. *Interaction in the Classroom.* London: Methuen, 1976.

Delamont, S., & Hamilton, D. Classroom research: A critique and a new approach. In M. Stubbs & S. Delamont (Eds.), *Explorations in Classroom Observation.* London: J. Wiley & Sons, 1976, 3–20.

Dumont, R. V. Learning English and how to be silent: Studies in Sioux and Cherokee classrooms. In C. B. Cazden, V. P. John, & D. Hymes (Eds.), *Functions of Language in the Classroom.* New York: Teachers College Press, 1972, 344–369.

Fanselow, J. F. Beyond *Rashomon*—conceptualizing and describing the teaching act. *TESOL Quarterly,* 1977, *11,* 1, 17–39.

Fiahive, D. E., & Moore, R. Critical variables in assessing ESL teacher effectiveness. Paper presented at the thirteenth annual TESOL convention, Boston, Mass., March, 1979.

Flanders, N. A. *Analyzing Teaching Behavior.* Reading, Mass.: Addison-Wesley, 1970.

Frake, C. O. A structural description of Subanum "religious behavior." In W. H. Goodenough (Ed.), *Explorations in Cultural Anthropology.* New York: McGraw-Hill, 1964.

Freedman, E. S. Experimentation into foreign language teaching methodology. Paper presented at meeting of the British Association for Applied Linguistics, York, September, 1975.

Freudenstein, R. How to analyze a foreign language lesson. Paper presented at the tenth annual TESOL convention, New York, March, 1976.

Gaies, S. J. The nature of linguistic input in formal second language learning: Linguistic and communicative strategies in ESL teachers' classroom language. In H. D. Brown, C. A. Yorio, & R. H. Crymes (Eds.), *On TESOL, '77. Teaching and Learning English as a Second Language: Trends in Research and Practice.* Washington, D. C.: TESOL, 1977.

Gardner, P. L. Research on teacher effects: Critique of a traditional paradigm. *The British Journal of Educational Psychology,* 1974, *44,* 2, 123–130.

Gardner, R. C., & Lambert, W. E. *Attitudes and Motivation in Second-Language Learning.* Rowley, Mass.: Newbury House, 1972.

Garfinkel, H. *Studies in Ethnomethodology.* Englewood Cliffs, N. J.: Prentice-Hall, 1967.

Genesee, F. The role of intelligence in second language learning. *Language Learning,* 1976, *26,* 2, 267–280.

Giorgi, A. *Psychology as a Human Science. A phenomenologically based approach.* New York: Harper & Row, 1970.

Hatch, E., & Long, M. H. Discourse analysis, what's that? In D. Larsen-Freeman (Ed.), *Discourse Analysis.* Rowley, Mass.: Newbury House, in press.

Henzl, V. Linguistic register of foreign language instructon. *Language Learning,* 1973, *23,* 207–222.

Hymes, D. Models of the interaction of language and social setting. *Journal of Social Issues,* 1967, *23,* 2.

Jarvis, G. A. A behavioral observation system for classroom foreign language skill acquisition activities. *Modern Language Journal,* 1968, *52,* 335–341.

Keating, R. F. *A Study of the Effectiveness of Language Laboratories.* New York: Columbia University, Institute of Administrative Research, Teachers College, 1963.

Krashen, S. D. The monitor model for second-language acquisition. In R. C. Gingras (Ed.), *Second Language Acquisition and Foreign Language Teaching.* Arlington, Va.: Center for Applied Linguistics, 1978, 1–26.

Krashen, S. D., Seliger, H. W., & Hartnett, D. Two studies in adult second language learning. *Kritikon Litterarum,* 1974, *3,* 220–228.

Levin, L. *Comparative Studies in Foreign-Language Teaching.* Stockholm: Almqvist & Wiksell, 1972.

Lofland, J. *Analyzing Social Settings.* Belmont, Ca.: Wadsworth, 1971.

Long, M. H. Wait and see. Paper presented at the annual CATESOL conference, Los Angeles, Ca., April, 1979.

Long, M. H., Adams, L., McLean, M., & Castaños, F. Doing things with words—verbal interaction in lockstep and small group classroom situations. In J. F. Fanselow & R. H. Crymes (Eds.), *On TESOL '76.* Washington, D.C.: TESOL, 1976, 137–153.

Macfarlane, J. M. Focus analysis. (Some notes towards a system of F. L. classroom observation.) In R. L. Allwright (Ed.), *Working Papers: Language Teaching Classroom Research.* University of Essex, Department of Language and Linguistics, September, 1975, 131–145.

McEwan, N. Z. An exploratory study of the multidimensional nature of teacher-student verbal interaction in second language classrooms. Unpublished doctoral dissertation, University of Alberta, 1976.

Mchoul, A. The organization of turns at formal talk in the classroom. *Language in Society,* 1978, *7,* 183–213.

Mehan, H. Accomplishing classroom lessons. In A. V. Cicourel et al., *Language Use and School Performance.* New York: Academic Press, 1974, 76–142.

Mehan, H. Ethnography. In *Bilingual Education: Current Perspectives. Social Science.* Arlington, Va.: Center for Applied Linguistics, 1977, 73–89.

Mehan, H. Structuring school structure. *Harvard Educational Review,* 1978, *48,* 1, 32–64.

Mehan, H., Cazden, C. B., Coles, L., Fisher, S., & Maroules, N. The social organization of classroom lessons. (CHIP Report 67) La Jolla, Ca.: University of California, San Diego, Center for Human Information Processing, December, 1976.

Mehan, H., & Wood, H. *The Reality of Ethnomethodology.* New York: Wiley, 1975.

Merleau-Ponty, M. Phenomenology and the science of man. In J. Edie (Ed.), *The Primacy of Perception.* Evanston, Ill.: Northwestern University Press, 1964.

Moskowitz, G. *The Foreign Language Teacher Interacts.* Minneapolis, Minn.: Association for Productive Teaching, 1970.

Moskowitz, G. The classroom interaction of outstanding foreign language teachers. *Foreign Language Annals.* 1976, *9,* 135–143, 146–157.

Moskowitz, G., & Hayman, J. L. Interaction patterns of first-year, typical, and "best" teachers in inner-city schools. *The Journal of Educational Research,* 1974, *67,* 5, 224–230.

Naiman, N., Fröhlich, M., & Stern, H. H. *The Good Language Learner.* Toronto: Ontario Institute for Studies in Education, 1975.

Nash, R. *Classrooms Observed.* London: Routledge & Kegan Paul, 1973.

Nearhoof, O. Teacher-pupil interaction in the foreign language classroom: A technique for self-evaluation. Unpublished research paper, quoted in F. M. Grittner, *Teaching Foreign Languages,* New York: Harper & Row, 1969, 328–330.

Nelson, L. N. The effect of classroom interaction on pupil linguistic performance. Unpublished dissertation, University of California, Los Angeles, 1964.

Oller, J. W., Jr. Research on the measurement of affective variables: Some remaining questions. Paper presented at the thirteenth annual TESOL convention, Boston, Mass., March, 1979.

Oller, J.W., Jr. & Perkins, K. Intelligence and language proficiency as sources of variance in self-reported affective variables. *Language Learning,* 1978, *28,* 85–97.

Ochsner, R. A poetics of second language acquisition. *Language Learning,* 1979, *29,* 1, 53–80.

Oskarsson, M. Comparative method studies in foreign language teaching. *Moderna Sprak,* 1972, *66,* 350–366.

Oyama, S. The sensitive period and comprehension of speech. *Working Papers in Bilingualism,* 1978, *16,* 1–16.

Paulston, C. B. Structural pattern drills: A classification. *Foreign Language Annals,* 1970, *4,2,* 187–193.

Pelto, P. J. *Anthropological Research. The Structure of Inquiry.* New York: Harper & Row, 1970.

Phillips, S. U. Participant structures and communicative competence: Warm Springs children in community and classroom. In C. B. Cazden, V. P. John, & D. Hymes (Eds.), *Functions of Language in the Classroom.* New York: Teachers College Press, 1972, 370–394.

Politzer, R. L. Foreign language teaching and bilingual education: Implications of some recent research findings. Paper presented to the ACTFL annual conference, San Francisco, Ca., November, 1977.

Riley, P. Discourse networks in classroom interaction: Some problems in communicative language teaching. Paper presented at the BAAL seminar, University of Bath, April, 1977.

Rogers, C. The effect of indirect teacher behavior on achievement by students in foreign language skills. Unpublished dissertation, Rutgers University, 1972.

Rosenshine, B., & Furst, N. The use of direct observation to study teaching. In R. Travers (Ed.), *Second Handbook of Research on Teaching.* Chicago: Rand McNally, 1973, 122–183.

Rothfarb, S. H. Teacher-pupil interaction in the FLES class. *Hispania,* 1970, *53,* 2, 256–260.

Sacks, H. An initial investigation of the usability of conversational data for doing sociology. In D. N. Sudnow (Ed.) *Studies in Social Interaction.* New York: The Free Press, 1972.

Scherer, A. C., & Wertheimer, M. *A Psycholinguistic Experiment in Foreign Language Teaching.* New York: McGraw-Hill, 1964.

Schneebaum, T. *Keep the River on Your Right.* Grove Press, 1969.

Schumann, F. M. Diary of a language learner: A further analysis. Paper presented at the second Los Angeles Second Language Research Forum, October, 1978.

Schumann, F. M., & Schumann, J. H. Diary of a language learner: An introspective study of second language learning. In H. D. Brown et al. (Eds.), *On TESOL '77*. Washington, D. C.: TESOL, 241–249.

Seliger, H. W. Does practice make perfect? A study of interaction patterns and L2 competence. *Language Learning*, 1977, *27*, 2, 263–278.

Shultz, J. It's not whether you win or lose, but how you play the game. Working Paper 1. Cambridge, Mass.: Harvard University, Graduate School of Education, Newton Classroom Interaction Project, 1976.

Sinclair, J. McH. and Coultard, R. M. *Towards An Analysis of Discourse*. London: Oxford University Press, 1975.

Smith, L. M., & Geoffrey, W. *The Complexities of an Urban Classroom*. New York: Holt, Rinehart & Winston, 1968.

Smith, P. D., Jr. *A Comparison of the Cognitive and Audiolingual Approaches to Foreign Language Instruction. The Pennsylvania Foreign Language Project*. Philadelphia, Pa.: The Center for Curriculum Development, 1970.

Spradley, J. P. *You Owe Yourself a Drink: An Ethnography of Urban Nomads*. Boston, Mass.: Little, Brown, 1970.

Stubbs, M. Teaching and talking: A sociolinguistic approach to classroom interaction. In G. Chanan & S. Delamont (Eds.), *Frontiers of Classroom Research*. Slough: National Foundation for Educational Research, 1975, 233–246.

Stubbs, M. Keeping in touch: Some functions of teacher-talk. In M. Stubbs & S. Delamont (Eds.), *Explorations in Classroom Observation*. London: John Wiley & Sons, 1976, 151–172.

Stubbs, M. & Delamont, S. (Eds.) *Explorations in Classroom Observation*. London: John Wiley & Sons, 1976.

Telatnik, M. A. The intensive journal as a self-evaluative instrument. Paper presented at the twelfth annual TESOL convention, Mexico City, April, 1978.

Tucker, G. R., Hamayan, E., & Genesee, F. H. Affective, cognitive and social factors in second language acquisition. *Canadian Modern Language Review*, 1976, *32*, 3,

Walsleben, M. Cognitive and affective factors influencing a learner of Persian (Farsi): A journal of second language acquisition. Unpublished paper, English 272K, University of California, Los Angeles, 1976.

Weeks, T. E. Discourse, culture and instruction. Paper presented at the discourse analysis section, AERA, 1976.

Wesche, M. B. Learning behaviors of successful adult students on intensive language training. Paper presented at the first Los Angeles Second Language Acquisition Research Forum, February, 1977.

William, S. M. Interaction analysis and achievement: An experiment. In J. R. Green (Ed.), *Foreign-Language Education Research: A Book of Readings*. Chicago: Rand McNally, 1973, 153–165.

Williams, J. D. Some problems involved in the experimental comparison of teaching methods. *Educational Research*, 1965, *8*, 26–41.

Wolcott, H. Criteria for an ethnographic approach to research in schools. *Human Organization*, 1975, *34*, 2, 111–127.

Wragg, E. C. Interaction analysis in the foreign language classroom. *Modern Language Journal*, 1970, *54*, 116–120.

Wright, C. J., & Nuthall, G. A. Relationships between teacher behaviors and pupil achievement in three experimental elementary science lessons. *American Educational Research Journal*, 1970, *7*, 477–491.

Questions for Discussion and Activities

1. Long defines the investigation of classroom learning as "research on second language learning and teaching all or part of whose data are derived from the observation or measurement of the classroom performance of teachers and students." What other components do you think impinge on classroom learning that are external to the classroom? How might the relationship between classroom and non-classroom elements in language learning be investigated?

2. What methods might be used to validate findings of various classroom observation instruments? What expectations might you have from certain types of teacher/learner interaction if the observed category of interaction is relevant to second language acquisition? For example, would performance on a discrete point grammar test be a good measure of the effectiveness of certain kinds of teacher behavior? What else would or would not?

3. Long, citing Adelman and Walker (1975), suggests using "triangulation" to control for observer bias. How might this methodology be employed in the L2 classroom?

4. Observe and tape a ten-minute segment of a language lesson using an observational instrument. Categorize your responses and then interview the teacher and possibly some students about what went on during your observation. Do the retrospections of the teacher or students support your observations?

5. Keep a participant observer's diary or record of a foreign language class you are in as a learner. What insights can you gain from this in your role as a teacher?

6. Become a member of a small group activity in an ESL class. Write up your observations either during or immediately after the experience. What aspects of the activity do you think are not accessible to the non-participant observer?

PART II

Learner Strategies and Learner Variables

3

Risk-Taking
and the Language Learner[1]

Leslie M. Beebe

If you are a roller skater, a skier, a stunt person, a helicopter pilot, a casino gambler, or even a smoker, you have probably been told more times than you would care to remember that you are taking risks. If you are not involved in any of the activities that we stereotype as gambles, you are still a risk-taker as far as the psychologist is concerned. As Daryl Bem points out, there are many risk-taking situations in everyday life which involve neither danger nor gambling. You take a risk when you get married, guess at an answer on a test, speak up in a group, or substitute a turtleneck for a tie (Bem, 1971, pp. 4–5). To Bem's examples, I would add that you take a risk every time you open your mouth in a foreign language, or for that matter in any learning situation where you are called on to perform. Without realizing it, even the most conservative individual takes risks. Every human being takes risks. However, not every human being takes the same number of risks and makes equally risky choices. These factors are a function of many variables. Before discussing the variables that affect risk-taking behavior, it is necessary to define risk-taking in general and to establish the connection between risk-taking and language learning.

Risk-taking may be defined as a situation where an individual has to make a decision involving choice between alternatives of different desirability; the outcome of the choice is uncertain; there is a possibility of failure. In the words of Kogan and Wallach, two of the leading researchers on risk-taking, "These two aspects of decision situations, the lack of certainty and the prospect of loss or failure, lend a risky character to the decision-making process" (Kogan and Wallach, 1967, p. 113). Daryl Bem phrases it a slightly different way: "Taking a risk . . . may be viewed as a selection of one alternative or course of action from among many in which the consequences of that choice could leave the individual in a worse position than if he had selected otherwise or not selected at all" (Bem, 1971, p. 5).

I have long believed that the good language learner is one who is willing to take risks. Learning to speak a second or foreign language involves taking the risk of being wrong, with all its ramifications. In the classroom, these ramifications might include a bad grade in the course, a fail on the exam, a reproach from the teacher, a smirk from a classmate, punishment or embarrassment imposed by oneself. Outside the classroom, individuals learning a second language face other negative consequences if they make mistakes. They fear looking ridiculous; they fear the frustration coming from a listener's blank look, showing that they have failed to communicate; they fear the danger of not being able to take care of themselves; they fear the alienation of not being able to communicate and thereby get close to other human beings. Perhaps worst of all, they fear a loss of identity. Given these realities, we must conclude that all second and foreign language learning involves taking risks.

In this paper, I shall move from these introductory remarks on risk-taking to a brief overview of the psychological literature on risk-taking behavior, and a look at some of the literature in linguistics and ESL which seems to be related. After the review of the literature, I shall discuss my own empirical research on risk-taking among Puerto Rican elementary school children. Finally, I shall conclude by discussing the implications of the research on risk-taking for the ESL classroom and the study of second language acquisition theory.

Review of the Literature on Risk-Taking

The social-psychological literature

Several concepts are basic to the understanding of risk-taking behavior: expected value, expected utility, and subjective probability (Bem, 1971). Expected value is a mathematical calculation of the objective value of gamble. Bem cites a stereotypical example—flipping a coin. Gamblers have a 50% probability of winning and a 50% probability of losing. As long as they bet equal amounts of money on winning and losing, they will come out even. When they bet different amounts, they can calculate mathematically how much money they can expect to win or lose.

Usually, however, gambling is not such a simple matter. Expected utility, or the gambler's subjective value attached to the situation, often affects behavior. The old adage, "Better safe than sorry," is often quoted in gambling situations where the expected value is negative, but an individual places high subjective value on making a bet. Bem cites buying auto accident insurance as an example. Most citizens buy it, despite a negative expected value. They anticipate losing money, but they prefer the certainty of paying regular yearly premiums to the possibility of losing a fortune.

Besides allowing subjective utility to override objective value, human beings allow subjective estimates of probability to override objective knowledge of actual probability. People who refuse to fly because they fear their plane will crash often know very well that the probability of being killed in a car accident is greater. Yet they continue to drive their cars every day and refuse to fly in an effort to stay alive.

Bem (1971) divides external factors influencing risk-taking behavior into three categories: the situation, the individual, and the social setting. Following this useful categorization, let us take a look at the literature on risk-taking in somewhat more detail than Bem has done.

Factors involving the individual, sometimes grouped with personality factors, include motivation to achieve, need for approval, age, sex, locus of control, and self-esteem. Herlizer and Cutter (1971, p. 281, in Larson, 1977, pp. 19–20) suggest that risk-taking is not a stable personality variable itself and has only a "fragile series of personality correlates." Nevertheless, claims have been made about correlations between personality and risk-taking behavior. Atkinson (1958) and Atkinson and Feather (1966) review research which is known as the McClelland-Atkinson position, based on the theory of achievement motivation developed by McClelland, Atkinson, Clark, and Lowell (1953). This position claims that persons with a high motivation to achieve are, contrary to popular belief, moderate, not high, risk-takers (Kogan and Wallach, 1967). These individuals like to be in control and like to depend on skill. They do not take wild, frivolous risks or enter no-win situations. They also shy away from low-risk situations. On the other hand, low need achievers, persons who strongly fear failure, and those with a high need for approval, are likely to take courses of action which are extremely risky or extremely conservative. They are less likely to change their risk-taking behavior even when it leads to failure. Kogan and Wallach (1967) admit that the Atkinson theory of achievement motivation has been repeatedly tested out and confirmed, but they insist that it is not conclusive since the studies involved competitive classroom games only, did not control for individual differences in skill, and did not study chance conditions. The methods of calculating achievement motivation influenced the results too.

Age and sex have also been considered personal characteristics that might affect risk-taking. Contrary to a popular stereotype, men overall did not have significantly higher risk-taking levels. However, men and women did tolerate higher risk levels in behaviors considered "appropriate" respectively to their sex (Wallach and Kogan, 1959). As for age, elderly adults were more conservative than college students in their risk-taking preferences (Wallach and Kogan, 1961).

Locus of control, a construct developed from social learning theory by Rotter (1966), has been claimed to be a relatively stable personality variable in comparison to risk-taking. People displaying internal locus of control attribute their outcomes (what happens to them) to internal causes, i.e., their own actions.

Those displaying external locus of control tend to attribute their outcomes to fate, luck, chance, or powerful other people (Bridge et al., 1979). The question has been asked: What is the relationship betweeen internal locus of control and risk-taking behavior? Joe (1971) reports that two studies show that internals are more cautious and conservative in risk-taking than externals. Two studies claimed the opposite, one with a significant result. And two studies found no significant relationship. Joe believes the evidence is in favor of internals as more cautious and conservative.

As for the relationship between self-esteem and risk-taking, there is no conclusive evidence, but Führer (1974, in Larson, 1977) makes the claim that consistent, successful risk-takers in her study were internal, cautious, and had middle-level self-esteem. In general, it seems that situational variables influence the study of risk-taking to a greater degree than personality variables.

Situational variables include the degree of skill versus chance affecting the outcome, the influence of prior experience (success versus failure, and the number of trials), the value of the reward, and the degree of interest the participant has in the task. The degree of skill versus chance affecting the outcome seems to be the major variable studied by psychologists. In their review of the literature, Kogan and Wallach conclude that "a skill context appeared to stimulate a moderate level of risk taking, whereas a chance context seemed to induce . . . extremely risky or conservative strategies" (1967, p. 128).

The value of the reward seems to be another important situational determinant of risk-taking behavior. A penny may not have the same influence as a dollar reward. Likewise, the seriousness of a possible loss (e.g., death, losing one's job) influences a decision. Kogan and Wallach believe that real payoffs lead to greater conservatism in decision-making than imaginary incentives. They also claim that the cost of failure is a greater deterrent than the value of success as an incentive.

Prior experience (success versus failure) may or may not be a situational determinant of risk-taking behavior. Edwards (1962) claims it is not. Kogan and Wallach (1967), however, claim that previous losses and wins do affect risk-taking. It seems highly unlikely that individuals would be oblivious to repeated success or repeated failure.

In addition to individual personality factors and situational factors, there are factors involving social setting which affect risk-taking behavior. This category encompasses the vast literature on group versus individual settings. J.A.F. Stoner (1961), in his unpublished master's thesis, was the first to describe the phenomenon of the "risky shift." This refers to the finding that individuals take greater risks in group decisions than they do by themselves on the very same task. There is a great deal of evidence that the risky shift exists, but very little agreement as to what explains it. Madaras and Bem (1968) discuss four alternative hypotheses to explain it, concluding that Brown (1965) is probably right in proposing the "cultural value for risk" hypothesis. Brown claims that the society values risk-taking. Individuals in group discussion will alter their risk levels to appear and feel just as risky as the next person. After reporting Brown's hypothesis, Madaras and Bem provide empirical evidence that there is, in fact, value placed on risk. They also discovered exceptions, however, involving a conservative shift. They concluded that a conservative shift resulted from specific circumstances in which there was a moral value competing with the value for risk, a group pessimism phenomenon, or a feeling or responsibility to others for possible failure. In other words, the risky shift did exist; so did the conservative shift under specific circumstances.

Despite the volumes of literature documenting the risky shift, there has never been a consensus on its explanation, or even full agreement that it would exist under all conditions outside experimental situations. Even with the examples of the conservative shift, however, it seems that language teachers interested in fostering risk-taking cannot ignore the probable positive effects of group discussion.

Literature in linguistics and ESL related to risk-taking

Although research on risk-taking is no longer in vogue in psychology, the phenomenon of risk-taking is frequently mentioned in recent research on applied linguistics and second language pedagogy. It is clear that several areas of linguistic and pedagogical research may be illuminated by the definition and study of risk-taking. These include the problem of the silent student, the risk of speaking for the second language teacher, the study of motivation, the characteristics of the good language learner, the Monitor Model, and the acculturation model of second language acquisition.

The Silent Student. William Labov has maintained for years that black students who don't speak much to teachers in class or during oral interviews should not be labeled "nonverbal" (Labov, 1969). He claims that these "silent" students operate on the assumption that anything they say can be used against them. They remain silent whenever possible or use other means to avoid answering the question. I have noticed the same kind of behavior from many ESL students in schools. They answer simply "yes" or "no" without elaborating; they answer "nothing" or "I don't know"; sometimes they pause frequently. Perhaps the black students and ESL students who display this kind of behavior have something in common. They are often found to be quite talkative with their peers, but quiet with teachers (or others they perceive as teachers). In the case of black students, Labov has shown that many of those who teachers claimed were "nonverbal" displayed a rich variety of verbal behaviors in their peer groups. The same is true of the ESL students when they are free to speak as they like. Perhaps what the two groups have in common is their perception of the risks involved in speaking. In the classroom, the person who believes that anything he says may be held against him is one who perceives talking in class as a high risk–low gain proposition. With his peers, speaking is a low risk–high gain situation.

The Risk of Speaking for the Second Language Learner. One of the reasons why many second language learners are shyer speaking a second language around peers from their own language group than around native speakers and teachers is that they perceive the risk of looking foolish as greater in the presence of peers from their country. They figure that they cannot be expected to compete with native speakers, but they may be compared unfavorably to their peers.

Heyde's pilot study on self-esteem and oral performance (1977, p. 232) suggests that subjects with high self-esteem have higher ratings from both themselves and their teachers on their oral production than subjects with low self-esteem. Heyde does not directly link self-esteem and risk-taking although her review of the literature encourages my hypothesis that there is a relationship. Heyde (1977, p. 230) cites Fitts's report of research (1972, pp. 36–42) that motivation is related to self-esteem. She also cites Gardner and Lambert's correlation between integrative motivation and proficiency, especially oral-aural proficiency (1972, p. 30, in Heyde, 1977, p. 228). Heyde argues that speaking best reflects self-esteem "since speaking is an active skill which requires *risking* (emphasis mine) evaluation by others of the speaker's grammar, pronunciation, language facility, and often personal worth" (Heyde, 1977, p. 228). Heyde then connects self-esteem to motivation and motivation to risk.

I, too, would argue that risk is an inevitable part of speaking. To demonstrate this, we need only consider Lambert's research in Montreal (Lambert, 1967). Groups of judges were asked to evaluate the personality characteristics of speakers by listening to their voices on audio-tape. The judges were not told that they were hearing two readings, one in French, one in English, by speakers who were bilingual. This procedure, known as the matched guise technique, allowed Lambert et al. to discover biases of the judges. Judges consistently rated speakers in their French Canadian guises lower than in their English Canadian guises. The French Canadian guises were rated by French Canadian student judges as less intelligent, dependable, likable, and as having less character. This research demonstrates that speaking involves risking a negative evaluation.

Risk-Taking and Motivation in Language Acquistion. Charles Curran (1976) has outlined a five-stage growth process in Counseling-Learning, moving from total dependence of the learner on the counselor in Stage I to total independence from the counselor in Stage V. Curran alludes to the increase in security during the first three stages, and the difficulty that the learner experiences in passing on to and through Stage IV. Curran discusses "resurgence of aggression," a "stronger determination to overcome barriers," and open hostility which is often present in Stage IV. Rardin (in presentations at Teachers College, Columbia University, 1976, 1977) speaks of the difficulty, and frequent inability, that many immigrants experience in moving on to Stage IV. Some immigrants, no matter how many years they live in the country of the target language, do not proceed to Stage IV. The study of risk-taking may shed light on this immigrant phenomenon. In Stage I, learners feel a sense of high risk–high gain. There is the risk of making mistakes and failing to communicate, but there is the gain of learning to communicate. Once they pass through Stage III and become able to communicate their ideas, they may perceive proceeding on to Stages IV and V as low gain. The gain could be low because they are already able to make themselves understood and fulfil their instrumental needs.

If they continue to progress in acquiring native-like competence in the language, they may perceive a high risk as well. It is no longer the initial risk of sounding foolish in one's child-like state of linguistic dependence. It is now the risk of a threat to one's ethnic identity.

I contend that fossilization (Selinker's term, 1972, for non-native structures that do not change to become more like the target language as time goes on) and difficulty in moving on to Stage IV arise from a risk-taking situation where learners perceive high risk–low gain. In other words, learners experience a crisis in motivation because they evaluate the situation as a bad gamble.

A similar phenomenon hits people living temporarily abroad, but the circumstances differ from group to group. Many Peace Corps Volunteers, for example, learn only a corpus of useful expressions they need to live comfortably. After mastering these, they do not progress further. Their instrumental needs have been met. Other Peace Corps Volunteers continue to make progress. The latter are usually those who have an integrative motivation. We might take a new look at instrumental versus integrative motivation in light of risk-taking. Limited instrumental goals may be met very quickly. After they are met, the situation becomes one of low gain and high effort, if not high risk. However, if the goal is integration, there is a high gain attached to continued progress.

While living in Thailand, I informally observed that missionaries, whose motivation was strongly integrative as well as instrumental, were most successful among foreigners in learning to speak Thai well. Researchers also succeeded in acquiring the skills they needed to complete their research. Library researchers learned to read; interviewers learned to speak. Very few researchers learned to write Thai well. There was no instrumental need for most of the diplomatic corps to learn Thai, and integrative motivation is a painful proposition for people who stay only two to four years in a foreign country and then move to another part of the world. A perceived threat to national identity is present, leaving a situation seen as risk without sufficient gain.

The Good Language Learner. Some of the most intriguing research of recent years deals with the characteristics of the good language learner. Naiman, Fröhlich, and Stern (1975) have researched this topic, and they allude to risk in several places. Joan Rubin, in a ground-breaking article, claims that good language learning depends on at least three variables: aptitude, motivation, and opportunity (1975). She does not refer to risk-taking *per se,* but her discussion of each of these variables alludes to aspects of risk-taking or cites authors who mention risk.

Aptitude is the source of much debate. As Rubin points out, Carroll argues that aptitude is invariant (Carroll, 1960, in Rubin, 1975), whereas others, like Rubin, believe that students can be helped to become better language learners.

Rubin cites seven general strategies (or techniques used to gain knowledge) which good language learners seem to employ. She underscores three of these in her discussion of the abilities the poor language learner needs to develop. Although they are never called risk-taking, they discuss aspects of risk-taking.

The first strategy considered by Rubin to be a part of high aptitude is being a good guesser. Clearly, guessing is part of risk-taking, if we think of risk-taking as making a decision when the outcome is uncertain and the prospect of failure is there. Buying stocks, playing poker, having your hair cut, and speaking in a foreign language, all involve some guessing about a result that is unknown and risky.

Rubin cites the willingness "to appear foolish in order to communicate and get the message across" as a second crucial strategy of successful language learners (1975, p. 43). A willingness to appear foolish is a willingness to take a risk. It is a gamble on being worse off after you have spoken than you were before. Although this strategy is surely related to risk-taking, and I agree with Rubin that good language learners have it, I think that most good learners also have a healthy self-esteem which leads them to be less prone to expecting that their normal errors make them look foolish. In other words, I think they perceive speaking as a more moderate risk than do unsuccessful language learners who may view it as extremely high or low risk. This might be predicted since research suggests that success in business correlates with moderate risk-taking behavior (Bem, 1971).

The third strategy which, according to Rubin, reflects the high aptitude of the successful language learner is using knowledge to make up new sentences, i.e., using acquired competence. Here again, there is a connection to risk-taking. Although silence could be a risk in some contexts, risk-taking in learning to speak a second or foreign language must involve the learner trying out new structures he or she is unsure of.

After aptitude, Rubin claims that motivation is the second crucial variable in good language learning: " . . .the good language learner seems to have a high motivation to communicate, no matter where he is" (Rubin, 1975, p. 43). Since the outcome of attempted communication in a second language is particularly uncertain, and the more elementary the learner, the more uncertain the outcome and the greater the possibility of failure to communciate, it seems quite certain that motivation to speak is related to willingness to take risks.

Rubin's third crucial variable in good language learning—opportunity to practice—can also be related to risk-taking if we recognize that "the good language learner takes and creates opportunities to practice what he has learned while the poorer learner passively does what is assigned . . ." (Rubin, 1975, p. 44). This point can also be viewed in terms of Krashen's distinction between input and intake (Krashen, 1978). The good language learner allows more input to become useful intake. This probably involves active listening to language that is beyond the learner's proficiency—a process which could be threatening and involve some risk on a personal level.

Naiman, Fröhlich, and Stern (1975) maintain that the good language learner emphasizes fluency over accuracy in the earlier stages of learning. This willingness to make a mistake for the sake of comunicating effectively is similar to personality characteristics cited by Rubin. Another personality factor suggested by Naiman, Fröhlich, and Stern is extroversion. They quote a teacher who said, "One good characteristic is to be outgoing, to be willing to take risks" (1975, p. 81). Other teachers, though a smaller number, mentioned introversion as a characteristic of successful learners. No consistent personality profile emerged from the study, but the majority of comments favored the view that the successful learner is not afraid of making an error and not afraid of speaking when uncertain of the exact syntax.

The Monitor Revisited. Krashen (1978) developed his notion of individual variation in the amount of monitoring done by a learner. Krashen's Monitor Model posits that there are two separate systems for gaining knowledge of a second language. Individuals may subconsciously "acquire" language through the creative construction process used by children in first language acquisition. This process is completely unconscious, informal, and separate from conscious, formal "learning" of linguistic rules. Krashen's model asserts that language users may edit their output by using their "Monitor." They draw on conscious knowledge of linguistic rules to edit their speech. The amount they "monitor" (i.e., edit) varies with the individual. Krashen describes extreme cases of monitoring: overusers and underusers. He suggests that extreme overusers are so overly concerned with correctness that they sacrifice fluency. Extreme underusers are so uttterly oblivious to conscious linguistic knowledge that they do not utilize it to advantage even when conditions favor it. These learners are unaffected by information about the target language which they learn in class. Krashen suggests that successful Monitor users (i.e., optimal users) are those who edit when it does not interfere with communication.

The Monitor Model should be revisited after a look at the psychological research on risk-taking. It is possible that Krashen's cautious overuser is a low risk-taker. His Monitor underuser is a high risk-taker. The optimal Monitor user calculates the appropriate time and place for monitoring. This is like the moderate risk-taker who takes enough risks to move ahead, but does not take wild chances. J.W. Atkinson's research on motivation and risk-taking suggests that individuals who are high in achievement motivation (e.g., successful executives) prefer competitive situations with a moderate probability of success. They get satisfaction from adopting risky goals with a 50% approximate chance of success and feeling that it is their skill, not chance, that leads to their success in reaching the difficult goal (Atkinson, 1958, 1964; Atkinson and Feather, 1966, in Carney, 1971, pp. 52–53). Contrary to popular belief, high need achievers are not high risk-takers, but most probably moderate risk-takers. Kogan and Wallach (1967, p. 181) suggest that under certain circumstances they can even be conservative risk-takers. Those who have a high fear of failure tend to be extremely high or extremely low risk-takers (Bem, 1971, pp. 12–13).

If these individuals also crave approval from others or worry about their self-image, they will avoid moderate risks, acting consistently, but irrationally, in a very risky or very conservative way (Kogan and Wallach, 1967, in Bem, 1971, pp. 13–14).

Krashen's discussion of individual variations in use of the Monitor is an abstract model of three categories: Monitor overusers, Monitor underusers, and optimal Monitor users. It reports case studies and does not attempt to say a great deal about the personality of individuals in each category. Krashen simply describes the overuser as self-conscious and introverted, the underuser as outgoing and uninhibited. He relates Monitor use to the onset of Piaget's Formal Operations stage. It seems that understanding of Monitor use would be greatly enhanced by reference to the vast amounts of psychological literature on personality characteristics such as extroversion/introversion and risk-taking, as well as to Piaget's work. The literature shows that individuals do not have a fixed risk-taking propensity. On the contrary, risk-taking varies according to the situation (e.g., the degree of chance versus skill involved in the risk) and the social setting (e.g., the presence of a group). It is possible that the underuser (who may be viewed as a high risk-taker) will modify his or her behavior under certain circumstances. The overuser (viewed as a low risk-taker) will become riskier if put in groups and subjected to conditions for the risky shift phenomenon whereby members of a group are riskier in making group decisions than they are when making their individual ones.

The Acculturation Model Revisited. Schumann's Acculturation Model (1978) claims that social and affective (psychological) factors constitute acculturation, and acculturation is the major causal variable in second language acquisition. Learners can be placed on a continuum of social and psychological distance or proximity to the target culture. Those learners with high social and psychological distance, i.e., those who have low contact with target language speakers, are the ones who will have the most difficulty acquiring the target language.

It is possible to reinterpret the variables that make up social and psychological distance as factors that affect the learner's perception of the risks involved in learning a new language. Let us look, for instance, at social dominance patterns. Couldn't the situation of belonging to a subordinate group be considered one in which the risk is very high? Risk is a situation in which the outcome is uncertain, and there is a possibility of failure. High risk means that there is a high probability of failure. Belonging to an economically, culturally, or politically subordinate group would involve high risk in that the chance of full integration and reaping the full benefit of communication would be perceived as low, even if one learned the target language.

Perhaps the reason that a small second language group, not very cohesive, with low enclosure, is conducive to second language learning is that the learner from this situation perceives less risk of losing a peer group when learning the new language. The fact that the two groups have a positive attitude toward each other, rather than a negative one, could mean that the learner perceives a lower risk and a higher gain in attempting to assimilate or adapt to the target culture. In some way, each of Schumann's social variables can be related to a learner's perception of risk in the situation. Psychological (affective) variables also relate to risk in that they involve one's perception of a threat to ethnic identity or self-identity (the ego).

Having looked at several areas of applied linguistics and ESL which can be reinterpreted in light of the research on risk-taking, let us now turn to the second section of this paper. This section reports on the findings of an empirical study which attempts to define risk-taking in terms of linguistic performance and then find evidence for it in sociolinguistic data.

Interviewer Ethnicity, Accuracy, Avoidance, and Risk-Taking: An Empirical Study

The major variables in this study were the ethnicity and language competence of the interviewer, and the accuracy rates, avoidance scores, and risk-taking levels of the interviewee. The interviewers were a monolingual, native English-speaking Anglo, A Spanish-dominant Hispanic, and an English-dominant Hispanic. Accuracy was measured in one instance as correctness on DO insertion in WH questions. Later, a more global measure, number of correct T-units, was adopted. Risk-taking was first measured only for WH questions and then broadened in the most recent study to reflect amount of talk and volunteering. The study demonstrated that levels of risk-taking were significantly higher for bilingual children with the monolingual English-speaking interviewer. The accuracy rates were significantly lower with that interviewer. And topic avoidance was significantly lower in that situation. Before examining these findings in detail, let us turn to the methodology, background research, hypotheses, and questions for the study.

The data reported here are based on a study of twenty Puerto Rican bilingual (Spanish-English) third graders in the New York area. The children were selected by stratified random sampling from one school. Ten of the children had gone through the school in the monolingual track; ten had gone through in the bilingual track. In each program, monolingual and bilingual, five children were boys, five girls. Each child was interviewed in English four separate times: once by a monolingual English-speaking interviewer, twice by Hispanic bilingual interviewers—one of them a Spanish-dominant interviewer, the other an English-dominant interviewer—and finally in a group of three children with all three interviewers present. The interviews were all conducted inside the school during school hours. This provided a constant setting and easy access to the children, but it had the disadvantage of obtaining less interviewee talk and generally more formal talk than was elicited during exploratory interviews held on a weekend in Central Park. The interviews all began with questions designed to initiate conversation and ended with ESL exercises using cue cards and colored picture stimuli to elicit WH questions and progressive aspect markers. The topics selected were controlled in number and content across interviewers.

The data in this study are based on both the conversational data and the WH-question exercises. In the case of the WH questions, they are restricted to a subsample of nine of the original twenty children. They are further narrowed down to comparisons between the monolingual interviewer and the Spanish-dominant interviewer. In the case of the conversational data, the findings are based on the entire original sample with the exclusion of one male child in the bilingual program who was so severely handicapped emotionally that the data obtained were unusable. Comparisons are restricted to the interviews with the monolingual interviewer and the English-dominant interviewer.

I have elsewhere discussed the finding (Beebe, 1980) that a subsample of nine bilingual children, the group who were having great difficulty with WH questions, displayed higher accuracy with the Spanish-dominant interviewer but greater risk-taking with the monolingual-interviewer. The difference in accuracy rates between interviewers did not turn out to be statistically significant, but the risk-taking scores were in fact statistically significant. I therefore argued only that risk-taking varied as a function of interviewer ethnicity. More recent work, however, has obtained significant differences in accuracy as well as risk-taking.

In earlier papers (Beebe, 1977, 1978) I have demonstrated that Chinese-Thai bilinguals have more accurate pronunciation when speaking Thai to an ethnic Thai than when speaking Thai to an ethnic Chinese who is bilingual in Thai and Chinese. Phonological data of this sort seem to be quite straightforward. The same relationship obtains with the Puerto Rican children presently being studied. They are consistently more accurate in pronunciation when they speak to the native speaker of English.

This relationship reverses, however, when grammatical structures are examined or when correctness on a more global level is considered. Why? No one really knows for sure, but one plausible hypothesis is risk-taking. Risk-taking, which has been defined in social psychology as a choice with an uncertain outcome and a prospect of failure, cannot be so easily defined in second language learning as in, say, roulette. All productive use of a second language involves some risk. There is always some uncertainty in the act of pronouncing for the adult acquirer who will probably never attain fully native pronounciation. There is always the possibility of failure to communicate in either speaking or writing. How, then, do we define risk-taking?

Thus far, although many of us in ESL use the term risk-taking, no one has attempted to give a general definition. I have defined it in purely structural terms (Beebe, 1980) for the specific context of one structure—WH questions with the auxiliary DO inserted (e.g., *Where did* she see that fire?). I have measured risk-taking by calculating the number of times subjects attempted to insert DO in a WH question over the number of WH questions they produced.

$$\text{Risk-Taking} = \frac{\text{number of times DO attempted}}{\text{number of questions produced}}$$

The use of DO could be correct or incorrect, required or not required in that context. The important factor was that the child attempted it when uncertain as to its proper use. All children knew the auxiliary DO, recognized and understood it, but they all had difficulty producing it correctly. Since the ability to use DO correctly in WH questions is acquired later than the ability to communicate the question, and it is a difficult grammatical structure, it was considered an appropriate choice for an initial attempt to operationalize the notion of risk-taking and measure it in second language acquisition.

The results of this inquiry are seen in Table 1. The nine subjects in the subsample of children who were having difficulty with DO insertion in WH questions displayed significantly greater risk-taking rates with the monolingual interviewer than with the Spanish-dominant interviewer (p. < .01 on a dependent t-test, one-tailed). They favored the Spanish-dominant interviewer

Table 1. Rates of Risk-taking in Production of WH Questions by Nine Bilingual Children with the Monolingual and the Bilingual Interviewer

| | Interviewer | | | |
| | Monolingual | | Bilingual (Spanish-dominant) | |
Children by Program and Sex	n	%	n	%
Monolingual Program				
Male				
Alberto	21/29	72	10/23	43
Mark	14/30	47	7/20	35
Female				
Dorren	7/30	23	3/32	9
Samantha	8/29	28	0/14	0
Bilingual Program				
Male				
Luis	12/22	55	14/26	54
Richard	9/31	29	8/29	28
Female				
Jenny	6/30	20	3/24	13
Nydia	20/30	67	15/26	58
Carmen	0/30	0	0/29	0
$\overline{X}$		=38		=27

Key: n = the number of times DO insertion was attempted (right or wrong, needed or not) divided by the number of questions produced by that subject

% = Risk-taking rates (calculated like percents)

$t_8 = 3.068; p < .01$

N = 9 subjects

(though not significantly) in their accuracy rates with DO insertion in WH questions.

The results led to further research questions about risk-taking:

1. What are some more general measures of risk-taking?
2. What is the relationship between measures of risk-taking and ethnicity of the interviewer?
3. How do other measures of risk-taking relate to accuracy rates?
4. What is the relationship between avoidance and risk-taking?

Virtually all attempts at productive use of a new language meet the psychologist's definition of risk-taking—an act involving uncertainty and a possibility of failure. That is, for most people, just opening their mouths in a second language constitutes a risk. I searched the literature, however, in an attempt to find more specific (and more measurable) definitions of risk-taking. Larson cites the humanist point of view that "all learning is risk-taking behavior" (1977, p. 2). It may be true that all learning involves some risk, but we would not want to measure learning (e.g., give achievement tests) and consider this a measure of risks taken. Kleinmann (1978) says risk-taking is a variable that future studies of avoidance will have to examine in detail, but does not attempt to define it. Madden et al. (1978, pp. 112–113) contrast avoidance with guessing strategies. Guessing is defined as a "trial and error" approach. The authors do not explicitly equate guessing with risk-taking, but in a paper by Bailey, Madden, and Eisenstein (1979) the authors imply that the guessing they describe is a kind of risk-taking, where risk-taking means hypothesis testing (p. 18). Guessing about correct structure (i.e., using a structure without being sure it is correct) seems to be the prevalent working definition of risk-taking in ESL, but nowhere is it explicit in the literature.

"Guessing" could be used to describe the behavior of the nine children who attempted to use DO in WH questions even though they had not fully acquired it. In addition, studies could be designed to discover: (1) the role of guessing in learning; (2) the relationship between degree of acquisition and guessing behavior. However, for this paper, other linguistic measures were sought which might constitute additional evidence of risk-taking, even if they were not considered to be identical to risk-taking.

Two measures were selected as evidence of risk-taking: (1) the amount of interviewee talk; (2) the amount of information volunteering. The amount of talk was defined as the number of T-units used by the child with each interviewer. (T-units were calculated using an adaptation of Loban's "communication unit," 1976.)[2] The amount of information volunteering, called the number of "volunteers," was defined as the number of times each child volunteered some new information not explicitly required by the question asked, divided by the total number of T-units. Topic changes and extra information voluntarily supplied by the child thus counted as "volunteers." In addition, for the few children who launched into lengthy monologues on one topic, every eighth T-unit became an artificial boundary for the onset of a new "volunteer."

The findings showed that the amount of talk was significantly greater with the monolingual interviewer than with the English-dominant interviewer. The findings were significant at the .0005 level on a dependent t-test (one-tailed). (Data on the Spanish-dominant interviewer are not yet available.) If amount of talk is assumed to be an indirect measure of risk-taking, these data confirm the hypothesis that the children take significantly more risks with a native speaker of the target language and a non-Hispanic member of the target culture. The findings corroborate those on WH questions with the Spanish-dominant interviewer.

Table 2. Amount of Talk by Nineteen Bilingual Children with the Monolingual and the Bilingual Interviewer

	Interviewer	
		Bilingual
	Monolingual	*(English-dominant)*
Children by		
Program and Sex	*n*	*n*
Monolingual Program		
Male (5)	885	346
Female (5)	509	331
Bilingual Program		
Male (4)	457	294
Female (5)	721	388
Totals	2572	1359

Key: n = number of T-units
t_{18} = 5.019; p < .0005
N = 19 subjects

On the measure of volunteering information, the results were also positive. The data confirmed the hypothesis that children would volunteer significantly more often with the monolingual interviewer than with the English-dominant Hispanic interviewer. On a dependent t-test (one-tailed), the result was t_{18} =2.114; p < .025. However, the coding of T-units containing volunteered information was much more subjective than the counting of T-units used to calculate amount of talk.

Another crucial question in this research concerned the correlation between the accuracy of the children's speech and the ethnicity of the interviewer. General accuracy was calculated in terms of the correctness of T-units:

$$\text{Accuracy} = \frac{\text{number of correct T-units}}{\text{total number of T-units}}$$

Table 3.   Rates of Volunteering by Nineteen Bilingual Children with the Monolingual and the Bilingual Interviewer[a]

	Interviewer			
	Monolingual		Bilingual (English-dominant)	
Children by Program and Sex	n	%	n	%
Monolingual Program				
Male (5)	78/885	9	20/346	6
Female (5)	36/509	7	23/331	7
Bilingual Program				
Male (4)	24/457	5	11/294	4
Female (5)	47/721	7	23/388	6
Totals	185/2572	7	77/1359	6

Key: $n = \dfrac{\text{number of volunteered T-units}}{\text{total number of T-units}}$

$t_{18} = 2.114; p < .025$

$N = 19$ subjects

[a]All except four of the nineteen subjects volunteer more with the monolingual interviewer than with the English-dominant bilingual interviewer. The averages given here seem to obscure the pattern, but the summary format is maintained for consistency.

The data confirmed the hypothesis that the bilingual children would be significantly more accurate with the English-dominant Hispanic interviewer. On a dependent t-test (one-tailed) $t_{18}=4.377; p < .0005$.

Table 4.   Accuracy Rates of Nineteen Bilingual Children with the Monolingual and the Bilingual Interviewer

	Interviewer			
	Monolingual		Bilingual (English-dominant)	
Children by Program and Sex	n	%	n	%
Monolingual Program				
Male (5)	559/885	63	269/346	78
Female (5)	353/509	69	269/331	81
Bilingual Program				
Male (4)	288/457	63	191/294	65
Female (5)	411/721	57	237/388	61
Totals	1611/2572	63	966/1359	71

Key: $n = \dfrac{\text{number of correct T-units}}{\text{total number of T-units}}$

$t_{18} = -4.429; p < .0005$

$N = 19$ subjects

In addition to this finding, the data confirmed the hypothesis that children would avoid significantly more with the English-dominant Hispanic interviewer than with the monolingual interviewer. On a dependent t-test (one-tailed), t_{18} =2.414; p < .025.

Table 5. Rates of Avoidance of Nineteen Bilingual Children with the Monolingual and the Bilingual Interviewer

	Interviewer			
	Monolingual		Bilingual (English-dominant)	
Children by Program and Sex	n	%	n	%
Monolingual Program				
Male	37/885	4	27/346	8
Female	30/509	6	50/331	15
Bilingual Program				
Male	28/457	6	25/294	8
Female	48/721	7	46/388	12
Totals	143/2571	6	148/1359	11

Key: $n = \dfrac{\text{number of instances of topic avoidance}}{\text{total number of T-units}}$

$t_{18} = -2.476$; p < .01
N = 19 subjects

In Beebe (1980) a marginally significant result was obtained on avoidance of DO insertion in WH questions with the Spanish-dominant interviewer. In that research, avoidance was defined as non-use of a structure in a context where the structure was obligatory (for the grammaticality of the question) but not attempted.

$$\text{Avoidance} = \frac{\text{number of obligatory contexts where DO insertion is avoided (obligatory, but not attempted)}}{\text{number of WH questions produced for the exercise}}$$

In the continuation of the research, reported here, an attempt was made to find a more global measure of avoidance. The avoidance of the previous study was strictly structural, and only one small structure was coded. Here, the avoidance is not specifically structural although, in fact, structural avoidance may be a motivating factor in semantic avoidance.

Avoidance, here, was calculated as the sum total of topic avoidance (three types) plus message abandonment. These categories are adaptations of the communication strategies proposed in Tarone (1977).

$$\text{Avoidance} = \frac{\text{topic avoidance}_{1,2,3} + \text{message abandonment}}{\text{total number of T-units}}$$

Topic avoidance was divided into three types. All three involved no real response to a question the child was believed to understand, but apparently chose not to answer. One kind of avoidance was silence. Another was an answer of "I don't know," "I don't remember," or simply "No" in a situation where the child must have known the answer and would have had to honestly answer "Yes" (e.g., Q: "Have you ever been in a fight/argument with a friend? With a brother or sister?" A: "I don't know" or "No.") The third kind of avoidance was the repetition of the interviewer's question with a trailing-off intonation showing comprehension, but being followed by no real response. For example, the interviewer said, "What would you do if you had a million dollars?" The child responded, ". . .if I had a million dollars? . . ." There was a subjective element to the coding of all three types of topic avoidance. The same was true of coding message abandonment. The intentional failure to finish a response was coded as message abandonment, whereas a response cut off by the interviewer's interruption (or concurrent talk) was not considered avoidance by message abandonment.

To sum up the findings, then, the data showed that there was significantly greater correctness and significantly more avoidance with the English-dominant Hispanic interviewer. (Correctness and avoidance were not significantly correlated with each other, however.) With the monolingual interviewer, there was a significantly greater amount of talk than with the English-dominant Hispanic interviewer, and there was a marginally significant increase in the amount of volunteering, These last two measures were assumed to be evidence of risk-taking. Thus, we can say that while there was greater accuracy with the Hispanic interviewer, there was greater risk-taking with the monolingual interviewer.

The point of this research is not to stereotype these phenomena as good or bad, but (1) to describe the influences of interviewer ethnicity on risk-taking, (2) to understand the forces that motivate risk-taking, and (3) to ascertain the effects that it has on learning. None of these is a simple question. None has a simple answer. And none has been fully answered by this research alone. But speculation as to the answers is still useful.

We may speculate that there is a causal connection between interviewer ethnicity and risk-taking. We know that there is a correlation, but we are limited, as in all social science research, in the ability to infer a causal link. Not only that, but there are other possible explanations. One possible explanation for the correlation between higher risk-taking and a monolingual interviewer is that conversation in English with a monolingual English speaker is a natural communicative setting, whereas speaking in English to a Hispanic interviewer for any Hispanic child (even to an English-dominant Hispanic interviewer) may seem unnatural. Another possible explanation for more risk-taking (measured by more talk and more volunteering) with the monolingual was that the monolingual was more experienced in interviewing. Of course, we can always argue that amount of talk and volunteering do not reflect risk-taking, but this is a question of definition.

Despite these explanations for the consistent correlation between measures of risk-taking and the presence of a monolingual interviewer, we suspect that something deeper must be going on. If the controls of the study are reasonably solid, we hope to explain the data using more general theoretical considerations.

In this study, it seems that we must examine the higher risk-taking scores with the monolingual interviewer in relation to the accuracy scores with that interviewer. The accuracy scores were lower with the monolingual interviewer for grammatical and semantic measures but higher for phonological measures. We must also take into account the fact that the children had higher syntactic complexity scores for WH questions with the monolingual interviewer. An explanation for more talk, more volunteering, and more complexity with the monolingual can be found within Accommodation Theory (Giles, 1977; Giles and Smith, 1979). According to this theory, we unconsciously adjust our speech as a means of communicating our intentions, moods, loyalties, etc., to our interlocutors. If we want them to think well of us, and wish to gain their approval, we will change our speech style to become more similar to theirs (Giles and Smith, 1979; p. 47). The bilingual children in this study may have attempted to make their speech converge toward that of the monolingual interviewer. At first glance, one might predict higher accuracy with this interviewer; but it was not as simple as that. The result of attempted convergence was higher risk-taking scores (measured by amount of talk, amount of volunteering, and complex WH question structure) but lower accuracy. This was true when grammatical structures were measured. It did not happen in pronunciation of vowels and consonants since much less was being coordinated. In the area of phonology, where complexity is less of a factor, there was in fact greater accuracy with the native speaker. It is in the area of grammar and semantics where attempted convergence toward the interlocutor—in this case, the attempt to match native complexity—leads to lower accuracy. Accommodation Theory can thus be used to account for higher *pronunciation* accuracy with the monolingual interviewer in claiming that there was phonological convergence toward a native model. In the area of grammar and semantics, it is claimed that there was an attempt at convergence toward the complexity of the native speaker's (i.e., the monolingual's) speech. This would account for the higher risk-taking rates.

The research described in this paper is still in progress. Thus far, it has established a statistically significant correlation between interviewer ethnicity and amount of talk, amount of volunteering, complexity of WH questions, and risk-taking in WH questions. That is, there was a significant increase in all measures related to risk-taking in the presence of a monolingual non-Hispanic interviewer.

At this point it is not certain how close we have come to measuring risk-taking *per se* in speaking English as a second language. We have measured phenomena which would seem to be strong indications of risk-taking. Ultimately, I hope we will be able to measure risk-taking in another way. We would first need to be able to measure syntactic development in the sense that Larsen-Freeman (1978) has suggested. Larsen-Freeman argues that we need a second language acquisition index of development which allows us to posit stages through which learners pass in acquiring a second language. These stages would be "defined in purely linguistic performance terms" (p. 135). If we had this index of development, we could view risk-taking as the attempt to speak beyond one's own stage of acquisition. For a child at $Stage_n$, it would be taking a risk to attempt linguistic structures in $Stage_{n+1}$, or, for that matter, structures normally acquired in *any* more advanced stage. If we could do this, we could describe risk-taking objectively in terms of linguistic performance. This would not exclude additional subjective or objective analysis of affective factors in the situation.

Even if future attempts at more direct measures of risk-taking do not prove fruitful, the present study has succeeded in showing that the socio-linguistic setting (in particular, interviewer ethnicity) is a crucial variable affecting amount of talk, amount of volunteering, syntactic complexity attempted in WH questions, and structural risk-taking in WH questions. This is in accordance with the literature on risk-taking which indicates that risk-taking, although partially a personality variable, depends primarily upon the situation. The evidence that this is true in language learning is encouraging to the ESL teacher who can facilitate a helpful degree of risk-taking by controlling the classroom environment.

Now let us turn to a discusson of the implications this research has for the classroom.

Research on Risk-Taking: Implications for the Classroom

Virtually every classroom practice can be reexamined in light of the research on risk-taking. Several problems exist in doing this, however. Let us look at some of these problems before discussing classroom practice. First of all, we do not know the optimal level of risk-taking. We know that high-need achievers (i.e., those with a high motivation for achievement) are likely to be moderate risk-takers and that successful business people are most commonly moderate risk-takers. These findings lead us to suppose that if we are to define and encourage an optimal level of risk-taking in classrooms, we should probably choose moderate risk-taking. Still, research has not led us to this conclusion. We know that successful executives favor moderate risk-taking, but we do not know if their risk-taking behavior led them down a path of success. Nevertheless, given the definition of risk as possibility of failure, our common sense leads us to favor moderate risk-taking as a goal in the classroom. High risk-taking involves not just possibility of failure but rather probability of failure. Low risk-taking involves hoping for guaranteed success, not a realistic strategy in today's world, and certainly not a desirable outcome of the educational process. Thus, we endorse moderate risk-taking as the optimal behavior, where students strive for success, keeping a limited reliance on chance and a realistic appraisal of their own skill.

Another problem, besides determining an abstract optimal level of risk-taking, faces us in drawing implications of risk-taking research for the classroom. This problem is one of establishing what constitutes a moderate risk for a specific learner in a specific situation. What is a high risk for one student may be a low risk for another. The student's level of achievement will certainly affect this. As discussed earlier, an index of development is prerequisite to creating an objective measure of risk. In addition, affective factors in the student's situation and personality will determine in part the subjective appraisal of risk. At present, we do not have an integrated objective or subjective measure of risk that takes into account individual differences.

A third major problem facing us is that we really do not know if there will be positive effects of facilitating risk-taking for low risk-takers and encouraging students to take moderate risks. At this stage, with no integrated measures of risk in language-learning situations and no longitudinal studies of student performance in relation to risk, we must rely upon experience and intuition. Experience and intuition lead us to assume that moderate risk-taking in language learning is the best overall strategy. There are still circumstances, however, where riskier or more conservative strategies should be adopted.

Finally, there are problems with making assumptions about fostering optimal levels of risks. These problems relate to cultural differences among students in a second language class. If we accept the hypothesis that our culture values risk highly, we must expect that other cultures place different values on it. We cannot assume that students from various cultural backgrounds will share the same values or perceive the same risks. There will be cultural preferences for cooperation versus competition. Lupfer et al. (1971) found that cooperating friends were more likely to take risks than competing friends, but this is not necessarily universal. Different groups (e.g., women versus men, young people versus elderly people, upper class versus lower class) can be expected to value risk differently and perceive its appropriateness for their group differently. They will probably respond to different types of rewards as well, depending on their motives for learning.

These problems identified, we must examine the implications of risk-taking research for classroom practice. This research affects virtually all areas, including testing and general teaching methodologies. Let us first take a look at testing.

Testing

The inverse correlation between risk-taking and accuracy, reported in the second section of this chaper, suggests that there is a trade-off situation. If teachers want students to attempt difficult structures, to talk a great deal, and to volunteer new information when communicating, they must expect that accuracy levels will go down. These behaviors increase the risk of making an error, and naturally, more errors will be made.

But we must ask: So what? A popular viewpoint today is that errors do not matter. Communicating (i.e., getting the point across) is what counts. The traditonal view is that accuracy is important to high academic standards, central to good discipline, and important for efficient communication. Clearly, a compromise position is needed.

Research shows that risk-taking and accuracy are negatively correlated. We must therefore choose between the two. One principled way to do this is to distinguish among the goals of language use in different settings. If the goal is to communicate as much as possible, risking error by using partially acquired structures is highly justifiable. If the goal is to demonstrate high grammatical accuracy on a composition test, the best strategy is to avoid using difficult structures (Schachter, 1974), i.e., to avoid taking risks. Students in these circumstances will get higher scores if they stick to structures they know well. If, on the other hand, students are taking multiple choice or fill-in-the-blank tests, guessing (risk-taking) is generally advisable. In some cases, however, especially on standardized tests, there is a penalty for wrong answers.

This complicated system is very confusing. Students cannot be taught one strategy and simply use it everywhere. What seems important is for the teacher to clarify the value of risk-taking in various communicative and testing situations in the classroom. When students take a composition or other free production test, we should either separate appraisals of communicative success and accuracy or adjust an integrated appraisal to account for risk-taking and avoidance, not just accuracy.

Methodology

There are implications of research on risk-taking both for general areas of language teaching methodology and for specific approaches to teaching. Of the general teaching areas, feedback and the teaching of reading are two that stand out. Frank Smith has long been known for the view that "all aspects of reading, from the identification of individual letters or words to the comprehension of entire passages, involve the reduction of uncertainty" (1971, p. 2). Smith says a reader must establish a criterion, a notion he or she takes from signal detection theory. The criterion is the amount of information the readers insist upon before making a decision about the identification of a symbol or the meaning of a passage. Some readers require almost absolute certainty before making a decision. These must be low risk-takers. Others are willing "to take a chance and make a decision on minimal information, even at the risk of making a mistake" (1971, p. 23). These people must be high risk-takers in reading. Smith emphasizes the necessity of taking chances in the reading process (1975). He writes, "The more often you want to be right, the more often you must tolerate being wrong" (1971, p. 24). In sum, Smith sees good readers as those who take risks. Effective readers test out their hypotheses, eliminating some of the alternative interpretations with information from the printed page, but they are also willing to tolerate vagueness.

The general study of feedback is also related to risk-taking. Teachers providing correction to students must bear in mind the task that they have set or that students have set for themselves. If students understand an exercise to be communicative, and they reveal personal views, they seek a substantive reaction from the teacher, not a correction of the technical accuracy of their words. Many students seem not to hear teacher corrections. This may be because they are not at a sufficiently advanced level to possess productive use of the rule in question. But, frequently, it is because their attention is focused on the risks (the uncertainty) involved in the act of communicating their meaning, not on the chance of making an error in syntax or pronunciation. They want a reaction to meaning, not an evaluation of form. Often, providing the former creates a natural communicative setting. Later, the topic of discussion may turn to technical accuracy, and then the teacher may effectively comment on form. What seems important is that the feedback responds first to the area where the student perceives a risk. Of course, there is always a risk of both failure to communicate and failure to be accurate in speaking a second language, but usually one or the other is the primary focus of attention, not both. Teachers must respond to this perception of risk if they want students to attend to their feedback.

Research on risk-taking can be related to virtually every aspect of the language classroom, including specific pedagogical approaches. The research cannot (and should not) be used to evaluate approaches since an approach is such a complex set of behaviors. However, reviewing approaches in terms of risk-taking may illuminate some new perspectives.

Perhaps we can set aside the notion of gain in the context of approaches to second language teaching. Students will perceive the same general reward in learning a new language regardless of the teaching methodology adopted. On the other hand, however, gain may be a factor since it could be related to students being able to say what they want to say. That is, it could be related to the chance to communicate one's thoughts in a language classroom. Students who strongly wish to communicate their own ideas will perceive a greater gain (or reward) in communicative practice than in mechanical drills. Whatever their perception of gain, risk is still a variable in their reactions to various approaches.

One of the most common complaints about the audio-lingual approach was that it was boring. Viewed in terms of risk and gain, we might guess that because audio-lingual learning was limited primarily to mechanical drill, students perceived it as a low risk-taking situation. There is very little risk, comparatively, in repetition and mindless manipulation based on habit. There is also low gain, in that students are not permitted to talk about what they feel like communicating. Primarily, they repeat the words of others. The chance of error is low. The risk of exposing one's personal views to criticism is virtually nil. Yet research suggests that high-need achievers prefer moderate risk to low risk situations. They also prefer situations requiring skill. Mechanical manipulation of utterances is probably not viewed as skill. Thus, the extremely low risk situation created by audio-lingual methodology may explain the complaints of boredom.

Proponents of the delayed oral practice approach (e.g., Gary, 1978) claim that an extended period of listening in the early stages of second language learning leads to better speaking skills, even though practice in speaking is delayed. They also claim that reading and writing improve. If indeed delayed oral practice does have these positive effects, there may be cognitive explanations such as those suggested by Postovsky (1975, in Gary, 1978). In addition, however, proponents argue for affective advantages to delayed oral practice. There is one possible affective advantage they do not mention, however. That advantage lies in the delay of complex situations which involve too high a risk for the beginning learner to handle comfortably. Gary calls oral sentence production at early stages "stressful and embarrassing" and says it "reduces the learner's concentration and effectiveness" (1978, p. 191). Perhaps the stress is due to forcing learners to enter a high risk situation when their skill is still low. They therefore perceive it as a game of chance, primarily.

The Silent Way often evokes one of two reactions. One of them is a strong hostile reaction. This may be due to the fact that students feel a high risk when left almost completely to their own devices and made to accept full responsibility for their learning. On the other hand, many students have a strong positive reaction to Silent Way, saying they were "on the edge of their chairs" the whole time. This reaction may come from students who perceive their linguistic skills as higher and view the situation as one requiring skill and moderate risk. Then again, it could be typical of those who enjoy high risk situations.

Risk-taking may also be relevant to students' reactions to Community Language Learning. The security provided by the group and the sense of community that develops may make it possible for students to take risks—even high risks—without feeling as threatened as normal. The shift, discovered by Stoner (1961), toward riskier behavior in a group than in individual situations may help students take risks they would not otherwise feel comfortable taking. Furthermore, the freedom to communicate one's own ideas (our own thoughts being the ones we are most highly motivated to communicate) may constitute a high gain situation.

If we look beyond specific approaches to second language teaching, we can find advantages in the recent trend toward the use of communicative drill rather than mechanical drill. Although students may perceive the same gain (learning a language) no matter what the methodology used, they will not necessarily see the same gain or value in what happens in the process of learning. Communicative drills may be more effective than mechanical drills in part because the perceived gain, or value attached to communicating one's own ideas, may motivate more speaking and involve some risk-taking.

Although it is not possible at this stage to describe an optimal level of risk-taking for all individuals and situations, it has become clear that extremely high risk-taking is not desirable. On the other hand, we still believe in the old adage: "Nothing ventured, nothing gained." It is hoped that this discussion of risk-taking will help teachers identify risk in language learning settings and assess the effects of their classroom practices from this new perspective.

Notes

1. This research was funded by a grant from the Spencer Foundation and sponsord by Teachers College, Columbia University. I gratefully acknowledge this support. In addition, I would like to thank Melanie Schneider, Ramon Valenzuela, Liz Rios, and Celsa Renta for thir research assistance, and Dympna Bowles and Moira Chimombo for substantial contributions to the data analysis and the conceptual framework of the paper.

2. Loban created the "communication unit," which is basically a T-unit designed for the study of oral language. He writes:

the words comprising a communication unit will fall into one of the following threc categories:

1. each independent grammatical predication

2. each answer to a question, provided that the answer lacks only the repetition of the question elements to satisfy the criterion of independent predication

3. each word such as "Yes"or "No" when given in answer to a question such as "Have you ever been sick?"

Categories 2 and 3 are only necessary in oral language; Hunt's T-unit is based upon written language so he does not need to deal with *answers to questions* and *yes* or *no*, (Loban, 1976, pp. 9–10)

Consequently, a sentence consisting of an independent clause and a dependent clause constitutes one communication unit (or T-unit, as they are called here). A sentence consisting of two independent clauses constitutes two units in Loban's system. Just as Loban had to adapt Hunt's system of calculating T-units for the purpose of studying oral language, we had to adapt Loban's system for the purpose of studying non-native speech. For example, in the case of category 2, non-native speakers often omit more than just the question elements, but the answer to the question is still considered a T-unit in our system. Or, again as a consequence of grammatical error, the non-native speaker uses the question element in category 2. It remains one T-unit.

References

Atkinson, J. W. (Ed.). *Motives in Fantasy, Action, and Society*. Princeton, N. J.: Van Nostrand, 1958.

Atkinson, J. W. *An Introduction to Motivation*. Princeton, N. J.: Van Nostrand, 1964.

Atkinson, J. W., and Feather, N. T. (Eds.). *A Theory of Achievement Motivation*. New York: Wiley, 1966.

Bailey, N., Madden, C., & Eisenstein, M. A comparison of production and imitation: On the formal and functional integration of closely related structures. Paper presented at Applied Linguistics Winter Conference, Teachers College, Columbia University, 1979.

Beebe, L. M.The influence of the listener on code-switching. *Language Learning*, 1977, *27*, 331–340.

Beebe, L. M. Dialect code-switching of bilingual children in their second language. In CUNY Forum in Linguistics, Special Issue: Papers on Bilingualism and Second Language Learning, 1978.

Beebe, L. M. Measuring the use of communication strategies. In R. Scarcella & S. Krashen (Eds.), *Research in Second Language Acquisition: Selected Papers of the Los Angeles Second Language Research Forum.* Rowley, Mass.: Newbury House, 1980.

Bem, D. J. The concept of risk in the study of human behavior. In R. E. Carney (Ed.), *Risk-Taking Behavior.* Springfield, Ill.: Charles C. Thomas, 1971.

Bridge, R. G., Judd, C. M., & Moock, P. R. *The Determinants of Educational Outcomes: The Impact of Families, Peers, Teachers, and School.* Cambridge, Mass.: Ballinger, 1979.

Brown, R. *Social Psychology.* New York: The Free Press, 1965

Carney, R. E. (Ed.). *Risk-Taking Behavior: Concepts, Methods, and Applications to Drug Abuse.* Springfield, Ill.: Charles C. Thomas, 1971.

Carroll, J. B. The prediction of success in intensive foreign language training. (mimeo), Cambridge, Mass.: Graduate School of Education, Harvard Univesity, 1960. Cited in J. Rubin, 1975.

Chastain, K. Affective and ability factors in second language acquisition. *Language Learning,* 1975, *25,* 153–161.

Curran, C. C. *Counseling-Learning in Second Languages.* Apple River, Ill.: Apple River Press, 1976.

Edwards, W. Subjective probabilities inferred from decisions. *Psychological Review,* 1962, *69,* 109–135.

Fitts, W. H. *The Self Concept and Performance.* Nashville, Tenn.: 1972. Cited in A. W. Heyde, 1977.

Führer, C. R. Skill-oriented risk-taking in disadvantaged preschoolers: A link in a behavioral pattern. Ph. D. dissertation, Teachers College, Columbia University, 1974. Cited in D. Larson, 1977.

Gardner, R. C., & Lambert, W. E. *Attitudes and Motivation in Second Language Learning.* Rowley, Mass.: Newbury House, 1972. Cited in A. W. Heyde, 1977.

Gary, J. O., Why speak if you don't need to? In W. C. Ritchie (Ed.), *Second Language Acquisition Research: Issues and Implications.* New York: Academic Press, 1978.

Gattegno, C. *Teaching Foreign Languages the Silent Way.* New York: Educational Solutions, 1963.

Giles, H. Social psychology and applied linguistics: Towards an integrative approach. *ITL: Review of Applied Linguistics,* 1977, *33,* 27–42.

Giles, H, & (Smith, P. M. Accommodation theory: Optimal levels of convergence. In H. Giles & R. N. St Clair (Eds.), *Language and Social Psychology.* Baltimore: University Park Press, 1979.

Heyde, A. W. The relationship between self esteem and the oral production of a second language. In H. D. Brown, C. A. Yorio, & R. H. Crymes (Eds.), *On TESOL '77: Teaching and Learning English as a Second Language: Trends in Research and Practice.* Washington, D.C.: TESOL, 1977.

Kleinmann, H. H. The strategy of avoidance in adult second language acquisition. In W. C. Ritchie (Ed.), *Second Language Acquisition Research: Issues and Implications.* New York: Academic Press, 1978.

Kogan, N., & Wallach, M. A. Risk taking as a function of the situation, the person, and the group. *New Directions in Psychology III.* New York: Holt, Rinehart and Winston, 1967.

Krashen, S. D. Individual variation in the use of the Monitor. In W. C. Ritchie (Ed.), *Second Language Acquisition: Issues and Implications.* New York: Academic Press, 1978.

Labov, W. The logic of nonstandard English. In J. E. Alatis (Ed.), *Monograph Series on Languages and Linguistics 22,* 1969.

Lambert, W. E. A social psychology of bilingualism. *Journal of Special Issues,* 1967, *23,* 91–109.

Larsen-Freeman, D. An ESL index of development. *TESOL Quarterly,* 12:4, 439–450, 1978.

Larson, D. Correlations between psychological studies of risk taking and humanist theories of learning with implications for second language learning. Unpublished paper, Teachers College, Columbia University, 1977.

Loban, W. Language development: Kindergarten through grade twelve. *NCTE Research Report No. 18.* Urbana, Ill.: National Council of Teachers of English, 1976.

Lupfer, M., Jones, M. Spaulding, L., & Archer, R. Risk-taking in cooperative and competitive dyads. *Journal of Conflict Resolution,* 1971, *15,* 385–392.

Madaras, G. R., & Bem, D. J. Risk and conservatism in group decision-making. *Journal of Experimental Social Psychology,* 1968, *4,* 350–365.

Madden, C., Bailey, N., Eisenstein, M., & Anderson, L. Beyond statistics in second language acquisition research. In W. C. Ritchie (Ed.), *Second Language Acquisition Research: Issues and Implications.* New York: Academic Press, 1978.

Naiman, N., Fröhlich, M., & Stern, H. H. *The Good Language Learner.* Toronto: Ontario Institute for Studies in Education, 1975.

Postovsky, V. A. The effects of delay in oral practice at the beginning of second language teaching. Ph.D. dissertation, University of California, Berkeley, 1975. Cited in Gary, 1978.

Rotter, J. B. Generalized expectancies for internal versus external control of reinforcement. *Psychological Monographs 80* (1, whole No. 609), 1966.

Rubin, J. What the "good language learner" can teach us. *TESOL Quarterly,* 1975, *9,* 41–52.

Schachter, J. An error in error analysis. *Language Learning,* 1974, *24,* 205–214.

Schumann, J. H. The acculturation model for second-language acquisition. In R. C. Gingras (Ed.), *Second-Language Acquisition and Foreign Language Teaching.* Washington, D.C.: Center for Applied Linguistics, 1978.

Selinker, L. Interlanguage. IRAL, 1972, *X,* 3.

Smith, F.*Understanding Reading: A Psycholinguistic Analysis of Reading and Learning to Read.* New York: Holt, Rinehart and Winston, 1971.

Smith, F. *Comprehension and Learning: A Conceptual Framework for Teachers.* New York: Holt, Rinehart and Winston, 1975.

Stoner, J. A. F. A comparison of individual and group decisions involving risk. Unpublished master's thesis, MIT School of Industrial Management, 1961. Cited in D. J. Bem, 1971.

Tarone, E. E. Conscious communication strategies in interlanguage: A progress report. In H. D. Brown, C. A. Yorio, & R. H. Crymes (Eds.), *On TESOL '77. Teachers of English to Speakers of Other Languages.* Washington, D.C.: TESOL 1977.

Wallach, M. A. & Kogan, N. Sex differences and judgment processes. *Journal of Personality,* 1959, *27,* 555–564.

Wallach, M. A. & Kogan, N. Aspects of judgment and decision-making: Interrelationships and changes with age. *Behavioral Science,* 1961, *6,* 23–36.

Questions for Discussion and Activities

1. In what way do you think risk-taking is related to Bialystok's description of inferencing? Are good inferencers necessarily risk-takers? Can you think of situations where a good learner might be a low risk-taker but a good inferencer or a high risk-taker and a poor inferencer?

2. In what way is the high risk-taker related to the High Input Generator discussed by Seliger in this volume? Are the two necessarily the same? What conditions would have to exist in order for a low risk-taker to be a High Input Generator?

3. Given Bem's characterization of the factors influencing risk-taking behavior, which can be affected by the teacher? Which factors lie beyond the teacher's control?

4. Why may it be the case that learners who are highly motivated to achieve may be poor in acquiring communicative proficiency in a language?

5. Examine a set of compositions written by L2 learners. Rank the compositions in terms of (1) grammatical accuracy, (2) expression of content and style. How do these rankings compare with what you know about the risk-taking style of the writers in oral language production?

6. While observing an ESL class, do you notice any difference in risk-taking behavior patterns if the students are in large groups or in small groups? Why do you think some students seem more likely to take risks in small groups?

7. Beebe states that "situational variables influence the study of risk-taking to a greater degree than personality variables." Study a group of bilingual children in an educational setting. Do you note differences of behavior for individual children when they are in their first language setting and when they are in the second language setting? Of the situational variables described in the literature on risk-taking, which do you think might explain your observations?

8. What are some ways that the language teacher might increase risk-taking by increasing reward while limiting the cost of failure?

9. What other explanations might be offered for the fossilizations in the grammars of high level bilinguals other than the high risk-low gain hypothesis suggested by Beebe?

4

Competitiveness and Anxiety
in Adult Second Language Learning:
Looking *at* and *through* the Diary Studies[1]

Kathleen M. Bailey

Problems in Research on Affect: Anxiety in Second Language Learning

Affective factors are generally assumed to influence second language acquisition (SLA). Yet there are many difficulties associated with research on such variables. The tasks of defining, manipulating, and quantifying affective factors pose serious problems for researchers. A case in point is anxiety. In reviewing the research on anxiety and second language learning, Scovel borrows from work in psychology by Hilgard, Atkinson, and Atkinson (1971) and defines anxiety as an emotional state of "apprehension, a vague fear that is only indirectly associated with an object" (Scovel, 1978, p. 34).

Empirical research on affect in language learning usually takes the form of correlation studies. An example which is relevant to the present study is a paper by Gardner, Smythe, Clement, and Glicksman (1976), who conducted research "concerned with delineating components of the integrative motive" (p. 199). One of those components in a formal instructional setting is what Gardner et al. have termed French Classroom Anxiety, or "feelings of anxiety in the French classroom situation" (ibid., p. 200). In that study data from a self-report survey of approximately one thousand high school students in seven communities across Canada were correlated with four measures of French achievement (aural comprehension, speech skills, final course grade, and opportunity to use French).

A negative correlation was found to exist between reported French Classroom Anxiety and scores on an oral production test of speech skills. Gardner et al. report, "The negative correlation of French Classroom Anxiety indicates that the more anxious students are less proficient in Speech Skills" (ibid., p. 202). This finding is not surprising, but it is restricted by a limitation of all correlational studies: one cannot identify the causal variable. Does anxiety impair students' oral fluency, or do they become anxious in oral production tasks because their speech skills are low? Whatever the relationship of French Classroom Anxiety to oral production, the trend varied among the grade levels of the students surveyed:

> Whereas French Classroom Anxiety plays a minimal role in Grade Seven, it becomes more dominant in the later grades. In fact, by Grade Eleven, French Classroom Anxiety is among the best three predictors of all four variables. It would seem therefore, that anxiety possibly plays a more important role as students begin to achieve a better grasp of the language. (ibid., p. 203)

An alternative interpretation of these findings is that older language learners are generally more anxious. (See Schumann, 1975, for a discussion of age and affective factors in SLA.)

Because affective factors, such as anxiety, are so complex, many studies have produced conflicting findings and varied terminology. In a paper which reviews the research on the role of anxiety in SLA, Scovel (1978) discusses several attempts to define affective factors. He summarizes by saying,

> . . . Most of the constructs and behaviors which have been misclassified as affective factors in the literature can be subsumed under the category "learner variables," either intrinsic or extrinsic to the learner, but affect, if we adhere to its traditional definition in psychology, is itself only one variable within intrinsic learner variables, and, therefore, if we are to proceed with an examination of the relationship of anxiety to foreign language learning, we must first of all realize that we are talking about only one affective variable among many intrinsic learner variables. (p. 130)

Scovel turns to Buddhist philosophy and borrows the concept of *vedanā* (feelings) in developing a broad definition:

> . . . Affective factors are those that deal with the emotional reactions and motivations of the learner; they signal the arousal of the limbic system and its direct intervention in the task of learning. (ibid., p. 131)

After discussing various studies of anxiety in SLA (many of which produced conflicting findings), Scovel suggests that "anxiety can be viewed, not as a simple unitary construct, but as a cluster of affective states, influenced by factors which are intrinsic and extrinsic to the foreign language learner" (ibid., p. 134). He then considers research on anxiety in the fields of athletics and applied psychology. Typically anxiety is measured by behavioral tests, self-report, or physiological tests, but Scovel cites Beeman, Martin, and Meyers (1972, p. 427) as saying that there is generally "a low correlation between clinically rated anxiety, self-rated anxiety, and psychometric anxiety" (Scovel, 1978, p. 136).

Scovel points out that the research in applied psychology has contributed a number of ideas which are relevant to SLA research on anxiety. For instance, research by Verma and Nijhavan (1976) revealed an interaction between IQ and anxiety level: "higher states of anxiety facilitate learning at upper levels of intelligence, whereas they are associated with poorer performance at lower IQ levels" (Scovel, 1978, p. 136). In addition, Beeman et al. (1972) found that "increased anxiety is likely to improve performance at later stages in a learning activity, but conversely hinders academic performance at earlier stages of the same activity" (Scovel, 1978, p. 136). Scovel feels that other conflicting findings can be accounted for by Spielberger, Gorusch, and Lushene's (1970) distinction between *state anxiety,* which is (relatively) momentary, and *trait anxiety,* a "more permanent predisposition to be anxious" (Scovel, 1978, p. 137).

Finally, Scovel notes that the issue of *facilitating* versus *debilitating* anxiety (Alpert and Haber, 1960) may be central to research on anxiety in SLA. These concepts are related to work by Chastain (1975), who investigated the correlation between language test scores and anxiety. His conflicting results led him to conclude that mild anxiety could be beneficial while too much anxiety could be harmful (Scovel, 1978, p. 132). This concept was tested in a study by Kleinmann (1977) in which subjects with high facilitating anxiety attempted to use syntactic structures unlike those of their native language, while subjects with high debilitating anxiety avoided such structures. Scovel explains facilitating and debilitating anxiety as products of the limbic system, "the source of all affective arousal" (1978, p. 139):

> Facilitating anxiety motivates the learner to "fight" the new learning task; it gears the learner emotionally for approach behavior. Debilitating anxiety, in contrast, motivates the learner to "flee" the new learning task; it stimulates the individual emotionally to adopt avoidance behavior. (ibid.)

Findings from psychological research on performance are related to the issue of facilitating and debilitating anxiety. In discussing the effect of an audience or the presence of coactors on task performance, Davis states that

> the performance which was *facilitated* involved tasks requiring well-learned behavior; social *inhibition* occurred where the *acquisition of new information* was required by the task. (1969, p. 16)

There is an important distinction here: "Learning is the acquisition of new responses, and performance is the emission of old (that is, well-learned) ones" (ibid.). To restate, then, inhibition occurs when learners must publicly produce new responses which are not yet well-learned. However, in language classes it is not unusual for students to be called upon to *perform* during the early stages of *learning.* Such demands for public performance could be premature and may lead to anxiety on the part of the learner.

Scovel ends his review on a note of cautious optimism. He feels that it is possible to isolate affective variables in SLA research and that anxiety is, in fact, a subject worthy of investigation. However, he also points out that the more we study language learning, the "more complex the identification of particular variables becomes" (1978, p. 140):

> ... Before we begin to measure anxiety, we must become more cognizant of the intricate hierarchy of learner variables that intervene: the intrinsic/extrinsic factors, the affective/cognitive variables, and then the various measures of anxiety and their relationship to these other factors. (ibid.)

Thus Scovel's paper addresses the problems of identifying and defining affective variables, with anxiety being the case in point. In a paper which focuses on methodological issues, Oller discusses the various difficulties involved in language learning research on the affective domain in general. The first problem is that the measurement of affective variables is "necessarily inferential and indirect" (1979, p. 9):

> While many sorts of behavior can be directly observed ... attitudes can only be inferred from behaviors or statements of the person in question. The difficulty of validating such inferences is increased by the need to establish some more or less stable set of values against which attitudes can be referenced. This need is complicated by the fact that attitudes are typically unstable sorts of things. (ibid., p. 10)

Because affective variables are usually not directly observable, data are often based on "inferences made by an observer concerning how the person really feels or thinks or would behave under certain circumstances" (ibid., p. 11).

One way of minimizing the problems of inference[2] in research on affective variables is to query the subjects directly, either in questionnaires or interviews. In these cases the subjects themselves provide the data on their attitudes and feelings. Since such feelings are often hidden, especially in adults, "the necessary reliance on self-reports would seem to be an entirely unavoidable weakness" of research on affective variables (ibid.).

Unfortunately, self-reports are often problematic because the subjects "tend to give answers that are associated with the respondents' perceptions of the predispositions of the researcher" (ibid., p. 17). That is, the subject may say what he or she thinks the researcher wants to hear. A related problem has been termed "self-flattery" by Oller and Perkins (1978), who showed that self-evaluations on given traits correlate with the subjects' judgments of the desirability of those traits. Oller states, "On the whole, it was possible to show that as much as 25% of the variance in self-ratings may be attributed to the self-flattery factor" (1979, p. 18).

In discussing the problems of inference and self-reports, Oller points to yet another serious issue in research on affective variables. He hypothesizes that questionnaires designed to assess affective variables may in fact be measuring language proficiency or intelligence instead (ibid., p. 16). It is beyond the scope of this paper to do more than mention this important and complicated issue. At this juncture it is sufficient to state that research into affective variables in language learning poses numerous challenging problems at all levels—definition, description, measurement, and interpretation.

Yet, for many people involved in language teaching and learning, the hypothesis that the affective domain is significant in second language learning is intuitively sound. It is a widely held belief that what the learner experiences in a language lesson is as important as the teaching method, the sequence of presentation, or the instructional materials. In responding to Oller's criticism of the research on affective factors, Tucker has said,

> Although we would all presumably agree with the proposition that affective variables (somehow defined) are important in some way during the course of foreign or second language learning or teaching, their precise description and measurement remains a problematic issue. (1979, p. 3)

Given the complexities of research on affective variables, finding out exactly what the learner experiences is a complicated venture. How can a researcher in a language classroom minimize the problems of observational inference and/or obtain valid self-report data from subjects? Given the variety of learners'needs, motivation, and learning styles, how can a classroom researcher discover what individual students really do and think and feel during the language lesson?

One recent response to this dilemma has been the use of intensive journals to provide the data base for studying personal and affective variables in language learning. The diary studies are first-person case studies: the researcher becomes the language learner in question.

The Use of Personal Diaries as Language Learning Research Tools

Early work using intensive journals as language learning research tools was conducted by Francine and John Schumann. While studying Arabic in Tunisia and Persian in Iran and California the Schumanns recorded "daily events and the thoughts and feelings related to them in a log-like fashion, paying particular attention to cross-cultural adjustments and efforts made and avoided in learning the target language, both in and out of class" (1977, p. 243). In keeping a language learning diary, the researcher/learner records anything and everything perceived to be important to his or her current learning experience. The diaries often include early impressions of the people and culture of the target language environment, the teacher and fellow students in a language class, comments about the learner's fears and frustrations, and the difficulties or successes experienced by the learner.

Several of the diarists have also documented their personal language learning histories in their reports. These accounts of the diarist's previous language learning experience are by definition retrospective. The language learning histories are included in hopes that they will contribute to an understanding of the personal factors involved in the current language learning experience.

In studying their own language learning, diarists assume the role of participant observers in ethnographic research. Methodologically speaking, the diary studies can be classified as belonging to the anthropological research tradition (Long, 1979). For both ethnographers and second language diarists, the research questions are not predefined, and open-ended note-taking is the typical data collection procedure:

Ethnographers do not set out to test particular hypotheses in any formal sense. Instead, they try to describe all aspects of whatever they experience in the greatest possible detail. This they accomplish principally by making extensive written notes, usually recording their observations as soon as possible *after* involvement in the day's activities in order to avoid compromising their own participant role. Note-taking is as systematic and thorough as the individual ethnographer cares to make it . . . . (ibid., p. 26)

Most of the diarists have kept written logs, although others have preferred to use tape-recorded comments for storing journal entries (Kheredmand, personal communications). Some find writing cumbersome and slow while others feel inhibited by the presence of a microphone and find they are better able to express themselves in writing. Diary research is largely introspective since the learner reflects on his or her own experiences;[3] however, some diarists (e.g., Bailey, 1978) in formal classrooms include commentary on other learners as well (Long, 1979).

In introspective research on personal variables, it is important for the diarist to record his or her feelings honestly and openly during the initial data-collection phase of a diary study. Otherwise, if the original journal is prematurely edited, significant information could be automatically censored if it were painful or embarrassing for the diarist.[4] The Schumanns point out that since the diaries

must be as candid as possible and entries are uncensored, they are essentially private documents. Therefore, for the study, this raw data was rewritten by each subject, keeping all relevant detail but eliminating highly personal entries. (1977, p. 243)

In practice it seems that very little is edited in the public versions of the diaries. The names of the participants are changed and comments damaging to others are usually deleted. However, one finds that writing about a painful or embarrassing incident often renders it harmless. In rewriting the journal, the diarist can take a clinical view of the entries. Time, introspection, and the catharsis of writing usually divest the diarist of any painful personal involvement in the episodes reported.

Once the journal has been "revised" for public consumption, the researcher rereads the entries, looking for significant trends. An issue is usually deemed important if it arises frequently or with great salience (J. Schumann, personal communication). Papers reporting on the findings may or may not include the journal excerpts. Thus, simply stated, the process of doing a diary study entails five major steps:

1. The diarist provides an account of his or her personal language learning history.
2. The diarist/learner/researcher systematically records events, details and feelings about the current language-learning experience in a confidential and candid diary.
3. The journal entries are revised for public perusal. Names are changed and information damaging to others or extremely embarrassing to the learner is deleted.

4. The researcher studies the journal entries as data, looking for "significant" trends.
5. The factors identified as important to the language-learning experience are discussed, either with or without illustrative data.

Although diarists may try to relate their findings to theories of learning or language acquisition, the introspective diary studies that have been conducted to date have been largely heuristic. It is normally in the fourth step, the sifting of the data, that specific research questions are defined. In a broad sense, the diary studies are guided by one main question: "What factors are important in *my* language learning experience?" As personal variables emerge, the diarist continues to reread the data, seeking insights and further examples of the phenomena in question.

This chapter is an example of a language classroom diary study, or at least a part of one. It is based on a journal I kept while studying French as a foreign language in a low-level college reading class.

Competitiveness and Anxiety in an Adult Learning French

As a doctoral student in Applied Linguistics I was faced with the requirement of passing translation exams in two languages. I enrolled in French 2R, a reading and grammar course designed primarily for people who want to pass language exams rather than learn to speak French. The class met three hours a week on Mondays, Wednesdays, and Fridays, for ten weeks. There was no required lab session. I felt that such a course would provide me with the review I needed to prepare for the linguistics translation exam. Three years before enrolling in French 2R I had completed two quarters of introductory French. Those courses had been taught with the direct method. During the interim I had made no effort to study French.

The French 2R teacher was a female native speaker of French. During the previous quarter French 1R, the prerequisite course, had been taught by a more experienced teacher and four of the French 2R students had taken that class together. Thus they were familiar with one another, the textbooks, and a particular teaching style.

In conducting this research I kept a journal of experiences related to my language learning. Typical entries include comments about French class meetings, tests and homework, my classmates, conversations, commercials and television programs in French, class parties, etc. An initial analysis of the diary revealed three prevalent factors or themes which are discussed elsewhere (Bailey, 1979). These themes were (1) my response to the language learning environment, (2) my preference for a democratic teaching style, and (3) my need for success and positive reinforcement.

In rereading the diary I kept during the French 2R course, I noticed that I often compared myself to the other students in the class. A closer examination revealed a great deal of competitiveness on my part, although I would not have characterized myself as a competitive learner. This realization surprised me and led to two questions, both of which could be answered by the diary. First, I wanted to determine what specific evidence the diary provides of competition in the French classroom, or of competitiveness in my approach to learning French. Second, I wondered what effect such competitiveness may have had on my efforts to learn French. Excerpts from the journal are examined in order to answer these questions.

It appears that during the first two weeks of the ten-week course I was highly anxious about learning French because I felt I could not compete with the other students. After that period I became more confident but was still competitive with regard to tests and grades. Although the nature of my competitiveness changed during the quarter, it appears to have been important in my language-learning experience, at least in this formal instructional setting.

After just the first hour of the class, when much of the journal entry is devoted to my first impressions of the teacher and my entry-level French proficiency, I seemed to be "sizing up" the other students. The diary says,

> I have just come from the first class meeting. The teacher's name is Marie. She seems nice—young, enthusiastic, and willing to slow down for the students. She encourages us to tell her when we don't understand something. She also stops lecturing in French to give us grammatical explanations, and she often writes on the board when she sees we don't understand what she has said. . . . I am interested in the problems of one man in the class who has taken the ETS French exam twice and failed. He is desperate and somewhat discouraged. I hope I can encourage him. He is really trying. He talked to the teacher after class but he's using a lot of energy fighting with his own frustrations. There are only ten or twelve students in the class. The girl who had been in France seemed to try to allign herself with the teacher, but Marie made an effort to distribute turns evenly and not play favorites. I think this will be a good class for me and I'll try to write in my journal after each meeting. (1979, pp. 38–39)

It may be that in referring specifically to the woman who had been in France and the man who had failed the ETS test, I was identifying the sources of the greatest and least threat to me as a learner in that class. In the journal entries for the second meeting it is clear that I was experiencing what Gardner et al. (1976) called "French Classroom Anxiety":

> . . . Today I was panicked in the oral exercise where we had to fill in the blanks with either the past definite or the imperfect. Now I know what ESL students go through with the present perfect and the simple past. How frustrating it is to be looking for adverbial clues in the sentence when I don't even know what the words and phrases mean. I realized that the teacher was going around the room taking the sentences in order, so I tried to stay one jump ahead of her by working ahead and using her feedback to the class to obtain confirmation or denial of my hypotheses. Today I felt a little scared. I'm so rusty! (ibid., p. 40)

This fear of public failure seems to have been caused or at least aggravated by comparing myself with the other students (or with an idealized self-image), rather than by any fear of rebuke from the teacher. In fact, the journal entry for that same day shows that I actually ranked my French fluency against that of the other students:

> . . . I hope Marie will eventually like me and think that I am a good language learner, even though I am probably the second lowest in the class right now (next to the man who must pass the ETS

test). The girl who has been in France seems to think that she's too good for the rest of us, but she didn't do all that well today. I want to have the exercises worked out perfectly before the next class. Today I was just scared enough to be stimulated to prepare for next time. If I were any scareder I'd be a nervous wreck. I feel different from many of the students in the class because they have been together for a quarter with the other teacher. They also don't seem very interested in learning French. Today Marie was explaining something and some of the students looked really bored. (ibid., p. 41)

I was apparently very uncomfortable throughout the third class meeting as well. My feelings of inadequacy in comparing myself to the other students led me to seek out allies and react negatively to some students. On Friday of the first week, the third day of instruction, I wrote,

Today I decided to speak to the man who is so uptight about his ETS test. I was sad that he didn't come to class. I hope he doesn't drop the course. I said hello to another student in the hall (Robert is his name) but he just nodded. I would have liked to have someone to commiserate with. . . . I am absolutely worn out. I floundered through the class, making at least four stupid mistakes out loud. I felt so lost! . . . Today my palms were sweating and I was chewing my lip through the entire class. My emotional state wasn't helped by the blond girl who sat next to me. She had already taken French 3 and was just looking for a three-unit course. She made several comments about how slow the class is and then decided this isn't the right course for her. I offered to buy her grammar book and I'm relieved she agreed to sell it to me: that means she won't be back. . . . I'm not having any trouble understanding Marie's grammar explanations. My grammar background is probably stronger than most of the students'. I'm just having trouble in recognizing and producing the spoken language. I want to work on French a lot over the weekend. (ibid., pp. 42–43)

These journal entries from the first week of the French course reveal a learner who was very uncomfortable and extremely anxious about the class. After only three hours of instruction I had ranked myself as the second lowest in a group of ten or twelve students. Yet I was consoled by the thought that even though my spoken French was poor, my knowledge of grammar was probably better than the other students'. In other words, although I couldn't compete with the others orally, I thought I would have an edge in the grammar competition.

Since the student who had to take the ETS test didn't come to class on Friday, I had become the lowest person in the rankings of French fluency. Seeing myself as weaker than the other students motivated me to study French in order to avoid the embarrassment of making public errors. However, the feeling that I couldn't compete in class became so intense that I soon withdrew from this painful situation. On the fourth day of instruction I wrote,

Today I skipped my French class. Last Friday after class I spoke to Marie and apologized for slowing down the class. I asked her how far they had gone the previous quarter in the grammar book, so that I could try to catch up over the weekend. She was very encouraging and said that I hadn't slowed the class down. Over the weekend I had planned to do a total review of the French grammar book, but I didn't get to it because I had so much departmental business to do. Last night I began reading the assigned chapter but I got bogged down and discouraged and I quit. Coming to school today I vowed to leave my office an hour before class so I could prepare. Some things came up though and twenty minutes before the class was supposed to start, I decided to skip class and use the time to review instead. Then I discovered I had left my French books at home! I feel very anxious about this class. I know I am (or can be) a good language learner, but I hate being lost in class. I feel like I'm behind the others and slowing down the pace. Since I didn't have the French books, I decided to go to the library and study for my other class. . . . I tried to read but I was so upset about the French class that I couldn't concentrate so I've just been writing in my journal. I *must* get caught up in French or I'll never be able to go back to the class. (ibid., pp. 43–44)

This journal entry shows that in this case, French Classroom Anxiety definitely interfered with language learning (at least in the short-term perspective) when I temporarily withdrew from the instructional setting. My *perceived* inability to compete with the other students was so strong that I either didn't heed or didn't believe the teacher's encouraging comments.[5] Apparently I felt that the other students had a "head start" on me because they had been studying French together for a quarter. The sense of competition is clearly revealed in the foot-race imagery used in the diary: "I apologized for *slowing down* the class" and asked "*how far they had gone*"so I could "try to *catch up.*" This racing imagery is particularly apparent in the comment, "I feel like I'm *behind the others* and *slowing down the pace.* . . . I must get *caught up* in French. . . ." Thus, the language with which I expressed my frustrations in the diary reveals the development of competition as a prevalent theme in my perceptions of this classroom situation. (It is unlikely that an observer or a videotape camera could have captured these intense feelings of inadequacy. It is also doubtful that I would have revealed them on a questionnaire.)

Today we had our first test. It consisted of two paragraphs in French, which we were to translate into English. These were followed by six sentences in French, also to be translated, and five multiple choice questions in which we were to choose the correct English interpretation of a word or phrase. I felt pretty good about this test. I finished and left while the others were still working. (ibid., pp. 52–53)

This last sentence is curious. Apparently I felt I had caught up with the group in terms of my French proficiency, but I never felt accepted by them. "Beating them" by finishing the test early may have been a basic form of revenge. I was very surprised, however, when the teacher returned the exams. The journal entry says,

Today we went over the exam we took last week. I got a "B+." The grade was all right with me but I was amazed to see that I had skipped one sentence within a paragraph and the entire middle section of the test. I just didn't notice those six sentences to be translated into English. No wonder I finished before the others! It is strange that I did finish early but I didn't go back over the test. I honestly thought I had done my best on the entire test. In retrospect, I am pleased to have gotten a "B+" after having jumped over so much of the exam. I wonder what grades the others got. (ibid., p. 53)

In fact, this entry reveals an error on my part: I *had noticed* those parts of the test; otherwise I wouldn't have been able to describe them in the entry cited above. The diary shows that I had unwittingly skipped those sections even though I had been aware of them at some point during the test.

This pattern of rushing through tests persisted throughout the quarter. When the second test was returned I wrote,

> Much to my surprise I skipped part of the test again. I missed an entire section by not copying it onto the paper I handed in. I even had correct notes about the sentence on the ditto sheet, but I neglected to follow through on them. Why am I so careless as a test-taker in French? (ibid., p. 63)

At the time I didn't realize that my competitiveness in test-taking situations was causing me to do poorly. I attributed the gaps in my test-taking behavior to a lack of monitoring, insensitivity to context, or just plain carelessness. Yet none of these explanations was intuitively appealing. After the third classroom examination I wrote,

> I am disgusted with myself for skipping something once more. This time it was just a phrase in the passage that I could not translate, but the silly thing is that the term was included on the vocabulary list provided. Thus I missed a section on the translation because I misinterpreted a term that was actually defined for me! This is more evidence that I am not as good a test-taker in a foreign language as I am in my native language. (ibid., p. 83)

Although I couldn't identify the cause of this gapping, I tried to disrupt the pattern by concentrating on systematically completing the tasks on the fourth test, the final examination. This time I was more successful. At the beginning of the exam I seemed to be competing with the task, but when the first student left I was tempted to compete with her, which would have damaged my performance on the test. In this journal entry, as in the first two weeks of the course, competitiveness and anxiety again coincide. Here it is difficult to tell which is the cause and which the effect.

To summarize, then, the diary contains numerous indications that, at least in the French 2R class, I was a competitive language learner. Sometimes this competitiveness hindered my language learning (as in the case of debilitating anxiety when I avoided contact with the language by skipping class) and at other times it motivated me to study harder (as in the case of facilitating anxiety when I completed an intensive review so I would feel more at ease during oral classroom work). Journal entries which reveal this competitiveness have involved the following characteristics:

> 1. Overt—though private—comparison of myself with other students (e.g., self-ranking, use of comparatives and superlatives, comparison in particular skill areas, etc.)
> 2. Emotive responses to such comparisons (anxiety when I didn't compare favorably with the others and elation when I did), including emotional reactions to other students (e.g., the girl who'd been to France, the girl whose grammar book I bought, etc.); connotative uses of language (for instance, the foot-race imagery) in the diary entries sometimes reveal this emotion
> 3. The desire to outdo the other students; here realized as the tendency to race through exams in order to finish first
> 4. Emphasis on tests and grades, especially with reference to the other students
> 5. The desire to gain the teacher's approval
> 6. Anxiety experienced during the language class, often after making errors on material I felt I should have known (i.e., a discrepancy between an idealized self-image and a realistic assessment of myself as a language learner)
> 7. Withdrawal from the language-learning experience when the competition was overpowering.

In many cases, these manifestations of competitiveness coincided with comments about French Classroom Anxiety, but whether as a cause or as an effect—or in a cyclic relationship—is difficult to determine.

Competitiveness and Anxiety Among Other Language Learners

The excerpts from my French class journal are concerned with one perceived characteristic of one language learner. The question is often raised as to whether the findings of the diary studies are generalizable. That is, can the findings be attributed to a larger population of language learners? In order to answer this question, let us consider the work done by other diarists in language-learning situations.

Three caveats are in order here. The first is that in reading the diary studies one notices various degrees of introspection and observational acuity among the authors. The obvious conclusion is that some of the studies are more accurate and hence more reliable than others. Second, some of the papers reviewed here (Fields, Jones, Lynch, Scheding, and Walsleben) included the rewritten diaries, or substantial excerpts from them. Others (Bernbrock, Moore, Plummer, and F.E. Schumann) are discussions of trends in the diaries and do not include the actual journals. (Leichman's (1977) paper is a summary of her journal.) In these latter cases I may sometimes be drawing inferences from the diarists' comments, since I am not examining primary data. Finally, these ten papers were all written in English by adult native speakers of English. The "sample" is further restricted by the fact that, except for Moore and Fields, the diarists cited are all language teachers themselves. As readers of these studies we should probably assume that these diarists possess a certain degree of linguistic sophistication as well as the dual perspective of teachers-turned-learners. The purpose of considering these papers is to see what evidence, if any, the various diary studies provide of the relationship between competitiveness and anxiety in other language learners.

Francine Schumann (1978) identifies competition versus cooperation as a major trend in the diary she kept in Tunisia and Iran. She reports that she felt guilty when her husband was studying and she wasn't. She also says,

> This guilt was a result of my competitive feeling that if I didn't work as much as he did, he would get further ahead. . . . Instead of causing me to work harder, this competitiveness resulted in my feeling frustrated and led to a reduced effort. (pp. 5–6)

The Schumanns were able to resolve this problem by working together with materials that appealed to both of them. Francine Schumann further suggests that language-training programs that involve couples (e.g., Peace Corps training) should recognize the competition/cooperation phenomenon in order to "maximize cooperation and minimize competition" (ibid., p. 7). This last statement shows that, for Francine Schumann, cooperative language-learning situations are perceived as preferable to competitive situations.[6]

A British psychologist named Terence Moore studied his own behavior and reactions when he moved to Denmark to assume a post at the University of

Aarhus. Unlike the researchers who have kept diaries to study language learning, Moore used his "personal experience of being partially deprived of the normal modes of communication" (1977, p. 107) to gain insights into "the problems of the immigrant, the deaf, the aphasic, the person confined to a 'restricted code,' and especially perhaps to the child in the class where work is too difficult for him" (ibid.). Moore discusses the problems he encountered in the areas of (a) decoding and comprehension, (b) encoding and expression, and (c) the effects of and his reactions to restricted communication (ibid., p. 108). It is in this last area that Moore makes comments which are pertinent to the present study. Quoting from notes he made when he joined a Danish class, he writes,

> This is a good reminder of how a child feels when a lesson goes over his head. One feels bewildered; ashamed and inferior when everyone else appears to understand except oneself; sympathetic, a little victorious and anxious to help when it happens to someone else; humiliated when one has to admit ignorance openly, however kind the teacher is . . . (ibid., p. 109)

Although I don't have enough information to conclude that Moore is a competitive learner, it is clear that comparing himself to others in the oral language lesson was a source of some anxiety for him. Moore's conclusion is relevant to the issue of hidden affective variables which a diary study may reveal. Of his restricted communicative ability he writes,

> My experience has shown me how communication failure . . . can produce mystification, frustration, and many counterproductive emotional and behavioral responses. Because these are mostly silent, however, the magnitude of the problem has in my opinion been seriously underestimated. It calls for an imaginative and multifaceted approach by social and educational psychologists jointly with the teaching profession. (ibid., p. 110)

Cheryl M. Fields, writing in *The Chronicle of Higher Education,* has reported on her experiences as a participant observer in a language class. Her article is based on a diary she kept while taking an introductory Spanish course, the small group option offered by a Berlitz school. She enrolled ostensibly to learn enough Spanish to be able to conduct interviews in Mexico, but also to do a story on non-academic language-training programs. Fields, who had studied French for two years in college, says of herself, "I'd never studied Spanish before and had no particular aptitude for foreign languages—an understatement if I ever had uttered one" (1978, p. 4). Yet for her, knowing a second language would have been desirable:

> I always felt ashamed when I went to Europe and found that people there seemed to routinely speak at least two or three languages. (ibid.)

Fields's early entries about the Spanish class (like mine in the French 2R journal) are filled with comments about her classmates. After the first session she wrote,

> My first Spanish lesson was both reassuring and a little troubling. The other person in the class is a young woman who has never studied a foreign language before, and despite the fact that her mother is Mexican, knows absolutely no Spanish. . . . As a result the instructor spent a lot of time helping my classmate pronounce every word and attach the proper article. That didn't

bother me particularly, but I hoped my classmate would quickly catch on to the basics. . . . It was clear that Berlitz didn't or couldn't match people in their group lessons according to their language sophistication. I certainly didn't know much but my grounding in traditional language training had given me an obvious starting edge I hadn't imagined I had. (ibid., p. 4)

Fields's choice of words here when she refers to "an obvious starting edge" is an example of the connotative power of language revealing something about the diarist's attitude.

At the end of the second meeting Fields again overtly compares the students' performances:

A third person joined the class during the second lesson. The new fellow had had two years of high school French and had taken Chinese in college, so he quickly caught on as the instructor reviewed the first lesson. The instructor. . . carefully divided her attention during class. But she introduced a number of new words and concepts as the fellow and I progressed, even though it was clear that the other woman wasn't catching on as quickly. (ibid.)

At this early stage of language learning the speed with which she learned a structure or grasped a concept seems to have been important to Fields. She has already used the phrase, "to catch on quickly" three times in discussing her Spanish class. After the above entry the reader senses that Fields saw herself as better than the female student and roughly equal to the male student. But at the fourth class meeting a new person joined the group. Field wrote, apparently with some envy,

A fourth person joined the class today. Although it was the fourth lesson he had no trouble catching up with the rest of us because he had spent several months in Spain and had studied Spanish briefly in Madrid. He spoke with what is known as "the Castillian lisp." . . . The other woman in our class was absent and the fellows and I made pretty good progress. The new student commented during the break that he hoped the other man and I weren't confused by his lisp. We weren't; we couldn't understand anything he said, so there was nothing to be confused about. (ibid.)

Again the image of the language class as a race emerges in the diary. After this entry Fields continued to be sensitive to the presence of other students in her Berlitz class. Three weeks after the first class she wrote, "There were only two of us in class last night and things went smoothly. . . ." Two weeks after that she wrote, "The other woman in the original group hasn't been here for several lessons." (ibid., p. 5)

Like Francine Schumann, Fields seems to have been competing with her husband, who was not, in this case, a member of the class. There are two revealing comments about her husband which indicate that she envied his abilities as a Spanish speaker. Following the first Berlitz class Fields wrote,

After much patient repetition, my husband—one of the few people I had ever known to emerge from two years of college language training able to speak the language and with a good accent—had taught me to "roll my r's." (ibid., p. 4)

A month later, after gaining some functional proficiency in Spanish, Fields wrote,

I wish I could practice my Spanish more, but when I try to speak it to my husband, I find there are a lot of common verbs I still don't know. Also, since I can use only the present tense, my husband finds my conversational attempts disconcerting at times. He keeps trying to tell me the future or past tenses of the verbs I use, but that doesn't do me much good, since I don't know the rules for formalizing them. (ibid., p. 5)

Again it would be premature to say that Fields is a competitive language learner. It is safe to say, however, that she actively compared herself to other learners in the classroom, envied her husband's abilities and wished to be able to communicate better in a second language than she really could. She may have been competing with the other students, her husband, and/or an idealized vision of herself as a fluent foreign language speaker.

Brian Lynch (1979) kept a journal of his experiences in a college Spanish class. Although this study focuses primarily on his learning strategies, there are entries documenting overt comparison with his classmates. These entries frequently deal with his efforts to achieve correct pronunciation:

Following the exam we went over some oral exercises in which individuals were called upon to deliver a series of substitutions out loud. One of the drills I was called upon for included "trabajo" and "hijas"—the difficult velar fricative which no one in the class seems to be able to produce. At first I did produce the fricative quite well, surprising myself, and I sensed a reaction from the students around me—just recognition, not good or bad—but I was immediately self-conscious and struggled between wanting to produce the correct form and not wanting to sound funny. The next few times I did not produce the fricative well at all. . . . Here the classroom is not an environment where your peers are producing, or I believe even trying to produce, the correct speech sounds. Most people in the class seem not to care about speaking fast. (Lynch, 1979, pp. 30–31)

Lynch attributed this difference between himself and his classmates to motivation: "Most of these students are taking Spanish as a requirement and therefore aren't motivated in any integrative way to learn to speak Spanish without an accent" (ibid., p. 31). Because he saw himself as both integratively and instrumentally motivated, Lynch continued to be concerned with achieving native-like pronunciation and fluency. In one entry he ranked himself as third among the students in pronunciation ability and made some observations on his two competitors:

. . . I have the impression that I speak with a better accent, i.e., produce Spanish phonology better, than almost everyone else in the class. Only two exceptions come to mind—Señorita F., . . . who occasionally makes errors involving the use of French words instead of Spanish, and an Iranian student who seems to have studied Spanish before and has a larger vocabulary than the rest of the class. He is the person who approached me . . . to ask if I thought the teacher was any good. . . . (His) complaint was that the class was moving too slow. My reaction was that if it was moving too slow, no one in the class would be making mistakes on the simple matters that even he was guilty of from time to time. (ibid., p. 38)

Later in Lynch's journal competition is specifically mentioned, although not as a major trend and only with regard to pronunciation:

. . . We took turns reading the lesson out loud by paragraphs. Only one person read very well and that was Señorita F. . . . She is the only person who speaks with something resembling an authentic Spanish accent—and at times I have been aware of competing with her. Today she read so well that I felt a sudden urge to compliment her. It was nice not to feel competitive about it, and for once I felt a positive motivation as a result of the classroom environment (even if it was only one person). When I was called upon to read I was inspired to try and speak as clearly as possible and with good pronunciation. . . . Overall I was pleased with the results. I didn't feel like I was competing with Señorita F., but I was definitely serious about sounding good. (ibid., p. 56)

This entry is noteworthy in that Lynch, like Francine Schumann, sees the absence of competitiveness as a positive change.

The public performance aspect of his Spanish class seems to have been a source of some anxiety for Lynch:

I was aware today of the difference in my speaking ability between being called on in class and speaking out loud while studying (or even reading or speaking to someone outside of class). In class, where you are performing and being judged by instructor and classmates, there is much more tenseness and I became very much afraid of making mistakes, and I am not as aware of how closely I am approximating correct Spanish pronunciation. Sometimes the horrible accents I hear others using in class . . . shock me. It almost seems like they don't even want to overcome the accent problem. Today made me aware that in the classroom drills I tend to focus off speaking with a correct accent because I am so preoccupied with the right form of the answer— and that I may be sounding as poor as most of the class. (ibid., p. 41)

Lynch's fear of public failure was apparently aggravated by the reactions of one vocal student. The following entry reveals the type of hostility I experienced in my French 2R class:

One of the tangents we got off onto today actually involved only one student and the teacher, as near as I could tell. At least there were a few people who I noticed were looking around bored, annoyed, or laughing at the somewhat ridiculous questions this person tends to come up with regularly. This same person has the annoying (not just to me I believe) habit of exclaiming out loud in a "whiny"tone, "No-oo-o" when someone in class gives the wrong answer—a tone which seems to say, "How *could* you say *that* !"Until today I thought I was the only one who reacted this way to her, but I noticed a comrade or two sharing my look of irritation and smiling at me in recognition. (ibid., p. 44)

Here the word *comrade* provides an example of the connotative power of the language used in the diary entries.

Lynch felt that his fear of public failure contributed to poor oral performance, especially in short responses to questions:

I noticed that I still continue to stutter quite a bit—a problem I don't seem to have in English. It's usually (perhaps always) when I'm called upon for a one-sentence response. I tend to get very nervous and it takes me a few seconds before I can even start to speak, even when it's a relatively simple task or phrase. I'm obviously very afraid to make a mistake in front of the class—and I always feel very embarrassed about stammering. When I read a long passage or get involved in more of an on-going conversation, this seems to be less of a problem. (ibid., p. 53)

Earlier in the semester Lynch had observed that he had more difficulty in pronouncing the first few responses. After a warm-up period he found that he loosened up and felt more fluent (ibid., p. 29). One can hypothesize that in reading a longer passage or being involved in a prolonged conversation, Lynch has time to calm himself, relax and control his anxiety, which in turn improves his oral performance.

Another example of overt comparison with other students arose in Lynch's communicative use of Spanish during a classroom lesson. When called upon to form a question, Lynch asked the teacher in Spanish what he had read the day before. Although the question contained an accent error, it

> got the teacher onto the subject of V. Nabokov—and as it turned out, I was the only person in the class who had heard of him. I was asked to say who he was, in Spanish—a good test of my communicative abilities. . . . I was fairly happy with my answer. It was slowly constructed with many "uh's"and a questioning to the teacher on two of the words . . . but I did manage to deliver a whole sentence and use the preterite. . . . After class the professor initiated a conversation with me, in English, about my plans for next year. I was flattered by his interest. We talked about ESL (which he taught at night for twelve years) and about opportunities for travel that the field affords me. (ibid., pp. 50–51)

In this instance the teacher rewarded Lynch's performance by (a) prolonging his turn by setting a new task,[7] and (b) engaging him in social conversation, in which they discovered their common interest in ESL. Here it is apparently Lynch's difference from the other students (i.e., his unique knowledge of Nabokov) which led to these rewards.

Lynch's journal includes numerous remarks on tests and graded assignments, but never with reference to the other students. For him a key issue seems to have been whether a grade was inaccurately high. The following comments reveal Lynch's desire for true grades (i.e., an accurate assessment of his progress):

> Today in class we had our exams (lesson 3) returned. Mine was scored as "O/A" even though I forgot three accent marks. (ibid., p. 26)

> Today I handed in the rough draft of my Spanish essay, and, to my surprise, was greeted with a tentative "A+ excelente" reaction from the professor. I think he was pleased with my content mostly as he had made twenty or so corrections on my grammar and word choice –which despite the "A+ excellent" marking upset me very much . . . (ibid., p. 42)

> After getting my test back I noticed that he had scored mine as "−1, A", which I was sure was a mistake since I had remembered making so many (errors) . . . (ibid., p. 49)

Thus, Lynch's diary portrays a relatively secure language learner who is not highly prone to competitiveness. Only in instances of oral classroom performance (i.e., cases of potentially high anxiety and fear of public failure) do overt comparisons with other students emerge.

In a review of diary studies by six language learners, Snell (1978) identifies the attitude of the language learner toward other students as a source of competition for a number of the subjects. It appears that a language learner may face competition from other sources too. As well as competing with other students, the learner may compete with the teacher's expectations or with an idealized self-image. Evidence of these possibilities appeared in my French class diary when I wrote, "I hope Marie will like me and think that I am a good language learner. . . ." (Bailey, 1978, p. 41) and later, "I know I am (or can be) a good language learner, but I hate being lost in class" (ibid., p. 43).

Competition with other students and with one's idealized self-image can often be intertwined with the desire to gain the teacher's approval. For example, in keeping a diary of her experience while studying Indonesian as a foreign language, Hindy Leichman (1977) reports a fear of public failure and a need for success:

> When in class I still had the fear of being called on. I was afraid that I would fumble on the
> material I had worked so hard to learn. Each time I did fumble, I became a little less confident.
> On the other hand, each time I understood what was being said, I felt better. . . . In almost every
> class hour I would fluctuate between feelings of success or failure. (p. 2)

Apparently part of her sense of failure is based on her past history as a language learner—a history which is not documented in this particular paper. But part is attributable to the diarist's comparison of herself with the other students, rather than to a purely linguistic assessment of her fluency. In discussing the Indonesian classroom Leichman writes,

> From the beginning I believed that the other students were not struggling as much as me. Very
> often they would process the question and start to answer before I had a chance. This scared me
> because I did not know what I was doing wrong not to be able to think as quickly as them. So
> many of my hang-ups about language learning were my own perceptions of what I do and what
> others do. Unfortunately, I did not know which were distortions of the truth; maybe others were
> struggling as much, maybe I was speaking as fluently or at least not any worse than everyone
> else. So much depended on how I viewed myself and others. Very often I would try to stop
> concerning myself with how I thought they were doing and try concentrating on me. (1977, p. 3)

The paper does not include a language-learning history, but Leichman says she was not successful in her earlier attempts to learn a foreign language. Thus she had to overcome her own negative expectations.[8] She wrote, "Throughout the course there was a struggle within myself between my old feelings (of failure) and my desire for success" (ibid., p. 6). The impact of the word *struggle* here provides further evidence of her emotional state.

Leichman also identifies tests and grades as a source of apprehension for her. In discussing an exam she took in the Indonesian course she said,

> I had not done nearly as well as I had hoped, and was ashamed to let anyone see my grade. . . .
> During the review I volunteered to put something on the blackboard because I wanted the teacher to
> consider my class participation more than my test grade. (ibid., p. 4)

Here the learner seems to be competing for the teacher's approval as well as performing well in comparison to the other students. Leichman wrote that her performance on this exam "caused a temporary backslide" (ibid.) in her study of Indonesian. That evening she tried to study but couldn't concentrate:

> I just kept thinking that there was no point in learning the vocabulary since I would only fail
> again. I felt resentment at having to spend so much time studying when it did not pay off. Why
> should I study if I only do badly on a test? Eventually my feelings won over my better judgment
> and I gave up. (ibid., p. 4–5)

Leichman's journal entry for the next class period reveals the power of grades:

> The next day I did not want to go to class. I still was upset about the test and was unprepared
> emotionally to be confronted by other students as to my grade. Since it was a Tuesday, we were
> getting back our logs about the week before. I was scared that I would not do well on it and that
> would only compound my existing feelings. When I saw a good grade I was not only relieved, I
> was encouraged. Maybe I could not do well on tests, but I could succeed in other requirements of
> the course. I volunteered a lot during the review and left my paper open so anyone (and
> everyone) could see I had done well. (ibid., p. 5)

That day Leichman was successful in the Indonesian class and wrote that she didn't mind doing her homework that night because she had been successful in class.

Several of the other classroom diary studies also make reference to grades and tests. In a paper based on a diary which he kept while learning to read Thai in an individualized course, Chris Bernbrock (1977) recalls that he "could only manage to obtain mediocre grades" while studying French and Latin in high school, and that he saw "language studies as something to be avoided because he could not excel in them" (p. 1). Bernbrock also reports that a test grade led him to withdraw from a Russian course in college:

> After having failed to perform in a distinguishing manner on the mid-term examination, the learner withdrew and resigned himself to reading Dostoyevsky in English translation. (ibid., pp. 1–2)

Yet in an immersion situation in Thailand, the student "learned Thai quite well and was proud of his ability to use the language" (ibid., p. 2). Later Bernbrock was able to pursue the individualized programmed course in reading Thai syllables. In this course he worked alone with a professor who had studied Thai. They agreed on a reasonable syllabus—in effect, a learning contract. Bernbrock was also tutored by his wife, a native speaker of Thai. Of this experience he wrote,

> In this particular course I did not have to worry about my performance compared to other students or what the teacher expected of me. . . . I experienced none of the anxiety or fear of making mistakes that was so detrimental to my attempts to learn languages in the past. (ibid., p. 9)

Here Bernbrock explicitly identifies competition with other students and with the teacher's expectations as problems in his former efforts to learn a foreign language. In reflecting on his experiences Bernbrock suggests that a language course syllabus should "encourage learners to measure up against the goals of the course rather than measure up against the other learners" (ibid., p. 5). (The assessment method Bernbrock suggests is basically a type of criterion-referenced testing, as opposed to norm-referenced testing of achievement.) Like Francine Schumann and Brian Lynch, Bernbrock sees competition as undesirable in a language-learning situation.

It is difficult to determine the origins of a learner's responses to perceived competition. In reading journal studies that include a retrospective discussion of the diarist's language-learning history, one is often tempted to indulge in a little armchair psychology. The influence of the family seems to play a role in some learners' attitudes about performing in a language classroom. For example, as Snell points out (1978), Marjorie Walsleben's efforts to learn Persian seem to involve a long-standing rivalry with her younger sister. In comparing her own background as a language learner with that of her sister, Walsleben says,

> I was very envious of her apparent ability to be at ease when attempting to speak French or

> Spanish. . . . With a thinly disguised competitive reaction, I began a self-study of German. (1976, pp. 6–7)

Walsleben's sensitivity to competition is apparent in the discussion of a beginning Persian class she took as a graduate student. Like me in the French 2R class, she rated herself as being one of the less fluent members of the group:

> Two of the students had lived and worked in Iran and could speak Farsi to some extent; ten of the students were already familiar with the language through association with Persian friends; seven of the students were actual "beginners." I classed myself with the group of seven. (ibid., p. 13)

This last characterization of herself is curious since Walsleben had several Persian friends and some exposure to the language at the time she recorded this entry.

Walsleben saw her inability to compete with her more proficient classmates as causing her a great deal of anxiety. This anxiety is directly attributable to the stressful competitive nature of oral public performance in the Persian class. Walsleben reports that the class became polarized into the group that "knew" Farsi and the group that did not:

> Three of the more voluble students delighted in "racing" each other to see who could repeat the choral drills first and loudest. My anxiety level increased daily and I developed a feeling of frustration and incompetence which was only intensified by my wanting so very much to speak the language. (ibid., p. 15)

Whether or not this anxiety affected her language learning is open to debate. It is clear that she felt it did. As is often the case in the journal studies, what the diarist perceives as real may be more important to that person's language-learning experience than any external reality. At any rate, Walsleben's introspection led her to conclude, "I never feel that I do my best work or make my best efforts when I am anxious, insecure or feel threatened in any way" (ibid., p. 18).

The remarks above are excerpted from Walsleben's detailed language-learning history. In keeping a personal journal of a subsequent Persian class she often commented on her conflicting desire to gain the teacher's approval and her frustration with the way he taught and the tests he assigned:

> As class was dismissed (the teacher) assigned a vocabulary test for the following Wednesday to be derived from the thousand-word glossary that accompanied the first-year Persian text. I said that I felt such a test was unreasonable. . . . I knew that I did not have twenty-five hours to spend studying for such a vocabulary test, yet I was frustrated because I wanted to perform well on the test. I felt torn between wanting to somehow show him that I could do well, yet feeling that such a test at that point would not truly reflect anyone's basic productive capabilities. (ibid., pp. 23–24)

Later she wrote, "I knew I would not do well on the test, and it bothered me though I continued to feel it was a meaningless exercise" (ibid., p. 25). Throughout the remaining journal entries Walsleben comments on the frequent vocabulary tests, but these quizzes do not become objects of competition between her and the other students in this particular class. In fact, Walsleben's diary reveals a very empathic learner who was concerned with the feelings of the other students. Her own feelings of frustration were aimed at the teacher and his teaching methods, which she felt were wasting her time. Apparently she was not alone in this opinion. Toward the end of the journal Walsleben documents a classroom blow-up, triggered by yet another vocabulary test:[9]

> After the break (the teacher) announced that he would give the vocabulary test, "If that's okay." Shirley stated again her difficulty in studying uncontextualized words for a vocabulary test, and (the teacher) explained that he nonetheless felt that it was a justifiable way of building up our vocabularies. When he repeated that he was going to give the test and looked at me when he said, "If that's okay," I responded tersely, "You're the professor, but in my opinion it's a poor use of time." That was the proverbial last straw. For the next hour and a half the whole class was embroiled in a very emotional exchange of opinions dealing with what the class was and was not, what it could and should be, who would let whom do what.

> My seven weeks of pent-up anger and frustration made my voice quaver and my hands tremble so that I could not lift my coffee cup without spilling the coffee. (The teacher's) voice too was unsteady. I was terribly uncomfortable, feeling like the class "heavy" and feeling little or no support from the other members of the class at first. At one point, when I saw David's and Ramona's faces flush with what I interpreted as being discomfort, I tried to stop talking, but by then (the teacher) insisted that we continue.

> Gradually our voices became lower and more calm, and one by one, the students expressed their own opinions and suggestions. But when we finished talking, I was feeling an internal conflict between my belief that (the professor) had *heard* our criticisms and suggestions and my doubt that he would actually do anything in response to them. I felt exhausted and empty. (ibid., pp. 34–35)

Besides Walsleben two other students in the class were experienced language teachers, and throughout the journal there is much discussion of how the course should be taught. In this case it seems that the diarist is not competing with her classmates, but is struggling with the instructor for control of her language-learning experience. This idea is supported by the argument about "who would let whom do what" and her comment, "You're the professor." During the eighth week of the ten-week quarter she wrote,

> By Thursday I knew I would not go to class again—at least for the remainder of the quarter. . . . All quarter long I had spent hours and hours studying Farsi because I wanted to and was determined to keep progressing. Whenever I had several assignments to do I always did my Farsi first because to me it really was not work at all, but fun. Reading and translating was like working a puzzle. I had reread all the texts and marked all the relative clauses to see if I could grasp the pattern that was being used; it did not always appear to fit the rules (the teacher) had given us, so I wanted to ask questions about them whenever he reached the point where he intended to explicate grammatical points in the texts. I had also noted other grammatical questions in the text margins. But suddenly—it did not seem to matter. (ibid., p. 36)

Walsleben had not enrolled in this course for credit: she was there just to learn Persian. But she could not accept the teacher's methodology because of her own training as an ESL teacher. The over-emphasis on tests in the course seemed unproductive to her and in spite of her high integrative motivation, Walsleben left the Persian class.[10]

Another unhappy experience is reported by Rebecca Jones, who studied Indonesian in an eleven-week intensive program while she was immersed in the target culture. The journal of her experiences reveals a sharp contrast between the positive environment in the home of her Indonesian host family and the discomfort and frustration she felt within the formal classroom situation. The competitiveness she experienced in the Indonesian course is evident throughout the journal.

Much of Jones's unhappiness with the program started in an early encounter with the director. A diary entry made at the beginning of the course says,

> I can't believe Dr. Fox. He has just informed me that I am lucky that I am one of the ten participants in this program as I was a borderline case and on Indonesian tests I took to get admitted to the program I wasn't that good. Then he said it was because I hadn't used his books, *that* was the main problem. I can barely write this down. One of my friends warned me. If he likes you, you will do fine; if he doesn't, WATCH OUT. So I have to swallow my pride and hide my feelings and try to make him like me and avoid him or ignore what he says. I feel like telling exactly what I think of him, but that would do nothing but alienate me from the program and antagonize him more. (1977, p. 27)

Thus from the beginning of the course, Jones had to compete with the negative expectations communicated to her by the director. To salvage her pride she had to do better than he expected her to do—better than her test scores predicted she would do. Later in the week she wrote,

> . . . We have been divided into two groups, "good" and "not so good." I'm in the "not so good" group with Peter, Cindy and Laura. Those in the upper group are those who used Fox's book in the United States, who are his students, or who previously had been in Indonesia longer than three months. (ibid., p. 31)

Her status as a member of the less advanced group was apparently upsetting to Jones, who had been to Indonesia twice before—once as an exchange student for three months.

In Jones's case the prorgram director seems to have promoted the competition by overtly comparing the students in the class. Apparently hurt by this action, Jones wrote,

> Dr. Fox stated in front of the entire group that he was pleased with Peter's memorization of the dialogue; Laura's was OK; and he was not pleased with mine *at all*. In other words, he said, "A for Peter, B for Laura and C for Becky." That had the effect of turning me off entirely from the rest of the lectures for the rest of the day. I am writing in my journal and not listening at all. . . . (ibid., p. 36)

Peter and Laura, the two learners with whom Jones is compared, were both in the "not so good" group of students. According to the diarist, this public humiliation caused her to mentally withdraw from instruction for at least the remainder of the day. The director's comment was apparently very damaging to Jones's attitude about the program as a whole. At the end of this episode she wrote,

> I am building up a lot of resentment and negative feelings. If I learn Indonesian, it is in spite of Dr. Fox and this program. The program has the tendency of stripping away all support and exposing all my inadequacies in Indonesian. It crushes my ego, *especially when I wanted to be top in the class*. (ibid., p. 36) (emphasis mine)

This last comment is an example of an overtly stated desire to outdo the other students (like my predicting I would be the best student in the French 2R class). However, Jones was facing some severe obstacles: it seems she was competing with an idealized self-image as well as with her classmates and the director's negative expectations.

The competitiveness that developed in Jones's Indonesian classes spilled over into her free-time activities as well. During the second week of the program she wrote,

> I went downtown tonight with Sony and Laura. My Indonesian was good and I felt confident. I spoke in Indonesian all night and felt secure in my use of it. This is probably because I compared myself to Laura, whose language is terrible. She has difficulty understanding anything. I felt more confident because I know she is not going to correct my Indonesian. (ibid., p. 34)

Like me in the French 2R class, Jones seems to capitalize (emotionally and—indirectly—linguistically) on the presence of another learner with whom she can compare herself favorably.

Jones's first edge in the classroom competition appeared when the group began to study Jawi, Indonesian in Arabic script. Of this experience she wrote,

> Jawi began today. I did better than the others, except Glenn, because of my previous study of Jawi in Hawaii. I feel good because of that. (ibid., p. 46)

There is no further reference to Jawi in the edited diary, so the reader doesn't know if the Jawi writing practice continued to be a source of success for Jones. However, like me in the French 2R class, Jones found some satisfaction in ranking herself differentially (against the other students) in the various language skills. Nearly two months after the beginning of the course, Jones wrote,

> In comparison with the other members of the group, I would say that my pronunciation is the best, but my vocabulary is by far the most limited because I've stopped doing the readings. (ibid., p. 57)

In discussing the trends in her journal, Jones, like Francine Schumann, identifies her competitiveness with the other participants as one of the major personal factors influencing her language learning experience:

> Prompted by Dr. Fox's and the Indonesian staff's behavior toward me in the classroom situation, I began to feel more and more in competition with the other participants. A curious form of sibling rivalry developed among us. Dr. Fox . . . functioned in the role of the parent with all of the learners acting as children, competing in order to achieve recognition and attention. . . . I disliked this competitiveness in the classroom as I was not the top student and could not achieve my need for positive reinforcement and reassurance. So I essentially stopped working altogether on my language learning in the classroom situation. In order to gain favor with the parent figure of Dr. Fox, I turned my energies to organizing parties and trips for the group and totally abandoned anything more than a polite attempt in keeping up with the lessons. (ibid., pp. 77–78)

Thus, Jones saw the competitive climate in her Indonesian program as detrimental (or at least not conducive) to language learning. Although her Indonesian fluency improved (as measured by pre- and post-testing, as well as by her own estimation), she attributed this gain to her life with the Indonesian host family and to being immersed in the target language environment, rather than to the classroom instruction. Because she could not compete with many of the other students in the formal instructional setting, she chanelled her energies into other ways of pleasing the director/parent figure.

In a paper based on a diary she kept while studying Indonesian as a foreign language, Deborah Plummer (1976) also discusses the teacher as a parent figure. In reviewing her journal entries, Plummer identified three phases in her classroom language-learning experience. These stages were determined more by affective factors than by linguistic ability. Plummer's journal reveals that in the first phase of classroom language learning she adopted a childlike persona, which (she felt) enabled her to learn more easily:

> The best way I can describe my psychological state in the class is childlike. At the beginning I felt free from adult responsibility. I was expected to bring to the class no previous knowledge of the language. All of the students began at the same level. I felt like I could play. I knew I was not expected to make no errors in my L2 speech so I took advantage of my freedom. This does not mean that I made errors on purpose. It simply means that I was able to experiment and learn in the way I find easiest, that is, learning by doing. . . . (Plummer, 1976, p. 5)

Plummer's attitude toward the Indonesian teacher in this first phase seems to have promoted this childlike state. In discussing the professor she wrote,

> She became very much of a parental figure to me, in whom I could place my trust. I knew that she understood the changes I went through each day from 9:00 to 9:50 A.M. Before and after that time I was an adult who could express herself on an intellectual linguistic level, but during class I was an adult who struggled to talk about elementary concrete objects in the most simple, childlike speech. Instead of being frustrated by such a dichotomy, I found it much easier to adopt a childlike identity in the new language. I consider this a major factor in promoting the learning of the target language. Because of the threats a second or foreign language class often poses, this new identity helped preserve my adult ego and self-confidence. (ibid., pp. 5–6)

Plummer's description of herself in the first phase of her language-learning experience is remarkably similar to Walsleben's discussion of the highly vocal students who annoyed her so much in her Persian class:

> My childlike behavior in class was manifest in a variety of ways. what I was most conscious of was shouting out words. I particularly liked playing with the new sounds of the target language.[11] I liked repeating words and phrases after the professor and I did so in a loud voice. I liked trying to be the first to get it out. . . . I found myself just wanting to talk and make noise and play with the language until it became a part of me. . . . I realize that in such a language class there needed to be order. The professor, very much like a parent, let those of us play who needed to, but there was an understood limit and discipline. (ibid., p. 6)

During the first phase Plummer also reports that she had a "language-learning buddy" (i.e., a cooperative coactor):

> We usually sat together and laughed about the sounds of the new words as we shouted them out. . . . We incorporated Indonesian words into English phrases and took the liberty to invent some words. It was very much like child-play with language. . . . Our goal was to use Indonesian communicatively. (ibid., pp. 6–7)

Plummer and her language-learning buddy were apparently aggressive and fun-loving in their approach to learning Indonesian. Yet Plummer too was extremely sensitive to competition in the language classroom. At one point she saw herself as being out of favor with the instructor, for reasons she cannot (or does not) explain. This period she identifies as the second phase of her language learning:

> Outside of class I had felt very distant from the professor—an abrupt change from the in-class parental figure. In and out of class she was a person I highly respected and from whom I sought recognition and approval—as if she were a parent. . . . I felt that I had lost her recognition, approval and favor. I lost my self-confidence and most of all I lost my childlike feeling. I was an adult. As an adult I was responsible for my actions and my L2 errors became ego deflating and wounding. In my mind errors were no longer to be laughed at. (ibid., pp. 8–9)

During this second phase Plummer also reports a change in the relationship with her friend:

> He began sitting away from me and his attention was on another friend. I knew him better than anyone in the class so as a result I felt very much alone and isolated. I did not have much desire to communicate so my new language was useless. (ibid., pp. 9–10)

Plummer reports that she continued to be sensitive to the attention other students received and was bothered by one person in particular. In her journal she wrote, "More than anything, I was jealous." This entry provides an example of the kind of hidden emotions sometimes experienced by learners in language classrooms.

Eventually Plummer discussed these feelings with her professor in an oral exam situation. The teacher apparently responded appropriately because Plummer saw this discussion as another turning point in her language-learning experience:

> Phase III began after this session. I began to feel a little more self-worth and acceptance from my parental figure. She was more sensitive to my needs in class and her subtle attention, unnoticed by others, was very encouraging. I began enjoying the class again. She tried not to let any students dominate the class, which was difficult to do with the few very verbose students. I found those students very intimidating because I could not compete with them for the professor's attention. (ibid., pp. 10–11)

Although Plummer was unable to completely recapture the childlike attitude she had perceived as so beneficial to her early language learning, she saw herself as progressing in Indonesian. Because she had discussed her unhappiness with the teacher, she was able to regain a certain equilibrium in the class, although the competition from the highly vocal students continued to bother her.

In contrast, a diary study conducted by Susan Scheding (1978) in an introductory German class seems to portray an unanxious language learner. Scheding's description of herself leads one to think that Walsleben, Leichman, Bernbrock, Plummer, and I might not be comfortable in a language class with her. On the first day of her college German class she wrote,

> The teacher handed out the syllabus and discussed quizzes, grades, etc. I could feel the anxiety among my fellow students during this discussion, but it doesn't affect me. Many of these students are probably taking German to fulfill some sort of university requirement. I'm hoping to have a good time. . . . (1978, p. 4)

Scheding's approach to classroom language instruction is to seek out as much input and correction as possible. On the fourth day of the class she wrote,

Somehow I have the feeling that not everybody is participating in the oral drills. I can't really see, as I sit in the front and the chairs are in the traditional rows behind me. But there are thirty students in here and I seem to be awfully loud. . . . Why would anyone want to sit in the back of a language class anyway? I always sit close to the instructor in the beginning in order to make sure I'm hearing correctly. Besides, sitting in the front means the teacher is likely to correct me if I mispronounce a word, even in choral drill. This is something the students in the back can't benefit from. (ibid., p. 5)

Like me in the French 2R class, Scheding compares herself to the other students, but since she is a confident language learner, the results are quite different. Scheding often comments on the lack of challenge in her German class. The following entries are representative:

We spent most of the hour on grammar explanations. Even though they were in German, I found myself getting impatient with this. Why explain the obvious? I just have to tell myself that for some students it must not be so obvious. . . . (ibid., p. 6)

We reviewed for the quiz on Monday. This was very boring. The teacher seemed to avoid calling on me in class; he was looking for those students he is unsure of. But if no one else answered, he usually looked at me. . . . (ibid., p. 7)

The quiz was returned. I did very well, as I had expected. The teacher reassured those students who did poorly. I sympathize with those who are struggling. . . . Foreign language learners may not have to deal with culture shock, but most must face other anxieties, and one of them is grade anxiety. (ibid., p. 8)

Other entries reveal Scheding's annoyance when her classmates would ask picky questions or break into English during the German class.

Before enrolling in this particular course, Scheding had studied Spanish, Latin, French, Mandarin Chinese, Ameslan (AmericanSign Language), Indonesian, and Quecha. Her self-image was one of a successful language learner. Yet even a confident learner can experience anxiety in a situation where he or she feels incompetent (i.e., unable to compete). Scheding's journal provides a nice illustration of this idea. She reports that she had arranged to miss one class period and the regular teacher had told her he doubted she'd have any trouble with the new material when she returned. However, on returning to the German class, Scheding was surprised:

Today for the first time all quarter, I experienced the kind of anxiety I once used to experience in language classes when I wasn't prepared and had to go anyway. I had been away skiing with (the teacher's) blessings. During this time they had begun a new chapter. I had made arrangements with (the teacher) to make up the work, but (he) wasn't there today. We had a substitute and *he* didn't know I'd been away. He called on everyone several times during the hour and I really didn't know what was going on. I felt very anxious from the beginning, wishing he wouldn't call on me and keeping my head down, as though absorbed in the book. (It's the old ostrich syndrome: if I can't see him, he can't see me.) This hour passed very slowly and I was glad when it was over. (ibid., pp. 11–12)

Thus, with her confidence temporarily damaged by not knowing as much as her classmates (or as much as she normally knew), Scheding, like the other diarists, felt inadequate and anxious. This diary entry supports the distinction between state and trait anxiety, made by Spielberger, Gorusch, and Lushene (1970).

Although not prone to state anxiety, Scheding's temporary incompetence generated state anxiety.

Except in this one instance, the diary portrays Scheding as a highly confident language learner who compares herself favorably with her classmates because of her past experiences in learning languages (like Fields in the Berlitz class but with much broader exposure to language learning). Scheding may not have experienced much competitiveness because there was no need for her to compete. She was already at the top of her class, in her own opinion as well as the teacher's. And except for the one occasion when she was unprepared and vulnerable, there was no discrepancy between her real self and her ideal self.

Describing and Defining Affective Factors in Second Language Learning

The purpose of this review has been to see what evidence of the relationship between competitiveness and anxiety these ten diary studies provide. In discussing my own journal I listed seven characteristics of the entries involving competitiveness. Those characteristics, with some additions, have appeared in the journals of the other diarists as follows:

1. *Overt self-comparison of the language learner*
(a) with classmates (Bailey, Bernbrock, Fields, Jones, Leichman, Lynch, Moore, Plummer, Scheding, Schumann,Walsleben); (b) with other language learners not in the classroom (Fields, Walsleben); and (c) with personal expectations (Bailey, Bernbrock, Fields, Walsleben).

2. *Emotive responses to the comparisons* in (1) above (Baily, Bernbrock, Fields, Jones, Leichman, Lynch, Moore, Plummer, Scheding, Schumann, Walsleben), including (a) hostile reactions toward other students (Bailey, Lynch, Plummer); and (b) connotative uses of language in the diary (Bailey, Fields Leichman, Lynch) which reveal the diarist's emotional state.

3. *A desire to out-do other language learners* (Bailey, Jones), including (a) racing through examinations (Bailey); and (b) students shouting out answers in class (Plummer, and reported on by Walsleben).

4. *Emphasis on or concern with tests and grades*[12] (Bailey, Bernbrock, Leichman, Lynch, Walsleben) (a) especially with reference to other students (Bailey, Leichman); or (b) with a discussion of how tests interfere with language learning (Leichman, Walsleben); although (c) one "unanxious" student (Scheding) documents a notable lack of concern with tests and grades.

5. *A desire to gain the teacher's approval* (Bailey, Jones, Leichman, Plummer, Walsleben), including (a) perception of the teacher as a parent figure (Jones, Plummer); and (b) the need to meet or overcome a teacher's expectations (Bernbrock, Jones).

6. *Anxiety experienced during the language lesson* (Bailey, Bernbrock, Jones, Leichman, Lynch, Moore, Plummer, Scheding, Walsleben).

7. *Withdrawal from the language-learning experience* (Bailey, Bernbrock, Jones, Schumann, Walsleben), which can be either (a) mental (Jones) or physical (Bailey, Bernbrock, Walsleben); and (b) temporary (Bailey) or permanent (Bernbrock, Jones, Walsleben); (c) one diarist (Leichman) wanted to withdraw temporarily but continued to attend the language class.

The components of this description could be used in a correlation study to design a questionnaire or scale for measuring competitiveness and anxiety. In addition, some of the manifestations of competitiveness listed above may be directly observable by classroom researchers. For example, teachers may overhear discussions of grades, or notice students rushing through tests. Observers could identify students who shout out answers in classroom drills, or who withdraw from the learning environment following public humiliation or failure. But attributing such behaviors to the learners' competitiveness is still an inferential step, and the other items on the list may be examples of the hidden classroom responses Moore has called "a melee of emotions, rational and irrational" (1977, p. 108). Thus the diary studies, if they are candid and thorough, can provide access to the language learner's hidden classroom responses, especially in the affective domain.[13]

It is not my purpose to argue in favor of introspective diary studies over empirical research on second language learning. In fact, these two approaches to knowing can provide us with very different types of information, and each methodology can inform the other, as I have tried to show.[14] In discussing what he calls the "anthropological approach" and the "interaction analysis approach" to investigating language classroom processes, Long calls for "future research on classroom language learning which uses a combined approach, thereby avoiding some of the limitations of each and taking advantage of the strengths of both" (1979, p. 40). Ochsner has also argued forcefully for the use of both traditions—nomothetic (empirical) science and hermeneutic (here, introspective) investigation—in SLA research. He describes a poetics of SLA which would allow us to "develop a perceptual bilingualism; that is, the ability to study SLA from at least two points of view" (1979, p. 71).

As research on classroom language learning progresses, we must question first the form and then the content of the diary studies. The medium, the methodology, is introspective and descriptive—not necessarily predictive. Cause and effect are determined by the diarist's perceptions rather than by controlling and manipulating variables. This being the case, what is the value of the diarists' conclusions? Can they be generalized, and what can they teach us about language learning?

Based on this review we may conclude that the findings of the diary studies can be *compared,* whether or not they can be *generalized.* In fact, it may not even be desirable to try to generalize from the results of such language learning journals. Their main purpose is to discover what factors influence the individual diarist's language learning. As Long has pointed out, the diary studies are concerned with individuals in unique learning environments, so generalization of their findings to other learners and environments is precluded on the basis of the studies themselves. They may be relevant to many or even all learners, in other words, or idiosyncratic. (1979, p. 36)

Of course, in the complex, real-life world of the language classroom, given enough details of history, motivation, aptitude, etc., every student can be viewed as functioning in a unique learning environment. For this reason, the question of generalizability, as the term is used in the empirical research tradition, is inappropriate here.[15] Thus, it is primarily in the area of *personal variables* (Schumann and Schumann, 1977) or *learner variables* (Scovel, 1978) that the diary studies can contribute to our knowledge of second language learning (Long, 1979; Schumann and Schumann, 1977).

But questions of content, here the personal affective factors under consideration, must also be raised. What good does it do us to investigate competitiveness in language classrooms when competition surrounds us and permeates our lives? Caillois (1961) describes competition as both "a law of nature" (p. 46) and "a law of modern life" (p. 50). (Indeed the entire free enterprise system is based on economic competition.) He sees competition as a product of *agon,* the desire to win, which is one of four primary attitudes toward play among humans.[16] In a treatise on the play element in culture, Huizinga (1950) describes the agonistic impulse as innate and practically universal:

> From the life of childhood right up to the highest achievements of civilization, one of the strongest incentives to perfection, both individual and social, is the desire to be praised for one's excellence.... Doing something well means doing it better than others. In order to excel, one must prove one's excellence; in order to merit recognition, merit must be made manifest. Competition serves to give proof of superiority. (p. 63)

Such competition is well known, indeed integral, to prevalent trends in education. Reporting on ethnographic field work in elementary school classrooms, Roberts and Akinsanya (1976) characterize competition as one of "the most prominent emotions" of children:

> ... It is difficult to see how, in the present state of our culture, competitiveness can be overlooked. It would seem, perhaps, that the important outcome to avoid is that the competitiveness should become destructive of peers, while reinforcing dependence on the teacher. (p. 181)

Huizinga too discusses competition in knowledge as a universal theme:

> The urge to be first has as many forms of expression as society offers opportunities for it. The ways in which men compete are as various as the prizes at stake. ... The astonishing similarity that characterizes agonistic customs in all cultures is perhaps nowhere more striking than in the domain of the human mind itself, that is to say, in knowledge and wisdom (1950, p. 105).

If competition is practically all-pervasive, how can studying competitiveness contribute to our understanding of second language acquisition?

The answer lies in the complex relationship of competitiveness and anxiety, and then of anxiety to language learning. For several of the diarists cited above, entries which may be interpreted as revealing competitiveness or a perceived inability to compete often reveal anxiety as well. This trend leads us to the already obvious conclusion that Gardner et al.'s term "French Classroom Anxiety" (1976) should be broadened to the more general term "Language Classroom Anxiety."

At this point we should recall Tucker's comment regarding the present "state of the art" in research on affective variables:

> Although we would all presumably agree with the proposition that affective variables (somehow defined) are important in some way during the course of foreign or second language learning or teaching, their precise description and measurement remains a problematic issue (Tucker, 1979, p. 3).

Using the description above we can distill a definition of competitiveness as it occurs in the language classroom. Competitiveness is the desire to excel in comparison to others. The *others* are typically the learner's classmates, but as these diaries have shown, a learner may compete with an idealized self-image or with other learners not directly involved in the language classroom (a spouse, a friend, a sibling, etc.). Competitiveness arises when the comparison is emotive rather than objective.[16] If the comparison is invidious (i.e., if the learner perceives himself as lacking), such competitiveness can lead to anxiety. It may also lead to active *competition,* either through increased personal efforts to master the language or through striving to out-do other students (e.g., racing through tests, shouting out answers, over-emphasizing grades, etc.).

As Long notes, ethnographic field work—to which the diary studies are closely related—"is primarily a hypothesis-generating, not hypothesis-testing, undertaking" (1980, p. 27). This paper suggests the hypothesis that Language Classroom Anxiety can be caused and/or aggravated by the learner's competitiveness when he sees himself as less proficient than the object of comparison. Anxiety can also lead to competitiveness in the form of increased efforts to learn the language. (Such competitiveness, in Scovel's terms, is an intrinsic learner variable, which is influenced by extrinsic factors, including the behavior of the teacher[17] and other learners.) A corollary to this hypothesis is that as the learner becomes, or perceives himself as becoming, more competent (that is, better able to compete), his anxiety will decrease. Several of the diary entries cited above suggest that as anxiety decreases, the quality and quantity of performance increases, and vice versa. Thus I am suggesting a cyclic relationship between anxiety and negative competitiveness (i.e., invidious comparisons with other learners in which the learner perceives himself as lacking and attaches emotional significance to that perception). In formal instructional settings, if such anxiety motivates the learner to study the target language, it is *facilitating.* On the other hand, if it is severe enough to cause the learner to withdraw from the language classroom (either mentally or physically, temporarily or permanently), such anxiety is *debilitating* (Alpert and Haber, 1966; Kleinmann, 1977; Scovel, 1978). An over-simplified schematic representation of this complex relationship is presented in Figure 1.

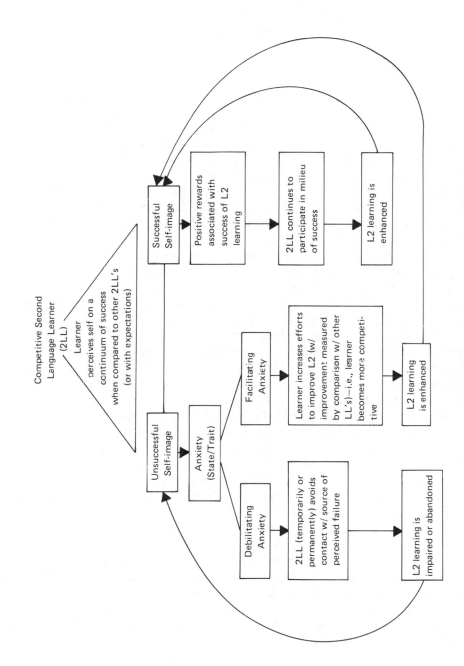

Figure 1. Competitiveness and the second language learner

At this point we should recall Tucker's comment regarding the present "state of the art" in research on affective variables:

> Although we would all presumably agree with the proposition that affective variables (somehow defined) are important in some way during the course of foreign or second language learning or teaching, their precise description and measurement remains a problematic issue. (1979, p. 3)

Thus, one value of the first-person diary studies is that the researcher /learner/diarist begins to study an affective factor by acknowledging its presence and psychological reality in the journal entries. He or she can then use the rich details of these entries to describe and define the variable under consideration. This approach to knowing is quite different from that of traditional empirical research, in which an investigator must operationally define his terms before beginning an experiment.

A second advantage is that, like other longitudinal case studies, the diary studies can provide developmental data. But since the diaries are first-person accounts, such data can yield information on the instability of attitudes discussed by Oller (1979, p. 10). Because the journals are systematic chronological records of personal responses to language learning situations, attitudinal changes can be traced through the sequential entries. An example is Susan Scheding's sudden state anxiety on the one day she was not prepared to participate in her German class. The gradual decrease in the comparison of myself with other students in the French 2R class is another.

A third advantage is linked to the complaint that the diary studies are not generalizable. Because they provide an in-depth portrait of the individual diarist, his or her unique history and idiosyncracies, the diary studies can give teachers and researchers insights on the incredible diversity of students to be found even within a homogeneous language classroom.

Finally, the journal studies enable the researcher/learner to document, and perhaps overcome, avoid, or counteract factors that are apparently detrimental to his or her language learning. There is some evidence that even the act of writing in the diary, whether or not the learner ever systematically reviews the entries, can be therapeutic for the learner. Ultimately, if we can use the diaries to identify the events and emotions leading up to changes in affect, we may be able to control or induce such changes. For instance, if we can determine the perceived causes of Language Classroom Anxiety, we might then be able to reduce this reaction or eliminate it entirely. Following the research of Gardner et al. cited above (1976), we can hypothesize that reduced Language Classroom Anxiety would lead to improved oral production on a measure of speech skills. Of course, we can also hypothesize that improved oral production would lead to a reduction in Language Classroom Anxiety. Either way, the diary studies allow us to see the classroom experience as a dynamic and complex process through the eyes of the language learner.

Notes

1. A portion of this paper was presented at a workshop for teachers at the American Language Institute, San Diego State University, on October 13, 1979. The title is based in part on work by Robert Ochsner (1979), who argues that we must "look *at* SLA; however, we must also learn to see *through* it" (p. 71). I am indebted to Robert Ochsner, Diane E. Larsen-Freeman, and Michael H. Long, who gave me references, constructive criticism, and moral support. I also appreciate the guidance of my teachers, José L. Galván and John H. Schumann.

2. See Long (1979) for a discussion of the degree of inference involved in various observational instruments used in language classroom research.

3. See Boring (1953) for an overview of the history of introspection as a tool of scientific psychological inquiry.

4. Throughout this chapter I use the terms *diary* and *journal* interchangeably. In addition, the terms *diarist, language learner,* and *researcher* typically refer to one person since that individual is functioning in all three roles.

5. In a related phenomenon, research on friendship groups in classrooms showed that

a student's perception of holding low status—more than the fact of actually having such status— was related to incomplete use of intellectual abilities and to holding negative attitudes toward self and toward the school. (Schmuck and Schmuck, 1971)

6. The issue of competition and cooperation in language learning has also been discussed by Stevick (1976) in describing the Silent Way. He points out that one positive feature of this method "is the absence of destructive competition: when students are depending on one another, the unique contributions of each are clearly recognized and valued by all, for even the slower students will, from time to time, remember something or figure something out that has escaped the others" (p. 142).

7. See Allwright (forthcoming) for a discussion of the relationship between *turns, topics* and *tasks* in the language classroom.

8. Schmuck, and Schmuck, in discussing group processes in the classroom, cite a definition of *expectations* from Finn (1972, p. 320):

Expectations are evaluations—whether conscious or unconscious—that one person forms of another (or of himself) which lead the evaluator to treat the person evaluated as though the assessment were valid. The person doing the expecting typically anticipates that the other person will act in a manner consistent with the assessment. (Schmuck and Schmuck, 1971, pp. 42–43)

9. See Bailey (1979) for a description of a similar classroom incident which was also touched off by the students' reaction to a test.

10. Francine Schumann also discusses withdrawal from learning due to nonacceptance of the teaching method:

I hated the method. My anger bred frustration, a frustration which I acutely felt as my goal was to be a star performer in class, and I found it impossible to be so under these circumstances.

Instead of resorting to a solution which would allow me to cope with this learning environment and learn in spite of the method, my reaction was to reject it and withdraw from learning. This withdrawal was gradual and displayed itself in a variety of ways. Some days I would assume such a low profile in class, making no attempts to participate, that only my physical presence allowed that I was indeed a member of the group. Other days this withdrawal took the form of my cutting-up during the lesson. Eventually the withdrawal led to my leaving class early, walking out on exams, and on some days not showing up at all. (Schumann and Schumann, 1977, p. 244)

11. See Peck (1977, pp. 86–90) for a discussion of adults and language play.

12. Davis discusses the research on feedback as it relates to the quality of group performance:

If the task permits individual contributions to be recovered or graded in the final group product, then *individual* members may be selectively rewarded accordingly. Alternatively, the group may be paid off *as a whole.* The result . . . is that cooperative behavior is usually evident in the latter kind of group, while a competitive interaction style typically characterizes the former sort of group. (1969, p. 81)

In a language classroom, achievement or improvement is normally measured on an individual basis by examination. Therefore, the language classroom is more closely related to the former type of group, in which members are rewarded selectively (i.e., by grades) than to the latter, in which the group members receive group "pay-off."

13. In discussing the research on group processes, Davis states:

It is possible to distinguish two basic methods for obtaining data concerning interpersonal behavior: (a) the observation of interpersonal behavior by trained observers, and (b) the self-report of the individual member concerning his own reaction to others and his perceptions of the reactions of fellow group members to each other. (1969, p. 7)

To the extent that each individual diarist can be considered a "trained observer," the diary studies can tap both of these sources of information.

14. See Bellack (1978) for a comparison of these two traditions, which he calls "mainstream scientific ideology" and "interpretive ideology," in research on teaching.

15. Long (1979, pp. 35–36) summarizes the arguments regarding generalizability in social science research.

16. In classifying games Caillois proposes "a division into four main rubrics, depending on whether, in the games under consideration, the role of competition, chance, simulation, or vertigo is dominant. (He calls) these *agôn, alea, mimicry* and *ilinx,* respectively" (1961, p. 12).

Stevick adopts the framework of Transactional Analysis to explain the three ego states—the Parent, the Adult, and the Child—and their roles in (adult) language learning. He describes the ego state of the Child as being "interested in comparisons, and particularly in establishing that 'Mine is better' than anybody else's" (1976, p. 68). The Child state also involves the "display of emotions, either pleasant or unpleasant" (ibid.). Many of the diarists cited above experienced such emotions, which were largely hidden in the classroom but vented in the journal entries.

17. The exact role of the teacher in promoting competitiveness and/or Language Classroom Anxiety is as yet unclear. In discussing group processes in (content) classrooms, Schmuck and Schmuck suggest that the actions of authoritarian teachers "encourage high dependency, high competition among students, feelings of some powerlessness, and at times, feelings of being alienated from the subject matter" (1971, p. 75). They also say that, "the teacher who encourages high amounts of dependency or competition through influence behaviors often is reaping debilitating outcomes for students" (ibid.). In pursuing the issue one step further, Schmuck and Schmuck point out that teachers too are susceptible to what Scovel calls "the effect of affect" (1978, p. 129):

If teachers have feelings of comfort and rapport in relationships with colleagues, they are supported in their feelings of self-worth and are better able to relate positively to students. Feelings of hostility, competition or alienation lead to anxiety and low levels of tolerance with students. (Schmuck and Schmuck, 1971, p. 196)

References

Allwright, R. A. Turns, topics and tasks: Patterns of participation in language learning and teaching. In D. Larsen-Freeman (Ed.), *Discourse Analysis in Second Language Acquisition.* Rowley, Mass.: Newbury House, 1981.

Alpert, R., & Haber, R. Anxiety in academic achievement situations. *Journal of Abnormal and Social Psychology,* 1960, *61,* 207–215.

Bailey, K. M. Mon journal de la classe de Français: An introspective analysis of an individual's language learning experience. Unpublished manuscript, University of California, Los Angeles, English Department (ESL Section), 1978.

Bailey, K. M. An introspective analysis of an individual's language learning experience. In S. Krashen & R. Scarcella (Eds.), *Research in Second Language Acquisition: Selected Papers of the Los Angeles Second Language Research Forum.* Rowley, Mass.: Newbury House, 1979.

Beeman, P.,Martin, R., & Meyers, J. Interventions in relation to anxiety in school. In C. Spielberger (Ed.), *Anxiety: Current Trends in Theory and Research.* New York: Academic Press, 1972.

Bellack, A. Competing ideologies in research on teaching. Ahlstrom, Berglund, Dahllof, & Wallin (Eds.), *Uppsala Reports on Education 1.* Department of Education, Uppsala University, 1978.

Bernbrock, C. An introspective study of second language learning. Unpublished manuscript, English Department (ESL Section), University of California, Los Angeles, 1977.

Boring, E. G. A history of introspection. *Psychological Bulletin,* 1953, *50,* 3, 169–189.

Caillois, R. *Man, Play and Games.* Translated from the French by M. Barash. New York: The Free Press, 1961.

Chastain, K. Affective and Ability Factors in Second Language Acquisition. *Language Learning,* 1975, *25,* 153–161.

Davis, J. H. *Group Performance.* Reading, Mass.: Addison-Wesley, 1969.

Fields, C. M. How Berlitz Taught Me Spanish Rápidamente. *The Chronicle of Higher Education,* 1978 (July 17, pp. 4–6, and July 24, p. 7).

Gardner, R. C., Smythe, P. C., Clement, R., & Glicksman, L. Second language learning: A social-psychological perspective. *Canadian Modern Language Review,* 1976, *32,* 198–213.

Huizinga, J. *Homo Ludens: A Study of the Play-Element in Culture.* Boston: Beacon Press, 1950.

Jones, R. A. Psychological, social and personal factors in second language acquisition. Unpublished MA thesis, English Department (ESL Section), University of California, Los Angeles, 1977.

Kheredmand, J. Personal communication, spring, 1979.

Kleinmann, H. Avoidance behavior in adult second language acquisition. *Language Learning,* 1977, *27,* 93–107.

Leichman, H. A diary of one person's acquisition of Indonesian. Unpublished manuscript, English Department (ESL Section), University of California, Los Angeles, 1977.

Long, M. Inside the "black box": Methodological issues in research on teaching. Paper presented at the 1979 TESOL Convention, Boston, Mass., 1979.

Lynch, B. The adult second language learner: An introspective analysis of an individual learning Spanish as a second language. Unpublished manuscript, California State University, San José, 1979.

Moore, T. An experimental language handicap (personal account). *Bulletin of British Psychological Society,* 1977, *30,* 107–110.

Ochsner, R. A poetics of second language acquisition. *Language Learning,* 1979, *29,* 53–80.

Oller, J. Research on the measurement of affective variables: Some remaining questions. Paper presented at the Colloquium on Second Language Acquisition and Use Under Different Circumstances, 1979 TESOL Convention, Boston, Mass., 1979.

Oller, J., & Perkins, K. Intelligence and language proficiency as sources of variance in self-reported affective variables, *Language Learning,* 1978, *28,* 85–97.

Peck, S. Play in child second language acquisition. Unpublished master's thesis, English Department (ESL Section), University of California, Los Angeles, 1977.

Plummer, D. A summary of a foreign language learning diary. Unpublished manuscript, English Department (ESL Section), University of California, Los Angeles, 1976.

Roberts, J. I., & Akinsanya, S. K. *Schooling in the Cultural Context: Anthropological Studies of Education.* New York: McKay, 1976.

Scheding, S. A diary of foreign language learning: German 1. Unpublished manuscript, English Department (ESL Section), University of California, Los Angeles, 1978.

Schmuck, R. A., & Schmuck, P. A. *Group Processes in the Classroom.* Dubuque, Iowa: William C. Brown, 1971.

Schumann, F. E. Diary of a language learner: A further analysis. Paper presented at the Los Angeles Second Language Research Forum, University of Southern California, Los Angeles, October, 1978.

Schumann, F. E., & Schumann, J. H. Diary of a language learner: An introspective study of second language learning. In H. D. Brown, R. H. Crymes, & C. A. Yorio (Eds.), *Teaching and Learning: Trends in Research and Practice.* Washington, D.C.: TESOL, 1977.

Schumann, J. H. Affective factors and the problem of age in second language acquisition. *Language Learning,* 1975, *25,* 209–235.

Schumann, J. H. Personal communication, spring, 1979.

Scovel, T. The effect of affect on foreign language learning: A review of the anxiety research. *Language Learning,* 1978, *28,* 129–142.

Snell, R. A review of six diary studies. Unpublished manuscript, English Department (ESL Section), University of California, Los Angeles, 1978.

Spielberger, C., Gorusch, & Lushene. *State-Trait Anxiety Inventory.* Palo Alto, Calif.: Consulting Psychologist Press, 1970.

Stevick, E. *Memory, Meaning and Method.* Rowley, Mass.: Newbury House, 1976.

Tucker, G. R. Comments on J. W. Oller, Research on the measurement of affective variables: Some remaining questions. Paper presented at the Colloquium on Second Language Acquisition and Use under Different Circumstances, 1979 TESOL Convention, Boston, Mass., 1979.

Verma, P., & Nijhawan, H. The effect of anxiety, reinforcement and intelligence on the learning of a difficult task. *Journal of Experimental Child Psychology,* 1976, *22,* 302–308.

Walsleben, M. Cognitive and affective factors influencing a learner of Persian (Farsi) including a journal of second language acquisition. Unpublished manuscript, English Department (ESL Section), University of California, Los Angeles, 1976.

Questions for Discussion and Activities

1. Bailey briefly discusses Oller's criticism of the research on affective variables in language learning. Which of the problems Oller cites are especially pertinent to (a) classroom research on language learning in general, and (b) diary studies in particular? (Oller's paper has recently been published in R. Andersen (Ed.) *New Dimensions in Second Language Acquisition Research.* Rowley, Mass.: Newbury House, 1981.)

2. Bailey's chapter includes excerpts from the first week of her French diary. What do these descriptions suggest about the early meetings of language classes?

3. Although she claims that the diary studies reveal insights about individual differences in language learning, Bailey compares textual excerpts from ten other diarists. To what extent are you, as a reader, convinced that this sort of textual comparison is (a) feasible, and (b) legitimate?

4. Bailey discusses *state* and *trait* anxiety, as well as *debilitating* and *facilitating* anxiety. What do these terms mean? In what ways do these concepts overlap? What other examples of state and trait variables can you think of? Would you expect one type to be more important in second language acquisition research?

5. In the last section of her chapter, Bailey discusses some of the advantages of diary studies as a research mode. What might be some of the disadvantages? What objections could be raised against them from the perspective of a researcher trained exclusively in true experimental techniques?

6. Keep a diary of your language learning (or teaching) for one week. See what you discover and what methodological difficulties you encounter.

7. Could the issue you focused on in your diary study have been better researched (or researched at all) via some other method? Why (not)?

8. Design a study to investigate an affective variable of interest to you. How could first-person diary studies be used to enhance your research?

9. Bailey claims that "the components of this description of competitiveness could be used ... to design a questionnaire or scale for measuring competitiveness and anxiety." Try to design such a questionnaire based on the information in this chapter.

5

Inferencing: Testing the "Hypothesis-Testing" Hypothesis[1]

Ellen Bialystok

The most pervasive theoretical stance in the literature on second language learning follows from cognitive theories in which some kind of active mental process is involved in learning a language. Behaviorist, or "habit-formation," theories receive little serious endorsement in current literature. Similarly, the deference of major issues in language acquisition to the operation of innate "language-acquisition" structures is also inadequate for the explanation of critical problems. The difficulty in embracing cognitive theory, however, is that it leaves to the researcher the task of specifying the nature of those mental processes that are responsible for learning and the manner in which they achieve their effect.

The impact of cognitive theory on issues in second language learning has been energetically promoted by Dulay and Burt and their colleagues (e.g., Dulay and Burt, 1974, 1977). They argue that second language learning, like that for a first language, may be conceived as a "creative-constructive" process in which the learner generates rules and structures through an evolving grammar. This position is compatible with the notion of "interlanguage" (Selinker, 1972), which now permeates most accounts of second language learning, as well as with hypotheses aimed at explaining the acquisition and production of a second language (e.g., Krashen, 1976; Bialystok, 1978).

If we accept the premise that the learner's language system is "created" through an active cognitive process, then the increased competence in the language that occurs depends at least as much on this active participation as it does on instruction through traditional methods. Moreover, it should be possible to identify some of the creative strategies learners employ for this purpose and to predict the consequences of their use. It should also be possible to differentiate learners on the basis of their use of such strategies and to relate specific aspects of achievement to the use of particular strategies.

In this chapter one such strategy, inferencing,is described and its effects examined for a particular task in a second language; specifically, the role of inferencing in comprehending written text is examined. In the first section, the inferencing strategy is described and discussed in terms of three types of inferencing. The second section examines the nature of reading in general and second language reading in particular. In the final section, evidence from a study which investigates the role of inferencing in second-language reading comprehension is reported.

Inferencing as a Strategy for Language Learning

The term "inferencing" was coined by Carton (1971) who defined it simply: "attributes and contexts that are familiar are utilized in recognizing what is *not* familiar" (p. 45). In this definition, the unfamiliarity was restricted to the lexical *term;* the *concept* represented by that term must be known by the inferencer. Following Carton, we have elaborated the definition for the strategy by placing it within the context of a language processing model. We have defined inferencing strategy as "the use of available information to derive explicit linguistic hypotheses. The information used for this purpose may be linguistic or non-linguistic, it may be taken from the speaker or from the environment, and it may relate to the structure or the meaning of the language" (Bialystok, 1979). Thus, the strategy describes one aspect of the creative process of language learning which may be recruited when the actual expressions or meanings are not known; attempts are made to generate or understand language on the basis of knowledge of language (target, native, and other) and of the situation. The process may also be called "informed guessing" or "hypothesis testing" in that an attempt is made to try out a possible solution to a linguistic problem.

Although the term "inferencing" has been created and is not in fact a word in ordinary language, it is worthwhile to consider the conventional definition of the verb "infer" from which the term has been adapted. Webster's Dictionary (1972) defines "infer" as follows: "to derive as a conclusion from facts or premises" (p. 432). The definition continues by explaining the difference between "infer" and some of its common synonyms:

> *Infer* implies arriving at a conclusion by reasoning from evidence; if the evidence is slight the term comes close to *surmise; deduce* adds to *infer* the special implication of drawing a particular inference from a generalization; *conclude* implies arriving at a logically necessary inference at the end of a chain of reasoning; *judge* stresses critical examination of the evidence on which a conclusion is based; *gather* suggests a direct or intuitive forming of a conclusion from hints or implications usually in the absence of clear evidence or plain statement. (p. 432)

Within the context of their ordinary use, the terms "surmise" and "gather" best approximate the meaning intended by the strategy of inferencing. The evidence upon which the inference is based is usually minimal, and the logic that connects the evidence to the hypothesis often questionable. But the result of the process is a proposition about the target language which may be offered in a linguistic interaction and evaluated through feedback from a native speaker, and may stimulate language learning by virtue of its creation. Even if the proposition fails, that is, the hypothesis is not supported, learning may result.

Thus, the strategy inferencing is used in the restricted sense of the ordinary language to apply to those inferences that are based on little evidence and for which necessary conclusions do not follow. Consider, for example, a learner of French who finds it necessary to convey the meaning of "typewriter" and does not know the correct word in French. A first hypothesis may be to "Frenchify" the English pronunciation, since some French words may be derived in exactly that manner. In the case of "typewriter," however, this strategy would fail and a new attempt would be necessary. The next hypothesis may be to capture aspects of the meaning as in *"instrument à écrire."* This attempt may succeed in conveying the meaning although it is not in fact the correct French form. The correct French form for typewriter, *"machine à écrire,"*[2] may even be supplied by the French-speaking partner in the conversation. Thus, based on information about how things are expressed in English (considering that "typewriter" may be glossed "something that writes") and a primitive knowledge of French, an inference can succeed in conveying the intended meaning and possibly also in providing the learner with a new word.

The diversity of activities subsumed by the general strategy "inferencing" is large because of both the many possible types of information upon which an inference can be based and the many logical or deductive processes which can be used to generate an inference. Carton (1971) has identified three categories of inferences as a function of the type of information used: intra-lingual, those inferences based on the nature of the target language; inter-lingual, those inferences based on relationships to other languages, for example, through cognates; and extra-lingual, those inferences based on the content and context of the message.

By extending Carton's distinctions to include hypotheses about the processes involved in inferencing, we have posited three types of inferences which are attributable to three different sources of knowledge. These we have called inferencing from Implicit Knowledge, inferencing from Other Knowledge, and inferencing from Context. The terms Implicit Knowledge and Other Knowledge refer to information sources in our model of second language learning (Bialystok, 1978).

Briefly, *Implicit Knowledge* refers to the unanalyzed, intuitive information the learner has about the target language, even though that information cannot be stated in the form of rules, principles, or regularities. The existence of the information, nonetheless, is evident through the learner's ability to form grammatical utterances and to judge the acceptability of strings in the target language. *Other Knowledge* refers to information about languages other than the target language, especially the native language, as well as the learner's general knowledge of the world. The *Context* includes both the linguistic and physical aspects of a situation which provide cues to meaning. Thus, in a conversation, the context given by the preceding language as well as by the presence of concrete objects may form the basis of an inference. Inferencing from each of these three sources will be considered separately.

Inferencing from implicit knowledge

Part of the process of inferencing involves making explicit what is already known vaguely or incompletely. There may be a great resource of such intuitive information about a target language, especially when the formal structures have not been systematically learned or the rules explicitly articulated. Thus, it is often possible for a learner to speak the language with a fluency that apparently exceeds expectations derived from standard measures of proficiency. The deliberate examination of this intuitive information for the purpose of abstracting rules or systems constitutes an important form of inferencing. Carroll (1977) has described just such an activity as important to language learning: "A most important strategy to adopt is that of always attempting to convert passive knowledge into active, productive knowledge" (p. 5).

Inferences from Implicit Knowledge are similar to the "intra-lingual inferences" described by Carton. In both cases, the hypothesis to be tested is based on the target language system, and the deduction is guided by an understanding of linguistic regularity. The information derived in this manner may relate to any of syntax, semantics, or phonology. For example, a learner of English as a second language can exploit the morphological information that the ending *-ly* signals an adverb, the ending *-or* refers to an agent, and the ending *-tion* is a cluster indicating a noun and is pronounced in a certain way.

If regularity is to be abstracted from intuitive information and inferences based on that regularity, then the representation of intuitive information must be structured and systematic. That is, even though the organizing principles are not apparent, the information represented in Implicit Knowledge nonetheless honors the systematic constraints of language. This organization permits the underlying structure to be recovered through examination of the information.

The "explication" of the information in Implicit Knowledge is part of the general process of language learning. It constitutes, for example, one of the two means by which information is accumulated for Explicit Knowledge, the source of *analyzed* linguistic information. The representation of information in this explicit form is hypothesized to be required for the performance of certain kinds of formal linguistic tasks, and the ability to perform such tasks is a component of overall linguistic competence (see Bialystok, 1978, for description). In this sense, the inferencing strategy is an integral aspect of the learning process; the learner gains control over information which was already possessed but in another form.

The articulation of this information in the Explicit Knowledge source permits the learner to operate upon it in a way not possible when the information is unanalyzed or intuitive. The development of skills associated with literacy and "metalinguistic knowledge" in general requires an elaborated concept of language in which the system, or code, is transparent. Although the conversational use of language proceeds perfectly well from an intuitive source, the manipulation of the linguistic system and the performance of transformations, deductions, and analyses with language, depend on this specialized knowledge of the linguistic system. The linguistic structures may be learned directly through methods such as formal instruction, but they may also be inferred by examining the information in Implicit Knowledge.

Inferencing from other knowledge

Although the source of Other Knowledge includes a great variety of information, such as knowledge of the world, knowledge of the subject matter, and so on, it is probably the knowledge of other languages that is most useful for inferencing. Over-reliance on such information is a common hazard in language learning, and its inappropriate use is called "interference" in error analysis (e.g., Richards, 1973). The strong version of the interpretation of interference errors is in contrastive analysis, in which attempts are made to predict such occurrences through linguistic examination of the native and target languages (Lado, 1957). But the strategy of inferencing from other languages, especially the native language, remains a viable form of promoting communication and understanding in a target language.

The most straightforward example of inferencing from Other Knowledge is in the use of cognates to interpret or convey meaning. The availability of cognates, however, is often limited, especially when the two languages do not share a family membership, and the language learner trying to speak in the target language may have no means of deciding *a priori* which target-language words will map onto the native language in that manner. In addition, words that appear to be cognates by virtue of their surface forms do not necessarily share sufficient semantic features to permit them to be used interchangeably. An example of this is the confusion between the French "*la cave*" (cellar) and the English "the cave" which is discussed later in the chapter. Even differences in connotation can preclude the adoption of similar-looking words from other languages. Consequently, more creative and more uncertain types of inferencing from Other Knowledge must be explored.

When a word is transposed directly from another (usually the native) language, then the strategy is called transfer, and the effectiveness of the strategy would likely depend on the extent to which the two languages were mutually intelligible. The attempt to modify the native language item so that it conforms in some way to the target language qualifies as an instance of inferencing. The modifications can be made in phonology by assigning a target-language pronunciation to a native-language term, in morphology by tagging the native-language term with a marker from the target language, or in semantics by transliterating a native-langue expression into simple vocabulary of the target language. These strategies are more or less effective as a function of many variables, but consistent attempts to use this variety of inferencing, possibly in conjunction with other strategies, will ultimately promote communication.

Inferences based on knowledge of other languages are particularly useful when the native and target languages are related. In a study of high school students learning French as a second language, it was found that the students in the class who spoke fluent Italian had a significant advantage over their non-Italian classmates in a test of French reading comprehension (Bialystok and Fröhlich, 1977). After the test, the students admitted that they had relied heavily on their knowledge of Italian to provide cues to meaning in the French passages.

To some extent, Other Knowledge is involved in many inferences that occur. Part of Other Knowledge is the learner's metalinguistic knowledge of language in general. This expertise with language is accumulated through more experience with language and probably through experience with more languages, but the knowledge itself is not related to a specific language. Thus, a learner with a great deal of metalinguistic knowledge will know more about language and how to use language than will a learner with a less developed capacity in this area. This linguistic skill must be related to the learner's ability to understand and abstract the regularities in language, and it is on these abilities that inferencing depends.

Preliminary evidence from a large study on communication strategies suggests that there is a relationship between the number of languages the learner knows and the ability of the learner to inference in another language.[3] Adult learners of French as a second language were given a test of inferencing in which they had to guess the meaning of Danish passages. None of the subjects in the study spoke Danish, and their responses were based on the information they could infer through the context, the structure of the language, and their knowledge of other languages. The single best predictor for success in the analysis thus far appears to be the *number* of languages the learner knows; all those subjects who claimed to know three or more languages, even though none of the languages was Danish, scored high; all those subjects who claimed to know only English and French scored more poorly on the Danish test.

Finally, since language is used to convey meanings, then prior knowledge about the meanings would clearly facilitate the process of inferencing. For example, it is easier to read a passage about respiration in the frog if one is familiar with biology. Forming inferences on the basis of related knowledge is an important approach to language learning and use.

Inferencing from context

The context in which language occurs is clearly a critical cue to interpreting the language. Removing language from such a context, in effect "decontextualizing" the language, has been assigned an important causal role in both the difficulty experienced by adults in learning a second language in an artificial environment (Macnamara, 1973a) and the difficulty experienced by some children in acquiring literacy skills or in coping with schooling in general (Olson, 1977). Thus, the presence of a context should be advantageous in efforts to use and learn a second language; specifically, the context should provide a useful basis for inferencing.

The context is created by both the language and the physical environment in which it occurs. The linguistic aspects of the context are the meanings that are shared and the points that become more apparent as the interaction proceeds; the physical aspects are the presence of concrete items referred to in the discourse, the facial expressions and gestures of the interlocutors, and the activities and events surrounding the interaction.

The exploitation of the context, both linguistic and physical, is not only critical to learning and using a second language but also has been posited as a fundamental process for first language learning. Macnamara (1972), for example, states that

> infants learn their language by first determining, independent of language, the meaning which a speaker intends to convey to them, and by then working out the relationship between the meaning and the language. To put it another way, the infant uses meaning as a clue to language, rather than language as a clue to meaning. (p. 1)

He goes on to provide evidence from the development of phonology, syntax, and semantics that the child must understand language on the basis of the objects present in the environment, the social aspects of the interaction, and so on, before the meaning can be extracted from the code directly.

Brown (1956) argues for the same point in his description of the "Original Word Game." The players in this game "form hypotheses about the non-linguistic categories eliciting particular utterances" and proceed to test these hypotheses in their own language production. To a large extent, these hypotheses are based on the presence of objects in the physical world as well as the paralinguistic aspects of language, such as intonation and gesture.

In a study by Clark (1973), children one and a half to five years old were examined for their comprehension of the spatial relation terms "in," "on," and "under." The experimental task required the children to manipulate a group of toy objects so that they formed a relationship specified by one of the three spatial terms in the instruction. What Clark discovered was that the children interpreted the instruction, not on the basis of their understanding of the spatial terms, but on the basis of their knowledge of the objects and the usual relationships into which those objects can enter. Thus, if the two objects were a crib and a toy animal, the child would reliably place the animal *in* the crib, regardless of the instruction, because that would be a reasonable interpretation of the relationship based on the child's knowledge of the world. Children were assigning meaning to the language on the basis of the information contained in the environment.

These processes used by children are not unlike the inferencing strategies used by adult second language learners. The use of each of the linguistic and physical aspects of the context serves to promote the development of second language skills.

The linguistic context is composed of the accumulation of the linguistic information pertaining to the interaction. The interaction may be between a learner and another speaker, or between a learner and a text, but in both cases the continuation of the interaction is facilitated by what has preceded. For example, in reading a text, the task may apparently become easier as the learner becomes more familiar with the point being advanced by the author, the style in which the passage is written, and the experience of reading in the target language. These all constitute features of the linguistic context, and all provide the basis for inferencing when the learner encounters difficulty.

One form of inferencing in this manner is in the clarification or disambiguation of unclear terms. For the former, the meaning of target language terms may become apparent when the learner encounters the word in a context; for the latter, the precise meaning of terms which are being used in an unconventional way may be interpretable only in context. Native speakers, too, regularly use the linguistic context for these purposes.

The physical context provides one of the most important bases for the formation of inferences. Language spoken in an environment rich in referential objects is by far more comprehensible and more interpretable than language spoken without such support. Similarly, a speaker lacking sufficient vocabulary or adequate command of the language to convey certain meanings can incorporate aspects of the physical environment into the language and increase the possibility for communication. Ostensive definition to objects in the environment is a simple and effective means of conveying an idea for which a lexical item is lacking.

While children reliably use inferencing from context in their attempts to learn language, adults may be more reluctant to place the responsibility for meaning in the environment. The process of schooling, in fact, probably discourages such a strategy through its reliance on logical relationships and explicit meanings conveyed in decontextualized essays. Second language learners may benefit by identifying more closely with prelinguistic infants than with highly educated adults. Macnamara (1973b), in fact, makes a similar point and suggests that the "teacher . . . would be wise to provide as many aids as possible to his meaning. And he should encourage the pupils to guess. This probably implies that he should be slow to give the child the meaning in the child's native tongue" (p. 60). What is also implied by Macnamara's statement is that the teacher should provide the student with the opportunity to inference from context.

Reading in First and Second Languages

The development of target language reading skills has long been a concern of second language learners and teachers. The ability to easily read and understand written text is an essential component of language proficiency. Pedagogical efforts to improve this reading competence must be based on a conceptualization of the reading process; instructional heuristics may be derived only through a theoretical perspective.

While great advances have been made in the theory of reading and the problems of learning and teaching reading (e.g., Gibson and Levin, 1975; Carroll and Chall, 1975), the application of these theories to specific problems of reading in languages other than the native language has been limited. Yet second language learners continue to grapple with the problem of attempting to understand information written in a textual form (as opposed to transcribed speech) in a language in which their competence is restricted. On the basis of current theories of reading, it appears that the inferencing strategy may have a role in facilitating the comprehension of written text in a second language for learners. What, then, is the theoretical perspective on reading, and to what extent can it be applied to second language reading?

Psycholinguistic theories of reading

In current theories of reading, the reader is assigned a fundamental and active responsibility for the interpretation of meaning (e.g., Goodman, 1968; Smith, 1971). The meaning abstracted from the text is the outcome of the interaction between the printed page and the reader's cognitive processing capacities. As stated by Smith et al. (1976), reading is the "active process of *constructing* meaning from language represented by graphic symbols (letters) systematically arranged" (p. 265, emphasis mine). The reader continuously samples information in the text, forms predictions about items, structures, and relationships that follow, and arrives at the meaning through a hypothesis-testing procedure. The redundancy provided by language makes this technique both efficient and reliable.

The basis of the process is the ability of the reader to utilize certain cues both inside and outside of the passage in order to determine its meaning. Goodman (1968) identifies four cue categories: cues within words (sound-letter relationships, spelling patterns); cues within the flow of languages (word-order patterns, agreements, contextual meanings); cues within the reader (language facility, experience, general conceptual background); and cues external to both the language and the reader, such as pictures, charts, and direct prompting. The role of this final category he explains as follows:

> Pictures are cues which may be decoded as a substitute or supplement to language. Prompting is actually recoding done by someone other than the reader . . . These external cues get between the reader and written language. In a sense they interfere with the vital recoding process. (p. 25)

Hence, the reader attempts to decode the written message by incorporating information from a variety of cue sources into tentative hypotheses about meaning.

The process described by these psycholinguistic theories of reading is similar to the process posited to underlie the inferencing strategy: information outside the text is used to interpret the meaning of the text. If this conceptualization of reading is not language-specific and forms the basis for reading in a second as well as a native language, then it is possible that second language learners could improve their ability to read and understand written material through the deliberate use of inferencing. It must be established, then, that second language reading can be described by the same model as that used for a native language.

Second language reading

While little research has directly addressed the issue of the compatibility of models of native language reading with the processes of second language reading, the extrapolation of evidence from different sources permits one to make judgments on the question.

In studies examining the development of reading skills in bilingual education programs, it has consistently been reported that there are large positive correlations between reading ability in both native and target languages (Cziko, 1976; Swain, Lapkin, and Barik, 1976; Tucker, 1975). This relationship suggests that the skill of reading is not tied to a specific language and that, once mastered, it may be used to read in any language. Such transfer of skill would require that the process of reading be the same for both languages. Genesee (1979) cautions, however, that the degree of such transfer depends on the similarity between the two languages; the more similar the languages the more likely and the more extensive will be transfer of reading skill. Yet in general it seems reasonable to conclude that the processes directing first language reading are responsible as well for reading in other languages.

Other evidence pertaining to second language reading has been reported by Cowan (1976). Second language learners reading passages in their target language were tested to see if they made the kinds of errors of prediction that would occur if they were reading according to the constraints of the psycholinguistic model and testing hypotheses based on their native language. That is, to what extent do first language expectancies falsely bias the second language learner to form inappropriate hypotheses in the target language? A sampling of syntactic or semantic information in the text would lead a skilled reader to expect certain syntactic or semantic features to occur because of native language regularities. The violation of these expectancies in the target language would indicate that the reader had formed hypotheses appropriate for the native language and consequently was reading the target language through the same strategy. The results indicate that the errors committed reflected predictions based on the native language. Thus, not only was an hypothesis-testing strategy being used, but the information upon which the hypotheses were based could be identified as emanating from the native language.

A careful analysis of some of the differences between native and second language reading has been undertaken by Macnamara (1970). English-speaking students learning Irish were given complex problems to solve in written form in both languages. Although all the components of the problems could easily be solved in both languages, performance in solving the complex problems was significantly worse for the Irish version than for the English. Macnamara attributed this difference to the deficiency of three components of the reading skill when reading the Irish: the rate of interpreting words; the rate of interpreting structures; and the ability to anticipate sequences of words. The process of reading and the strategies required for efficient reading, however, were not different in the two languages and are related to the processes involved in inferencing. Presumably improvement in these three component skills would mitigate the difficulty for the Irish problems.

If we then adopt this hypothesis-testing model of reading, it should be possible to intervene in the reading process and assist the second language learner in the "psycholinguistic guessing game" (Goodman, 1968) by helping the reader form good hypotheses about meaning. The presence of information that can provide a basis for good inferences should improve the learner's ability to extrapolate or construct meaning from written text. This possibility was examined in the following experiments.

Inferencing in Reading Comprehension

Although they are only tentative propositions about meaning, inferences must still be based on some information. The hypothesis is that providing information that could potentially form a basis of meaningful inferences will improve the reader's ability to understand the text. For the present study, this information was provided by means of certain cues which were given in conjunction with target language reading passages.

Since the extent to which understanding passages is independent of understanding the vocabulary used in those passages is unclear, the learner's comprehension of difficult lexical items within the passages was also examined. Hence the impact of the experimental cues could be assessed for their ability to promote good inferences at both the passage and the lexical levels. Moreover, some insight into the relationship between these levels of comprehension for second language reading may be gained.

The study was conducted with English-speaking high school students learning French as a second language.

Experiment 1

Four cue conditions were created and examined for their effects on the learners' ability to understand the general meaning of a passage and on their ability to translate difficult lexical items in the passage. Some of the cues were aimed at the lexical level and some were aimed at providing information of a more general nature.

In the first cue condition, a picture which summarized the gist of the passage accompanied the text. While the main point of the passage was conveyed graphically, none of the information depicted could directly assist the learner in answering the questions that followed. In this sense, the picture provided a context without divulging the answers to the questions. Incorporating the two sources, that is, the picture and the passage, however, should simplify the task of answering questions.

The second cue condition examined the extent to which comprehension of the passage improved when all lexical items used in the passage were known. The intention was to compare the comprehension attained in this case with that achieved through inferencing the gist of the passage through more general contextual cues. Thus, the second cue condition provided the learners with dictionaries containing all the difficult words in the passages plus a number of distractors. The dictionaries contained a total of about 350 words.

The third cue, called the lesson condition, was intended to equip subjects with the means of producing better inferences. Subjects were given a fifteen-minute lesson on "how to inference" in which three ways of inferencing were explained with examples. Subjects were told that they could inference through information they have about the target language using cues in prefixes, suffixes, and so on; through information they have about other languages, especially their native language, using cognates; and through information provided by the context of the passage. Sentence-completion examples, such as cloze sentences, were used to demonstrate how informational redundancy in the context could be exploited. The students were involved in the lesson by a question–answer format where they were encouraged to guess and attempt to infer the meanings of the sample items.

Finally, to provide a comparison for the performance under the various treatments, the final condition contained no cue. The subjects read the passages and answered the questions without assistance.

Method. Subjects. Four different classes of grade-ten students studying French as a second language were each assigned to one of the four cue conditions. The total sample size was seventy-nine subjects.

The four classes were from different schools in Toronto and were not entirely equivalent in their academic, social, or economic statuses. One class was from a working-class neighborhood, two were middle-class, and one was in a private girls' school. However, since the French history of all students was fairly equitable, it was decided to proceed with a comparison among these groups.

Materials and tests. Four humorous stories, each about 150 words in length, were selected for the study and modified for level of difficulty with the assistance of French language teachers.

Following each passage were two test sheets. The first contained five questions about the general meaning of the passage requiring short-answer responses. Both the questions and answers were given in English. The second contained five difficult vocabulary items from the passage which were to be translated into English.

Design and procedures. Students were visited in their classes and given the four passages to read in *one of* the four cue conditions. For the lesson condition, the lesson preceded distribution of the materials.

The instructions for all subjects were to read each passage and, where applicable, to utilize the accompanying cue, and then to answer the comprehension questions and vocabulary items without referring to the materials. Both sets of questions for each passage were answered before proceeding to the next passage.

Each subject received two scores out of five, one for the comprehension questions and one for the vocabulary items, for each of the four stories.

Results and Discussion. Since the groups receiving each of the treatments were not equivalent, comparisons among groups for overall performance levels remain tentative. Nonetheless, significant differences were obtained, and these are reported in Table 1.

Table 1.   Mean Score out of 5 for Question and Vocabulary Items

		Question		Vocabulary		
Condition	N	Mean	s.d.	Mean	s.d.	Mean
No Cue	16	2.50	1.13	2.30	1.43	2.40
Picture	28	2.68	1.28	1.76	1.14	2.22
Lesson	20	3.76	0.97	3.30	1.05	3.53
Dictionary	15	4.07	0.78	3.68	0.95	3.88
Mean		3.25		2.76		

Across all conditions it was more difficult to translate the vocabulary items than to answer the comprehension questions ($F(1,75) = 39.01$, $p < .01$).

The interaction between type of cue and type of question was significant ($F(3,75) = 4.55$, $p < .01$). That is, cue information differentially facilitated solutions to the two criterion tests. The picture improved performance on the comprehension test only and the dictionary and lesson improved performance on both the comprehension and the vocabulary tests.

These results may be interpreted by considering that inferences or information designed to facilitate comprehension at a lexical level is useful as well for improving comprehension at a global level. The lesson, for example, dealt primarily with word meanings. Inferences generated at a global level, as with the picture condition, provide direct access to passage meaning without helping to interpret particular vocabulary items.

Strategies for Translating.   Because of the danger of over-interpreting the between-group comparisons in performance, a detailed item analysis which sought to identify the different *strategies* used in the four treatment conditions was conducted on five of the vocabulary items. These items, which were selected because they appeared to elicit interesting errors, were as follows:

1. *la salle de séjour* (living room)
2. *la cave* (cellar)
3. *le signe de paix* (peace sign)
4. *coûter* (to cost)
5. *rencontrer* (to meet)

The summary of this analysis is reported in Table 2. The total number of possible responses for these items in each of the conditions was calculated by multiplying the number of items (5) by the number of subjects per group. These figures appear in the first column of the table and were the basis for all the proportions subsequently calculated.

Table 2.   Types of Responses to Five Selected Vocabulary Items

Condition	N	Total Possible Responses	Proportion Omitted	Proportion Correct	Proportion Incorrect	Proportion Guesses
No Cue	16	80	.30	.30	.14	.26
Picture	28	140	.45	.26	.13	.16
Lesson	20	100	.05	.36	.23	.36
Dictionary	15	75	.03	.63	.17	.17

The proportion of the target items that were omitted completely by the subjects is listed in the column "proportion omitted." An attempt to translate the item produced one of three response types—a correct translation, an incorrect translation that suggests no comprehension whatsoever of the item, and an incorrect translation that in some way captures or approximates the meaning, called here a "guess."

Although a formal comparison of the differences reflected in these proportions was not permitted by the data, trends and differences are nonetheless apparent. While subjects in the dictionary and lesson conditions left blank almost no item, subjects in the no cue and picture conditions were less willing to translate the items of which they were unsure.

The proportion of correct responses across the groups deviates only for the dictionary condition; for the other three groups subjects were correctly translating approximately the same number of these five items. Even for the lesson condition where more responses were registered, the proportion of those that were accurate translations is only slightly higher than it is for the other two groups. The dictionary condition, not surprisingly, leads to a high number of exact translations.

The proportion of incorrect responses for each group indicates that the greatest number of errors is found in the lesson condition. As well as increasing the number of correct responses, the instruction to inference increased as well the number of incorrect responses.

The extent to which subjects were able or willing to guess possible translations for the difficult items in the four conditions is reflected in the proportion of guesses recorded. The most extensive use of guessing was observed from the subjects in the lesson condition, and the consequences of these guesses are also manifested in the correct and incorrect columns.

While the lesson and dictionary conditions both encouraged subjects to attempt to translate more of the items than did the other two conditions, the motivation in each case was different. The increase in responses in the dictionary condition is attributed to the learner's knowledge of the exact meaning through reference to an official source. The increase in the lesson condition is attributed to the learner's willingness to generate and test hypotheses about possible meanings, some of which were clearly wrong.

Item Analysis.   To further illustrate the specific biases induced by the four conditions, consider in greater detail the responses elicited to two of the items— "*la cave*" and "*rencontrer.*"

The context for the occurrence of "*la cave*" in the passage was that a father who was paying little attention to his son's questions about the location of the Alps told his son that perhaps he could find the Alps "*dans la cave.*" This contextual information was differentially accommodated in the four cue conditions.

For three of the conditions at least half of the subjects guessed that the translation for "*la cave*" was "the cave." In the lesson condition, subjects were explicitly told that cognates were useful for inferring meaning; in the no cue and picture conditions subjects were likewise misled by the surface similarity of these items. In the dictionary condition, however, not a single student was seduced by this superficial similarity, and instead they consulted a dictionary to establish the exact meaning. This strategy difference suggests that the subjects in the other three conditions who proposed "the cave" as the translation, were probably aware that they were testing an obvious although precarious hypothesis and their uncertainty about its validity would have led them to a dictionary, were one available.

More appropriate inferences were made *only* by subjects in the lesson condition. Some of the inaccurate but contextually reasonable guesses offered by these students included "atlas," "book," and "map."

The translation of the item "*rencontrer*" also proved problematic to the subjects, and different strategies for dealing with this item were observed for the different cue conditions.

Reasonable guesses for this item were considered to be words that were related in some way to either of the components of the target item. Acceptable guesses, then, included the meaning of "re" or "again" with some appropriate verb, or focused instead on the "*-contrer*" stem and led to inferences such as "tell," or "encounter." The proportion of times any of these alternatives were offered by the subjects in each group are as follows:

No cue	0.25
Picture	0.21
Lesson	0.85
Dictionary	0.47

In the absence of an exact solution, subjects in the lesson condition were more willing to utilize aspects of the difficult item in an attempt to understand or approximate its meaning. While this additional effort produced incorrect responses as well, the benefits of inferencing were still clearly evident for improving comprehension of both word and passage meanings.

Experiment 2

In order to make valid comparisons in the overall performance across the four treatment conditions, particularly with respect to the reading comprehension test, the experiment was replicated using a repeated-measures design. The subjects in this study performed in all four cue conditions and answered both comprehension and translation questions for all passages.

To accomodate this design, a proliferation of reading passages was required. Accordingly, twelve stories were composed so that each subject would read three stories in each cue condition. A Latin Square design was used to distribute the passages equally among the four conditions by considering them as four sets of three passages each. Hence, all subjects read all the passage sets, but four different passage-cue pairings were used.

The passages were reassessed and restandardized by high school French teachers to assure that they were of equal difficulty, that the level was appropriate for the grade tested, and that they were suitable for the students in the study.

The dictionaries for the dictionary cue condition were expanded and included about 1,000 words in the new version.

Method. Subjects. Eighty grade ten students participated in this experiment. These students were from four different classes in the same school which was located in a middle-class neighborhood in Toronto.

Designs and Procedures. Students were tested in two groups of two classes each in a large room in their school. Two testing sessions were used so that students performed in two of the cue conditions at each session. The order in which the cue conditions were presented was fixed—the first session tested picture and dictionary and the second tested no cue and lesson. The placement of the lesson in the last condition prohibited subjects from explicitly applying these strategies to the task in any of the other conditions.

Following from the previous experiment, scores were calculated for each of the question and vocabulary items in each of the cue conditions. In the present experiement, however, differences between conditions were a within-subjects variable.

Results and Discussion. Analysis of variance on the cue condition by criterion test, with the three stories as a repeated measure, was performed. The mean scores out of five for each type of question in the four cue conditions are presented in Table 3.

Again, subjects were more successful with the comprehension questions than with the vocabulary items in all the cue conditions, ($F(1,76) = 240.54$, $p < .001$), although the interaction between cue condition and criterion test revealed different patterns of effect ($F(3,228) = 4.18$, $p < .01$).

Table 3.   Mean Score out of 5 for Question and Vocabulary Items

| | Question | | Vocabulary | | |
Condition	Mean	s.d.	Mean	s.d.	Mean
No Cue	2.83	1.23	1.91	1.01	2.37
Picture	3.25	1.16	2.15	0.96	2.70
Lesson	3.05	1.27	2.03	0.99	2.54
Dictionary	3.03	1.34	2.43	1.08	2.73
Mean	3.04		2.13		

N = 80

For the comprehension questions, lowest scores were observed in the no cue condition; better performance was elicited for the dictionary and lesson conditions (Newman-Keuls: $p < .05$); and the best results were obtained for the picture cue condition (Newman-Keuls: $p < .05$). Translation of the vocabulary items was enhanced only in the dictionary condition (Newman-Keuls: $p < .05$).

These results differ from those in the previous experiment in two ways—the picture cue was actually *better* than the lesson and dictionary for aiding global comprehension rather than just being equally effective, and the lesson failed to significantly improve scores on the vocabulary translation test.

In the first experiment the picture cue was given to the class that happened to be the lowest achieving academically of the four classes in the study. The overall performance of this class was significantly below that of the other three classes, all of which were comparable with each other. Nonetheless, the picture cue for this deviant class made their comprehension scores equivalent to those obtained in the lesson and dictionary classes; were the students in the picture cue class more competent initially, then we might expect that the picture cue could allow them to surpass the other students in answering the comprehension questions, as was evident in the second experiment.

The lesson condition in this experiment was less effective in assisting with the translation items than it had been in Experiment 1. The reason for this suppressed effect may be that the lesson was given to a larger group of students, it was somewhat shorter than that used previously, and there was little class participation, that is, it was essentially a lecture. These conditions were imposed by restrictions on the time available and the administrative necessity of testing a large class. Thus, only the dictionary condition was able to effectively assist subjects with their interpretation of word meanings.

Effects of inferencing on comprehension

The study demonstrates that the interpretation of a written passage depends not only on the text alone but also on the information given in a variety of sources. Thus, providing readers with supplementary information increases their comprehension of the passage. Further, readers can be trained to utilize this information more effectively, as demonstrated in the lesson condition.

The information in the cues was differentially informative to the two criterion tasks. In general, lexical information increased comprehension at both the global and lexical levels while global information was primarily useful only for general comprehension.

The distinction between the global and lexical levels for the cues clarifies as well a possible discrepancy between the findings for the picture cue obtained in the present study and those reported in the literature for native language reading. Several studies with children learning to read in their native language have shown only a fragile facilitating effect on comprehension through the provision of picture cues (Denburg, 1975; Willows, 1978). In these studies, reading and comprehension were improved only if the picture was of a certain degree of complexity, in a certain spatial relation to the text, and so on. Pictures not conforming to strict criteria were either non-facilitative or even detrimental. The index for comprehension, however, was always assessed at the *lexical* level, and the picture always represented a particular lexical item in the passage, either a thing (noun) or relation (verb). In the present study, however, the pictures were constructed to represent information of a general contextual nature and were found to be facilitative only for general comprehension; lexical comprehension was not improved. The traditionally limited role for pictures in children's reading may thus be obviated by using instead global pictures which provide a general context for the passage. Although no improvement would be expected in the comprehension of specific word meanings, such possibilities for improving global comprehension should be explored.

The results of the present study suggest that the deliberate provision of different kinds of contextual information and instruction in inferencing techniques are pedagogically expedient in second language reading comprehension. The lesson provided subjects with a heuristic device for dealing with difficult information; stable long-term effects of this instruction were neither measured nor expected. But the evidence from this limited situation is promising; students were able to understand the techniques described in the presentation and to apply them to similar material on their own. Continuing investigations should examine the following: the most effective forms for such lessons; indications of their more long-range effects, that is, the modification of a language learner's approach to language, thereby producing, in effect, a better "inferencer"; and the generalizability of this inferencing strategy to various tasks. Similarly, a systematic analysis of what techniques of cuing and contextualizing teachers routinely employ can contribute to an understanding of how to promote more effective native and non-native language reading.

The implied recommendation for second language reading programs which follows from this study is that cues such as those tested in the present study should accompany target language reading passages. In addition to the demonstrated empirical validity of the argument, the suggestion is also consistent with the spirit of current trends in language development. Children learning a first language do so in a contextual environment; adults learning a second language often lack such environmental support. Part of the demonstrated success of children's language learning as opposed to adults has been attributed to that difference. Similarly, the suggestion that adults be provided with a context to facilitate language comprehension simplifies their language learning task by making it more congruent with the child's experience.

The original predictions were based on the assumption that language learning and language use are cognitive activities that engage many aspects of the learner's conceptual system. While it may be possible for neurolinguists to localize the human language capacity in particular cortical regions, it has not yet been possible for psycholinguists to similarly delimit the boundaries of conceptual information that is brought to bear in a language task. Language learners can, and should, and probably do, use information from a wide range of sources to promote easy and efficient use of a language. Perhaps a more empirical approach by learners accompanied by greater trust in their judgments would be expedient for language learning; like scientists, language learners must "test the hypotheses" derived from inferences.

Notes

1. The research reported in this chapter was supported by a grant from the Department of the Secretary of State, Canada. The author gratefully acknowledges the assistance of Maria Fröhlich, Joan Howard, and Cora Palmer who assisted with the testing and analysis of the experiments.

2. I am indebted to Maria Fröhlich for pointing out that the success and availability of various types of inferences depend upon the relationship between the native and target languages. A German speaker, for example, could directly arrive at the correct form *"machine à écrire"* by inferring a transliteration from the German word for typewriter, *"Schreibmaschine."*

3. Ellen Bialystok, Maria Fröhlich, and Joan Howard, work in progress at the Modern Language Centre, Ontario Institute for Studies in Education.

References

Bialystok, E. A theoretical model of second language learning. *Language Learning*, 1978, *28*, 69–83.

Bialystok, E. The role of conscious strategies in second language proficiency. *Canadian Modern Language Review*, 1979, *35*, 372–394.

Bialystok, E., & Fröhlich, M. Aspects of second language learning in classroom settings. *Working Papers on Bilingualism*, 1977, *13*, 1–26.

Brown, R. The original word game. Appendix in J. Bruner, J. Goodnow, & G. Austin, *A Study in Thinking*. New York: Wiley, 1956.

Carroll, J. B. Characteristics of successful second language learners. In M. Burt, H. Dulay, & M. Finocchiaro (Eds.), *Viewpoints on English as a Second Language*. New York: Regents, 1977.

Carroll, J. B., & Chall, J. S. (Eds). *Toward a Literate Society*. New York: McGraw-Hill, 1975.

Carton, A. S. Inferencing: A process in using and learning language. In P. Pimsleur & T. Quinn (Eds.), *The Psychology of Second Language Learning*. Cambridge: Cambridge University Press, 1971.

Clark, E. V. Non-linguistic strategies and the acquisition of word meanings. *Cognition*, 1973, *2*, 161–182.

Cowan, J. R. Reading, perceptual strategies and contrastive analysis. *Language Learning*, 1976, *26*, 95–109.

Cziko, G. A. The effects of language sequencing on the development of bilingual reading skills. *Canadian Modern Language Review*, 1976, *32*, 534–539.

Denburg, S. M. The interaction of picture and print in reading instruction. Doctoral dissertation, University of Toronto, 1975.

Dulay, H., & Burt, M. A new perspective on the creative construction process in child second language acquisition. *Language Learning*, 1974, *24*, 253–278.

Dulay, H., & Burt, M.Remarks on creativity in language acquisition. In M. Burt, H. Dulay, & M. Finocchiaro (Eds.), *Viewpoints on English as a Second Language*. New York: Regents, 1977.

Genesee, F. Acquisition of reading skills in immersion programs. *Foreign Language Annals*, 1979, *12*, 71–77.

Gibson, E. J., & Levin, H.*The Psychology of Reading*. Cambridge, Mass.: MIT Press, 1975.

Goodman, K. S. The psycholinguistic nature of the reading process. In K. S. Goodman (Ed.), *The Psycholinguistic Nature of the Reading Process*. Detroit: Wayne State University Press, 1968.

Krashen, S. D. Formal and informal linguistic environments in language acquisition and language learning. *TESOL Quarterly*, 1976, *10*, 157–168.

Lado, R. *Linguistics across Cultures*. Ann Arbor: University of Michigan Press, 1957.

Macnamara, J. Comparative studies of reading and problem solving in two languages. *TESOL Quarterly*, 1970, *4*, 107–116.

Macnamara, J. The cognitive basis of language learning in infants. *Psychological Review*, 1972, *79*, 1–13.

Macnamara, J. Nurseries, streets and classrooms: Some comparisons and deductions. *Modern Language Journal*, 1973a, *57*, 250–254.

Macnamara, J.The cognitive strategies of language learning. in J. W. Oller & J. C. Richards (Eds.), *Focus on the Learner: Pragmatic Perspectives for the Language Teacher*. Rowley, Mass.: Newbury House, 1973b.

Olson, D. R. From utterance to text: The bias of language in speech and writing. *Harvard Educational Review*, 1977, *47*, 257–280.

Richards, J. C. Error analysis and second language strategies. In J. W. Oller & J. C. Richards (Eds.), *Focus on the Learner: Pragmatic Perspectives for the Language Teacher*. Rowley, Mass.: Newbury House, 1973.

Selinker, L. Interlanguage. *IRAL*, 1972, *10*, 209–231.

Smith, E. B., Goodman, K. S., & Meredith, R. *Language and Thinking in School* (2nd ed.). New York: Holt, Rinehart and Winston, 1976.

Smith, F. *Understanding Reading*. New York: Holt, Rinehart and Winston, 1971.

Swain, M., Lapkin, S., & Barik, H. C. The cloze test as a measure of second language proficiency for young children. *Working Papers on Bilingualism*, 1976, *11*, 32–43.

Tucker, G. R.The development of reading skills within a bilingual program. In S. S. Smiley & J. C. Towner (Eds.), *Language and Reading*. Bellingham: Western Washington State College, 1975.

Webster's Seventh New Collegiate Dictionary. Toronto: Thomas Allen & Son Ltd., 1972.

Willows, D. M. A picture is not always worth a thousand words: Pictures as distractors in reading. *Journal of Educational Psychology*, 1978, *70*, 255–262.

Questions for Discussion and Activities

1. What is meant by the "creative construction" hypothesis? How does it differ from non-cognitive explanations of language learning?
2. Collect some samples of learner English to demonstrate the creative construction hypothesis. What learner constructed hypotheses might explain your data?
3. Tape an interview with a low level learner of English or some other language in which the learner is forced to create new forms. Can you categorize the learner's errors into the three types of knowledge sources upon which the learner forms his or her inferences?
4. Given the importance of linguistic and non-linguistic context in encouraging more accurate inferencing, analyze a language textbook in terms of the supportive contextualization which the materials provide. What does such a view about the role of context say about the type of effective practice that should be carried out in language drill?
5. It is often stated that the reading ability of second language learners exceeds their ability to speak. How might this disparity of skills be explained on the basis of inferencing?
6. Analyze an ESL reading text. To what degree are the various mechanisms that encourage inferencing built in? How might the text be improved to allow for better inferencing?
7. Compare scientific writing to normal descriptive prose such as that found in newspapers or popular magazines. To what degree do you find linguistic and non-linguistic redundancy built into these texts?
8. What kinds of cues for inferencing from the categories discussed by Goodman would be most useful for beginning level second language learners? What kinds of cues would the advanced level learner be able to utilize?
9. How might the various conditions described in the Bialystok reading experiments be adapted to explore various cue conditions for inferencing in spoken language?

PART III
Teacher Speech

6

Foreigner Talk in the Classroom—An Aid to Learning?

Craig Chaudron

Recent research in second language acquisition has begun to consider the role of the learner's linguistic environment as input to his or her developing grammar. (Hatch and (Wagner-) Gough, 1976; Meisel, 1977; Gaies, 1977; Katz, 1977). As in studies of mothers' talk to children acquiring their first language (cf. Snow, 1977), the hypothesis has been forwarded that native speakers' accommodations in their speech to second language learners (known as foreigner talk—FT) will influence the learners' acquisition of various structures; for example, by simplifying morphological forms, syntactic word order, etc.

The strong form of this hypothesis, that the learner's syntactic development would be isomorphic with the types or frequency of structures encountered in the FT, has not, however, been seriously advocated by any L2 researcher (see, however, Boyd, 1975; Larsen-Freeman, 1976; Hamayan, 1978). Meisel (1977), in fact, has argued an alternative relationship; namely, that although superficial similarities may occur between FT and learners' developing interlanguage, this is the result not of a causal relation from the former to the latter, but of the operation of identical universal processes of simplification that underlie on the one hand language acquisition (cf. Corder, 1975; Schumann, 1978), and on the other hand, speech accommodation and reduction by fully competent speakers (cf. Giles, Bourhis, and Taylor, 1977).

Nevertheless, since the fact that native speakers simplify their speech to non-natives in various contexts has been well documented (Hatch, Shapira, and Wagner-Gough, 1978; Meisel, 1977; Gaies, 1977; Freed, 1978; Chaudron, 1979), a weaker form of the hypothesis of FT influence on L2 acquisition must be considered. This version would hypothesize that the simpler accommodations to the learner help improve the learner's chances to *comprehend* the meaning of the speech addressed to him or her.

Simplification

What needs first to be determined here, however, is exactly what constitutes simplification of a complex code in speech accommodation. Studies of foreigner talk in educational settings have considered phonological and morphological regularization (Henzl, 1973), less varied vocabulary (Henzl, 1973; Chaudron, 1979), canonically ordered clauses (Freed, 1978), and less subordination (Gaies, 1977; Freed, 1978; Chaudron, 1979); for example, as measures of simplicity at different levels of analysis. In some way, linguistic simplicity involves less varied, more common, and structurally more elemental or regularized linguistic material. Yet disputes will inevitably arise, for analyses will differ in their assumptions as to underlying linguistic structures or derivations, and consequently as to which structures are the simplest linguistically. Meisel points out, for example, that within a transformational framework

> There are a number of criteria for simplicity which apparently cannot be tied together into just one definition . . .
>
> 1. Simplification of surface structure, e.g., fewer elements occurring . . .
> 2. Derivational simplification . . .
> 3. Simplification of underlying structure . . .
> 4. Psychological simplification computed on the basis of processing time, memory span, number of errors, etc.
> 5. Perceptual simplification, facilitating the process of decoding an utterance, e.g., by non-violation of perceptual strategies . . .
>
> . . . simplification is used in many different and sometimes contradictory ways as illustrated by the following two examples:
>
> — additional rules may be needed to reduce the number of surface elements, thus complexifying the derivational history of the sentence; also, this reduction could entail perceptual complexity if too much information is lost.
> — additional surface elements, possibly introduced by additional rules, may result in more explicit and therefore simpler constructions—viewed from the standpoint of the listener who has to decode the utterance. (1977, pp. 88–89)

Similarly, in discussing baby talk, Ferguson (1977) has contrasted simplification (meaning some form of linguistic simplicity) with *clarifying* modifications, or cognitively more redundant speech.

There arises the difficult question whether linguistic simplicity, by whatever definition, amounts to the same thing as cognitive simplicity. After some initial successes, psycholinguistic researchers have been at pains to relate linguistic theory directly to the perception and cognition of language (cf. Fodor et al., 1974). Without a consistent and adequate measure of the possible levels of linguistic and cognitive complexity, such comparisons are very difficult to make.

Simplification in the Classroom

The concern of this chapter is thus to illustrate the conflict between simplification in the linguistic sense and simplification in the cognitive sense, both types being possible instantiations of the hypothesis regarding foreigner talk and its comprehensibility for second language learners.

The particular case of formal classroom instruction for English as a second language (ESL) students, as an important instance of the L2 learner's contact with the L2, will be looked at in some detail. Furthermore, the lessons to be discussed are predominantly lessons in various subject matter for special classes of ESL students, at both the introductory high school and first-year university levels.[1] Such classes are an increasingly common occurrence in North America and throughout the world.

For want of a better measure of linguistic or cognitive complexity, appeal will be made to (1) comparisons with similar speech directed to native speakers, (2) intuitions about the difficulty of comprehending the utterances, or in several cases (3) the apparent inability of the students to react appropriately to the teachers' utterances.

The following classroom discursive phenomena will be examined: vocabulary, anaphoric reference, questioning, topic development, and explanations.

Vocabulary

Taking briefly the case of vocabulary first, it should be evident that vocabulary can be simplified for the L2 learner by employing more frequent words or possibly simple circumlocutions. Direct, comparative evidence for this as a phenomenon was obtained in a fortunate series of recordings of the same university lecturer conducting a lesson on the same topic (a novel about Depression-era Canada) on the same day, first to native speakers and then to ESL learners. Although the exact lesson format was different, many instances of the identical content being explained occur, affording the following examples (1–5), where the (a) items are the expression used to native speakers, and the (b) items are those to non-natives:[2]

(1a) . . . clinging . . .
(1b) . . . hold on very tightly . . .

(2a) . . . it's ironic . . .
(2b) . . . it seems funny . . .

(3a) . . . we still have this <u>myth</u> . . .
(3b) . . . there's still this <u>feeling</u> in North America . . .

(4a) . . . if you worked hard, you would <u>make</u> it.
(4b) . . . if you could <u>work</u> hard, you would be <u>rewarded</u>.

(5a) . . . if you didn't make it, then that was a reflection on your <u>character</u>.
(5b) . . . if you're unemployed, if you're poor, it's your own <u>fault</u> somehow.

(emphases in original; all (a) examples from University/1st year/Canadian Culture—non-ESL; all (b) examples from University/1st year/Canadian Culture—ESL)

These examples illustrate the possibilities both for the employment of vocabulary that one could assume is more simple in terms of its commonness of usage, and for *simplifying* circumlocutions. Short of an accumulated measure of commonness of all words used in a given lesson, it is difficult to determine the simplicity of vocabulary use in that entire classroom.

Impressionistically, lessons to the lowest-level learners, in reception classes for new immigrants with little familiarity with English, look less complex lexically. Teachers evidently accommodate to the learners' knowledge of the language and of the culture. What is more easily noted in any lesson, however, are the ways that more difficult vocabulary is *clarified*, or elaborated upon, and made more *cognitively* simple through redundancy.

This is a much more common phenomenon in the ESL lessons in this data than in several comparable non-ESL lessons that were observed.

An earlier paper (Chaudron, 1979) illustrated a wide range of phenomena that teachers use to elaborate and explain vocabulary arising during the typical lesson to ESL learners. It was argued in that paper that several of the syntactic structures most often used for elaboration, in particular apposition, conjunction, and parallel structures, *can* lead to ambiguity "as to whether *new* meanings are being added or whether a particular word is being elaborated . . ." (p. 16). This ambiguity is exemplified in the following (6–8):

(6) (Apposition) . . . the <u>beaver</u> is known as a very in<u>dustrious</u> and <u>busy</u>, uhm, <u>hard</u>-working animal.
(High school/Grade 10/History)

(7) (Conjunction) . . . Canada was a <u>booming</u> and expanding and economically <u>rich</u> . . .
(University/1st year/Canadian Culture—ESL)

(8) (Parallelism) If you look at <u>wire</u> sculpture, if you look at pieces of sculpture . . .
(High school/Mixed grades 10–11/Art)

The L2 listener could easily perceive some of these as series of *new* predications. The redundancy no doubt allows the learner to capture the essential meaning being conveyed, while the listener may *not* have perceived the *particular* meaning of "industrious," "booming," or "wire," and their similarity to the clarifying, redundant synonyms. Conversely, the simplified vocabulary illustrated in the (b) examples (1b–5b) above may have conveyed a better immediate meaning, while losing the possibly more important nuances that the lecturer wanted to convey with words like "clinging," "ironic," and "myth," which were addressed to native speakers.

A similar conflict appears with the other discursive phenomena in these classes for ESL learners.

Anaphoric reference

The first example with anaphoric reference, taken from the matched university lessons, demonstrates that the native speaker appears to be simplifying his or her speech to the L2 learners. In a discussion about the differential treatment of unemployed in different Canadian provinces during the Depression, the professor said the following to native speakers:

(9) . . . they just-everybody from the prairies tended to go to B.C. because of the weather, an' because things were slightly better in B.C. anyway . . . And so, Vancouver w- was obviously horrified that these hordes of people were going to come in.
(University/1st year/Canadian Culture—non-ESL)

Whereas with ESL students the same point was made thus:

(10) But also th- the people tended to go from one province-they went from the poor provinces to the rich provinces. 'N' then when they got to the rich provinces they got upset 'n' said don't come here, we don't want you, (you know). Go back! So they- in order to force the people back to their homes, so they wouldn't have to give out so much relief.
(University/1st year/Canadian Culture—ESL)

Although British Columbia had been mentioned just prior to (10), the specific comparison with that province is lost here, and for the ESL learners a more general reference is made to "*rich* and *poor* provinces." The generalization of rich and poor may be advantageous, but it is not certain that the ESL students will be able to connect the two points (from "B.C." to "rich"), especially those several students who had not read the book. Moreover, a more significant problem with reference is illustrated in (10): ESL teachers employ a large number of anaphoric pronouns, *it, this, they,* and so on, in contexts that require a reasonably high degree of English competence in order to interpret the antecedents of the references. The rule is employed in (10) that a stressed pronoun ("*they* got upset . . .") will switch the referent from the current noun topic to an alternative interpretation. But it is not a given that the learners can so quickly retrieve this connection and relate "*they*" with "the *rich* provinces." To the extent that pronominalization may be considered a simplification,[3] it may have been better to have retained the more explicit, though possibly more complex, "Vancouver," or even, "the people of Vancouver."

Compare with these an even more blatant obfuscation of the intended referents in the same ESL class:

(11) . . . a lot of people are obviously sort of middle class. . . . And they're
afraid of the men, because they think that they are going to ha- start a riot,
and destroy property, uh, they get very suspicious when they come into a
small town, . . .
(University/1st year/Canadian Culture—ESL)

The sudden alternation of antecedents for "they" and "their" makes this
passage potentially quite difficult to interpret, given a developing L2 competence in the listener. It is not being suggested here, however, that such examples
are the *rule* in these classes. In many ways the classes to be used here for
illustration appear to be successfully simplifying the material. But the risk is
ever-present that the well-meaning native speaker will complicate the comprehensibility of the material.

To take some other examples of this potential problem with reference, note
the use of "it" in the following:

(12) Did you say I or we?
SS: I.
I. Usually his brother's with him, right, it's we. I run to school at noon.
Together. [meaning all students should pronounce together] I run to
school at noon.//
Students: I run to school at noon.
((Reception/Beginners/English)

Although it cannot be determined how well the students retrieved the referent for
"it," namely, "the correct sentence," or "the correct subject," it would have
made a much clearer statement if the teacher had in fact *said* that noun phrase.

Finally, (13) is an example of the difficulty of retrieving the referent for
"that." ESL learners commonly have trouble acquiring the distinction between
it, this, and *that,* and yet most teachers' speech is replete with longer passages in
which these words appear (several others will appear in examples below).

(13) He says [reading from class handout] "and what difficulties as well as
positive contributions can come out of these relationships." Do you think
that's important in *Duddy Kravitz*? Difficulties and   is that an important
hint, at all? How.
(University/1st year/Canadian Language & Culture)

The exact referent of these two "that"s remains a little unclear even to a native
speaker's interpretation, so it is no wonder the students failed to respond
immediately to these questions, and the teacher had to rephrase them
subsequently.

Questioning

This brings us to a third area, concerning the use of lines of questioning in
classrooms with ESL students. The problem of foreigner talk questioning in
native–non-native dyadic discourse has been examined by Hatch and (Wagner-)

Gough (1976), Freed (1978), and especially by Long (1980). Questions not only serve to get the non-native to interact, an essential task of the ESL classroom teacher, but they are also used to focus on topical relationships, especially in the classroom setting where they break down the lesson and different subtopics into manageable units. It is very frequently seen that a question will be posed announcing a general, encompassing, rhetorical theme, immediately followed by a more specific question that seeks the first bit of practical information needed in order to answer the more general question. Some examples are (14) and (15):

(14) If, a state, if a state only has, under 20 inches of rain in a year, [Student's Name] what kind of climate does it have? Is it like Canada, or is it like Lebanon?
(High school/Grade 10-beginners/Geography)

(15) What is a capital city? . . . [no appropriate response] OK. Ottawa is the capital city of Canada. Ottawa is the capital city of Canada. Just like what is the capital city of Italy?
(Reception/Beginners/Geography)

Following, example (15) several students were asked to identify their capital cities before the teacher summarized with, "Capital city is where the government is. Where the government is."

The simplification process here is not so evidently unique to foreigner talk, but it is highly likely to be employed, because the non-native students are regarded as needing this extra cognitive guidance. A primary difficulty with this approach to simplification is that the digression into practical knowledge often appears to obscure the general point. This is demonstrated in a continuation of example (14):

(16) S: Like Lebanon. . . .
    S: There is hot, you know . . .
    . . . OK. It's a hot state. [Meaning Nevada] Because Lebanon is very hot also, and there's very little rain. Uhm, [Student's Name] you said there's desert there, that's true,
    S: It will be the same as the capital.
    It will be the same as,
        The capital of Lebanon.
    A- the capital of Nevada? . . . [Ss attempt several inexact responses] OK. If you looked at something in the East Coast, uhm what would that climate be like, what would it look like there? . . . There's a lot of rain, but when you have a lot of rain, what do you have, then?
    S: Thunderstorm?
    No, what grows when you have a lot of rain?
    SS: - - - Forest.

Yeah, forests.
(High school/Grade 10-beginners/Geography)

Admittedly, this happens to be a lesson in *map reading*, but the possibly important characterization of the climate with little rain and of one with much rain is getting lost. "Dry" and "wet" never are mentioned, "tropical" is not considered, and although "desert" and "forest" are mentioned, a clear contrast of the different climates fails to be made in even these imprecise terms. An additional point worth noting here is the apparent misleading nature of the later questions, "What would it look like there," and "When you have a lot of rain, what do you have, then?" The students' response are what come typically when such simple questions are phrased with common vocabulary, "look like," and "have." Again, a more explicit phrasing, such as "what kind of plants would grow there?" would not have been too difficult for these learners.

Another clear example of loss of a major point is evidenced in a comparison of the two matched university lessons. A contributing problem is the fact that the instructor organized the ESL class differently by giving each student her or his own individual question to respond to. This tended to break up the continuity of the discussion, and the questions tended to be about more specific details in the novel that had been read. In the ESL class, the student's question was:

(17) S: Are there any kind people in the book? Uh,_ _ yes. The workers.
Yes. . . .
. . . the . . . the teachers.
Which one? Oh oh the teacher you mean. Wha- whatever his name is. . . .
Are there any other characters that were very, an- any people that wanted to help the men? . . . Who's the nicest person in the book in a sense? . . .
That you meet right at the beginning?
S: Uh, Harry.
Harry. Yes. Harry, you remember the man who has the coffee shop? He gives them free cups of coffee an' Mat thinks, I've only known him for one day, but he's the best friend I've ever had . . . 'n' then there's uh, one man who gives them a a ride somewhere because his children are also in a difficult position, 'n' this little old lady who (goes) up and gives them money, 'n' says I'm on your side boys 'n' so on. B' what's th- what's the usual attitide of the crowd, to the- . . . what do most of the people think of the strikers? I think that's somebody else's question anyway.
(University/1st year/Canadian Culture—ESL)

Compare this *list* of people with the similar point made in the non-ESL class (example (18)), where the line of questioning is contained within a larger question about the social atmosphere of the times:

(18) Wha- what do you think, wh- what kind of social atmosphere . . . your

ht had marked itself more by
ictionary meanings. Also, if the
n changed to something like the
re do you look for them?" the shift

ric to determine the simplicity or
uncers and shifters (though cf. Bates
r is it easy to determine in the present
ul. The point remains, however, that
y of announcing these points does not
e required for non-native listeners to

ggestions in the preceding examples that
instruction more cognitively simplified has
rtant points about the lesson.
nstrate this argument, that elaborations in the
ully done, may cloud the point being made with
sing information. This is particularly evident in
engthy explanations.
n geography class on scale, the teacher was
e between a graphic scale and a ratio scale, or the
e. The teacher takes great pains to demonstrate how
aying a ruler on a map first and then illustrating how
he same measure according to the ratio:

is one to 50,000, that means one centimeter here,
). If I put this ruler down and did it 50,000 times, I'd be
ne. And that's what it tells you. Or, it could be one ruler
own one ruler length from [School Name], which is here.
ld take me downtown. To the other side. [Of the city] Close
o if- it's one to 50,000 again. One ruler length, if I laid the
monstrates laying ruler down] all the way across an' I do it
n' I'd be at- close to High Park. That's why it's called a
raction, because it represents the distance as measured on
ou don't have to have units with it. It can be any unit you
re some place, and uh, you have an inch ruler, it'll work
f you have a metric ruler, it'll work with this scale. If you
it that we don't even know about, it'll work with this scale

impression of the social atmosphere of the day . . . Can you think of any examples of people who were very sympathetic? Were there uh what about, were there any very kind people?

S: There was uh, Harry, and the uh- what was that hamburger guy?

Yes. §(I didn't know) they had hamburgers then. I guess they did. § Yes Harry was th- the prime one who gave free, free coffee 'n' . . . Can you think of any other examples of people who (kind of) came forward [Student's Name]? . . . Yes. 'ts another one I remember, (it's) people were sympathetic because their own children were out of work and so on . . . But there was oth- a little woman who came forward, on- a little old lady who came forward and put money in their pocket or something. § So she's she's obviously meant to be (an) idealizing. § B' what- what did the wh- what does the writer seem to be doing though with the crowd in the book? (University/1st year/Canadian Culture—non-ESL)

In (18), the more symbolic nature of the kindness and niceness is made clear by the embedding of this question in the more general initial question, and by the mentioning of words such as "sympathetic" and "idealizing."

A final example of the possibilities for a loss of clarity from the use of precise questions that are meant to lead to the general question is illustrated in example (19):

(19) What's the result of the fact that they have different educational opportunities?

S: Created (as/a) different soc- different class in society?

Yes. Uh, is it created, or just simply keep it there? Maintain it there? Do we have a classless society at the moment?

S: Uh - - -

Pardon?

Yes.

We have a classless society. No upper 'r middle lower.

SS: I'm sorry - - -   - - -
(University/1st year/Canadian Language & Culture)

Here, the instructor's oblique question is intended to lead the student to a line of reasoning that eventually will answer the first question, but the leap of logic appeared to have been lost on these students.

The difficulty with the employment of specific procedural questions or of obliquely logical questions is that, while they may conform to the teacher's notion of a simplified structuring of knowledge, they may not be the simplest logical steps for a learner of ESL. They presuppose a sophistication in the learner's ability to acquire knowledge that may not match his or her classroom skills in ESL.

Topic develoment

A fourth problematic area in FT simplification in such classrooms has to do with the structuring or development of the topic. Teachers have numerous means at their disposal for establishing the topic or subtopic of discussion, from the formal and explicit

(20) We're going to look at number six today, and, if we have a chance we're going to look at some atlases.
(High school/Grade 10-beginners/Geography)

to the abrupt, fragmental,

(21) The scale used in atlases.
(Reception/Late transition/Geography)

An exploration of the variety of topic structuring devices is beyond the scope of this chapter. They include such syntactic phenomena as fronting, left-dislocation, extraposition, pseudo-clefting, and subordinate clauses; phonological phenomena such as stress or lengthening; demonstrative pronouns and quantifiers; repetition; sentence fragments; and many more. What is of interest in this current study, however, is the way in which teachers, in simplifying their maintenance of a continuing topic, or their announcement of a new topic or subtopic, do not succeed in cueing the learners to their intent.

For example, while examining how to use the Yellow Pages, the teacher in a Grade 10 English class was using a handout. The points on the handout had been discussed for a while, and then the teacher turned to a new aspect, to ask the students to imagine how they would find different items in the Yellow Pages. She had previously compared looking for something by walking up and down the streets to letting one's fingers do the walking, so it is not surprising in the following example (22) that the brief reminder of the ongoing topic, in this case the quite common topic announcer of a conditional subordinate clause with sentence-final falling intonation and a pause,[4] was not directly perceived by all the students as the condition for the following question; it could have been perceived as a *summary* of the just-completed work on the handout:

(22) ...when you're looking in the Yellow Pages, then. What is, what is the way look - - - for, finding, something, if you wanted to look, and find something like, where all the Chinese restaurants in Toronto are?

SS: - - (I'd look) in Chinatown.

How would you, [Laughter]
How would you find it in the Yellow Pages? Where would you look?

S: I think, that, (I don't)

Where would, where would you look?

S: What would I do?

Yeah, where would you look?

impression of the social atmosphere of the day . . . Can you think of any examples of people who were very sympathetic? Were there uh what about, were there any very kind people?

S: There was uh, Harry, and the uh- what was that hamburger guy?

Yes. § (I didn't know) they had hamburgers then. I guess they did. § Yes Harry was th- the prime one who gave free, free coffee 'n' . . . Can you think of any other examples of people who (kind of) came forward [Student's Name]? . . . Yes. 'ts another one I remember, (it's) people were sympathetic because their own children were out of work and so on . . . But there was oth- a little woman who came forward, on- a little old lady who came forward and put money in their pocket or something. § So she's she's obviously meant to be (an) idealizing. § B' what- what did the wh- what does the writer seem to be doing though with the crowd in the book? (University/1st year/Canadian Culture—non-ESL)

In (18), the more symbolic nature of the kindness and niceness is made clear by the embedding of this question in the more general initial question, and by the mentioning of words such as "sympathetic" and "idealizing."

A final example of the possibilities for a loss of clarity from the use of precise questions that are meant to lead to the general question is illustrated in example (19):

(19) What's the result of the fact that they have different educational opportunities? _ _

S: Created (as/a) different soc- different class in society?

Yes. Uh, is it created, or just simply keep it there? Maintain it there? Do we have a classless society at the moment?

S: Uh - - -

Pardon?

Yes.

We have a classless society. No upper 'r middle lower.

SS: I'm sorry - - -   - - -
(University/1st year/Canadian Language & Culture)

Here, the instructor's oblique question is intended to lead the student to a line of reasoning that eventually will answer the first question, but the leap of logic appeared to have been lost on these students.

The difficulty with the employment of specific procedural questions or of obliquely logical questions is that, while they may conform to the teacher's notion of a simplified structuring of knowledge, they may not be the simplest logical steps for a learner of ESL. They presuppose a sophistication in the learner's ability to acquire knowledge that may not match his or her classroom skills in ESL.

Topic develoment

A fourth problematic area in FT simplification in such classrooms has to do with the structuring or development of the topic. Teachers have numerous means at their disposal for establishing the topic or subtopic of discussion, from the formal and explicit

(20) We're going to look at number six today, and, if we have a chance we're going to look at some atlases.
(High school/Grade 10-beginners/Geography)

to the abrupt, fragmental,

(21) The scale used in atlases.
(Reception/Late transition/Geography)

An exploration of the variety of topic structuring devices is beyond the scope of this chapter. They include such syntactic phenomena as fronting, left-dislocation, extraposition, pseudo-clefting, and subordinate clauses; phonological phenomena such as stress or lengthening; demonstrative pronouns and quantifiers; repetition; sentence fragments; and many more. What is of interest in this current study, however, is the way in which teachers, in simplifying their maintenance of a continuing topic, or their announcement of a new topic or subtopic, do not succeed in cueing the learners to their intent.

For example, while examining how to use the Yellow Pages, the teacher in a Grade 10 English class was using a handout. The points on the handout had been discussed for a while, and then the teacher turned to a new aspect, to ask the students to imagine how they would find different items in the Yellow Pages. She had previously compared looking for something by walking up and down the streets to letting one's fingers do the walking, so it is not surprising in the following example (22) that the brief reminder of the ongoing topic, in this case the quite common topic announcer of a conditional subordinate clause with sentence-final falling intonation and a pause,[4] was not directly perceived by all the students as the condition for the following question; it could have been perceived as a *summary* of the just-completed work on the handout:

(22) ...when you're looking in the Yellow Pages, then. What is, what is the way look - - - for, finding, something, if you wanted to look, and find something like, where all the Chinese restaurants in Toronto are?
SS: - - (I'd look) in Chinatown.
How would you, [Laughter]
How would you find it in the Yellow Pages? Where would you look?
S: I think, that, (I don't)
Where would, where would you look?
S: What would I do?
Yeah, where would you look?

If you wanted to, if you wanted to find Chinese restaurants.

S: Chinatown.

S: - - - -

You would look under restaurants? OK.

(High school/Grade 10-beginners/English)

The fact that some of the students laughed does suggest that the point was perceived by some, but the teacher's difficulty in eliciting an answer does not speak well for the clarity of the question. Besides the possible difficulty with the topic condition expressed in the adverbial fragment at the beginning, there can also be problems for non-native speakers in recognizing "look" as meaning "look up/under in a book," rather than "look for in reality," or similarly, problems in being misled by the stressed quantifier, "*all.*" The teacher in this case does repeat the topic, but some more explicit suggestion is evidently necessary in her questions, such as, "under which heading," or the like. In fact, since the handout exercise had become a little too involved in details and vocabulary and had not focused on the issue of topical headings in the Yellow Pages, it would probably have aided this particular line of questioning if the teacher had established the extension of the topic from the few examples on the handout to the entire Yellow Pages, with a few simple examples of headings first.

Another example of an unsuccessful topic-shift is this case in a geography class (example (23)), where the teacher has written the word "scale" on the blackboard, having previously assigned the students the homework to look up its meanings in the dictionary. He attempted here, however, to delay the work on the assignment, but unsuccessfully:

(23) [T has said "I asked you took up this word in the dictionary.] [i.e. "scale"] There are"] . . . eight meanings for it, at <u>least.</u> [Writes "scale" on board] But, before we start talking about the meanings, we want to think about the meanings for geography first. The meanings of <u>scale.</u> And you find it on <u>maps.</u> Where do you look for it, where do you look for it?

S: Dictionary.

OK.

SS: Dictionary.

No, I-if you're looking at a map, OK let's do the dictionary meanings first then, if you want to do that.

(Reception/Low transition/Geography)

Part of this problem is, no doubt, the ambiguity of "look for it," as we saw above in example (22), especially in this case the referent of the pronoun, which could have been made more explicit ("a map scale"). But the attempted topic-shift in "we want to think about the meanings for geography first . . ." appears to have failed. This was perhaps an ill-advised attempt in the first place, but it could have succeeded if the teacher's preemptive statement had marked itself more by explaining that he did *not* want to talk about the dictionary meanings. Also, if the pronoun in "And you find it on maps," had been changed to something like the following, "You can find scales on maps. Where do you look for them?" the shift may have been more successful.

No one has developed an adequate metric to determine the simplicity or complexity of the wide variety of topic announcers and shifters (though cf. Bates and MacWhinney, 1979; Givón, 1978), nor is it easy to determine in the present data which are most cognitively successful. The point remains, however, that the fragmented and sometimes casual way of announcing these points does not always achieve the clarity that may be required for non-native listeners to comprehend the point.

Explanations

There have been occasional suggestions in the preceding examples that teachers' attempts to make their instruction more cognitively simplified has resulted in failures to make important points about the lesson.

Two last examples will demonstrate this argument, that elaborations in the linguistic material, unless carefully done, may cloud the point being made with too much redundant and confusing information. This is particularly evident in some instances of teachers' lengthy explanations.

In the one late transition geography class on scale, the teacher was demonstrating the difference between a graphic scale and a ratio scale, or the representative fraction scale. The teacher takes great pains to demonstrate how the ratio scale works, by laying a ruler on a map first and then illustrating how one would actually use the same measure according to the ratio:

(24) It says the scale is one to 50,000, that means one centimeter here, represents 50,000. If I put this ruler down and did it 50,000 times, I'd be over at Woodbine. And that's what it tells you. Or, it could be one ruler length. If I put down one ruler length from [School Name], which is here. Let's see, it could take me downtown. To the other side. [Of the city] Close to High Park. So if- it's one to 50,000 again. One ruler length, if I laid the ruler down, [Demonstrates laying ruler down] all the way across an' I do it 50,000 times an' I'd be at- close to High Park. That's why it's called a representative fraction, because it represents the distance as measured on the earth. And you don't have to have units with it. It can be any unit you want. So if you're some place, and uh, you have an inch ruler, it'll work with this scale. If you have a metric ruler, it'll work with this scale. If you have another unit that we don't even know about, it'll work with this scale too.

S: Sir!

Yes.

(but) you saying that if I go like 15,000 you- be close to High Park. But how do you know which direction to go?
(Reception/Late transition/Geography)

The difficulty here is that, while the demonstration was "graphic" enough, it is misleading about the usefulness of a ratio scale. No one would actually lay the ruler down 50,000 times; instead, the calculation is a simple mathematical one. Unfortunately, the teacher does not illustrate this simple operation for determining the distance between points; the ratio scale is left perhaps as a means of getting from one place to another in a rather laborious way. The student question that followed suggests this, that the *activity* of laying the ruler down has captivated *his* thinking.

Finally, from the matched university lessons comes a fairly clear indication that the lecturer has overdone the point for the ESL students. In his discussion with non-ESL students, he expands on a point in the following way:

(25) . . . this article I was reading made the point that in North America in general, uh, that- people started out with the idea of equal opportunity, you know that everybody who came here, because there was such abundance . . . because there was equal opportunity to become rich. It wasn't like Europe, where you had your family an' your social class an' your education an' all this sort of thing, against you, or for you. But in in Canada an' in the United States you could work away, and if you had the proper character, if you worked hard, you would make it. And therefore, of course, as the reverse of that, uh, the idea developed that if you didn't make it, then that was a reflection on your character! But then in a sense this a result of the individualism and uh, abundance that's here in North America. So that although it's not true, we still have this myth that everybody who works hard can get ahead. And uh, when the Depression came along of course it was a great shock to people. 'N' they therefore, made everything individual, 'n' they said, these people can't get jobs because they are lazy, because they are no good as individuals, because they have failed, not because social conditions beyond their control, have led to . . . their loss of work. But I think th-that is in fact a very important point about North American society that we have such a strong belief in individual competition and hard work and so on, that naturally, those (who) don't get jobs are judged in that way, (kind o') as person- personal failures rather than (as) social accidents.
(University/1st year/Canadian Culture—non-ESL)

We see here that the point is elaborated several times in different ways, but notice the ways in which the similar points have been elaborated on in the ESL class (example (26)). Here it is much more disorganized, with more digressions to exemplify vocabulary or particular relationships. The interconnections between ideas are also more difficult to interpret, owing to the greater fragmentation and lack of consistent topic maintenance, a point to be clarified further below. The ESL explanation (from which several points have been excised) took about twice the time of the native speaker explanation we have just seen in (25).

(26) ... aspect of uh, the book is interesting, as far in connection with what people have said about North American society. Uh, Canadian and American, but particularly American. Uh, in Europe, everyone of course was divided into social classes. Uh, you probably did what your father was going to do, uh, if you were a peasant, you accepted that ... But when, when America was was developed, people came here, there was all this land, lots of opportunity for making money, gaining wealth. And, because there was more than people needed, uh, everybody could have a lot. And therefore, people thought, if you could work hard, you would be rewarded! You would get ... what anybody would get if they worked hard and tried to make money. And this tradition has continued in North American society. And even though now ... there isn't endless opportunity, not everybody in America ca-can be rich! We can't all be millionaires. But there's still this feeling in North America that if you're unemployed, if you're poor, it's your own fault somehow. So they have a- this particular I mean this is perhaps true in many societies, but uh it's exaggerated in uh, North America because of the uh, abundance, the wealth, that was here. So that everybody, so it was thought, could be rich. ... That's why during the Depression, they- people did not get together, and try to help the people who were suffering from the Depression. They just thought, it's their fault, they're lazy, there's work if they if they would only take it. And, of course, in the Depression there wasn't work ... And they get- they have people come up to the- the streets and say, you lazy things, you could work if you wanted to. An' that's still a- still a common idea in Canada actually, isn't it. Not quite so bad now because we have unemployment. [Meaning insurance] But now the idea is that you know people are lazy and want to take unemployment. They don't want to do work when they can get unemployment. ... And yet, people because of this tradition blamed the people individually instead of saying, social conditions have produced general unemployment. That we should do something about that. They thought it's your fault. Not the fault of social conditions, you know ... in spite of- ... the fact that this attitude still exists to a certain degree ... you know they- they would think that if you're unemployed it's your own fault, uh, because you can't keep a job, you won't work hard enough and so on. That's still, still a common attitude.

   (University/1st year/Canadian Culture—ESL)

   The excessive amount of rephrasing is obvious here. Note in particular the continuing isolation in this example of the main point with varying disconnected expressions: "this tradition," "this feeling," "they just thought," "a common idea," "this tradition" again, "this attitude," and "a common attitude."

Compare these to example (25), where we only see "idea of equal opportunity," "idea" "a very . . . point," and "this myth," referring to the main point throughout. The maintenance of the main idea or topic through such an explanation would undoubtedly be facilitated by minimalizing the terms used to refer to it. But we see in the ESL explanation the more extreme possibilities for altering vocabulary and syntax to rephrase a point, a procedure which might not unfairly be dubbed as "supererogatory pleonasm."

Some disclaimers

Three points are worth making as disclaimers about what has been shown in the foregoing discussion of teachers' "foreigner talk" discourse. First, it has not been the intention here to castigate the teachers concerned for conducting incomprehensible lessons. On the contrary, the examples cited are drawn from a much broader selection of very successful explanations, elaborations, questionings, topic developments, and cohesive references. An examination of such instances would fill three times the space of this chapter. Furthermore, these teachers are personable, and sympathetic toward their students, and their lessons are evidently appreciated very much.

Second, most of the phenomena and problems displayed here are probably not peculiar to the classrooom with ESL students; teacher talk is itself a special register of a language. Every teacher is faced with the problems of conveying information with an explicit, lucid language, which will frequently necessitate simplifications and restructurings of the information. The suggestion here, however, is that greater efforts to simplify are made by teachers when faced with non-native speakers of the classroom linguistic medium.

Third, it is noteworthy that the data base for this study exemplifies few instances of FT as an ungrammatical version of the L1. Other studies have varied in this respect, some showing evidence of ungrammaticality in conversational speech (Hatch et al., 1978; Meisel, 1977) and others finding none (Freed, 1978). In this data the few instances of possibly ungrammatical speech are also potential performance errors that are not uncommon in any normal discourse (cf. Crystal and Davy, 1969). There is extensive evidence of fragments and other elliptic utterances, but these are typically grammatically well-formed, if not always entirely textually coherent. This is not to say that morphological and syntactic deviance will not occur in FT; rather, that teachers in such subject-matter classrooms are probably more aware of the need to communicate in a natural grammatical mode.

Conclusion

The point of the preceding should be clear. What has been illustrated are the highly conflicting demands on the native English-speaking teacher, who must at the same time present significant and coherent ideas and knowledge, but in a way that is comprehensible to learners who lack fundamental linguistic competencies such as attribution of referents to pronouns, recognition of synonymy, signals for topic-shifts, and so on. The pressure to ensure communication appears to lead at times to ambiguous over-simplification on the one hand, and confusingly redundant over-elaboration on the other. Some compromise between these two extremes would seem to be appropriate in most of the examples cited above. The teacher must be careful to be explicit and perspicuous, while meeting the learners' need for linguistic simplicity.

The intention in examining such difficulties is to promote better understanding of effective instructional methods in L2 classrooms. Informed decisions by teachers and teacher trainers as to the degree of simplification required in such classroom situations should lead to improved clarity of instruction. Prerequisite to such decisions is a better understanding of L2 learners' comprehension of the varying structures that teachers employ while attempting to simplify their instruction. This is a major goal of further investigations of foreigner talk in the classroom.

Notes

1. See Chaudron (1979) for details on the different classrooms investigated.

I would like to express my appreciation to the several people who have discussed this work in earlier versions, or who have provided me with many ideas and encouragement. These are in particular: Patrick Allen, Bruce Barkman, Ellen Bialystok, Norbert Dittmar, Maria Fröhlich, Eddie Levenston, Patsy Lightbown, Mike Long, Ron Mackay, Catherine Snow, and Merrill Swain.

Special gratitude is due the teachers in this study who so congenially gave their time to let me observe in their classrooms. Discussions with them were also most helpful in suggesting other areas of concern in ESL teaching. They must regrettably remain anonymous. Thanks are also due the principals and coordinators of the different schools and programs, in particular to Jean Handscombe and to Merlin Homer for their efforts on my behalf, and for their helpful comments on issues that are important to teachers.

2. References to cited classroom dialogue follow the format: School/Grade (level)/Subject, according to the data in Chaudron (1979). Typographical conventions are: underlined syllables indicate stress; underlined spaces indicate slight pause without falling tone; underlinings separately spaced indicate longer pauses; spaced hyphens indicate unintelligible material; material in parentheses indicates approximated speech content; ellipses indicate excised material; material in square brackets indicates transcriber's comments; material enclosed by §. . . § indicates low tone, *sotto voce* utterances; comma punctuation within utterances indicates falling tone pauses; single hyphens indicate broken utterances; final punctuation indicates syntactic mood, not necessarily final tone. Student speech is indicated by (S:).

3. The issue of pronominalization as simplification is of course debatable. Viewed as a deletion and replacement, it is possibly more complex in a derivational theory of complexity. However, since much of the current data suggests that teachers extensively pronominalize, it must be viewed as a surface linguistic simplification of the variety of material presented to the learners.

4. Cf. John Haiman's (1978) interesting article on conditionals as topics.

References

Bates, E., & MacWhinney, B. A functionalist approach to the acquisition of grammar. In E. Ochs & B. Schieffelin (Eds.), *Developmental Pragmatics.* New York: Academic Press, 1979.

Boyd, P. A. The development of grammar categories in Spanish by anglo children learning a second language. *TESOL Quarterly,* 1975, *9,* 2 (June), 125–135.

Chaudron, C. Complexity of teacher speech and vocabulary explanation/elaboration. Paper presented at the Thirteenth Annual TESOL Convention, Boston, Mass., March 2, 1979.

Corder, S. "Simple codes" and the source of the second language learner's initial heuristic hypothesis. Paper presented at the Colloque Theoretical Models in Applied Linguistics IV, Université de Neuchâtel; reprinted in *Studies in Second Language Acquisition,* 1975, *1,* 1, Indiana University Linguistics Club, Bloomington, Ind.

Crystal, D. & Davy, D. *Investigating English Style.* London: Longman Group, 1969.

Ferguson, C. A. Baby talk as a simplified register. In C. Snow & C. A. Ferguson (Eds.), *Talking to Children: Language Input and Acquisition.* Cambridge: Cambridge University Press, 1977.

Fodor, J. A., Bever, T. G., & Garrett, M. F. *The Psychology of Language: An Introduction to Psycholinguistics and Generative Grammar.* New York: McGraw-Hill, 1974.

Freed, B. F. Talking to foreigners versus talking to children: Similarities and differences. Revised version of paper presented at the Los Angeles Second Language Research Forum, UCLA, Los Angeles, 1978.

Gaies, S. J. The nature of linguistic input in formal second language learning: Linguistic and communicative strategies in ESL teachers' classroom language. In H. D. Brown, C. A. Yorio, & R. H. Crymes (Eds.), *On TESOL '77: Teaching and Learning English as a Second Language: Trends in Research and Practice.* Washington, D.C.: TESOL, 1977.

Giles, H., Bourhis, R. Y., & Taylor, D. M. Towards a theory of language in ethnic group relations. In H. Giles (Ed.), *Language, Ethnicity and Intergroup Relations.* New York: Academic Press, 1977.

Givón, T. Definiteness and referentiality. In J. H. Greenberg (Ed.), *Universals of Human Language: Volume 4: Syntax.* Stanford, Calif.: Stanford University Press, 1978.

Haiman, J. Conditionals are topics. *Language,* 1978, *54,* 3, 564–589.

Hamayan, E. Acquisition of French syntactic structures. Ph.D. dissertation. McGill University, Montreal, 1978.

Hatch, E. & (Wagner-) Gough, J. Explaining sequence and variation in second language acquisition. *Papers in Second Language Acquisition.* Special Issue No. 4 of H. D. Brown (Ed.,), *Language Learning.* Ann Arbor, Mich.: University of Michigan Press, 1976.

Hatch, E., Shapira, R., & Wagner-Gough, J. Foreigner talk discourse. *ITL: Review of Applied Linguistics,* 1978, 39–60.

Henzl, V. M. Linguistic register of foreign language instruction. *Language Learning,* 1973, *23,* 2 (December), 207–222.

Katz, J. T. Foreigner talk input in child second language acquisition. *Proceedings* of the Second Annual Los Angeles Second Language Research Forum, February 11–13, UCLA, Los Angeles, 1977.

Larsen-Freeman, D. ESL teacher speech as input to the ESL learner. *Workpapers in Teaching English as a Second Language,* 1976, *10,* UCLA, Los Angeles, 1976.

Long, M. H. Questions in foreigner talk discourse. Paper presented at the Fourteenth Annual TESOL Convention, San Francisco, 1980.

Meisel, J. M. Linguistic simplification: A study of immigrant workers' speech and foreigner talk. In S. P. Corder & E. Roulet (Eds.), *Actes du 5ème colloque de linguistique appliquée de Neuchâtel.* Geneva: Droz, 1977.

Schumann, J. *The Pidginization Process: A Model for Second Language Acquisition.* Rowley, Mass.: Newbury House, 1978.

Snow, C. Mothers' speech research: From input to interaction. in C. Snow & C. A. Ferguson (Eds.), *Talking to Children: Language Input and Acquisition.* Cambridge: Cambridge University Press, 1977.

Questions for Discussion and Activities

1. Chaudron discusses two possible roles for speech modifications by native speakers addressing non-native speakers. Foreigner talk may aid comprehension by the learner and/or determine the order in which various features of the second language are acquired. What kind of evidence would be needed to determine the true function(s) of foreigner talk? Do you know of any such evidence?

2. Tape-record a native speaker talking to a non-native as they engage in some kind of cooperative task; e.g., getting acquainted or playing a game. Do the same with two native speakers. Transcribe the tapes. What differences do you notice between the native speakers' speech when addressing native and non-native interlocutors? Are there any features of the native speakers' speech that are unique to the foreigner-talk corpus, or do the two corpora differ only in the relative frequencies of those features? Why is it necessary to obtain comparable native speaker–native speaker baseline data in studies of foreigner talk?

3. Chaudron recognizes the possibility that some of the features he describes as speech modifications made to non-native speakers may be characteristics of foreigner talk, teacher talk, or a hybrid. Design a study that would show which were which.

4. Conduct a pilot version of the study you designed in answer to question 3.

5. If necessary, modify the design for the study in light of problems your pilot study identified.

6. Tape-record a non-native speaker of some second language using that language to address (1) an equally advanced second language speaker of that language and (2) a less advanced speaker of the language. On the basis of your results, is the ability to use foreigner talk unique to native speakers of a language?

7. Compare the kinds of speech modifications made by native speakers talking to non-natives across languages. For example, we know that native speakers sometimes delete free and bound morphology (producing ungrammatical foreigner talk in English—see, e.g., C. A. Ferguson's article in *Anthropological Linguistics* 1975, *17*, 1–14). But what happens in languages (e.g., Mandarin) with little or no morphology there in the first place?

8. What other "simple codes" can you think of? What characteristics do they share? What distinguishes them? (You might consider some of the following: baby talk, caretaker speech, telegraphese, newspaper headlines, teacher talk, foreigner talk, pidgins, jargons, and the language of note-taking.) Are they all "simple," in fact? Are any elaborated versions of some standard form of a language? Do they serve different purposes?

9. Obtain a sample of foreigner talk and one or more of the other "restricted codes" you considered in answer to question 8. Analyze them, looking for shared and unique linguistic features.
10. It is often claimed that foreigner talk aids comprehension. Design a study that would test this hypothesis.

7

Foreigner Talk in Content Classrooms

Linda A. Schinke-Llano

Since Ferguson's (1975) article, the corpus of information on the phenomenon of foreigner talk (FT) has increased steadily. More than thirty studies have contributed to our knowledge of the phonological, morphological, syntactic, and discourse characteristics of foreigner talk.[1] Of those studies, eleven are classroom-based (Chaudron, 1978, 1979; Gaies, 1977; Hatch et al., 1975; Henzl, 1974, 1975, 1979; Long and Sato, 1981, and Chapter 12, this volume; Steyaert, 1977; Trager, 1978; and Urzúa, 1980). With the exception of the Urzúa study, all the classroom studies are based in ESL or foreign language classrooms, and all involve adult–adult communication. Thus, a major portion of second language learners, namely those in kindergarten through high school (K–12) settings, has yet to be considered in the FT literature.

Conservative estimates place the number of students in the U.S.A. of limited-English proficiency (LEP) at 3.6 million (Carnegie, 1979). These are students whose home language is one other than English and who have not yet developed the English language skills necessary to function at capacity in the all-English curriculum. Depending upon the district in which they are enrolled, LEP students receive a variety of programmatic treatments. Where numbers warrant and fiscal concerns allow, many students are enrolled in bilingual education programs. For a portion of the day in such programs, students receive instruction in ESL, in native language arts and culture, and in one or more content areas taught in the native language. In districts where bilingual education programs are not available, LEP students often receive either formal classroom instruction or informal tutorial assistance in ESL. Finally, many

LEP students have no special assistance whatsoever. Whatever the programmatic treatment (or lack thereof), all LEP students spend at least a portion of their school day in the all-English classroom.

If the nature of second language acquisition is ever to be understood completely, an examination of all second language environments in which the learner finds himself or herself is essential. For example, for the K–12 students in question, analyses are needed of the linguistic environment experienced in the community (Heath, 1980), the ESL classroom, and the all-English classrooms. Further, for the phenomenon of foreigner talk to be fully characterized, analyses of its use in a variety of functional contexts are needed—from casual conversation to formal ESL instruction to instruction in content classes.

To help achieve these goals, a study was designed which would characterize the linguistic enviroment experienced by LEP students in all-English content classes and which would, in turn, identify features of foreigner talk discourse peculiar to an instructional context. One portion of the study—that devoted to classroom observations—is reported here.

Method

The study was conducted over a six-week period at the end of the academic year in the public school system of a large industrial town in the Chicago area. The school system is highly integrated, both linguistically and racially. Subjects were twelve monolingual English-speaking classroom teachers situated in four schools. Four were fifth-grade teachers; four were sixth-grade teachers; and four taught fifth- and sixth-grade combination classes. All had classroom populations consisting of native speakers of English, non-native speakers fluent in their second language, and limited English-proficient (LEP) students. Instead of identifying the students as NNS (non-native speakers) as is done in much of the literature, the designation LEP is used throughout the study for two reasons. First, the term NNS can be misleading since a student's being a non-native speaker of English does not preclude his or her being fluent in the language and thus able to participate in classroom activities like a native speaker. Second, LEP was the designation used by the federal and state governments at the time of the observations, and the designation which served as the basis for programmatic treatment in the district.

All LEP students in the classrooms observed were Spanish-speaking; all participated in the district's bilingual program. Thus, the LEP students spent a portion of every morning and afternoon in the bilingual classroom; they returned to their home classroom for the remainder of the time. Although there was some variation among classrooms as to precisely what time the students returned from the bilingual classroom and as to which content area lesson they returned to, the pattern was consistent. According to the bilingual program director and to the four bilingual teachers (one per school at the fifth- and sixth-grade level), LEP students were to be as fully integrated as possible into the home classroom activities when present.

Those students following this programmatic pattern fell into the first three of six levels of language fluency as defined by the state "Rules and Regulations for Transitional Bilingual Education" (1976, pp. 3–4):

I. The student does not speak, understand, or write English, but may know a few isolated words or expressions.

II. The student understands simple sentences in English, especially if spoken slowly, but does not speak English, except isolated words or expressions.

III. The student speaks and understands English with hesitancy and difficulty. With effort and help, the student can carry on a conversation in English, understand at least parts of lessons, and follow simple directions.

IV. The student speaks and understands English without apparent difficulty but displays low achievement indicating some language or cultural interference with learning.

V. The student speaks and understands both English and the home language without difficulty and displays normal academic achievement for grade level.

VI. The student (of non-English background) either predominantly or exclusively speaks English.

Assessment of students according to these levels is completed during the annual state bilingual census conducted in March. These data then serve as the foundation for the following year's program. Thus, the LEP students observed in this study had actually been categorized over one year before. Exceptions, of course, were those students who had entered the system after completion of the census.[2]

Data collection

With respect to data collection, the twelve teachers were informed that observations concerning classroom language would be conducted. While the precise nature of the observations was not known, the teachers were aware that observations could not be made unless the LEP students were present. The teachers were audio-taped for approximately one hour each as they conducted a content lesson. Content lessons taped included science, mathematics, and social studies: in essence, any academic area in which English was the medium of instruction, not the target. Because of the length of lessons at this grade level and the schedules of the LEP students, it took two and, in a few cases, three visits to complete one hour of taping. In addition to the audio-tapes, field notes were kept of any comments made by the teachers outside of the lesson regarding the LEP students. The audio-tapes were then transcribed in preparation for coding and analysis.

Coding

Coding of the data focused on interactions between teachers and students. For the purposes of this study, an interaction consists of the turns taken by speakers on the same topic. This concept is similar to Sinclair and Coulthard's (1975) level of discourse called exchange: i.e., a structure in which more than one person contributes. A common classroom interaction sequence is composed of the teacher's initiation, a student's response, and the teacher's feedback. An example follows:

T: And where do we go during a tornado drill?
S: Basement.
T: All right. We go to the basement.

Occasionally, a portion of the interaction is non-verbal:

T: Now point to the southern hemisphere.
S: (Points to southern hemisphere on map.)
T: All right.

In addition, interactions vary in length from the brief ones just cited to much lengthier ones:

S: (Raises hand.)
T: Yes, ma'am.
S: Is that a topo ... whatever?
T: That's a top ... that's a topography map or topographical map. Right.
S: Because it has the mountains showing?
T: Because it shows what that earth is like in that area.
S: How 'bout that one?
T: That one over there is political, isn't it?

Once identified, all interactions were categorized as directed or non-directed. Directed interactions are those characterized by the teacher's turn-taking with a single student. The examples given in the previous paragraph are all directed interactions. Non-directed interactions, on the other hand, are those characterized by the involvement of many students or the entire class. The following are illustrations of non-directed interactions:

T: It begins with F.
Several: Fossil.
T: That's the first vocabulary word, so write it down. Galaxy.
Class: (Writes vocabulary word.)

In addition to interactions being designated as directed or non-directed, they were also coded according to their function. Four functional categories were used: instructional (I), managerial (M), disciplinary (D), and miscellaneous (X). Instructional interactions serve to request or convey information directly related to the content of the lesson. With respect to grammatical structures, the initiation of an instructional interaction sequence is usually signalled by an interrogative (generally a WH-question) such as the following:

What happens when a cold front moves into an area?

Why does the air move up?

How's the cold air come down?

In addition, affirmative commands may signal the initiation of an instructional interaction. For example:

Name the parts of the tooth.

Describe a sedimentary rock.

Give an example of an igneous rock.

Responses in instructional interactions are generally declaratives ranging from complete sentences to one or several word utterances:

It's reflected sound.

Acoustics.

Half the earth.

Managerial interactions, on the other hand, serve to convey information concerning procedures. They may be regarded as either relating to the lesson being conducted (ML) or to the classroom situation as a whole (MC). While both types of managerial interactions are usually initiated by affirmative imperatives, other structures appear as well. Examples of utterances which initiate ML interactions are these:

Continue reading.

You're gonna match the words with the definitions.

What page are we on?

Samples of utterances which initiate MC interactions are these:

Close the door.

Go get anything that's in my mailbox.

These go on my desk.

Disciplinary interactions, as the name indicates, serve to reprimand the addressee for his or her behavior. While instructional and lesson-related managerial interactions are initiated by both teachers and students, disciplinary and class-related managerial interactions are virtually always teacher-initiated. Although any grammatical structure can signal the initiation of a disciplinary interaction, affirmative and negative imperatives are most often employed:

Be quiet! And I flippin' well mean be quiet!

Don't do that!

You have to go the office and show Mr. (principal's name) what you've done today.

The final category, a miscellaneous one, comprises interactions not classifiable as instructional, managerial, or disciplinary. Relatively infrequent (1.5%), such interactions are primarily asides or digressions. Quite often they are characterized by humor which may be peculiar to the class:

T: Look at this. There is a mad (student's name) jar on the next page. It's got a wide mouth.

Class: (Laughter.)

    S: What's that? (referring to microphone on teacher's lapel)

    T: Me and Frank Sinatra we use small microphones so we can sing.

Analysis

Once coding of the data with respect to direction (directed or non-directed) and function (instructional, managerial, disciplinary, or miscellaneous) was completed, a three-stage analysis was done. First, the number of directed interactions for each teacher and for the total group was tabulated, including a breakdown of the number of interactions with each student. No distinction was made between teacher- and student-initiated interactions since, in either case, it is the teacher who determines if the interaction will take place. Histograms were used to illustrate the frequency distributions; means were computed for each teacher to determine the existence of a quantitative difference between interactions directed to LEP students and to non-LEP students. Finally, the Mann-Whitney U Test was employed to determine the significance of any variation in treatment. Throughout the study, $\alpha \leq .01$ was used.

For stage two, the analysis focused on the functional type of interaction. Again, tabulations were done for each teacher and for the group of twelve. Of the interactions directed to LEP students, what percentage are instructional, managerial (both ML and MC), disciplinary, and miscellaneous? What is the functional mix of those directed to non-LEP students? The χ^2 test was used to determine the significance of any differences observed.

In stage three, the length of interaction was considered. Are interactions addressed to LEP students brief (consisting of an initiation, response, and optional feedback) or extended (consisting of two or more turns for each speaker)? What length characterizes interactions with non-LEP students? Again, χ^2 analysis was used to ascertain the significance of differences demonstrated.

In summary, the purpose of the portion of the study reported here is to ascertain the quantity and quality of interactions addressed to LEP students in comparison with those addressed to non-LEP students in a content classroom setting. Such an analysis helps characterize the linguistic environment encountered by LEP students in the classroom, as well as the nature of foreigner talk in an instructional setting.

Results

Stage one

The first stage of data analysis pertains to the number of interactions directed to LEP and non-LEP students. Table 1 summarizes the data collected in the twelve classrooms. Fractional numbers in the student column resulted from a fluctuation in attendance: i.e., all students were not present for all taping sessions. A more detailed table (Table A) is included in the Appendix.

Table 1.   Directed Interactions

Number of students			Number of directed interactions			$\overline{X}$ (number of directed interactions per student)		
non-LEP	LEP	Total	non-LEP	LEP	Total	non-LEP	LEP	Total
267.25	22.75	290	1218	56	1274	4.6	2.5	4.4

Thus, each non-LEP student was interacted with an average of 4.6 times per hour. Each LEP student, on the other hand, was interacted with only 2.5 times per hour—slightly over half as much. Looking at the data another way, the non-LEP students, who represent 92.2% of the total number, participated in 95.6% of the interactions. In other words, the LEP students, who count for 7.8% of the population, had only 4.4% of the interactions.

This discrepancy is even more pronounced when the distribution pattern of interactions is examined. Table 2 presents the frequency of interactions in four groupings: zero, 1–3, 4–6, and 7 or more. Numbers given are percentages.

Table 2.   Frequency of Directed Interactions (in percentages)

Number of interactions	non-LEP	LEP
0	14.0	45.0
1–3	41.3	28.6
4–6	24.0	17.6
7+	20.7	8.8

Thus, while 45% of the LEP students are not interacted with at all, only 14% of the non-LEP students fall into this category. Conversely, although only 8.8% of the LEP students participate in 7 or more interactions per hour, 20.7% of the non-LEP students do. In addition, in each of the other categories (1–3 and 4–6 interactions per hour), non-LEP students are consistently involved in more interactions than their LEP counterparts.

When all 290 students are ranked according to the number of interactions observed, and the Mann-Whitney U Test is applied to the rankings, $p = .005$ (two-tailed) obtains. With $\alpha \leq .01$, the results are significant. That is, teachers in the study interact significantly less often with LEP students in their classes than they do with non-LEP students.

As often occurs when summary data are discussed, important individual differences are lost. One such example is the large variation among teachers with respect to the total number of directed interactions. (See Appendix, Table A, column 7.) Two main factors contribute to this variation: teaching style and lesson type. With respect to style, many teachers utilize a method dominated by teacher-talk; others exhibit more of a balance between teacher- and student-talk. In addition, certain teachers exert rigid control over which students will be called upon to speak; other utilize a more free-wheeling approach by addressing questions to the class as a whole and encouraging answers to be shouted out. The latter approach often results in a large number of total interactions, but a relatively small number of directed interactions. The type of lesson also affects the number of interactions. For example, a lesson in which material is being presented for the first time yields relatively few interactions. A review lesson, on the other hand, results in a high number of interactions.

Another example is the variation within each class regarding the number of times each student is interacted with. Generally speaking, many students are rarely interacted with, while a few students are interacted with frequently. These fluctuations corroborate the findings of Jackson and Lahaderne (1967) in their study of sixth-grade classes.

Curiously, if a χ^2 one-sample test is used to analyze the results for each teacher, only two teachers (T7 and T8) demonstrate significantly different treatment of the two groups of students ($p < .001$). Of the five teachers (T1, 2, 5, 6, 12) who exhibit a moderately different treatment of the two groups, one (T2) actually favors the LEP group. Finally, five teachers (T3, 4, 9, 10, 11) appear to demonstrate virtually no difference in their treatment of the two groups. These individual variations which contradict the findings for the group ($p = .005$) will be examined in the discussion section below.

Stage two

The second stage of analysis concerning the functional types of interactions yields further evidence of differential treatment of the two groups of students. Recall that the functional types of interactions are instructional (I), managerial —lesson related (ML), managerial—class related (MC), disciplinary (D), and miscellaneous (X). Table 3 summarizes the functional types of interactions for the group of twelve teachers. Numbers shown are percentages.

Table 3.   Functional Types of
Directed Interactions
(in percentages)

Type of interaction	Non-LEP	LEP
I	64.9	39.1
ML	23.5	44.0
MC	4.2	16.9
D	5.9	
X	1.5	

Thus, 64.9% of the directed interactions with non-LEP students are instructional, while only 39.1% of interactions with LEP students fall into this category. On the other hand, MC interactions represent only 4.2% of the interactions with non-LEP students, but 16.9% of those with LEP students. In short, slightly less than two-thirds of the interactions with non-LEP students are instructional; nearly two-thirds of the interactions with LEP students are managerial (both ML and MC).

χ^2 analysis of these figures yields p < .001. Thus, in both the first and second stages of analysis, evidence exists at a highly significant level that teachers as a group treat LEP students differently from non-LEP students in both quantity and quality of interactions.

Also similar to the first stage of analysis, the figures summarizing the group's behavior in the second stage mask interesting individual differences among the teachers. Table B in the Appendix presents the functional types of interactions by the teacher. As indicated by Table B, five teachers employed all functional types with non-LEP students, including the miscellaneous category; six employed four types; and one employed three types. With non-LEP students, however, a different distributional pattern is evident. Only one teacher utilized three functional types of interactions; four utilized two types; four employed only one; and three had no interaction whatsoever. Obviously, the range of interaction is diminished when LEP students are addressed. Interestingly, no teacher had disciplinary or miscellaneous interactions with any LEP student.

The χ^2 test was again used to analyze the figures for each teacher. Due to the large number of cells with zero frequency, a 2x2 contingency table was used which differentiated I interactions from ML, MC, D, and X. Of the nine teachers who addressed both groups of students, six (T1, 2, 6, 9, 10, 12) evidenced differential treatment with respect to functional type of interaction at a highly significant level (p < .001). Interestingly, the three teachers (T3, 4, 11) who did not treat LEP students significantly different with respect to functional type of interaction belong to the group that showed no significant difference in total number of directed interactions. Thus, there appears to be a positive relationship between the quantity and quality of interactions with LEP students. That is, as total class participation increases, so does the range of functional types of interaction.

Stage three

The final stage of analysis, examination of the length of interactions, results in additional support for the evidence of differential treatment of LEP and non-LEP students. Table 4 summarizes I, ML, and MC interactions according to their length. Recall that brief interactions generally consist of initiation, response, and optional feedback; extended ones have two or more turns per speaker. D and X interactions are not listed since they were not used with LEP students. Numbers given are percentages. Table C, which presents the detailed breakdown by teacher, is found in the Appendix.

Beginning with MC interactions, there appears to be an important difference in length of interactions between the two groups. However, this variation is due solely to T6's having one extended MC interaction with an LEP student. (See

Table 4.   Length of Directed Interactions
(in percentages)

Type of interaction	Length of interaction	non-LEP	LEP
I	brief	65.7	78.3
	extended	34.3	21.7
ML	brief	88.3	94.5
	extended	11.7	5.5
MC	brief	100.0	83.3
	extended		16.7

Table C in the Appendix.) Thus, two points can be made, First, it is the nature of the MC interaction to be brief. Second, if MC interactions are used with LEP students, they are of the same length as those used with non-LEP students.

The picture changes slightly with ML interactions. Like MC interactions, they are generally brief in nature. However, if extended interactions are used, they are used twice as often with non-LEP students. The single exception to this statement is T4 whose interaction lengths occur in nearly the same proportion for LEP as for non-LEP students. It was found earlier that T4 belongs to the group that does not treat LEP students differently either in total interactions or in functional type of interaction.

Since more variation occurs for ML interactions, and since frequencies are larger in each cell, a χ^2 two-sample test is appropriate here. Calculations yield $p < .10$. With $\alpha \leq .01$, the result is not significant; however, it is indicative of a trend toward differential treatment of LEP students in ML interactions.

Finally, the length of I interactions shows the strongest evidence of a difference in treatment between the two groups. Although the majority are brief, I interactions have the largest proportion of extended interactions of the three functional types examined. This trend is evident with both groups of students: for non-LEP, 34.3% of I interactions are extended; for LEP, 21.7%. Using a χ^2 test, $p < .05$ obtains. Again, with $\alpha \leq .01$, the result is not significant; yet, the trend toward differential treatment is intensifying. Recall that for MC interactions, no difference in treatment is evident; for ML interactions, $p < .10$ obtains; and for I interactions, $p < .05$ results. Thus, it appears that with respect to interaction length, the more complex the functional type, or rather the more important the functional type to the content of the lesson, the larger the difference in treatment between LEP students and non-LEP students.

In summary, the results of the portion of the study reported here show strong evidence that the teachers observed interact differently with the LEP students in their classes than they do with non-LEP students. First, in terms of total directed interactions, the result for the entire group is significant ($p = .005$), Next, regarding functional types of interactions, the result is again significant ($p < .001$). Finally, in terms of interaction length, although significance does not obtain for any of the functional types, we observe a trend of increasingly differential treatment from MC interactions to I interactions; that is, from the least crucial in the learning process to the most. A discussion of these results follows.

Discussion

While persuasive evidence exists that the LEP students observed are interacted with differently from their non-LEP counterparts, one cannot automatically assume that this occurs by virtue of their being limited-English proficient. That is, perhaps we are not witnessing the phenomenon of foreigner talk. A discussion of possible explanations of the results is advisable.

Before examining these alternative explanations, however, a closer look at those teachers who evidenced little differential treatment with regard to total interactions is important. Recall that the results reported for several teachers in stage one countered the results for the group. Table A in the Appendix shows that the mean number of interactions with LEP students for T9 and T11 is only slightly below the mean for non-LEP students. Further, four teachers (T2, 3, 4, 10) actually show means for LEP students above those for non-LEP. While individual differences among teachers indeed exist, the relatively large group that does not typify the trend is suspect.

One possible explanation is the impact of the researcher on the observational setting. For example, on both taping days, T10 called upon an LEP student to read first; T11 called on an LEP student to go to the board first to work a math problem. One doubts whether these are normal operating procedures. Further, T9 and T10 indicated that they spent a free period one day trying to determine what the researcher was observing. Although both claimed their classroom behavior was no different than usual, this discussion would suggest possible effects from the obtrusive observation procedure. Even T4, whose data show perhaps the most "democratic" interactions, may not have been behaving as usual. For example, when one LEP student was called upon to read, the other students reacted with surprise. The teacher had to quiet them down before the LEP student could read.

In the case of T3, the high mean is undoubtedly due, not to the presence of the researcher, but to the personality of one of the LEP students. Of five LEP students in the class, only one was interacted with; that particular student initiated interaction with the teacher eight of eleven times, a singular occurrence among all the LEP students observed.

Once the data from these teachers are put in perspective, one can turn to a discussion of the possible causes of differential treatment. With respect to total number of directed interactions, six conceivable explanations exist. First is the question of cultural bias. Teachers may not be interacting with LEP students because they are Mexican, Puerto Rican, or Spanish-speaking in general. This possibility is easily rejected, however, since all teachers interact with racial, ethnic, and linguistic minorities in their classes who speak fluent English.

Second, differences in treatment may exist because of a lack of volunteering on the part of LEP students. It was seen with T3 how an LEP student's initiation of interaction influenced the total interaction pattern. However, this premise can be rejected as well. In all the classes, non-LEP students who do not volunteer are frequently called upon. Further, in one instance an LEP student who did volunteer was totally ignored, despite the fact that the teacher (T12) was looking for someone to read who had not previously read.

A third possibility accounting for differential treatment may be an attitude on the part of the teachers that LEP students are not their "responsibility" since they participate in the bilingual program. While bilingual teachers indicate that LEP students are expected to participate in their home classrooms, certain exchanges and occurrences give credence to the notion that LEP students are not considered as regular participants. When T1, for instance, called on an LEP student to answer a question, the student was startled even though he was attending to the lesson. T10 requested a student to read by saying, "LEP1, can you read for us?"; the question was posed with an intonation expressing doubt. In T7's class where there were insufficient textbooks, the two LEP students were given texts only after the fast readers finished. And in T12's class, the following exchange (or lack of) took place with an LEP student who had been in the school six weeks:

    T: (To LEP2) Do you have a book?
LEP2: (No response.)
 S26: She doesn't understand English.
    T: (To S26) She doesn't read any English?
 S26: (Shakes head no.)

If, in reality, the issue of responsibility is an explanation, then it appears there are non-LEP students who are not the teacher's responsibility either. Especially in classes where no interaction with LEP students occurred, there were non-LEP students who were not interacted with as well.

A fourth explanation is related to the seating pattern of LEP students in the classrooms. If the room is thought of as being roughly divided into thirds (front, middle, and back—with front being closest to the teacher), the distribution shown in Table 5 is found.

Table 5.   Seating Position of
LEP Students

Front	Middle	Back	
T2	T5	T1	T9
T4	T8	T3	T11
	T10	T6	T12
		T7	

The rationale of the majority of teachers for seating the LEP students at the back of the room is understandable, if not acceptable. Since these students are in the classrooms only a portion of the day, seats closer to the teacher are given to those students present the entire day. Interestingly, those teachers (T2, T4) who seat the students in front also interact with them both quantitatively and qualitatively. Of the seven who seat LEP students in the rear of the class, four interact minimally; the remaining three belong to the group possibly influenced by the researcher's presence or affected by the presence of an extraordinarily outgoing student. While the correlation is not perfect, there does appear to be a relationship between seating position and degree of interaction. However, it is too simple to say that those in front get called on, and those in back do not. The seating pattern, instead, most likely reflects the teacher's perception of the LEP student's ability to participate in the class.

The fifth explanation is that teachers avoid interacting with LEP students for fear of embarrassing them. This reasoning, of course, assumes an inability on the part of the student to respond well or at all. Related to this is the final explanation. Teachers may not interact with LEP students because they do not want to take the time necessary for the interaction. This reasoning, again, assumes an inability of the LEP student to respond efficiently or effectively.

The attitude that LEP students are incapable of participating in class does appear to be operative among the teachers observed. Prior to their taping sessions, teachers 5, 6, 7, 8, and 12 all volunteered the information that their LEP students "do not participate." T3 said the same thing about all LEP students except the one who continually seeks assistance. Those assessments of LEP students are borne out, for there is little if any interaction with LEP students in those classrooms. Thus, perceptions about a student's abilities in a second language affect the quantity of interactions with that student.

The quality of interactions is also affected, as shown in the second and third stages of analysis. For example, one can surmise that relatively fewer instructional interactions occur with LEP students because teachers assume they cannot process the information. Further, when instructional interactions do take place with LEP students, they are briefer than those with non-LEP students. Again, an assumption of the student's inability to continue the interaction is underlying.

Thus, despite the alternative explanations to the contrary, it is apparent that the teachers exhibit differential treatment of the LEP students by virtue of their perceived inability to function in the content classroom. Adjustments in speech in such situations are clearly indicative of foreigner talk.

Conclusions

Several important findings have resulted from the portion of the study reported here. First, with respect to the total number of directed interactions, teachers treat LEP students and non-LEP students significantly differently ($p = .005$). Next, the difference in treatment of the two groups regarding functional types of interaction is also significant ($p < .001$). Finally, although the difference in length of interactions is not significant, an interesting trend appears. That is, the more crucial the functional type of interaction to the teaching process, the more differential the treatment of the two groups with respect to interaction length. Thus, LEP students in content classes are interacted with less frequently than their non-LEP counterparts. When they are interacted with, the interaction is generally managerial in nature, rather than instructional. And even when the same functional type of interaction occurs, it is briefer.

In short, it has been found that the linguistic environment for LEP students in all-English content classes is different from that for non-LEP students. Further, as a result of this study, several characteristics of foreigner talk specific to an instructional setting have been added to those already documented. While previous findings of phonological, morphological, and syntactic features of foreigner talk are indeed important, the characteristics examined here—frequency, type, and length of interaction—more appropriately define the instructional environment in which the K–12 LEP student finds himself.

Implications

When discussing results of studies, the question of generalizability is always foremost. Certainly, twelve subjects is not a large number; yet, the significance levels obtained indicate occurrences far removed from chance. It is likely, then, that the results are generalizable to all such middle-grade classrooms. One would caution, however, generalizing the results either to lower elementary or to junior or senior high content classes. Yet, if anecdotal evidence is admissible, it is the opinion of the researcher, based on six years of K–12 classroom observations, that the interaction patterns observed in this study are indeed typical.

If the typicality of these interaction patterns is accepted, the consequences are overwhelming. If LEP students are interacted with half as much in twelve hours as their non-LEP counterparts, if only a third of those interactions are instructional, and if all interactions are briefer, then the cumulative effect of this pattern over a month's or year's time is staggering. What, then, are the possible consequences of such differential treatment?

First is the question of self-esteem. While an LEP student's global self-esteem may not be directly affected by this reduced interaction during a portion of his or her school day, it is certainly conceivable that the student's situational self-esteem would be. Since it is widely held that self-esteem positively correlates with success in school, such differential treatment of LEP students should be of concern to educators.

Self-esteem aside, this interactional pattern has implications for the LEP student's second language acquisition and for his or her mastery of content subjects as well. While no studies to date prove that communication in a second language speeds its acquisition, it is strongly suggested that verbal interaction is as necessary for second language acquisition as it is for first (Long, 1980). Further, if a student is consistently left out of classroom instructional activities, it would not be surprising for him to lose interest and, consequently, to fall behind in his or her acquisition of content-area information. While one could never claim an absolute correlation, certainly the LEP students' exclusion from classroom activities cannot be beneficial, either for language acquisition or acquisition of content skills.

Finally, one important issue has not yet been discussed. It has already been stated that foreigner talk results because of perceptions on the part of the speaker that the interlocutor cannot function adequately in his second language. Yet, a crucial question, especially in the context of a school setting, is whether or not these perceptions are accurate. While the portion of the study reported here sheds no light on this question, a subsequent portion carried out with the same teachers and students strongly suggests that the perceptions operating are indeed mistaken. In a general conversational context, such misperceptions would not be serious. In an instructional situation, however, they may have consequences of the seriousness discussed in the preceding paragraphs.

In conclusion, that foreigner talk exists has been shown repeatedly in the past few years. That is has additional characteristics specific to an instructional context has been demonstrated here. As a result of these characteristics, LEP students in content classes experience a difference linguistic environment than their non-LEP counterparts. Such differential treatment may have consequences for self-esteem, second language acquisition, and mastery of content subjects. What remains is to determine precisely the nature of those consequences and, equally important, to determine if the perceptions upon which the differential treatment is based are accurate.

Table A. Directed Interactions

Teacher	Number of students non-LEP	Number of students LEP	Number of students Total	Directed interaction non-LEP	Directed interaction LEP	Directed interaction Total	$\overline{X}$ non-LEP	$\overline{X}$ LEP	$\overline{X}$ Total
T1	22.75	3.25	26.0	56	4	60	2.5	1.2	2.3
T2[1]	22.5	2.0	24.5	95 (71)	15 (11)	110 (82)	4.2 (3.2)	7.5 (5.5)	4.5 (3.3)
T3	17.5	2.5	20.0	68	11	79	3.9	4.4	4.0
T4	26.0	2.0	28.0	144	13	157	5.5	6.5	5.6
T5	24.5	1.0	25.5	154	0	154	6.3	0	6.0
T6	28.0	2.0	30.0	92	2	94	3.3	1.0	3.1
T7	18.0	2.0	20.0	158	0	158	8.8	0	7.9
T8[1]	19.0	2.5	21.5	143 (107)		143 (107)	7.5 (5.6)		6.6 (5.0)
T9	27.0	1.0	28.0	78	2	80	2.9	2.0	2.9
T10	21.0	1.0	22.0	68	4	72	3.2	4.0	3.3
T11	20.5	2.0	22.5	54	4	58	2.6	2.0	2.6
T12	20.5	1.5	22.0	108	1	109	5.3	.7	5.0
Totals	267.25	22.75	290	1218 (1158)	56 (52)	1274 (1210)	4.6	2.5	4.4

[1]These teachers were observed for 45 minutes. Extrapolations for a one-hour period were made from the observed frequencies given in parentheses.

Table B. Functional Types of Directed Interactions (in percentages)

Teacher	Student	Function I	ML	MC	D	X	Totals
T1	non-LEP	85.7	5.4		7.1	1.8	100.0
	LEP	50.0	50.0				100.0
T2	non-LEP	76.0	14.2	1.4	4.2	4.2	100.0
	LEP	18.2	54.5	27.3			100.0
T3	non-LEP	66.2	25.0	5.9	2.9		100.0
	LEP	54.5	45.5				100.0
T4	non-LEP	63.2	27.0	3.5	5.6	.7	100.0
	LEP	53.8	46.2				100.0
T5	non-LEP	77.3	18.2	1.3	3.2		100.0
	LEP						
T6	non-LEP	50.5	25.0	13.7	6.5	4.3	100.0
	LEP			100.0			100.0
T7	non-LEP	69.0	20.2	1.9	8.9		100.0
	LEP						
T8	non-LEP	83.2	70.5	.9	5.6	2.8	100.0
	LEP						
T9	non-LEP	71.8	21.7	1.3	2.6	2.6	100.0
	LEP	100.0					100.0
T10	non-LEP	44.1	35.3	1.5	19.1		100.0
	LEP		100.0				100.0
T11	non-LEP	83.2	5.6	5.6	5.6		100.0
	LEP	75.0		25.0			100.0
T12	non-LEP	43.5	51.9	4.6			100.0
	LEP		100.0				100.0

**Table C.   Length of Directed Interactions
(in percentages)**

Interaction	Teacher	Student	Brief	Extended
MC	T2	non-LEP	100	
		LEP	100	
	T6	non-LEP	100	
		LEP	50	50
	T11	non-LEP	100	
		LEP	100	
ML	T1	non-LEP	100	
		LEP	100	
	T2	non-LEP	90	10
		LEP	100	
	T3	non-LEP	88	12
		LEP	100	
	T4	non-LEP	70	30
		LEP	67	33
	T10	non-LEP	82	18
		LEP	100	
	T12	non-LEP	100	
		LEP	100	
I	T1	non-LEP	58	42
		LEP	100	
	T2	non-LEP	83	17
		LEP	100	
	T3	non-LEP	52	48
		LEP	67	33
	T4	non-LEP	75	25
		LEP	86	14
	T9	non-LEP	46	54
		LEP	50	50
	T11	non-LEP	80	20
		LEP	67	33

Notes

1. See Long (1980) for a review of findings.
2. It should be noted that the procedure for the identification of LEP students in Illinois changed with the 1980 census. Language fluency levels are no longer being used.

References

Carnegie Corporation of New York. *Bilingual education and the Hispanic Challenge.* In annual report, 1979.

Chaudron, C. English as the medium of instruction in ESL classes: An initial report of a pilot study of the complexity of teachers' speech. Ms. University of Toronto; Modern Language Center, OISE, 1978.

Chaudron, C. Complexity of teacher speech and vocabulary explanation and elaboration. Paper presented at the TESOL Conference, Boston, March, 1979.

Ferguson, C. Towards a characterization of English foreigner talk. *Anthropological Linguistics,* 1975, *17,* 1, 1–14.

Gaies, S. The nature of linguistic input in formal second language learning: Linguistic and communicative strategies in teachers' classroom language. In H. D. Brown, C. A. Yorio, & R. H. Crymes (Eds.), *On TESOL '77. Teaching and Learning English as a Second Language: Trends in Research and Practice.* Washington, D.C.: TESOL, 1977.

Hatch, E., Shapira, R., & Gough, J. Foreigner talk discourse. Paper presented at the Second Language Acquisition Forum, UCLA, 1975. in *ITL: Review of Applied Linguistics,* 1978, 39–60.

Heath, S. B. Ethnographic research. Paper presented at the TESOL Conference, San Francisco, March, 1980.

Henzl, V. M. Linguistic register of foreign language instruction. *Language Learning,* 1974, *23,* 2, 207–222.

Henzl, V. M. Speech of foreign language teachers: A sociolinguistic register analysis. Paper presented at the 4th International AILA Conference, Stuttgart, August, 1975.

Henzl, V. M. Foreigner talk in the classroom. *International Review of Applied Linguistics,* 1979, *17,* 2, 159–167.

Jackson, P. W., & Lahaderne, N. M. Inequalities of teacher-pupil contacts. *Psychology in the Schools,* 1967, *4,* 204–211.

Long, M. H. Input, interaction, and second language acquisition. Ph.D. dissertation, UCLA, 1980.

Long, M. H. & Sato, C. J. Classroom foreigner talk discourse: forms and functions of teachers' questions. Paper presented at TESOL Conference, Detroit, March, 1981. Also Chapter 12, this volume.

Sinclair, J. McH., & Coulthard, R. M. *Towards an Analysis of Discourse: The English Used by Teachers and Pupils.* Oxford: Oxford University Press, 1975.

State Board of Education. Rules and regulations for transitional bilingual education. Springfield, Ill., 1976.

Steyaert, M. A comparison of the speech of ESL teachers to native and non-native speakers of English. Paper presented at the winter meeting, Linguistic Society of America, Chicago, 1977.

Trager, S. The language of teaching: Discourse analysis in beginning, intermediate, and advanced ESL students. Master's thesis, University of Southern California, 1978.

Urzúa, C. Language input to young second language learners. Paper presented at the Second Language Acquisition Forum, UCLA, March, 1980.

Questions for Discussion and Activities

1. If you were the adviser to a school district faced with an influx of non-English-speaking children, would you recommend that they be mainstreamed at once, given an initial diet of ESL, or provided with a combination of language and content instruction? What empirical research do you know of to support any of these options, or any alternative you propose?

2. Would your recommendation change in light of the results of Schinke-Llano's investigation? If so, how? If not, why not?

3. Schinke-Llano identifies some potential causes of the variability at the level of individual teachers in her study. Evaluate these, and suggest additional causes. How could these explanations be tested?

4. Schinke-Llano outlines several examples of what has often been referred to in educational research as the "self-fulfilling prophesy." What are these examples? What analogous processes do you expect occur in second language classrooms, given the examples in this study and your own experience as a teacher or learner in such classes?

5. Schinke-Llano's units of analysis involve interactions of different lengths, types, and functions. Why should these units be important for predicting the success of LEP children in educational settings? Do you think the same units would be relevant in second language classrooms?

6. What evidence are you aware of from research on child language acquisition which would predict the importance of the length and type of exchange between child and caretaker in facilitating language development?

7. How likely is it that the LEP children's second language acquisition could benefit from input from teachers designed primarily for their native speaker classmates? What would the minimum requirements be in terms of the LEP children's participation in the classroom conversation before the teacher's speech would be likely to be useful in this way? (Some suggestions can be found in Long, 1981, and in Long and Sato, Chapter 12, this volume.)

8. Tape-record a content class, e.g., at your university, which includes non-native speakers among its students. What evidence can you find of (lack of) speech adjustments by the teacher for the (supposed) benefit of those students?

9. Schinke-Llano reports that LEP students rarely initiated interactions and when they did they were often ignored. How can you explain this pattern? What is the relationship of the LEP problem to the discussion by Seliger (Chapter 11, this volume) about the importance of learner interaction and the High Input Generator?

PART IV
Teacher and Learner Feedback

8

Teacher-Student Interaction in Bilingual Classrooms: Four Approaches to Error Feedback

Nancy Johnson Nystrom

Errors and Language Learning: The View from Here

Research to date offers no coherent rationale for adopting a particular methodology in teaching young English as a second language (ESL) students in bilingual programs. Teachers confronted with children whose second language competence represents a wide range of language skill have in the past relied heavily on methods gleaned from research on foreign language learning among adults. Yet, considering the results of morpheme and strategy acquisition research (Dulay and Burt, 1974a, b, c; Ervin-Tripp, 1974; Wong-Fillmore, 1976), there is good reason to believe that children learn a second language in a manner that is similar more to the process by which they acquire their native language than it is to that by which adults learn a foreign tongue. This implies that ESL teachers in bilingual programs should enlist methods of providing opportunities for language input and production that simulate the first language acquisition environment. Additionally, it suggests that teachers should encourage linguistic hypothesis-testing among their students, allowing them to take risks in their approximations of the target language.

If teaching practices are to respond to the trends in second language acquisition research and eventually to address the specific needs of children in bilingual programs, the language learning process must first be described in the most comprehensive manner possible. This study focuses on a crucial aspect of that process: teacher responses to student errors and the socio-linguistic variables that may influence those responses.

Studies of error correction in second language classrooms have typically considered adolescent or adult learners as the subjects of inquiry. These investigations have identified several characteristics of teachers' priorities in treatment of adult learners' errors. Among the multitude of types of feedback, individual teachers characteristically use various means to respond to learners' errors. Upon hearing an error, a teacher may, for example, rephrase the student's utterance, modeling the correct response, then implement a drill addressing the mistaken form. In almost all cases, teachers model at least part of the desired form when students produce incorrect utterances.

Across types of feedback and types of error, however, there is little consistency in teacher treatment of learner error. Some errors are ignored, while others of a similar type receive significant amounts of attention in the teacher's response. The repertoire of responses to error varies in quantity and kind for particular teachers, but it is possible to identify many teachers who seem to have access to a limited number of alternatives for responding to students' mistakes. In addition to inconsistencies in individual performance, teachers are often ambiguous in their delivery of error responses. They do not always make clear which form was wrong, or even whether the error was one of form or of meaning (Holly and King, 1971; Fanselow, 1977).

From work with teachers of adolescents in immersion programs, Chaudron (1977b) found that most teachers attended to content errors more than linguistic (morpho-syntactic) or phonological errors. In the adult ESL classroom, however, students reported that they prefer explicit correction of their oral errors, and they consider pronunciation and grammar errors as important targets for correction (Cathcart and Olson, 1976).

These results suggest that error correction is a highly variable aspect of student-teacher interaction. Not only does the teacher's response vary with the nature of his or her repertoire of responses, it also seems to vary with the contingencies of each interactional situation: the nature of the learning task, the level of language acquisition of each learner, and other features of the decision-making process a teacher appeals to in correcting a student's mistake.

Several theorists in the field of error feedback (Cohen, 1975; Long, 1977; Chaudron, 1977a) have advanced our understanding of the nature of this process by providing models of teachers' strategies in responding to learners' errors. Yet the fact remains that each interactive situation is quite complex, and teachers typically are unable to sort through the feedback options available to them and arrive at the most appropriate response. Characterizing the similarly complex dynamic occurring when teachers answer children's questions, Mehan (1974) proposes that the negotiation of each situation reflects the process of interpreting and integrating the rules for social interaction. In attempting to describe how teachers and students behave when an error is committed, then, one must consider the socio-linguistic context of the discourse.

To examine the interaction of feedback variables, twenty hours of videotape were collected in four first-grade classrooms in which bilingual students were being instructed in oral language development. During interviews, the teachers themselves identified the errors made by their students from the videotape. Error-response sequences were isolated, transcribed, categorized, and analyzed in an effort to understand the structure of these episodes.

The original research question was a descriptive one: How do teachers influence the language environment by responding to speech errors made by their students? Such a broad question would have been impossible to answer with the available knowledge base. This study was designed to refine the question and to identify significant variables that could account for what was observed.

The specific questions which the collection and organization of the data addressed are the following:

1. Did the teachers in the study regard language learning as mastery of form, as illustrated by their attention to correct language use, or did they care more about communication of meaning? In other words, did they attend less to grammatical errors than to unsuccessful conveying of the messages?
2. Did the language teachers attend to language error more or in different ways than the teachers in regular classes in which limited English proficiency (LEP) children were students; that is, where the target language is the medium, rather than the subject, of instruction?
3. Did the teachers tend to correct solicited student statements more frequently than spontaneous student statements?
4. Did the teachers tend to correct more frequently when other students heard the correction?
5. How might each teacher's individual correction style be characterized, and what attitude toward language teaching and learning does that correction style reflect?

Framework for Analysis

In determining what constituted an error-response episode, Chaudron's (1977a) descriptive model of discourse in corrective treatment of learners' errors provided a point of departure. Chaudron's model includes both the terminology and the assumptions of discourse analysis. Its unit of analysis, rather than being based on an arbitrary time segment, is based on the natural divisions in classroom discourse: the beginnings of a new class of utterances is determined by change in the person speaking, as well as by changes in the function of what is said. Thus, in the following episode, a number of interesting aspects of interaction emerge, which might have been obscured if temporal coding had been selected as the method of documentation:

T: i want you to look at this and tell me ONE THING that's going on in this picture. tell me in a complete sentence. ok, dione?

P: (gasps) /wants to be called on/

T: dione.

P: a pig.

T: (looks out of the corner of her eye/uncertainly/) a pig. can you tell me that in a complete sentence? you need to say more than just, "a pig." you need to see say, "i see a pig," or you need to say, uh, "the pig is doing something."

P2: a goat?

T: ok, tony?

In the first statement made by the teacher, she sets the task. The students are to tell her "ONE THING" (the capitals denote articulatory emphasis) that they see occurring in the picture. They are to state their observation in a complete sentence. She establishes the rules (or continues with previously established rules) for turn-taking in the classroom discourse by calling on the student who gasps for attention.

The student called on violates the complete sentence rule by saying, "a pig." The teacher then focuses her (and the class's) attention on the form of her utterance. Rather than attending to the content of what the child said, commenting on its appropriateness as an observation of what objects or events the picture contains, the teacher gives the student sentences that she would consider acceptable: "I see a pig," or "The pig is doing something." The pupil is not afforded another opportunity to correct her mistake.

Chaudron's model uses the units of discourse structure called "moves" by Sinclair et al. (1975). Each error and response incorporates an opening move, an answering move, and usually a follow-up move, and any number of subsequent cycles of these moves. In the case of the episode just cited, the opening move is accomplished by the teacher, who initiates the interchange by setting the task and calling on Dione. The pupil answers by committing an error of discourse: not using a complete sentence as the teacher required. The teacher's follow-up move includes the following dimensions: correction, including the identification of the source and the location of the error; repetition of the student's utterance in its original form; modeling of the types of utterances she would consider appropriate; prompting of the student ("You need to say more than . . . "); restatement of the instructions ("Can you tell me that in a complete sentence?"); and explicit instructions as to what the student should say ("I see a pig;" "the pig is doing something."). Overlapping this follow-up move is the teacher's initiation of another opening move, contained in her statement, "Can you tell me that in a complete sentence?" The student does not provide an answering move. Thus, the cycle is interrupted, another move is initiated, and the next turn is taken.

Analysis: quantitative results

Situated in the context of discourse analysis, then, the data (errors, responses, and error-response sequences) were subjected to two categories of analysis. Frequency counts gave an overall picture of the nature of error in each teacher's classroom, the types of responding to error, and a deeper look into the teacher's attitude toward correction by further classifying the responses as being overtly corrective, covertly corrective, or non-corrective. Knowledge about the teacher's response style was then compared to anecdotal reports attesting to communication features in each class. The setting of task, taking of turns, and nature of the topic of each classroom is thus discussed as a backdrop for the quantified results.

Each teacher identified the errors that initiated the set of error-response episodes used in the analysis of her response style. By restricting the set of errors to only those perceived as such by the teacher, it was hoped that a more reliable appraisal of error might be achieved. However, the limitation is that the data are skewed in the direction of those errors that occupy a high priority or are salient for the particular teacher. Teacher A-1, for example, noticed and identified a large percentage of errors of form (phonological, lexical, morpho-syntactic, discourse, and dialect) and a small percentage of content errors. We cannot make any generalizations about the predominance of form errors in this teacher's class, however; only those errors cited by the teacher upon viewing the videotaped lessons were used in the analysis of error treatment.

Neither can we make generalizations about an individual teacher's style of corrective treatment without looking at the types of lessons used for analysis. Three lessons of each teacher's entire repertoires of curriculum and techniques were used in this analysis. Prior to videotaping, teachers were asked to include in their lessons as many opportunities as possible for oral language interaction among teacher and pupils.

The following discussion presents frequencies of kinds of errors and responses, but the meaning to be derived from these numbers lies in the description of the contextual information about each classroom. Much of the knowledge which contributed to the description came from observations in the classrooms and the school at large, as well as from interviews with the teachers while they watched the videotapes.

Teacher A-1. This teacher, the bilingual teacher at School A, taught all the Spanish-speaking pupils in grades K through 5 for at least an hour per day. She had twelve Spanish-dominant students in her first grade class. These students left their regular classroom teacher for an hour and a half each day to go to Teacher A-1 for instruction in Spanish for Spanish-Speakers (SSS), with emphasis on reading and math. A typical day in the first grade SSS class began at 8:30 a.m., and included some initial group activity, such as singing an alphabet song or listening to the teacher read a story in Spanish. The group of twelve students was then divided into small groups, according to ability, for instruction in phonics or language experience activities. Teacher A-1 used a variety of activities and instructional devices (overheads, charts, record player) to assist her in instruction. Also assisting her was a Spanish-speaking aide, who typically worked with one of the small groups.

The three classes used in this analysis included the following activities:

1. The teacher and three students sit at a small table with three balls in front of them, discussing the number, size, and shape of the balls. Written on small cards are the words, "una pelota" (a ball) and "unas pelotas" (some balls).
2. The teacher and the same group of students work on sounding out words from a list of words projected overhead. (The only errors extracted from this lesson for the present study were those in which the students were not reading from the overhead.)
3. The teacher shows a small group of children some cards with pictures on them. The children are to identify the pictures by stating Spanish words. (The first child to identify the picture "wins;" the reward was unspecified, but these children were accustomed to winning candy on occasion.)
4. The teacher helps the students with a written exercise in their workbooks.
5. The teacher shows the students a poster with drawings depicting items with particular word-initial sounds.
6. The teacher introduces a story they are going to read, asking the children to raise their hands when they hear words beginning with particular initial sounds.

Table 1 shows that the errors that appeared salient to the teacher upon viewing her videotapes were predominantly phonological and lexical. The students in her class were Spanish-dominant and were engaged in activities in which language development was the topic for instruction. We can make the generalization that to Teacher A-1, language development is largely the practice of sounds and words, since the errors she cited were mostly phonological and lexical.

Table 1.   Error-type Profile for
Teacher A-1

Errors	Number	% of total
Phonological	13	28.8
Lexical	16	35.6
Morph-Syn	4	8.9
Discourse	5	11.1
Dialect	3	6.7
Content	4	8.9
Total	45	100.0

Teacher A-1 used a variety of techniques in handling students' errors. (See Table 2.) Seventy-eight percent of the students' errors were contained in utterances that were responses to the teacher's initiations. In other words, only 22% of the errors occurred in utterances initiated spontaneously by the students themselves. This, of course, is not unusual in classroom dynamics; the teacher controls the topic and the taking of turns. Thus, most of the errors occurred

Table 2.   Teacher Response Profiles (in percentages)

Teacher	A-1	A-2	B-1	B-2
Models	10	20	—	17
Drills	6	2	—	10
Repeats	10	16	—	12
Prompts	13	13	—	13
Explains	3	4	—	7
(Re)states instructions	3	12	—	8
Tells student what to say	14	10	—	5
Reduces	2	—	—	—
Expands	3	4	—	4
Correct Response				
Repeats	13	1	—	6
Explains	2	1	—	3
Accepts	13	12	—	10
Verifies	8	5	—	5
Total	100	100	0	100

within the context of typical classroom disourse with the teacher soliciting student responses by asking questions, requesting students to repeat responses, or giving visual cues which the students were to render into oral language.

Table 3 displays a simple breakdown of the responses to errors of form (all errors except content errors) for each teacher. The students in Teacher A-1's class, for example, committed 38 errors of form, which comprised 84% of the total number of errors she identified from the videotapes of her class. Of those 38 errors, 29% were corrected overtly immediately, and 24% were not corrected at all. The remaining errors were responded to by delaying treatment and/or transferring treatment to another student in the class.

Table 3.   Corrective Feedback to Errors of Form

Teacher	A 1	A-2	B-1	B 2
Number of errors	38	38	29	88
Percent of total errors for teacher	84	84	100	83
Percent corrected	29	74	—	30
Percent delayed/transferred	26	5	—	32
Percent corrected and delayed/transferred	21	8	—	14
Percent not corrected or delayed/transferred	24	13	100	24
Total	100	100	100	100

Thus, Teacher A-1 overtly corrected approximately the same proportion of errors that she ignored. The remaining 47% of the errors were reserved for later treatment, or were referred to other students for corrections. We can generalize from these results by saying that, overall, Teacher A-1 did not immediately intervene when students made mistakes of grammatical form. Rather, she ignored the errors or delayed treatment, giving the students an opportunity to correct themselves; or she gave other students the opportunity to correct their peers. By not overtly correcting errors, she provided an atmosphere of student participation in communication sanctions. In those cases where she did overtly intervene, Teacher A-1 used numerous follow-up moves, including modeling the desired student statement, repeating the error (sometimes changing its form and sometimes emphasizing with stress or pitch the change that had been made), prompting the student, and telling the student exactly what to say.

The overall effect of this teacher's attitude toward error cannot be determined from the present study. Two characteristics of student talk to be found in this classroom, however, were the preponderance of language play and the students' enthusiastic participation in conversation with the teacher. Most of the discourse errors committed by these students were rhyming games ("una tortuna" for "una tortuga") or inversion of consonants within a syllable ("un robador" for "un borrador"). Both of these characteristics suggest a classroom environment conducive to exploration and experimentation with language. If these are desirable features of a language development situation, one might hypothesize that overt corrective intervention as a unilateral error treatment strategy is not advisable.

Teacher A-2. The regular classroom teacher in charge of a class composed of the twelve Spanish-dominant students in Teacher A-1's classroom, as well as fifteen English-dominant students, offers an interesting contrast to Teacher A-1, especially with regard to the types of learning activities she used. Although her classroom was set up for small group activities, the type of teaching videotaped in her classroom involved the teacher working with the whole class or with individuals. The whole-class activities were

1. asking the students what they would buy if they had one dollar to spend;
2. asking the students to discuss an illustration of a farm scene which was on the blackboard at the front of the room; and
3. asking the students to set up categories to distinguish between solids, liquids, and gases.

The activities in which individual students engaged in conversation with her frequently involved telling her about a picture they had drawn. In some cases the children had drawn the picture on their own initiative; in other cases, the teacher had told them to draw a picture, sometimes relating to a specific topic, such as finishing the sentence, "I'm happy when . . ." Although both Spanish-and English-dominant children were present in this classroom, the Spanish-speakers were all at two tables in the back of the room. Since they did not produce many spontaneous responses during whole-class activities, the teacher often made an effort to call on them. Likewise, in activities in which she called individual students to her to discuss their pictures, she often asked the bilingual, or Spanish-dominant, students to participate in this way. A native Spanish-speaker herself, she frequently spoke to them in Spanish when they appeared not to understand. She also cued them in Spanish in order to elicit more language. There were times when she elicited responses from them in Spanish during whole-class activities, but the Spanish-speakers usually did not respond. The majority of the interaction with these students involved the teacher and one pupil in a modified Language Experience situation, where students dictated sentences to the teacher. Table 4 characterizes the kinds of errors identified by Teacher A-2.

Table 4.   Error-type Profile for Teacher A-2

Errors	Number	Percent of total
Phonological	10	21.7
Lexical	1	2.0
Morph-Syn	17	36.9
Discourse	17	36.9
Dialect	0	0.0
Content	1	2.0
Total	46	99.54

Table 4 indicates that morpho-syntactic and discourse errors predominated according to this teacher's identification of error from the videotapes. Most of the discourse errors were incomplete sentences and occasionally, overly complex sentences. All of the phonological errors were committed by Spanish-dominant students.

Table 2 shows that Teacher A-2, like Teacher A-1, used several different strategies in responding to her students' mistakes. Table 3, however, indicates that a large majority (74%) of the errors of form were responded to with direct corrective intervention. Only 13% of the form errors were left uncorrected, and in only one case out of 38 instances of form error did she transfer the correcting role to another student. These data partially reflect the number of times this teacher worked with individuals, since only seven of the errors occurred within the context of whole-class instruction. However, this in itself is a reflection of this teacher's attitude toward the use of peers to assist in providing language data.

Like Teacher A-1, this teacher initiated most of the error-response exchanges (93%). She rarely drilled; only one out of forty-six erroneous responses resulted in a form of routine practice as a correction technique. Otherwise, the pattern one can derive from her responses indicates a wide repertoire of feedback options, following the same basic pattern as Teacher A-1: soliciting, modeling, prompting, yet rarely transferring the corrective role to the other students.

Teacher B-1.   B-1 was the English reading teaching in School B. She spent all of the time she was videotaped reading aloud with her students. For this reason, the data set is small, including only those errors that were made between reading groups, or during discussion about a story from the reader. However, most of the errors were dialect errors; therefore they were counted twice—once as dialect errors and once for the linguistic function that obtained. The students in this teacher's class were of various degrees of Spanish and English dominance (3 Spanish-dominant; 6 bilingual; 20 English-dominant), there being many speakers of non-standard English, as well as the students who had been selected for the bilingual program.

The error-resonse episodes can be characterized without a table. The teacher identified a total of 29 errors, and 83% of these were dialect errors. Most of these dialect errors were morpho-syntactic (83% of the total dialect errors). There were 3 phonological errors, 3 lexical errors, and no content or discourse errors. The teacher did not correct *any* of the errors, nor did she transfer any to other students. She ignored every error that she found in her videotapes, using no modeling, drilling, or transferring correction to other students.

These remarkable results are mostly a reflection of the kind of activity in which errors were found. Most of the errors were spontaneous statements initiated by the students in transition situations: organizing the next group, asking to go to the bathroom, asking what page they were reading from. Yet this teacher revealed in the interviews that she did not regard her role as one of a correcting machine, and she also did not regard non-standard dialect (which accounted for most of the mistakes) as erroneous language.

Teacher B-2.   This teacher taught twenty-two Mexican-American students who were of a wide range of language dominance. The subject was Spanish reading. The kinds of oral language activities these students engaged in with her, however, were pre-reading oral language activities. When the study began, she had just begun working with these students in Spanish for the first time, although they had received one semester of Spanish instruction from Teacher B-1. Typically, Teacher B-2 had the students sitting in a circle on the floor. This configuration allowed them to focus on the visuals, usually drawn by her, that she displayed and used to provoke discussion. Table 5 illustrates the large number of errors her students committed, which she found upon viewing the videotapes.

Table 5.   Error-type Profile for
Teacher B-2

Errors	Number	Percent of total
Phonological	50	37
Lexical	17	13
Morph-Syn	10	6
Discourse	11	8
Dialect	28	21
Content	20	15
Total	136	100

The large proportion of phonological errors may be explained by the fact that these Spanish-speakers were not of a high degree of Spanish dominance. Their enthusiastic attempts at speaking Spanish often resulted in creatively mispronounced words and phrases.

Table 3 shows that Teacher B-2 corrected 30% of the errors of form, deferring correction to the other pupils approximately as often as she transferred correction. Like Teacher A-1, this teacher corrected less than a third of her students' errors of form, and the correlation techniques used were varied and numerous.

The large number of errors in the videotapes for this teacher partially account for the wide variety of response types. Yet it is significant that the percentages of overtly corrected errors correspond dramatically with those of Teacher A-1. In addition, anecdotal evidence suggests that both teachers engaged the students in active production of language. The statistics representing their attitudes toward error correction suggest a strong connection between inattention to overt correction of error of form and encouragement of classroom language production.

In summary, when one considers the error-response episodes from the perspective of broad discourse moves (opening, answering, and follow-up moves), the teachers' response styles are remarkably similar, except in the case of Teacher B-1. The traditional methods of corrective treatment: correcting the students' errors, modeling the appropriate form, providing practice through drills, and occasionally calling on other students to give the correct answer.

Teacher B-1's response style differs from the other three teachers' styles in that she did not elicit students' statements containing errors; she did not respond with any kind of correction of the errors; and she did not transfer treatment of the error to the other students in the class. Her response style can best be characterized as not intervening when a student made an oral language error.

The gross frequencies of response moves and the percentages of types of responses demonstrate, in all cases but Teacher B-1, the diversity of response types the teachers appealed to in handling their students' mistakes. Yet the frequencies obscure certain characteristics of the error-response sequences which are significant in developing profiles of the teachers' response styles. Additional information concerning the nature of the teachers' styles follows.

Qualitative analysis

The collection, organization, and analysis of the data for this study necessitated a year-long acquaintance with the four teachers. During the observations and interviews, they exhibited attributes that should be considered in the analysis of their styles in responding to students' errors. They also revealed attitudes toward language teaching and error correction. The account that follows is based on classroom observations and both structured and unstructured interviews. Examples are from the transcribed data.

Teacher A-1.   Because this teacher had single-handedly begun the bilingual program at School A, she often expounded her philosophy of teaching Spanish-speaking students. Her reported primary concern was in developing the self-concepts of her students by giving them opportunities for achieving academic success. The bilingual students in her classroom engaged in conversation with her throughout each lesson; they appeared to be comfortable speaking Spanish in her classroom and on several occasions incorporated spontaneous language play into their classroom talk. The following example illustrates this.

T: ¿que traigo un borrador? [Shall I bring an eraser?]
P: (continues working, then sits back): un *robador*. [a robber; anagram of word for eraser, "borrador"]
T: (from other side of room) borrador.
P: borrador.
T: (now next to P) siéntete derechito. [Sit up straight.]
P2: /playfully and quietly/ un mapiador. [an eraser.]
T: /reassuringly/ mapiador. borrador.
P2: borrador.
T: borrador.

This example shows the teacher's concern for correct language without discouraging language production on the part of the students. An important feature of her correction (and of her interaction style in general) is a warm, engaging, concerned manner, attending to the constant demands for attention made by her students with frequent physical contact and affectionate terms such as "chulo" [dear].

   Her standards for correct language were communicated to the students, but her explanations of what constituted correct language were tempered by her acceptance of the students' utterances. The following example demonstrates her attention to correct lexical usage. The students had been reading a sentence with an exclamation point at the end.

P: ¿por qué tiene ese *accento*? [Why does it have this accent?]
T: muy bien. quiere saber virginia por qué está este punto aquí. esto es un punto de exclamación, digan. lo vea aca también. miren. lo ven aquí. [OK. Virginia wants to know why this mark is here. This called an exclamation mark. You can see it there, too. Look. You see it there.]
Ps: sí. [Yes.]
T: en español se pone un punto de exclamación al último y al principio. porque a uds. les gustan mucho gritar. cuando ven este punto de exclamación entonces se griten, eh? [In Spanish you put an exclamation mark at the beginning and at the end. Because you like to shout so much. When you see this exclamation mark you shout, OK?]

   The teacher makes clear the appropriate term and gives the students an explanation of the content behind the lexical item. But her manner is personal and reinforces spontaneous production on the part of the students. From the pupil's perspective, the lengthy explanation might very likely be interpreted as a reward for the spontaneous, content-related question.

Teacher A–2. This teacher has been described as being demanding of complete sentences in oral production. Her work with the whole class in oral language activities was characteristically teacher-centered, in that she set the task and asked for contributions from students with raised hands. The students in her class always faced her during language activities, and they typically gasped and whined in order to be called on. The following example occurred during an exercise in which the students were to tell the teacher what they would buy with one dollar. The teacher prefaced the activity by describing the task, then telling the students they had exactly one minute to think. The minute was spent by most children in looking at the clock.

T: uh, what would you buy, uh, Chris?
P: *a machine gun.*
P2: what?
T: YOU SAY IT TO ME IN A COMPLETE SENTENCE. "i would buy a machine gun," ok, steven?

As in the other examples cited for this teacher, the message to the pupils is that they are to produce complete sentences in oral language activity. Very rarely did the teacher make a comment relating to the message content of the student's statement when they made linquistic errors in whole-class activities.

In work with individual pupils, the teacher's concern for correct language was apparent. She typically worked with the Spanish-speakers in her class by asking them to tell her about a picture they had drawn. Combining oral language development with a kind of language experience reading lesson, she often asked the students to describe their picture to her while she wrote down the words. (The missing component of the language experience activity was the essential "languaging" of the activity; the students merely dictated a sentence or two which they had composed on their own to complete the sentence, "I'm happy when . . .")

T: ok, come on.
P: *my mom bought me easter egg.*
T: ok. tell me the sentence. "i'm happy when . . ."
P: i'm happy when my mom /unintelligible/ easter egg.
T: easter EGGS. did she buy you ONE egg or lotsa eggs?
P: one egg.
T: she only bought you one egg?
P: yes.
T: was it a big one?
P: yeah.
T: a great big one?
P: (Nods.) yeah.
T: i'm happy when my mother—mom—bought me EASTER egg. (Writes.) bought me a an AN easter egg. Bought me an easter egg. Ok. let's say this again. i'm happy when . . .

P: my mom bought me a easter egg.
T: AN easter egg.
P: AN easter egg.
T: very good. go color that side of it.

Although the frequency counts for this teacher indicate a diverse repertoire of responses to student errors, the individual examples suggest a rigidity in her conception of correct language. Her view of correct classroom language is characterized by insistence on complete sentences and on student answers phrased according to a specific model. Thus, even though the teacher purportedly uses activities to encourage discussion, the resulting student language is in fact decontextualized from conversational intent, and the teacher's style of error treatment removes that language even further from conversational meaning.

Teacher B-1. This teacher's response style has already been cited as being anomalous to the other teachers' styles of responding. Most of her students' mistakes were dialectal in nature, and all of her responses ignored the mistakes. The errors occurred between oral reading activities and were usually spontaneous statements. The teacher never interrupted a student's meaning to focus on form. An example follows:

T: ok? who does not have a speaking part this time?
P: *i don't got* a speaking part.
T: ok. you know what you all can do?
P: what?
T: you will . . .
P: . . . make the noises, i know.
T: ok. let's practice.

This teacher identified errors from the videotapes which, she said, were not Standard English and thus could be considered errors. Implicit in her response style, however, is an acceptance of Non-standard English. By ignoring her students' "errors," she conveyed to them her concern for communication of messages instead of concern for correct, or standard, grammatical form.

Teacher B-2. This teacher structured oral language activities around recognition of sight words and identification of lexical items from pictures. Her style of handling students' errors typically included letting the student know the answer was incorrect, but preferring the provision of clues or transfer of the correction to other students, to correcting the mistake immediately herself. The following protocol exemplifies this strategy:

T: ok. este animal (points to lion). si acaso del digo que lo pinten, ¿de qué color lo van a pintar? [OK. This animal. If I told you to color it, what color would you use?]
Ps: café. [Brown.]
T: ¿café. o . . . [Brown? Or . . .]

P: chocolate. [Brown.]
T: no. chocolate, no. [No. Not brown.]
P2: *pleto.* [Black. /mispronounced/]
T: ¿eh?
Ps: negro. [Black.]
T: negro. no. ¿lo van a pintar negro? ¿de qué color? (points to picture of lion on wall.) miren. allá está un leon. ¿De qué color es? [Black. No. You'd color it black? What color? Look. There's a lion. What color is it?]
P: café. [Brown.]
T: ¿café? y tiene tambien . . . [Brown? And it also has . . .]
P: amarillo. [Yellow.]
T: amarillo. café y amarillo. [Yellow. Brown and yellow.]

This teacher has a definite answer in mind, and her students try enthusiastically to come up with the correct lexical item. In spite of this guessing-game type of activity, many spontaneous conversations arose in her class. This teacher encouraged language production from her students by encouraging competition for the right answer. Incorrect student utterances were treated matter-of-factly by identifying them as such and allowing the error-maker or another student to attempt the right answer. Her tone in correcting was uncritical to the students and created a classroom atmosphere which forced students to produce language in the hopes of winning the language game.

Summary: The Questions Reconsidered

From the discussion it appears that the correction styles of the four teachers are inextricably connected to their teaching styles in general. Teachers A-1, B-1, and B-2 exhibited personal characteristics which seemed to encourage a comfortable environment for experimenting with language. Teacher A-2, on the other hand, regimented the language environment to such an extent that her oral language development class could not be considered conducive to the students' testing of their linguistic hypotheses.

Using the quantitative and qualitative information presented, the research questions of this study can be answered in the following ways.

1. *Do the teachers regard language learning as mastery of form, as illustrated by their attention to correct language use, or do they care more about communication of meaning, attending less to grammatical errors than to unsuccessful conveying of messages?*

Teacher A-1 overtly corrected only 29% of the errors of form she identified from the videotapes. In 71% of the instances of error of form, she allowed for some other kind of corrective treatment. The fact that she did not intervene in so many of cases of error indicates that correct language was of less concern to her than encouragement of connected discourse.

To Teacher A-2, correct language was the primary concern. She overtly corrected 74% of the errors of form and did not intervene only 13% of the time.

Teacher B-1 cared little about correct language, as demonstrated by the consistent non-correction of error in her classes.

Teacher B-2 overtly corrected only 30% of the time. Like Teacher A-1, this teacher did not insist on immediate corrective feedback. She allowed other pupils to correct, or she delayed correction and did not interrupt the communication of meaning.

2. *Do the language teachers attend to language error more or in different ways than teachers in regular classes where LEP children are students?*

The two second language teachers, A-1, and B-2, seem to be the most similar in their responses to error. They corrected about the same numbers of errors and used similar intervention strategies. The two teachers of content other than language, A-2 (language arts) and B-1 (reading), represent extreme ends of the correction continuum. A-2 consistently corrected error overtly, and B-1 consistently did not correct error.

3. *Do the teachers tend to correct solicited student statements more frequently than unsolicited student statements?*

In each error response sequence, the source of initiation was coded. As in typical classroom discourse, most of the error-response episodes in this study were teacher-initiated. The only teacher whose students consistently made errors in student-initiated exchanges was Teacher B-1. As we have seen, her strategy was to ignore the errors made by her students. The present study shows, then, that for this teacher, unsolicited errors (as well as solicited errors) remained uncorrected.

4. *Do the teachers tend to correct more frequently or in different ways when other students hear the correction?*

Teacher A-2 was the only teacher who engaged in private interactions with her students in this study. These error-response sequences were typically longer than those encountered in whole-class activities with other teachers, and they incorporated more diversity in type of corrective treatment. They usually resulted in a drill until the student arrived at the appropriate response. The whole-class errors were almost all incomplete sentences for Teacher A-2, and these were treated with a restatement of the complete sentence rule by the teacher. Thus, this teacher corrected more intensively and with more diversity in private interactions than in whole-class instruction.

5. *How can each teacher's individual correction style be characterized, and what attitude toward language teaching and learning does that correction style reflect?*

Generalizing from the quantitative analysis of the error-response episodes, as well as from the qualitative understanding of each teacher's response style, the following statements can be made about the four teachers in light of research in first and second language acquisition.

The teacher who conforms most to the model of language input described by research in first language acquisition (Snow, 1972, 1977; Lindfors, 1980) is

Teacher B-1. She allowed her students to initiate the error-response episodes, and she ignored their mistakes. She attended to the meaning of what was said and occasionally provided, in her next response, the appropriate language form.

Teacher A-1 conformed to the traditional model of the second language teacher, using a variety of response types, but attending to error with a clear goal of correct language. She did, however, allow her students to play with language, and she was flexible in allowing them to initiate exchanges. Thus, she created an environment conducive to linguistic hypothesis-testing.

Teacher B-2 also corrected in the conventional manner of a language teacher. Language teaching, as defined by her responses to errors, was a game for which she provided the rules and kept score. Yet the students were not intimidated by her role as corrector of errors, often engaged in spontaneous conversations with her, and corrected one another.

The environment for language development created by Teacher A-2 fits neither the model of interaction for first nor second language acquisition. Language learning for the students in this class was confounded by the teacher's confounding of the rules of conversation and written composition. Her students were not allowed to use anything but that language which would be considered correct if it were written in a composition.

In summary, several points can be made with regard to the use of language in these four classrooms. Two teachers in this study (A-1 and B-2) interpreted their task as that of the second language teacher, often covertly correcting students' errors and drilling the appropriate response. Their students responded by talking a good bit in conversational language. The topic, however, was usually language itself, not communication of ideas or intentions. Teacher A-2 corrected overtly, instilling in her students respect for the rules of composition. Her students' oral language production was characteristically labored and stilted. Teacher B-2 ignored her students' mistakes, presumably because she did not consider dialect errors to be unacceptable communications. Her students used conversational Non-standard English in classroom discussions, and the topics of these discussions almost always involved non-linguistic content.

Thus, the covertly correcting teachers promoted a classroom climate in which the communication most closely resembled an adult foreign language classroom. That is, both the subject and medium of instruction was language. The overtly correcting teacher allowed a range of topics in classroom discussions, but the communication could not be considered conversational for its emphasis on correct form. The non-correcting teaching promoted conversational communication about non-language topics.

Research in first language acquisition suggests that interlocutor's attention to meaning, rather than form, as well as a willingness to allow the child to structure the linguistic interaction, may be critical to successful language acquisition. All the teachers in this study ultimately controlled the topic of classroom discourse, and only B-1 did not force classroom language into the realm of meta-communication, making correct language the real topic for discussion.

In current theoretical approaches to first and second language acquisition there exists the assumption that learners need to take risks in their production of the target language in order to test and modify their linguistic hypotheses. Three of the teachers in this study (A-1, B-1, and B-2) encouraged conversational language production with their students, but only one (B-1) effectively accepted all student mistakes.

Wong-Fillmore's (1976) study of second language learners indicates that peers are a valuable source of language input about the target language. The language input her study examined was the natural language occurring in play situations, not the language of teacher-directed lessons. However, it may be that peers who are native speakers of the target language are an important source of input in teacher-conducted lessons as well as child-initiated activities. Teachers A-1 and B-2 transferred to other students almost as many errors as they corrected themselves. Teacher A-2 overlooked a potential resource by transferring so few of the error detections and corrections to other students in the class.

Attitudes toward oral language development represent a continuum for these four teachers, as manifested in their responses to learner error. At one end of the continuum is overtly correcting Teacher A-2, whose vision of correct language stifles natural conversation with her students. At the other end is non-correcting Teacher B-1, who manifests the attitude that the errors made by her students are developmental, and overt corrective treatment will be of little help in modifying the learner's interim grammar. In the middle of the continuum are Teachers A-1 and B-2, who apparently see error as a function of interference from the native language. Their reliance on covert correction and language drill evidence this attitude.

A preliminary report by Hamayan (1980) confirms the presence of these three approaches to error feedback in the adult ESL classroom she studied. The teachers tended to explicitly correct phonological errors, while syntactic errors were most frequently ignored. For all grammatical types of error, implicit correction was the reaction less than one-third of the time. For the adult learner, and with the often-specialized nature of ESL classes for adults, explicit, immmediate intervention may be the most appropriate form of correction.

According to the hypothesis-testing model of second language acquisition, however, first grade students in a bilingual program should have access to a language environment which provides them with opportunities for meaningful language interaction. There should be available models of correct language, but peers in small group activities are often, as in the classrooms in this study, an untapped resource. The teacher who allows errors to go uncorrected may not be meeting the needs of her students if native-speaker peer interaction in the classroom is limited. But teachers who sacrifice communication in the name of correct language use should consider the consequences of their methods on the language development of their students.

References

Allwright, R. L. Problems in the study of the language teacher's treatment of learner error. *On TESOL '75, New Directions in Second Language Learning, Teaching, and Bilingual Education.* Washington, D.C.: TESOL, 1975.

Brown, R. *A First Language.* Cambridge, Mass.: Harvard University Press, 1973.

Burt, M. K., & Dulay, H. C., (Eds.). *New Directions in Second Language Learning, Teaching and Bilingual Education.* Washington, D.C.: TESOL, 1975.

Cathcart, R. L., & Olsen, J. E. W. B. Teachers' and students' preferences for correction of classroom conversation errors. In J. Fanselow & R. Crymes (Eds.), *On TESOL '76.* Washington, D.C.: TESOL, 1976.

Cazden, C. Environmental assistant to the child's acquisition of grammar. Doctoral dissertation; Harvard University, Cambridge, Mass., 1965.

Chaudron, C. A descriptive model of discourse in the corrective treatment of learners' errors. *Language learning,* 1977a, *27,* 1, 29–46.

Chaudron, C. Teachers' priorities in correcting learners' errors in French immersion classes. *Working Papers in Bilingualism,* January, 1977b, *12,* 21, 21–44.

Chaudron, C. Complexity of ESL teachers' speech and vocabulary expansion/elaboration. Paper presented at the Teachers of English to Speakers of Other Languages Convention; Boston, Mass., March, 1979.

Cicourel, A. V., et al. *Language Use and School Performance.* New York: Academic Press, 1974.

Cohen, A. D. Error analysis and error correction with respect to the training of language teachers. *Workpapers in Teaching ESL,* 1975, *9,* 107–125.

Coulthard, M. *An Introduction to Discourse Analysis.* London: Longman's, 1977.

Dulay, H. C., & Burt, M. K. Error and strategies in child second language acquisition. *TESOL Quarterly,* 1974a, *8,* 2, 129–136.

Dulay, H. C., & Burt, M. K. Natural sequences in child second language acquisition. *Language Learning,* 1974b, *24,* 1, 37–53.

Dulay, H. C., & Burt, M. K. A new perspective on the creative construction process in child second language acquisition. *Language Learning,* 1974c, *24,* 2, 253–278.

Ervin-Tripp, S. M. Is second language learning like the first? *TESOL Quarterly,* 1974, *8,* 2, 111–128.

Fanselow, J. *Beyond Rashomon—Foci for Observing Communications Used in Second Language Instruction.* ED 108 474. Bethesda, Md.: ERIC Documents Reproduction Service, 1976.

Fanselow, J. The treatment of error in oral work. *Foreign Language Annals,* 1977, *10,* 5, 583–593.

Hamayan, E. V. Teachers' reactions to students' language errors; a preliminary report. Paper presented at the Teachers of English to Speakers of Other Languages Convention; San Francisco, March, 1980.

Holly, F. M., & King, J. F. Imitation and correction in foreign language learning. *Modern Language Journal,* 1971, *55,* 494–498.

Johnson, N. K., & Gardner, C. H. Toward a prototype for training classroom ethnographers. *Education and Urban Society,* May 1980, *12,* 3, 367–382.

Lindfors, J. W. *Children's Language and Learning.* Englewood Cliffs, N.J.: Prentice-Hall, 1980.

Long, M. H. Teacher feedback on learner error: Mapping cognitions. In H. D. Brown et al. (Eds.), *On TESOL '77,* Washington, D.C.: TESOL, 1977.

Long, M. H. Inside the "Black Box": Methodological issues in classroom research on language learning. Paper presented at the Teachers of English to Speakers of Other Languages Convention, Boston, March, 1979.

Mehan, H. Accomplishing classroom lessons. In A. Cicourel et al. (Eds.), *Language Use and School Performance.*

Mehan, H. *The Reality of Ethnomethodology.* New York: Wiley, 1975.

Mehan, H. *Learning Lessons.* Cambridge, Mass.: Harvard University Press, 1978.

Piestrup, A. M. Black dialect interference and accommodation of reading instruction in first grade. Monograph, Language-Behavior Research Laboratory, University of California, Berkeley, 1973.

Ramirez, A. G., & Stromquist, N. B. ESL methodology and student language learning in bilingual elementary schools. Stanford University, 1978.

Sacks, H., Schegloff, E., & Jefferson, G. A simplest systematics for the organization of turn-taking in conversation. *Language*, 1974, *50*, 696–735.

Schegloff, E. A., Jefferson, G., & Sacks, H. The preference for self-correction in the organization of repair in conversation. *Language*, 1977, *53*, 2, 361–382.

Searle, J. R. *Speech Acts: An Essay in the Philosophy of Language*. Cambridge: Cambridge University Press, 1970.

Schaughnessy, M. P. *Errors and Expectations*. Oxford: Oxford University Press, 1977.

Shuy, R. W. Learning to talk like teachers. Paper presented at the American Educational Research Association Conference, Toronto, April, 1978.

Sinclair, J. McH., & Coulthard, M. *Towards an Analysis of Discourse*. Oxford: Oxford University Press, 1975.

Slobin, D. I. Questions of language development in cross-cultural perspective. Paper prepared for a symposium on Language Learning in Cross-Cultural Perspective, Michigan State University, 1968.

Slobin, D. I. Cognitive prerequisites for the development of grammar. In Charles A. Ferguson & Dan Slobin (Eds.), *Studies of Child Language and Development*. New York: Holt, Rinehart and Winston, 1973.

Snow, C. E. Mothers' speech to children learning language. *Child Development,* 1972, *43,* 549–565.

Snow, C. E. The development of conversation between mothers and babies. *Journal of Child Language,* 1977, *4,* 1, 1–22.

Snow, C. E., & Ferguson, C. A. *Talking to Children: Language Input and Acquisition*. Cambridge: Cambridge University Press, 1977.

Wong-Fillmore, L. The second time around: Cognitive and social strategies in second language acquisition. Ph.D. dissertation, Stanford University, Stanford, Calif., 1976.

Questions for Discussion and Activities

1. Consider the role of interaction in the first language acquisition environment. Adults typically encourage the maintenance of conversational meaning despite syntactically limited attempts from the child. What activities might support a similar environment in second language classes for children? for adults?

2. First language acquisition research (Snow, 1972, 1977) has consistently demonstrated the insignificance of imitation and repetition as primary strategies the child uses in constructing a linguistic system from the limited language (s)he hears. Assuming that children acquiring a second language use some of the same strategies as native language acquirers, how might the teacher in ESL classrooms respond to errors without relying on imitation and repetition of the correct response?

3. Cazden (1965) found that when children's language was responded to by means of extension (no explicit modeling of the adult form, but a move to the next conversational response to the content of the child's utterance), it resulted in greater gains in first language acquisition than when the response was expansion (modeling the adult form). How might the second language classroom teacher provide a similar response style to children's attempts at the target language?

4. Wong-Fillmore (1976) identified three stages in second language acquisition which seem to motivate and guide the young learner's strategies. Occurring earliest was a concern for establishing social relations; the next stage was a concern for communicating content; and the final stage was a concern for speaking the second language correctly. In what ways do the three types of error feedback (overtly correcting, covertly correcting, and non-correcting) allow the new arrival to the elementary school ESL classroom to progress through these stages?

5. Fanselow (personal communication) has suggested the possible importance of "wait time" (the length of time a teacher gives a student before correcting the error herself) upon commission of an error in oral language. If a teacher allows a longer interval between error detection and correction, what kinds of results might one expect to see in student participation in the second language classroom?

6. How would you test hypotheses regarding the effectiveness of various kinds of feedback patterns on the language acquisition of learners? Design a study which you think would test various hypotheses regarding the relationship between feedback and language acquisition.

9

Learner Feedback: An Exploratory Study of Its Role in the Second Language Classroom

Stephen J. Gaies

I would like to begin this chapter with some personal history. The observations that I want to relate were first made a dozen years ago. In the years since then, I have had occasion to observe the phenomenon over and over, as well as to hear of similar observations by colleagues. I relate these now as a backdrop to the research I will describe later in these pages.

My first teaching position was as a foreign language teacher in a suburban junior high school. During the 1968–69 school year (as well as in previous years and, I assume, for some years afterward), foreign languages were taught in this school district according to what can fairly be termed strict audiolingual orthodoxy. To the best of my recollection, whatever deviations were made from the lesson plans outlined in the teacher's manuals we used were made by all of us teaching at a particular level. Learning was to proceed in lockstep fashion, not only within a particular class, but also from class to class. Those who have studied or taught with the original A-L-M materials know only too well how regimented a process language learning was supposed to be; those who haven't would be tempted to regard much of what I might say in greater detail as hyperbole.

My point is not to pass judgment on audiolingualism. I had some very successful learners and some notably unsuccessful ones. Maybe their relative success would have been different if they had had a different exposure to French; maybe not. The fact that not all of my (or anyone's) learners succeeded was itself a blow to the original claims made on behalf of audiolingual methodology (claims that we realize retrospectively were based on extremely thin evidence). But even at the time, it was not the source of disillusionment, or even of great surprise. What was surprising to me at the time was how different students reacted to what went on in the classroom period, how very difficult it was to regiment the classroom, to standardize the convergence of student, teacher, and content.

Today, we are in almost universal agreement that successful formal language learning involves a careful matching of learner characteristics, the learning setting, and methodology. We recognize that not all learners respond identically to a particular teaching method; indeed, learners do not all respond similarly to formal learning itself. We are far from knowing what the critical variables are in this matter. We suspect, at least, that there must be a very complex set of them involved.

In regard to my early teaching experiences, I am struck now, as I was then, by the fact that even in that situation, where everything that could be done to standardize the language learning experience was done, some learners attempted to shape, to the extent that they could, the nature of their convergence with the syllabus and with me. While many learners were content to let the nature of that convergence be determined for them—in essence, to abdicate whatever control they might have exerted over what took place during the class period—for others, it was quite a different matter. By the questions they asked, by the tangents they caused us to pursue, and in a number of other ways, they influenced the nature of the time we spent. At various times, I attributed what this latter group of learners did to inquisitiveness, to interest, to restlessness, to recalcitrance, and to other "positive" and "negative" sources. Whether what they did contributed to the overall success of the class or detracted from it is both unanswerable and, for present purposes, irrelevant. That different learners affected the structure of the classroom differently is, I think, extremely important to recognize.

In subsequent teaching experiences, as a teacher of foreign languages and as an ESL teacher, I have noted the same phenomenon to an even greater degree. Even where attempts were continually made to equalize students' opportunity for participation and to structure the nature of that participation, not all learners ended up participating to the same degree—or in the same way. This was certainly true in full-class settings, but it was no less true in small-group and "tutoring" contexts. In the case of dyads especially, variation in the role learners assumed was evident. While some learners confined their participation to answering questions and following directions, others assumed much more responsibility for determining what was to take place during the learning session. They would take the initiative for setting and agenda, they asked questions, and they interrupted explanations which they felt were unnecessary or confusing. Above all, they never hesitated to indicate whether or not they understood what we were talking about.

Anecdotal observations such as I have just related inevitably lead to the question: To what extent are the patterns and phenomena observed characteristic of formal language learning in general? This question is the basis of our attempt to understand the nature of formal language learning. To answer it—to discover what is universal to the formal language learning process and to explain those phenomena which are variable—researchers in our field are turning their attention more and more to what actually goes on in the language classroom. This emphasis on description of classroom activity represents an important change in the focus of language learning research.

This reorientation has been outlined in detail, notably by Long (1979), and I will therefore summarize it in the briefest of terms. The change is in part a reaction to the failure of large-scale methodological comparisons to shed light on critical variables in formal language learning. It is also due to the difficulty of conducting such studies. Perhaps of greatest importance, though, among the factors which have led to the current emphasis on descriptive investigation of actual classroom activity is the growing conviction that we have yet to determine what precisely the critical variables in formal language learning are.

The classroom is, of course, a multi-dimensional phenomenon, and classroom-centered research in recent years has investigated a wide variety of variables. From the point of view of quantity, however, as well as by other criteria, a primary focus has been the study of teacher-learner verbal interaction: "the analysis of *initiative* and *response* . . . characteristic of interaction between two or more individuals" (Flanders, 1970, p. 35). Many who are otherwise unfamiliar with classroom-centered research have heard of one or another of the various systems of interaction analysis used in educational research in general or language classroom research in particular. The sheer number of these systems is in itself evidence of the interest in this area; and indeed, in spite of the fact that the proliferation of analytical systems and procedures is not without dangers (Rosenshine and Furst, 1973; Delamont, 1976), the feeling remains strong that classroom verbal interaction is critically related to the learning process and therefore worthy of continuing research.

The research on which this chapter reports is based on the assumption that the investigation of the ways in which teachers and learners interact verbally can lead to useful insight into the language teaching/learning process. The particular focus of the present study is on "learner feedback," which I will define for now as "information provided by a learner to a teacher about the comprehensibility and usefulness of some prior teacher utterance(s)." I will qualify this definition later, but for now it will suffice.

The importance of feedback in verbal interaction—its role in shaping discourse—has been extensively studied. Just how important feedback is can perhaps be best appreciated by examining an admittedly over-simplified (but for present purposes serviceable) model of communication.

Verbal communication is universally interactive: that is, it presupposes the participation of at least two individuals, each of whom will alternately play the roles of speaker and hearer. Change in roles proceeds by a series of turns (allocation of which is both culturally and contextually determined), so that, as we all know, A says something to B, who then says something to A, and so forth, until the interaction is concluded.

Let us suppose that two or more speakers engage in a verbal communication. By what means does such interaction proceed? Here we must recognize a fundamental fact about language. In *no* language does each object, event, or relationship have a unique "label" or "word" associated with it, such that in referring to any referent, a speaker merely has to choose the particular symbol associated throughout that community of speakers with the referent in question. Instead of consisting of a large series of one-to-one correspondences between referents (objects, events, relations) and names (words), every language provides its users with the means to designate a single referent with any of a number of different terms and to use a particular term to refer to any of a number of referents. There are many ways to demonstrate this. Consider, for example, that without the possibility of referring to a referent by more than a single name, the use of euphemism would not be possible; conversely, the use of metaphor is possible only when we recognize the possibility of using a single word to refer to more than one referent.

Thus, as Rosenberg and Cohen (1966) have pointed out, the selection of a name for a referent by a speaker cannot be judged to be "correct" or "incorrect" on an absolute basis. Rather, the notion of "correctness" in choosing a name for a referent (or in encoding a message) must involve consideration of the context in which the communication takes place. Many factors enter into the definition of a "communicative context." One of them—and for our purposes, the most important of them—is the other participant(s). In the most general sense, a "correct" designation of a referent is one that is useful in talking about a referent to one's listeners, one that enables a listener to understand what the speaker is referring to: "a listener is said to understand a speaker if he can correctly discriminate the referent from a set of nonreferents on the basis of a message supplied by a speaker" (Glucksberg and Krauss, 1967, p. 309).

Thus, if I (or any speaker) wish to refer to a particular whale, I may choose among a number of names: "a whale," "a killer whale," "*Orcinus orca*," "a whale about thirty feet in length that is black with a white underside," "a leviathan," etc. Indeed, I might even choose to refer to one particular whale by its name, "Namu." The essential point is that each of these names may be "correct" in some contexts and "incorrect" (that is, inappropriate) in others, depending upon what I wish to differentiate the referent from, the general context of the conversation, and the particular participants involved.

Our immediate interest is with the last of these variables, the participant(s). And here is the important point: In communication, it is the responsibility of speakers to evaluate in advance the effect of an utterance on their listeners by taking into consideration both the immediate context and everything with which the referent is likely to be confused. In other words, speakers need to put themselves in their listeners' shoes. When speakers do this successfully, the communication process is sustained.

Listeners also have a responsibility in this process. It is to evaluate speakers' messages and, in their turn, to transmit messages which indicate (explicitly or implicitly) how intelligibly the referent has been labeled—in other words, to provide feedback.

In normal verbal interaction, the roles of speaker and listener are constantly shifting, but at any moment, a participant must play one or the other role. In successful communication, messages concerning a particular referent will be influenced by the utterances of the other participant. If the referent was clearly distinguished from nonreferents, the name (word) used will in all likelihood be retained in subsequent messages; if not, an alternative will in all likelihood be sought.

When a speaker asks, "Do you know what I mean by a 'phoneme'?," he or she entertains some doubt that the name will serve to distinguish the referent to which the word refers from all nonreferents (for example, "morpheme," "sound," or "vowel"). The speaker is in fact inviting the other participants to influence directly (if only with a nod of the head or by some other nonverbal signal) the speaker's subsequent messages, in which the speaker will either continue to use this label or find some substitute (if only temporarily). What the speaker is asking the other participants to do is to provide "feedback": that is, to evaluate the speaker's use of certain names for particular referents.

Breakdowns in communication can be attributed either to the speaker or to the listener.[1] In the case of the former, the failure to gauge consistently what a listener knows about the extra-linguistic context will lead to ineffective choices of referents. This difficulty will be aggravated to the extent to which the speaker is inattentive to listener feedback.[2] Communication breakdowns attributable to the listener include those which are due to the failure of the listener to monitor a speaker's choices of referents: in other words, they can occur when the listener fails to provide feedback. The preference that many students express for a non-lecture approach in classrooms is an indication of many things, among them the desire to be able to orient the lecturer's choice of referents. In many cases, however, the importance of feedback is more than a matter of preference.

What I have outlined to this point applies, as I have indicated, to communication in general. If we narrow our attention to communication in which at least one of the participants is a learner of the language in use, we will discover yet an additional dimension to verbal interaction. Verbal interaction between speakers who do not have equal proficiency in the language in use entails an additional set of choices, since the more proficient speaker (in most cases, a native or native-like speaker) cannot assume that the code (the language in use) is fully shared by the less proficient participant. Thus, in addition to encoding messages in accordance with the assumed extra-linguistic knowledge of the listener and the other contextual variables involved, the speaker must also tailor messages to the perceived linguistic proficiency of the listener. For example, what a speaker might normally choose as a label might, in the speaker's judgment, involve a lexical item which is probably not known by the listener. An alternative will have to be found. Another example: The way in which a speaker would normally encode a message may involve a syntactic complexity which would, in the view of the speaker, tend to obscure the referent for a non-proficient listener. Thus, an alternative encoding must be sought. In the area of testing, the importance of this sort of thing has become more widely recognized. Thus, while for many students the directions, "Do not turn this page until told to do so," may be perfectly intelligible, for young learners a more comprehensible set of directions might be something like, "Turn this page only when I tell you to turn it" (Kennedy, 1972, p. 164–165). Such adjustments are also frequently necessary when the less proficient participant is an adult using a language other than his/her native one.

How speakers of a language adjust their speech in communicating with less than fully proficient listeners has been the object of concern of a large number of studies in recent years. Collectively, language "input" studies have provided strong and consistent evidence that in "natural" settings (Clyne, 1968; Ferguson, 1975) and in the language learning classroom (Henzl, 1973, 1975; Gaies, 1977, 1979; Steyaert, 1977; Chaudron, 1979) proficient speakers make considerable adjustments in language they direct at less proficient listeners. These modifications involve phonology, morphology, syntax, and vocabulary; furthermore, they vary with a striking degree of precision according to the perceived level of proficiency of the listener.

The linguistic adjustments made by teachers to the language they use in the second language classroom constitute an additional set of "input controls" or "filters" designed to facilitate communication and to maximize pedagogical effectiveness. Whether such input control is effective in achieving these purposes is a matter of speculation, as it is for the similar adjustments made by parents and other adults to the speech they address to children acquiring their first language (Drach, 1969; Ervin-Tripp, 1971; Snow, 1972; Brown, Salerno, and Sachs, 1972; Landes, 1975). What *cannot* be assumed—and this point is made repeatedly whenever the limitations of "input" studies are cited—is that what learners actually take in, and the rate at which it is taken in, is determined exclusively by teacher input control.

This point can be argued from several perspectives. Among these is the one adopted by Corder (1967):

> The simple fact of presenting a linguistic form to a learner does not necessarily qualify it for the status of input, for the reason that input is "what goes in," not what is *available* for going in, and we may reasonably suppose that it is the learner who controls this input, or more properly his intake (p. 165).

Corder goes on to suggest that "learner intake" may be governed by the "characteristics of (the) language acquisition mechanism" (p. 165): in other words, essentially by factors over which the learner can exert little direct control, if any.

In this chapter, I will explore the concept of learner "intake control" from a different perspective. I will assume that *by the feedback learners provide, they negotiate the nature of "input."* In other words, by their participation in verbal communication (in accordance with the general "rules" of the communication process outlined above) and in particular by their responses to the special linguistic adjustments made by their teachers on their behalf, learners regulate the nature of the content[3] to which they are exposed in the classroom and the rate at which it is presented.

The purpose, then, of the study reported on in the following pages was to describe the nature of learner feedback. The data for the study were collected in a total of twelve different ESL dyads (teacher, student) and triads (teacher, students). Altogether six different teachers (Ss) taught in these dyads and triads. Although the subjects were teaching in these settings as part of the required field experience of the graduate program in which they were enrolled, most of them had had prior teaching experience—in some cases, quite extensive. The students in these twelve settings varied considerably in age, in their purposes for learning English, and, as best as can be ascertained, in their motivation to develop proficiency in the language.

It is important to recognize that no attempt was made to control for individual differences among the various learners involved in these ESL settings. Indeed, the selection of these settings is an example of what is often termed "accidental sampling": that is, the selection of a sample which is conveniently at hand. Such a sampling procedure is often the only option available to a researcher, but it must always be kept in mind that the data gathered from such a sample are far less appropriate as a basis for generalization than data gathered in the context of more rigorous sampling procedures (e.g., random or stratified sampling). This point will be emphasized again in the discussion of the results of the study.

One advantage to the procedure used is that it allows the researcher to observe actual learning settings, as opposed to teacher-learner groups put together solely for research purposes. Groups of this latter kind cannot be assumed to reflect what goes on in "natural" classes. In that sense, such groups impose another sort of limitation on the generalizability of findings.

The dyads and triads observed in the present study had already been meeting for a number of weeks when the data were collected. In each setting, the activity used to elicit data was a problem-solving task in referential communication— that is, a task whose completion depended on the imparting of certain information by the teacher to the student(s). The task required the teacher to describe, without recourse to gesture, a series of six different graphic designs in such a way that the learner(s), who had all six designs reproduced on an answer sheet, could number the designs in the order in which they were described. Two tasks of this kind—one which had been used in earlier studies of the role of feedback in referential communication (Krauss and Weinheimer, 1966; Glucksberg and Krauss, 1966, 1967) and one designed specifically for the present study (see Figure 1)—were performed in each of the settings.

Figure 1. Designs used in a task in referential communication

In preparation for the administration of the tasks, the subjects, who were unaware not only of the purpose of the study but also of the fact that a study had in fact been planned, were instructed to inform their learner(s) that what they were going to do was not a test; in addition, the learners were to be encouraged to request any clarification or re-explanation they felt was necessary for them to complete the task successfully (see Appendix 1: "Instructions to the Teacher/Tutor"). The audio recordings made of these activities indicated that in each case learners were clearly informed that they could provide whatever feedback (though the word itself was never used) they felt was necessary.

Transcriptions of the audio recordings were made in preparation for the analysis of the data. In a descriptive study such as the one under discussion, a critical step is the selection of a framework within which the phenomena under investigation can be viewed and the establishment of categories which will reflect basic distinctions in the data collected. This is an important point, one that, even though it may be clear to many, will be emphasized again (see below). In regard to the present study, a decision had been made *a priori* to examine learner feedback within the general framework of interaction analysis: in other words, as utterances which interact with teacher utterances to shape classroom discourse. From this point of view, which hardly represents a novel way of looking at classroom language, any number of classification schemes might have been developed for categorizing learner feedback. In fact, however, it had been decided in advance that major categories of learner feedback would be established on the basis of the four types of "pedagogical moves" defined by Bellack et al. (1966) in their study of classroom verbal interaction patterns. These pedagogical moves, or utterance types, are labeled "structuring," "soliciting," "responding," and "reacting,"[4] and were shown by Bellack and his associates to be distributed among the participants in a traditional classroom setting in a highly consistent fashion. The use of these categories in the study of learner feedback was based on the assumption that they could serve as effectively for the classification of learner feedback—which constitutes some proportion of the total verbal activity in the classroom—as they had served for the analysis of classroom discourse as a whole.

With some modifications, this classification framework proved feasible. The system provided a means by which to distinguish among a number of kinds of learner feedback. Learner utterances which are overtly elicited through teacher questions (teacher soliciting moves) can be viewed as feedback essentially different (see Figure 2) from what has been labeled "unelicited" feedback.[5] "Elicited" feedback is primarily the product of the teacher's attempt to monitor the rate and flow of "content" (input) in the classroom "Unelicited" feedback, by contrast, is a primary means by which *learners* can shape classroom discourse and, in the process, adjust input to their ability and needs. Unelicited feedback can be divided into three fundamentally different subtypes: "soliciting" feedback, by which learners attempt to obtain information which they feel is necessary for comprehension; "reacting" feedback, by which learners indicate comprehension or non-comprehension of content;[6] and "structuring" feedback, by which learners attempt to reorient or redefine the basis for subsequent

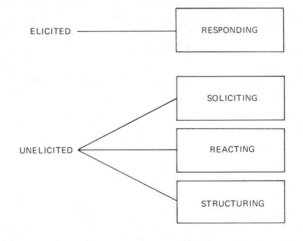

Figure 2.   Basic categories of learner feedback

interaction. It should be noted here that utterances were assigned to these major categories on the basis of functional properties rather than syntactic features. An interrogative sentence, for example, could be classified as soliciting, reacting, or structuring, depending on its communicative function.

These basic categories were selected in advance for the classification of learner feedback. In the data analysis, a number of subcategories were established on an *an hoc* basis for the particular data collected. These categories are displayed in Table 1. Examples of many of the subcategories can be found in the pages following.

Table 1.   Subcategories of Learner Verbal Feedback

Basic category*	Subcategory
Responding	Response to Direct Question
	Informational Response
Reacting	Comprehension Signal
	Confirmation by Repetition
	Confirmation by Paraphrase
	Confirmation by Definition
	Utterance Completion
	Non-Comprehension Signal
	Utterance Repetition (Non-Comprehension)
	Request for Definition
	Confirmation to Proceed
	Halt Signal
	Request for Repetition
Soliciting	Direct Question (Partial)
	Direct Question
	Information Search
Structuring	Redirecting Question
	Reorienting Feedback
	Initiating Act

*Based on Bellack et al., 1966.

Responding subcategories

Response to Direct Question. Learner responses classified into this category follow "closed" questions: that is, the response can be predicted by the teacher, or else the response is one of a relatively small number of alternatives.

Examples: T(eacher): Are you ready for #3?
   L(earner): Yeah.

   T: Start all over?
   L: Yeah.
   T: With #1 or #2?
   L: #2.

Informational Response. Responding feedback of this sort generally follows "open" questions and transmits information which cannot necessarily be predicted by the teacher.

Examples: T: If you had to describe #5 to somebody . . .
            L: It looks like a fish.
            T: Looks like a fish? Hmm. Well, maybe.
                How's it look like a fish?
            L: In back it's got a tail and . . .

            T: What kind of animal has horns?
            L1: Male, male cows.
            L2: Deer?

Reacting subcategories

Comprehension Signal. The learner indicates that a preceding teacher utterance has been understood.

Confirmation by Repetition. By repeating a single word or an entire utterance, with or without rising intonation, the learner signals comprehension (or tests whether the utterance has been correctly heard).

Confirmation by Paraphrase. In statement form, the learner indicates (or in question form, tests) comprehension by paraphrasing a word or utterance produced by the teacher.

Examples: T: And then finally the sixth design?
            L: The last one?

            T: Do you know what "worms" are?
            L: Worms? (Confirmation by Repetition)
            T: Yeah.
            L: When it's hot? (Confirmation by Paraphrase)

Confirmation by Definition. The learner indicates comprehension by defining a word used by a teacher.

Utterance Completion. The learner signals comprehension by anticipating the rest of a teacher's utterance.

            T: But if it's not clear . . . uh . . .
            L: (We) can ask.

Non-Comprehension Signal. The learner overtly indicates non-comprehension. This category includes signals made as a response to a teacher question.

Utterance Repetition (Non-Comprehension). Signals in this category are distinguished from those classified under "Confirmation by Repetition" primarily by paralinguistic and accompanying nonverbal signals.

Request for Definition. The learner indicates a specific element in a teacher utterance which cannot be processed.

Confirmation to Proceed. The learner interjects, either in the middle of a teacher utterance or between teacher utterances, a signal that the rate of input is acceptable and that the teacher can proceed. Such signals, which often take the form of "O.K." or "uhhuh," also imply comprehension of the utterance.

Halt Signal. The learner requests a temporary halt to the flow of input. Such signals either signal failure to comprehend or indicate a need for greater processing time.

Request for Repetition. Signals in this category are designed to increase the redundancy of the input (to facilitate processing or to check comprehension).

Soliciting subcategories

Direct Question (Partial). One element of a preceding teacher utterance is focused upon.

Example: T: You want to put your name on it?
           L: Do you want me to write on the paper?

Direct Question. The focus of the question is the entire preceding teacher utterance.

Example: T: ... actually four, there's one little triangle in the middle and then you have three outside triangles, O.K.?
           L: Unconnected?

Information Search. The focus is on something other than the immediately preceding utterance. The focus may be on information previously transmitted in the communication, or it may be on information not previously dealt with but relevant to the task immediately at hand.

Example: T: Now I have to collect your answer sheets, and then we go on to the next group.
           L: Do you want our name?
           T: Oh, yeah. Just your initials, just your initials, O.K.?

Structuring subcategories

Redirecting Question. A redirecting question is one that attempts to shift discourse to a different (but related) topic.

Example: T: ... and then the last one. By process of elimination you should be able to guess. But just in case, actually it looks like three triangles on the outside and then the way they all come together they form a little one on the inside, O.K.?
           L: What's #2?

Reorienting Feedback. This subcategory of feedback is corrective in the sense that it evaluates a teacher's attempt to select content requested by the learner(s).

Example: T: It's like the shape of an egg.
           L: O.K. Circle them?
           T: It's not quite a circle, but the shape of . . .
           L: I mean . . . what we do?

Initiating Act. The purpose of feedback in this subcategory is to shift to a new topic unrelated to either the specific or general task at hand. Utterances in this category reflect the greatest degree of discourse control assumed by a learner, since they attempt to redefine (at least temporarily) the basis for interaction.

Example: T: But, but this is related to the moth but it's usually more beautiful. It has many colors, and it's, it's a very lovely insect. Is it an insect? Yeah? O.K., O.K.
            L1: You don't know what's butterfly?
            L2: I'm sorry, I don't.
            T: Well now . . .
            L1: You know that one I could have shown you, you know. I found one in garbage.
            T: You found a butterfly in the garbage can?
            L1: Yeah.
            T: Really?

Before looking at the profile of the dyads and triads, which emerges from the descriptive framework just described, we might do well to consider carefully the nature of such categories. The reader should recognize a fundamental property of empirical research; namely, the relationship between categories and the data they used to classify. Such categories—whether they are selected in advance (as was the case with the four basic categories) or formulated specifically for particular data (as was the case with the nineteen subcategories)—are not inherent to the data; nor are they observable in the data. Rather, they reflect the particular order that a researcher chooses to impose on the data. The basis of organization is often largely determined, consciously or unconsciously, by prior experience and by the expectations that experience engenders.[7] In short, the reader should remember that there are many possible descriptions of particular data. Any one description will reveal certain patterns and obscure others; it will, quite simply, reflect one particular order that can be imposed on the data.

Tables 2 and 3 present profiles of learner feedback as it occurred in the dyads and triads, respectively. Altogether, 442 instances of learner verbal feedback were classified; of these, 239 occurred in the seven dyads, while 203 occurred in the five triads. Considerable variation from setting to setting in the amount of learner feedback provided can be observed. In the dyads, the number of

Table 2. Learner Feedback in Dyads

	Learner feedback category				
Dyad	Responding	Reacting	Soliciting	Structuring	Total
1 (1)*	15	31	2	4	52
2 (1)	2	1	—	—	3
3 (1)	—	7	1	—	8
4 (1)	9	16	9	10	44
5 (2)	10	52	14	8	84
6 (3)	1	14	9	1	25
7 (5)	1	16	4	2	23
Total	38	137	39	25	239

*The number in parentheses refers to the subject: for example, Subject 1 taught Dyads 1–4, while Dyad 5 was taught by Subject 2.

Table 3. Learner Feedback in Triads

	Learner feedback category				
Triad	Responding	Reacting	Soliciting	Structuring	Total
1 (2)*	3	18	5	—	26 (17,9)**
2 (3)	3	51	8	3	65 (55,10)
3 (4)	1	11	6	3	21 (14,7)
4 (4)	9***	22	4***	9	44 (26,18)
5 (6)	11	28	5	3	47 (30,17)
Total	27	130	28	18	203

  * The number in parentheses refers to the subject.

  ** The figures in parentheses indicate the distribution of total feedback moves between the two learners in each triad: for example, in Triad 1, one learner produced 17 feedback moves, while the other produced 9.

  *** These figures include one learner-learner move.

feedback moves ranged from a low of 3 to a high of 84; in the triads, the range was from 21 to 65.

These figures refer, of course, to verbal feedback alone. In view of the fact that audiotapes were used, nonverbal feedback could not be studied systematically. Nevertheless, the transcripts, along with subjects' comments after the tasks were performed, suggest quite clearly that while the subjects were sensitive in all cases to nonverbal feedback, in some settings heavy reliance on learner nonverbal feedback had already been established as a standing behavioral pattern.[8] Therefore, as already noted (see Note 4), while the present study assumes the value of investigating verbal feedback, it also recognizes that in some cases verbal activity may play a secondary or even minor role in the process of providing feedback.

Tables 2 and 3 profile verbal feedback in the four major categories as it occurred in the dyads and triads, respectively. While differences in the number of responding moves are more a reflection of what teachers were doing to structure discourse than of what learners were doing, the other categories reflect similarities and differences in the way and in the degree to which classroom discourse was influenced by learners during the performance of the tasks. The general tendency was for learners not to restructure discourse during the performance of the tasks, though in three settings this was done to some degree. How fully the dyads and triads proceeded through the tasks under the control of the teachers can be seen in the fact that, in the data for the five triads, there is only one instance of a learner feedback move directed at the other learner in the setting. Overall, the portrait of a teacher-centered approach, which is precisely what one would expect in a task in referential communication in which one party—the teacher—has certain information to impart to another—the learner(s)—emerges clearly. Learner control of discourse was accomplished primarily through their use of questions, by soliciting from the teacher the information they felt necessary, rather than by reorienting the manner in which the tasks were performed or, in the case of the triads, establishing extensive learner-learner interaction.

On the other hand, a striking difference exists in the number of reacting moves made in various settings. Any number of factors can be postulated to account for this difference: among them, the degree to which teachers relied on nonverbal signals, the difficulty of the tasks for various learners (although all of the learners eventually completed the tasks successfully), learners' relative interest in the tasks, their perception of their teacher's desire or need for verbal feedback (in other words, the interaction patterns already established in particular settings), and particularly tactics employed by teachers in describing the designs.

The data on learner feedback can be summarized as follows:

1. Collectively, the learners made use of feedback in all four of the major categories; not all individual learners, however, used all four types of feedback.
2. There was considerable variation from learner to learner in the amount of feedback provided.
3. In both dyads and triads, reacting moves were by far the most frequent form of feedback, structuring moves occurred the least frequently and were the least evenly distributed, with 3 of the 12 settings accounting for 63% (27 out of 43) of these.
4. In each of the triads, one learner provided considerably more feedback than the other.

The description of learner verbal feedback presented above needs to be supplemented, of course, by an examination of the effect it produces on classroom discourse. In the present study, the post-feedback utterances of teachers were classified. An attempt was made to adapt a previously used set of categories (Glucksberg and Krauss, 1967) of post-feedback responses. A five-category system was developed for the present study to compare a teacher utterance that in some way led to learner feedback with the teacher utterance that followed learner feedback. The categories are listed and defined below:

examples of post-feedback utterances in each category are provided in Appendix 2.

1. *Verbatim Repetition:* exact (or virtually exact) repetitions of the descriptions which led, directly or indirectly, to learner feedback.
2. *Reduced Repetition:* the use of the same reference phrase (description) by the teacher, but in shortened form.
3. *Expanded Repetition:* the reference phrase used by the teacher in the pre-feedback utterance is explained in some way (for example, by focusing on a particular word and defining it).
4. *Restructuring:* the pre-feedback description is abandoned and replaced by a new reference phrase. "Restructuring" reflects the belief on the part of the teacher that the original symbol used to designate a particular referent cannot be used successfully in the immediate setting.
5. *Question:* an alternative to a repeated, modified, or new description; in this way, the teacher seeks to elicit additional feedback which may be used in further description.

A total of 124 post-feedback teacher moves was recorded. This data is presented in Table 4. Here too, there was considerable variation in the total number of moves from setting to setting, ranging from a low of 1 to a high of 21.

Preliminary analysis of the data reveals little in the way of a relationship between learner feedback and teacher post-feedback behavior. There is no discernible relationship between the number of learner feedback moves in a particular setting and the number of post-feedback moves in that setting. Furthermore, there is no evidence that any particular category of learner

Table 4. Teacher Post-Feedback Moves

Setting	Post-feedback category					
	R*	RR	RE	ReS	Q	Total
Dyad: 1	3	1	6	3	—	13
2	—	—	1	—	—	1
3	6	1	1	—	—	8
4	—	—	1	—	—	1
5	4	—	9	2	1	16
6	1	—	—	3	2	6
7	2	—	4	—	—	6
Triad: 1	3	3	5	4	—	15
2	—	—	3	3	1	7
3	5	2	6	1	1	15
4	1	—	10	2	2	15
5	5	3	5	4	4	21
Total	30	10	51	22	11	124

* R = Verbatim Repetition; RR = Reduced Repetition;
RE = Expanded Repetition; ReS = Restructuring;
Q = Question

feedback is linked to any category of post-feedback teacher utterances. The most striking example of this is the post-feedback category of "restructuring." One would expect that utterances of this type would ordinarily follow learner feedback signaling non-comprehension. An examination of the transcripts shows, however, that teacher restructuring followed feedback indicating comprehension almost as often as it followed signals that the learner(s) did not understand what the teacher had said. In fact, the only immediately apparent pattern that can be detected is the tendency of teachers to expand descriptions rather than to reduce them in length (51 instances of the former compared to only 10 of the latter).

The purpose of the pilot study described in these pages was to explore learner verbal feedback with the eventual goal of developing the outline for a larger study. The data gathered in the pilot study is, as has just been discussed, hardly suggestive of clear-cut generalizations. In any case, however, the data base for the pilot study can hardly be assumed to be representative of all ESL teacher/learner situations.

Despite the failure of this initial analysis of the data to yield more in the way of insight into the relationship between learner feedback and its effect on teacher behavior, there is good reason to view prospects for further research in this area with optimism. The pilot study reported on in these pages had, as its primary goal, the description of learner verbal feedback as it occurred in a particular set of ESL learning settings. In terms of the questions it raises and the possibilities for further research, the present study would seem to have been well worth doing. In the paragraphs to follow, I will list the issues which the present study has raised, directly or indirectly, and the possibilities for follow-up research in this area.

One of the first questions which the present study raises is how similar the feedback behavior of the learners in the ESL dyads and triads observed is to that which might be observed in other settings of comparable size or in larger learning settings. In other words, does learning-group size bear on the issue of learner feedback? A study designed to explore such a question—indeed, any follow-up study which attempted to control one or more of the variables which were not controlled for in the pilot study—would also be able to test the descriptive generality of the categories and subcategories of learner verbal feedback used in the pilot study. Put differently, do the subcategories used in the present study—subcategories which were empirically derived from a set of data—work equally well with other data?

A related question is whether or not the kind and amount of feedback provided by language learners vary according to the nature of the activity taking place in the learning setting. Intuition suggests that this would be so, but empirical research would be more likely to provide us with usable findings. Clearly, in the settings observed, in which teachers and learners were involved in activities that were highly structured from the start—in which the alternatives for performing the tasks were extremely limited from the outset—the occurrence of structuring feedback was understandably infrequent. What role does structuring feedback play in language learning tasks which are less teacher- or materials-centered?

Another issue which could be usefully explored on the basis of the findings of the pilot study is whether or not a relationship exists between learner characteristics and the type of feedback provided. The data discussed in these pages suggest that learners have available to them, and exploit to various degrees, a number of types of feedback. Through the feedback they provide, learners are able to regulate to some extent the content to which they are exposed and the rate at which that content is presented. Do different learners exploit the possibilities to various degrees? Is there a relationship between "learning style," for example, and the use of different categories of feedback? In view of the lack of control of learner variables in the pilot study, the latter question cannot be answered on the basis of the data gathered. That it would be valuable to explore in further research is suggested by the attention directed by previous studies (Brown, 1973; Guiora et al., 1975; Seliger, 1977; Tarone, 1977) to the interrelationship of cognitive style, personality, and language learner behavior.

Still another issue is raised by the present study; namely, the relationship between teacher behavior and learner feedback. Do particular characteristics of teacher verbal activity either stimulate or reduce learner feedback? There is evidence in the pilot study data that certain features of teacher verbal activity—beyond the basic attempt to make content comprehensible—have much to do with the amount and kind of feedback learners provide. One such feature might be used here by way of illustration: a feature I will label "enriched redundancy." It involves, among other things, multiple descriptions of a single referent, unrequested repetitions, and an abnormally frequent use of questions to check comprehension (often in the form of pause markers).[9] Whether such teacher behavior is effective or not is not the issue here. Whether and how such features affect the opportunity for learners to regulate the nature and flow of content in the language learning setting is, and it would seem to be worthy of further investigation.

Further research on any of these questions would, as already mentioned, further test the adequacy of the category systems used, in the same way that the pilot study tested the applicability of Bellack et al.'s set of basic classroom moves to the description of learner feedback. This is not to suggest, of course, that alternative descriptive frameworks ought not to be investigated. One possibility would be to develop analytical units which would enable us to describe learner feedback in terms of "cycles." Such units would not restrict the researcher to analyzing a learner feedback utterance primarily in terms of the teacher utterances which precede and follow it; rather, larger units of discourse (in which two, three, or possibly more learner feedback utterances can be described as forming a single "event") might prove to provide greater descriptive (and eventually explanatory) insight.[10]

In summary, then, the pilot study reported on here provides a point of departure for the study of learner feedback. Based on the observation of actual classroom activity, the study describes ways in which language learners participate in the structuring of classroom discourse. The description presented, while not itself sufficient for developing generalizations about learner feedback and its effect on classroom language learning, has nonetheless raised questions which might be profitably explored in research designs out of which generalization may be appropriately drawn.

Appendix 1. Instructions to the Teacher/Tutor

You will need the following in order to perform this exercise with your student(s):

1. a cassette tape recorder and a blank cassette tape;
2. two (2) student answer sheets, in envelopes labeled #1 and #2;
3. two (2) examiner packets, in envelopes labeled #1 and #2; and
4. a pencil for each student.

Instructions for Administering the Exercise:

1. Load the recorder and begin recording even before you explain the instructions for the exercise to the students. BE SURE THE RECORDER IS RECORDING SATISFACTORILY.
2. Seat yourself and the student(s) facing each other, but at all times make sure that the student(s) cannot see your examiner packet and that you cannot see the student answer sheets.
3. Explain the task to the students. Tell them to take out answer sheet #1. On it they will see six (6) designs. You, the examiner, are going to describe these designs one by one, and they are to mark the order in which they are described by numbering the designs 1, 2, 3, 4, 5, and 6 (it doesn't matter where they put the numbers, as long as it is clear which design is given which number). Tell them they are free to indicate whether they have understood your description and to ask any questions which will help them identify the designs.
4. You are to describe the designs in the order specified in the examiner packet. You are free to ask students whether they have understood a description. MAKE IT CLEAR TO THE STUDENTS THAT YOU ARE WORKING AS A "TEAM" IN THIS EXERCISE. Do *not*, however, use hand or other body movements in your descriptions. Also, do *not* look at how a student has numbered his/her answers.
5. After Exercise #1 is completed, do Exercise #2. When both exercises are completed, put the material back into the folders and turn off the recorder. Of course, if you wish, you may check to see how well your student(s) did.
6. ABOVE ALL, REMIND STUDENTS TO ASSIST YOU DURING THE EXERCISE BY ASKING QUESTIONS AND INDICATING

THEIR UNDERSTANDING OR LACK OF UNDERSTANDING OF A DESCRIPTION.

7. Please do not discuss this exercise with anyone. Thank you very much for your cooperation and participation.

Appendix 2. Examples of Pre- and Post-Feedback Teacher Utterances

All excerpts given as illustrations are teacher utterances. For purposes of economy and clarity, intervening learner utterances have been omitted. There is, however, a minimum of one learner feedback move between each pre- and post-feedback pair.

1. *Verbatim Repetition.*

   Pre-feedback: It sort of looks a little bit like an "L." and . . . but not quite, like the, the foot of foot of the "L" has been chopped off.

   Post-feedback: It sort of looks like an "L" only the foot of the "L" has been chopped off.

2. *Reduced Repetition.*

   Pre-feedback: It looks like two horns of an animal. Do you know? an animal that has horns on top of its head? They're like ears, only they're on top of its head. O.K. Um, so they look like two horns that are coming up, and they practically meet. And then on, on the bottom is a . . . sort of a boat-like shape, O.K.? sort of like a rowboat. O.K.? So at the bottom you have a rowboat, and coming out of the rowboat you have two horns that almost meet on top, they almost make a circle, almost make a circle. Inside the circle it almost looks like a heart, a Valentine's Day heart, a heart? You know, for Valentine's Day?

   Post-feedback: O.K. It's that kind of a look to it. O.K. So you've got really basically two horns coming up to meet at the top.

3. *Expanded Repetition.*

   Pre-feedback: #5 looks to me like a goldfish that's carrying a block in his mouth.

   Post-feedback: It's a little fish, O.K., a very little fish, and people keep them in tanks. They're pretty, many different colors, sometimes they have very pretty tails, and things. O.K. Looks like a goldfish, except that there's something, like, where the mouth of the goldfish would be, he's carrying a, a brick, or a block, some, some rectangular object.

4. *Restructuring.*

   Pre-feedback: #4, uh, looks something like a dish that's turned upside down.

Post-feedback: It, it also looks something like an egg-shape, you know, half an egg shell.

5. *Question.*

Pre-feedback: Something like an animal with two teeth and a lemon-shaped head.

Post-feedback: What is a lemon?

Notes

1. I am excluding from consideration breakdowns due to distortion in the conducting medium—for example, a faulty telephone connection, illegible handwriting, and extraneous noise—which have to do with the acoustic (or graphic) dimensions of communication.

2. Such breakdowns have been the object of considerable research. Indeed, it has been asserted (Glucksberg, Krauss, and Weisberg, 1966) that nursery-school-age children typically engage in "nonsocial encoding"—that is, speech that is unedited for particular listeners and comparatively unresponsive to listener feedback. Part of the language development process, then, involves learning how to avoid speaker-based breakdowns, how to produce "social speech"—that is, messages encoded with regard to the listener.

3. It must be recognized that in the language classroom,—where the target language is not only the vehicle by which information is conveyed but also a product of the underlying system to be acquired by the learners (as Henzl says, "an instantaneous application of the subject matter, a model illustrating and reinforcing the information transmitted in the instructional process" (1975 p. 3)—the term "content" refers both to the information transmitted and to classsroom language itself.

4. Examples of each of these can be found in the description of the subcategories developed for the present study; see pages 200–202.

5. The focus of the study on verbal interaction should not obscure the fact that classroom discourse is shaped and regulated to a large degree by paralinguistic and nonverbal signals. Given this, the reader should recognize that the distinction between *verbally* elicited and *verbally* unelicited feedback is a distinction which, however useful it may be, may well be something of a misrepresentation.

6. This definition of "reacting" moves is somewhat different from the one used in the Bellack et al. (1966) study. In that study, reacting moves were those utterances that evaluated the correctness or appropriateness of other utterances. Here, learner utterances that are classified as "reacting" are also evaluative in nature, but it is the *comprehensibility*, rather than the *correctness*, of a preceding utterance that is being judged.

7. Indeed, there is growing recognition of this fundamental limitation in traditional modes of inquiry. In many fields it has led to a revitalization of "qualitative" or ethnographic research. Among other things, this research methodology has as a goal the development of theory and organizational categories based on the first-hand participation of the "observer/researcher" in the field. (See, for example, Glaser and Strauss, 1967.)

8. This assumption is justified in part by the fact that the dyads and triads had been in progress for a minimum of two months before the study was undertaken. The groups were not artificially contrived for research purposes, and it is therefore reasonable to assume that the behavior observed reflected to a large degree the ordinary patterns of behavior in the settings.

9. An example of such "enriched redundancy" can be found in Appendix 2, in the example of "Reduced Repetition" (Pre-feedback description).

10. An example of the alternatives available can be seen in the study of corrective feedback; compare Fanselow (1977), in which the unit of analysis is a correcting move following a learner error, with Salica (1980), in which the attempt is made to identify corrective cycles (based on Chaudron's (1977) model of corrective discourse).

References

Bellack, A. A., et al. *The Language of the Classroom*. New York: Teachers College Press, 1966.

Brown, H. D. Affective variables in second language acquisition. *Language Learning*, 1973, *23*, 2, 231–244.

Brown, R., Salerno, R. A., & Sachs, J. Some characteristics of adults' speech to children. Report No. 6, Language Acquisition Laboratory, University of Connecticut, 1972.

Chaudron, C. A. A descriptive model of discourse in the corrective treatment of learners' errors. *Language Learning,* 1977, *27,* 1, 29–46.

Chaudron, C. Complexity of teacher speech and vocabulary explanation/elaboration. Paper read at the Thirteenth Annual TESOL Convention, Boston, Mass., February, 27–March 4, 1979.

Clyne, M. Zum Pidgin-Deutsch des Gastarbeiter. *Zeitschrift für Mundartforschung*, 1968, *35*, 130–139.

Corder, S. P. The significance of learner's errors. *International Review of Applied Linguistics*, 1967, 5, 161–169.

Delamont, S. *Interaction in the Classroom*. London: Methuen, 1976.

Drach, K. The language of the parent: A pilot study. The structure of linguistic input to children, Working Paper No. 14, Language Behavior Research Laboratory, University of California, Berkeley, 1969.

Evrin-Tripp, S. An overview of theories of grammatical development. In D. Slobin (Ed.), *The ontogenesis of Grammar*. New York: Academic Press, 1971.

Fanselow, J. F. The treatment of error in oral work. *Foreign Language Annals*, 1977, *10*, 583–593.

Ferguson, C. A. Toward a characterization of English foreigner talk. *Anthropological Linguistics*, 1975, *17*, 1–14.

Flanders, N. A. *Analyzing Teaching Behavior*. Reading, Mass.: Addison-Wesley, 1970.

Gaies, S. J. The nature of linguistic input in formal second language learning: Linguistic and communicative strategies in ESL teachers' classroom language. In H. D. Brown, R. H. Crymes, & C. A. Yorio (Eds.), *On TESOL 77*. Washington, D.C.: TESOL, 1977, 204–212.

Gaies, S. J. Linguistic input in first and second language learning. In F. R. Eckman & A. J. Hastings (Eds.), *Studies in First and Second Language Acquisition*. Rowley, Mass.: Newbury House, 1979, 185–193.

Glaser, B. G., & Strauss, A. L. *The Discovery of Grounded Theory: Strategies for Qualitative Research*. Chicago: Aldine, 1967.

Glucksberg, S., & Krauss, R. M. What do people say after they have learned how to talk? Studies of the development of referential communication. *Merrill-Palmer Quarterly of Behavior and Development*, 1967, *13*, 309–316.

Glucksberg, S., Krauss, R. M., & Weisberg, R. Referential communication in nursery school children: Method and some preliminary findings. Journal of Experimental Child Psychology, 1966, *3*, 333–342.

Guiora, A., et al. Language and person—Studies in language behavior. *Language Learning*, 1975, *25*, 1, 43–62.

Henzl, V. M. Linguistic register of foreign language instruction. *Language Learning*, 1973, *23*, 2, 207–222.

Henzl, V. M. Speech of foreign language teachers: A sociolinguistic analysis. Paper read at the Fourth International Congress of Applied Linguistics, Stuttgart, West Germany, August 25–30, 1975.

Kennedy, G. The language of tests for young children. In B. Spolsky (Ed.), *The Language Education of Minority Children*. Rowley, Mass.: Newbury House, 1972, 164–181.

Krauss, R. M., & Weinheimer, S. Concurrent feedback, confirmation, and the encoding of referents in verbal communication. *Journal of Personality and Social Psychology*, 1966, *4*, 3, 343–346.

Landes, J. E. Speech addressed to children: Issues and characteristics of parental input. *Language Learning*, 1975, *25*, 2, 355–379.

Long, M. Inside the "black box": Methodological issues in classroom research on language learning. Paper read at the Thirteenth Annual TESOL Convention, Boston, Mass., February 27–March 4, 1979.

Rosenshine, B., & Furst, N. The use of direct observation to study teaching. In R. Travers (Ed.), *Second Handbook of Research on Teaching*. Chicago: Rand McNally, 1973, 122–183.

Salica, C. Testing a model of corrective discourse. Progress report presented to M. A. Colloquium, TESL Department, University of California, Los Angeles, May 16, 1980.

Seliger, H. W. Does practice make perfect?: A study of interaction patterns and L2 competence. *Language Learning*, 1977, *27*, 2, 263–278.

Snow, C. Mothers' speech to young children. *Child Development*, 1972, *43*, 549–565.

Steyaert, M. A comparison of the speech of ESL teachers to native speakers and nonnative learners of English. Paper read at the Fifty-Second Annual Meeting of the Linguistic Society of America, Chicago, Ill., December 28–29, 1977.

Tarone, E. E. Conscious communication strategies in interlanguage: A report. In H. D. Brown, R. H. Crymes & C. A. Yorio (Eds.), *On TESOL 77*. Washington, D.C.: TESOL, 1977, 194–203.

Questions for Discussion and Activities

1. Learners' provision of feedback, Gaies claims, is how they negotiate the input. Why is the nature of language addressed to learners believed to be an important variable in second language acquisition?
2. Consult a book on research methods. What is meant by "accidental," random, and stratified sampling? What are the advantages and disadvantages of each procedure?
3. Gaies's subjects were "unaware not only of the purpose of the study, but also of the fact that a study had in fact been planned." What could be the effect on the validity of a study of (a) subjects knowing they are research subjects, and (b) subjects knowing the focus of the research? What measures can be taken to avoid or control for these problems?
4. Gaies's dyads and triads had been working together for at least two months before the data were collected. In many laboratory studies of this kind, subjects meet only once for the purpose of the investigation. In what ways could prior familiarity with one's partner(s) affect conversation and, in turn, the external validity of a study?
5. Write directional hypotheses concerning the differences you predict between conversations among friends and strangers based on your answer to question 4. Then tape-record two dyads working on Gaies's task, one that is formed of two people meeting for the first time, and one that consists of two friends or people who know each other well. Transcribe the conversations and apply Gaies's categories to the data. Test your hypotheses. What other differences between the conversations do you notice which might be due to the variable of prior acquaintance of the speakers?
6. Gaies had native speakers describe the pictures to non-native speakers. What differences would you expect to observe in the verbal feedback they received if their partners had been other native speakers? Why?
7. Replicate Gaies's study using two native speaker-native speaker dyads. Test the predictions you made in answering question 6. How can native speaker baseline data help a researcher better understand non-native speaker speech patterns?
8. Gaies found considerable variability in the amount of verbal feedback learners gave. How could this relate to Seliger's distinction between high and low input generators?
9. Compare the functions of teacher and learner feedback as described by Nystrom and Gaies in this book. In what ways are they similar? In what ways are they different?

PART V

**Input, Interaction, and Acquisition
in the Second Language Classroom**

10

Exploring Relationships between Developmental and Instructional Sequences in L2 Acquisition[1]

Patsy M. Lightbown

The study described in this chapter was designed to investigate relationships between the language L2 learners hear and the language they produce. The specific aspect of language under investigation is the use of a group of grammatical morphemes which have figured in much recent L2 research. The subjects of the longitudinal study are French Canadian adolescents who have little contact with English outside the classrooms in which they are taught English as a second language (ESL) for a few hours a week.

Grammatical morphemes in ESL learners' speech

Many empirical studies in recent second language acquisition research have focused on the accuracy with which ESL learners use certain grammatical morphemes. In most of these studies, results have been reported in terms of rank order correlations between accuracy orders for the different morphemes in the speech of different groups of learners. The similarity of these accuracy orders has led a number of researchers to hypothesize that there is a "natural sequence" in ESL morpheme acquisition. That is, they believe there is evidence that learners of different ages (children and adults), from different first language backgrounds, and with different kinds and amounts of ESL instruction and exposure to English, will acquire this group of grammatical morphemes in essentially the same order (Dulay and Burt, 1974; Bailey, Madden, and Krashen, 1974; Larsen-Freeman, 1976).

The analysis of the data in virtually every study was based on Brown's (1973) obligatory contexts methodology. The investigator examines a learner's utterance to determine the extent to which the grammatical morphemes in question are supplied in contexts where they are required. For example, if the learner points to a picture of baby birds in a nest while saying "the baby bird are hungry," an obligatory context for the noun plural has been created but not fulfilled. The number of times a morpheme is used correctly is divided by the total number of contexts requiring its use in the learner's speech. The result is an accuracy score for that particular morpheme.

Most of the studies supporting the "natural sequence" hypothesis were cross-sectional in design, and most of them obtained the data by engaging the subjects in a structured conversation based on the Bilingual Syntax Measure (Burt, Dulay, and Hernandez, 1975). Some researchers have suggested that the "natural sequence" findings are at least partly explained by the nature of the BSM's predetermined set of questions (see, e.g., Larsen-Freeman, 1975; Porter, 1977).

In a review of the morpheme acquistion literature, Krashen (1977) attempted to refute suggestions that the "natural sequence" in morpheme accuracy studies was an artifact of the Bilingual Syntax Measure. He cited studies in which data from written compositions and spontaneous speech yielded the same results as the BSM. Krashen's explanation for Larsen-Freeman's findings, showing differences between BSM results and results based on data elicited by other means, was that adult second language learners have two ways of internalizing knowledge of the target language: (1) *acquisition,* an unconscious process which resembles the child's development of the first language, and (2) *learning,* a conscious process in which the learner's attention is on the forms of the language. According to Krashen, Larsen-Freeman's results from tasks other than the BSM (and sentence imitation) were based on "learned" knowledge which would vary from individual to individual according to the amount and kind of instruction each has had and his or her predisposition to draw on this knowledge. But learners would only draw on "learned" knowledge when they were given time to reflect and when their attention was focused on linguistic form. When, as in the BSM, their attention is not drawn to form, learners would be more similar to each other because their output would be based on their "acquired" knowledge which, Krashen hypothesizes, is very similar among learners. Thus the order in which the morphemes are taught in ESL classes would not alter the "natural sequence" of morpheme acquisition, a sequence determined by unconscious processes (Dulay and Burt, 1978).[2] Krashen proposes, in fact, that the analysis of data from spontaneous language will always yield a morpheme accuracy order reflecting this sequence, and that only data from discrete-point grammar tests, in which the learner's formal knowledge is purposely tapped, will show a different order.

Nevertheless, a number of questions remain concerning the interpretation of the "natural sequence" claims. For example, evidence from some longitudinal studies tends to disconfirm the hypothesis that relative *accuracy* in the cross-sectional results predicts the sequence of *acquisition* for groups or individuals (e.g., Hakuta, 1974b; Rosansky, 1976). Further, the accuracy order based on the obligatory contexts methodology often leaves a substantial amount of data unaccounted for. As Hatch (1978), Andersen (1977), and others have pointed out, learners may not only use a particular form correctly in obligatory contexts but also incorrectly in other contexts. "Overuse" or inappropriate use of a particular form indicates that the learner has an incorrect or incomplete understanding of the functions of the form and the limits of its use.

Relationships between language heard and language produced

In L1 research, mother' speech has been studied together with the language of the child (Moerk, 1977; Cross, 1977; Newport, Gleitman, and Gleitman, 1977). However, even though the importance of studying the input to L2 learners has been emphasized by a number of researchers (especially Wagner-Gough and Hatch, 1975), we know of no L2 studies in which the input to specific learners or groups of learners has been analyzed in relation to those learners' language development over time. Larsen-Freeman (1976a,b) has suggested that the so-called "natural sequence" in morpheme accuracy may be determined largely by the frequency with which certain morphemes occur in the input. She found a significant positive correlation between ESL learners' morpheme accuracy orders (Larsen-Freeman, 1975) and the frequency of the same morphemes in the speech adult native speakers addressed to their children (Brown, 1973).

Hatch (1974) and Lightbown (1980) showed a close relationship between sequence of emergence of certain questions in the speech of L2 learners and the frequency of these questions in speech addressed to them, but these studies were based on data from L2 investigators' speech rather than from the learners' peers or classroom teachers, from whom they presumably received most of their input.

Larsen-Freeman (1976b) found positive correlations between the rank order of frequency of nine grammatical morphemes in the speech of two university ESL teachers and the accuracy orders which she obtained in her 1975 study. However, there was no information about the absolute frequency of occurrence of the various morphemes, and, while the correlations are positive and sometimes significant, morphemes that are widely separated on the accuracy orders (for example, -ing and 3rd singular) are separated by only one rank in the teachers' speech. Furthermore, the high accuracy progressive auxiliary was eighth of the nine morphemes in frequency of occurrence in the teachers' speech. Thus, it would be very difficult to conclude that the accuracy orders were *caused* by the frequency orders (see Dulay and Burt, 1978, for discussion of this issue).

It is evident that an adequate study of input to learners is extremely difficult in most settings, especially those in which learners receive a great deal of informal exposure to the language. The problem of obtaining an adequate and representative sample of the language learners hear seems almost insurmountable. The ESL classroom setting, however, is one in which the problem may be dealt with more successfully, especially when learners have little contact with the target language outside the classroom. Although a number of researchers are currently working toward the analysis of classroom interaction (see, e.g., Chaudron, 1977a, b, and chapter 6, this volume; Gaies, 1977), most classroom interaction studies have been carried out separately from language acquisition studies. That is, the relationship between the input and learners' production of language has been guessed rather than investigated specifically. Even in studies of the effectiveness of language teaching approaches or methods, what actually occurs in the classroom is rarely investigated explicitly. Indeed, Long (1980) and this volume have suggested that we know almost as little about what goes on in the classroom as about what goes on in Chomsky's hypothetical language acquisition device which is often referred to as a "black box."

Background of the Present Study

The study reported here was carried out within the framework of a larger research project[3] in which both cross-sectional and longitudinal approaches are being used to trace the development of English by a group of French-speaking students living in Quebec communities where there are relatively few opportunities for young people to come in contact with English-speakers. A few of the students have a friend with whom they speak English or an English-speaking coach on their baseball or hockey teams. For most of the learners, however, exposure to English outside ESL classes is limited to a few television programs and popular music.

The subjects ranged in age from 11 to 17. In the first year of the study, they were in grade 6, 8 and 10. Students who did not change schools or drop their English course (optional in grade 11) were followed in the second year of the study (in grades 7, 9, and 11). In the first year there were 175 subjects; in the second year there were 100. All the students had begun studying English in grade 4 or grade 5.

The Morpheme Accuracy Study

One aspect of the research has been the study of learners' use of the various functions of -s morphemes (which seem to be a source of confusion and error for all groups of learners from grade 6 to grade 11) and the progressive marker -ing. In the first cross-sectional study, we investigated only the -s morphemes (Lightbown, Spada, and Wallace, 1978). In that study, we observed that, if we looked at verb morphemes and noun morphemes separately, our subjects' relative accuracy in using -s morphemes conformed in general to the "natural sequence" hypothesis.[4] That is, students were very accurate in supplying the copula (it's a girl) and progressive auxiliary (she's holding some balloons), but their performance on the third person singular (she wants a cookie) was quite poor. Performance on the noun plural (some balloons) was far better than performance on the possessive, which occurred very rarely.

If noun and verb morphemes were combined, there was one difference between the relative accuracy we observed and the "natural sequence" literature. In every group, our subjects' performance on the plural was considerably worse than their performance on the progressive auxiliary.[5]

In a subsequent study (Lightbown and Spada, 1979), we added the progressive morpheme -*ing* to the list of morphemes analyzed. We then noted other differences between our results and the "natural sequence" results. First, the grade 6 students were more accurate in using the -*ing* in obligatory contexts than the older, more advanced, groups (see Figure 1). Furthermore, when we considered -*ing* as well as -*s* morphemes, we found that for the group as a whole, our accuracy orders no longer conformed well to the "natural sequence" hypothesis. The "natural sequence" hypothesis (as summarized by Krashen, 1977) would have predicted the order shown on the left in Figure 2. Our accuracy order, for the group as a whole, is shown on the right.

Thus, the results of our cross-sectional study differed from the predicted "natural sequence" in two ways: (1) accuracy on the plural was considerably worse than accuracy on the auxiliary; and (2), except for the grade 6 group, accuracy on -*ing* was extremely low relative to the -*s* morphemes.[6] Furthermore, longitudinal results from the grade 6 group (when they were in grade 7) showed a decline in -*ing* accuracy, and thus supported our hypothesis that the poorer performance on the -*ing* by the older students reflected a developmental phenomenon for these classroom-instructed learners, rather than a difference between groups of learners in the cross-sectional study.

In addition to the observation that our results did not match those of previous studies in terms of accuracy, we were struck by the extent to which learners used certain forms in *inappropriate* contexts. For example, we noted that, while the learners as a group were 80–100% accurate in supplying the copula -*s* and auxiliary -*s* in obligatory contexts, some also tended to use an -*s* inflection in contexts where it was not required, for example, in a sentence such as "the girls want a cookie" in describing a picture in which there was only one girl. We had also noticed in an earlier interview that the grade 6 learners sometimes overused the -*ing* inflection on action verbs, occasionally using -*ing* where the simple present -*s* or no inflection would have been correct (for example, "she's jumping" in response to "what does she do?"). On the other hand, students in grades 8 and 10 used -*ing* much less frequently. They tended instead to use uninflected verbs, for example, "the girl take a cookie" even in contexts requiring the progressive.

The present study extends our previous research through a more detailed examination of longitudinal data from the grade 6–7 subjects. We have sought to account for our results by examining the use of the -*ing* and -*s* inflections in the classroom speech of the subjects' grade 6 teacher and in the textbooks used in grades 4, 5, 6, and 7. Because the subjects were known to have little exposure to English outside the classroom, we expected to find that the use of -*s* and -*ing* morphemes observed in our subjects' speech could be accounted for largely by characteristics of the classroom language.

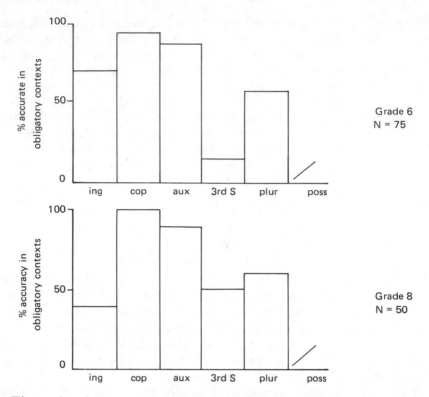

Figure 1. Accuracy of -*ing* and -*s* morphemes in picture card game. Cross-sectional sample

Subjects and Procedures

Subjects. The subjects for the present longitudinal study are the students who were in grade 6 during the first year of the research project. The original grade 6 group consisted of 75 students in three classes in the same school with the same teacher. They had, in fact, had the same teacher and the same materials—*Look, Listen & Learn* (Alexander and Dugas, 1972–3)—throughout their ESL instruction. Through grades 4, 5, and 6 they had 80 to 120 minutes of English per week. In grade 7 they used Book I of the *Lado English Series* (1971, Canadian edition) in their English classes which met for approximately 200 minutes per week.

When the students entered grade 7 (the first year of secondary school in Quebec), nearly half of them were scattered in different public and private secondary schools. Of those who were enrolled in the nearest secondary school, we have longitudinal data on thirty-six who were present for three recordings of the oral communication game which was used as the principal instrument for data collection (see below). Thus, the longitudinal (grades 6–7) sample consists of thirty-six students.

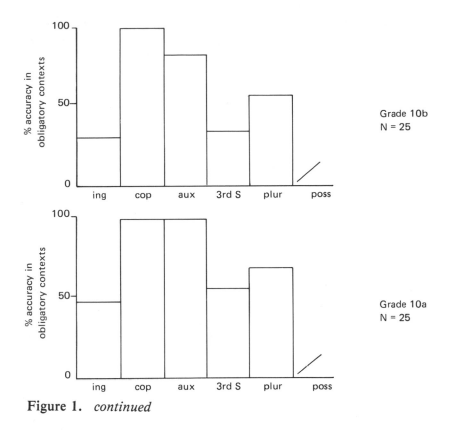

Figure 1. *continued*

The subjects of this study differ from subjects of previous morpheme studies in several ways and thus offer an opportunity to investigate further the claim that, in the acquisition of a set of English grammatical morphemes, there are "natural sequences" which transcend the learners' native languages, instructional history, and age. Our subjects differ first in that they are French-speakers. While a number of L1 groups are represented in previous research, most are Spanish-speakers and there are no groups of French-speakers among the subjects. A second difference is that our subjects rarely used English outside the ESL classroom setting, whereas subjects of previous studies appear to have received both instruction and informal exposure or informal exposure alone. Finally, our subjects are different by virtue of their age—11 to 14 years—since most subjects of previous research have been considerably younger (5–8) or older (adults, especially foreign students at university level).

Learners' language data. The data from the learners were obtained from recordings of an oral communication game—the picture card game. This game was played with seven sets of cards with simple drawings on them.[7] Each set had four cards which were very similar in subject and design but differed in their

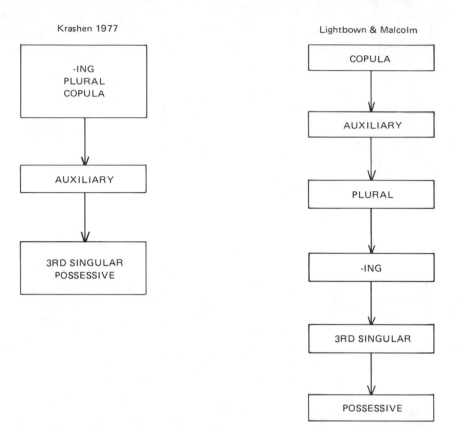

Figure 2.   Adaptation of Krashen's (1977) "Proposed 'Natural Order' for Second Language Acquisition" compared with accuracy order observed in this study. In Krashen's order, morphemes in the same box are not considered to have a fixed order relative to each other.

details (see the Appendix, p. 241, for an example). Each student played the game three times; once in grade 6 in April, twice in grade 7 in December, and in May.

The game was played by two participants—the student and the interviewer, a member of the research team. The interviewer had two copies of each set of cards, one arrayed in front of her and the other placed face down in front of the student. The student took one card from each set and described it to the interviewer. The interviewer tried to guess which one the student was describing and verified her choice by matching her copy of the card with the student's. All interviews were audio-recorded and transcribed.

Each picture was specifically designed with the purpose of providing obligatory contexts for the use of -*s* and -*ing* morphemes. Thus, although the students could successfully play the game without using these structures, the clearest and most precise description of each picture would include one or more of them. Because of the game-like nature of the task, we expected students to be less concerned with correctness of form than with communicating information. In this setting, we hoped to bias the students toward what Krashen (1976) would call "acquired" language, that is, language which has not been filtered through the learner's conscious knowledge of linguistic rules which he could use only under test-like conditions.

When we had analyzed the results for the grade 6 administration of the picture card game, we became aware that, for two of the -s morphemes we wanted to analyze, 3rd person singular and possessive, obligatory contexts were extremely rare. We therefore made some changes in the task for the second administration.

In order to provide more contexts for the possessive on the second administration, we added a new set of picture cards and slightly altered another set. On each card in the new set, there was a drawing of a gift-wrapped package with a name tag on it. After students had described their picture (e.g., it's a present. It has green paper and a red bow), the interviewer would ask "whose present is it?" The altered set of picture cards showed birthday party scenes (children with party hats around a birthday cake on a table). We altered this set by adding a banner over the children's heads with the words "happy birthday Pat" or "happy birthday Jack." This permitted the interviewer to ask each student, "whose birthday is it?"

It should be noted that the above questions to elicit the possessive were the only predetermined specific questions used in the game. Otherwise, the interviewer tried to say as little as possible without leaving the learner in an awkward long silence. She would simply say, "tell me about your picture" and then say no more unless the student reached an impasse, at which point the interviewer might help out by asking more specific questions such as "how many children are there?" or "how old is Jack?"

In order to increase the number of potential obligatory contexts for the 3rd person singular, we chose to go outside the picture card game which tended to create contexts for the progressive -ing form of verbs. For this, we prepared five pictures which were different in size, format, and style of drawing from those used in the picture card game. When each student had completed the picture card game, the interviewer introduced the additional pictures by saying, "Now, I'm going to show you some other pictures. These are pictures of a little boy who likes to do the same thing every day. I want you to tell me what he does every day." Then, as she showed the student each picture, she would ask specifically,

1. What does he do first?
2. Then what does he do?
3. What does he do next?
4. What does he do in the winter?
5. What does he do in the summer?

Students' responses to these questions in the "little boy" context were always tabulated separately from those elicited in the picture card game, since the "little boy" data exist only for grade 7 administrations of the game. Unless otherwise specified, results referred to throughout the paper are from the picture card game only.

Classroom data. When our subjects were in grade 6 we were able to audio-record and transcribe fifteen class sessions for each of the three grade 6 groups at intervals of approximately two weeks over the course of the school year. Because the learners had the same instructor, we had a substantial sample of their teacher's speech and of the language they heard and produced in the classroom. In grade 7, however, the students were placed in fifteen different sections with three different teachers, making it virtually impossible for us to record a sample of classroom speech that would adequately represent the input to all the learners.[8]

The grade 6 classroom recordings have provided us with a large corpus of classroom data. For the present study, we have analyzed the fifteen classroom recordings from one of the grade 6 classes. Because the ESL instruction for all three classes had the same format and covered identical material in the textbook, these samples are representative of the teacher's speech to all the grade 6 students. The total corpus of classroom data contains approximately 45,000 running words.

The grade 6 teacher was a native speaker of neither French nor English but of another Romance language. Her English was near native-like in terms of grammatical accuracy and her pronunciation was also very good. She also spoke French during the English classes although her French was not quite as fluent or as accurate as her English.

Analysis of learners' language. Use of *-s* morphemes.   Five categories of obligatory contexts for *-s* morphemes were analyzed:

1. copula	She's happy.
2. auxiliary (in progressive construc-	The girl *is* holding three balloons.
tion)	He's opening the box.
3. 3rd pers. singular	She wants a cookie.
	The girl has a red skirt.[9]
4. plural	Two trees and two houses.
5. possessive	The boy's hat.

In the overall counts of accuracy in obligatory contexts, both contracted *'s* and uncontracted *is* are included for the copula and auxiliary. Our practice has been to count as obligatory contexts for the auxiliary *only* utterances containing a verb with *-ing* inflection. Thus, "she's blow the candle" would not be counted as a correct auxiliary. On the other hand, we counted as obligatory contexts for *-ing* inflection (discussed below) *all* obligatory contexts for the progressive, whether or not the auxiliary was supplied. This was based on our assumption that *-ing* added to the main verb is the more salient and essential marker of the progressive; that is, we felt that native listeners would recognize "she blowing the candles" as a (slightly ill-formed) progressive construction, but would not so consider "she's blow the candles." In addition, we noticed that some subjects tended to add -s to clause-initial noun phrases even if the following verb was stative; for example, "she's have three balloons" might occur alongside "she's blow the candles." Given the inappropriate -s in the first sentence, it does not seem sensible to treat the -s in the second sentence as a correct occurrence of the progressive auxiliary. Thus, we recorded occurrences of "inappropriate -s" separately for subsequent analysis.

A preliminary observation of the apparent frequency of utterances in which inappropriate -s occurred following the first noun phrase led us to hypothesize that some learners might have developed an interlanguage rule whereby all sentence-initial or clause-initial noun phrases required an -s inflection. To test this hypothesis we isolated all the clause-initial noun phrases and determined the frequency with which -s or is was added to them, characterizing the conditions under which -s was added, for example, whether to a noun or to a pronoun.

Use of -*ing* inflection.   The learners' speech was also analyzed for accuracy and frequency of the -*ing* inflection. Accuracy was determined by measuring the correct use of the -*ing* in obligatory contexts. Because of the nature of the task, describing pictures, there were many obligatory contexts for the use of the progressive -*ing* (e.g., I see a girl, she's hold*ing* three balloons; there's a boy, he's open*ing* a box).

We also examined the overall frequency of -*ing* relative to other inflections. In addition to the -*ing* used correctly in contexts for the progressive, we kept a record of correctly used present participles (e.g., it's a boy holding a box), and -*ing* used inappropriately; that is, where another form was required. Such inappropriate use was rare in the picture card game, of course, since the descriptions usually created contexts for the progressive. However, questions about the pictures of the "little boy who does the same thing every day," provided obligatory contexts for the 3rd person singular. If, in response to the interviewer's question "what does he do first?," a student said "he's getting up," the -*ing* would be considered inappropriate. Data from the "little boy" questions were tabulated separately, as noted above.

Analysis of textbooks and of classroom speech. For the analysis of the verb forms used in the textbook series *Look, Listen, and Learn,*[10] a record was made of the form or forms (uninflected, -*ing* inflected, or -s inflected[11]) in which every verb appeared in the textbooks. The form in which each verb appeared first and its form in each subsequent appearance were noted. A less detailed analysis was done of the verb forms in the *Lado English Series* (1st Canadian edition), Book I.

In addition to investigating the verb inflections, we also examined the noun inflections (plural and possessive) which appeared in the learners' textbooks.

This analysis, however, does not represent as detailed an inspection of the textbook data as does the analysis of verb inflections.

In six selected samples of the grade 6 teacher's speech, all verbs were identified and categorized according to their form—uninflected or inflected with -*ing*, -*s,* or other inflection. In four of the six samples, the teacher's use of verbs was further divided according to whether the verb was "text-determined" (i.e., taken directly from the textbook) or used as part of some other classroom interaction. In the transcripts of fifteen half-hour class sessions, verbs which the students used in the picture card game were identified in the teacher's speech and analyzed in terms of their form. In addition, the frequency of a number of grammatical morphemes was analyzed in the teacher's speech for comparison with students' use of the same morphemes and the observed frequency of their use in other studies. Finally, we looked at the relative frequency of occurrence of contracted and uncontracted forms of the copula and auxiliary in the teacher's and students' classroom speech.

Results and discussion

Verb morphemes: Copula, auxiliary, 3rd person singular, -ing. Accuracy on the copula was always very high (see Figure 3). It was also the most frequently used of the -*s* morphemes. Because of the nature of the picture card game, students frequently introduced their picture descriptions with *it's* or *there's.* Thus while copula -*s* accounted for over half of all the correctly used -*s* morphemes, the actual form of about half these copula constructions was *it's* or *there's.* Accuracy on the progressive auxiliary was also very high and was used with a variety of noun and pronoun subjects. The auxiliary, however, occurred

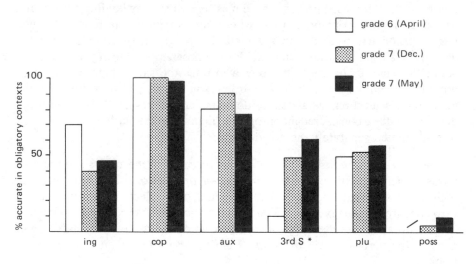

*Includes has.

Figure 3.   Accuracy of-*ing* and-*s* morphemes in picture card game. Results for 36 longitudinal subjects

far less frequently than the copula. (Note once again that we did not consider an obligatory context for the auxiliary to have been created when -ing did not occur on the following verb.)

As noted above, there were also occurrences of nouns or pronouns with a following -s morpheme where the -s was inappropriate, e.g., "she's have three balloons." An initial analysis showed that the majority of inappropriate -s morphemes occurred on noun phrases in the clause-initial position. Inappropriate -s occasionally occurred elsewhere (e.g., "the boy sit down the chairs" but such use was less frequent. We hypothesized that some students might have inferred from their classroom drills with copula and auxiliary that all English sentences have an -s morpheme attached to the clause-initial noun phrase.

Attempting to characterize this occurrence of inappropriate -s in more detail, we examined each clause-initial noun phrase in the grade 6 and grade 7 (December) data. We examined the form of the noun phrase (noun or pronoun) and its following morpheme ('s,[12] is or ∅—no following -s morpheme). The categories 's and is were correct if the obligatory context was for copula or progressive auxiliary, and incorrect in other obligatory contexts (for example, "she's holding three balloons" versus "she's want some cookies"). The category ∅ was correct when the obligatory context was for neither copula nor progressive auxiliary (e.g., "she has three balloons"). Table 1 shows results which generally confirm the preliminary observation in that a large majority of clause-initial noun phrases were followed by 's or is. The tendency to add an -s morpheme to a clause-initial noun or pronoun was stronger overall in grade 6 (82% of combined nouns and pronouns) than in grade 7 (71%). In both grade 6 and grade 7, singular nouns in clause-initial position were far more likely to be followed by is than 's, while the opposite was true for pronouns. Furthermore, when 's was attached to a singular noun, it was often inappropriate. In the grade 7 data, 21 of the 22 noun + 's constructions were inappropriate, e.g., "a girl's have three balloons." On the other hand, is following a noun was almost always (93%) a correct copula or auxiliary.

Table 1.   Percent of Singular Clause-Initial Noun Phrases
Followed by 's, is, or ∅: Picture Card Game,
36 Longitudinal Subjects

Noun Phrase Type	Following Morpheme	Grade 6 Percent	Grade 7[a] Percent
pronoun (he/she/it)	's	87	68
	is	2	1
	∅	11	31
		(194 clauses)	(259 clauses)
singular noun	's	21	14
	is	57	62
	∅	22	25
		(181 clauses)	(208 clauses)

[a]December

Results in the pronoun category show a substantial change from grade 6 to grade 7. Whereas 87% of the singular pronouns were followed by 's in the grade 6 data, 68% were followed by 's in grade 7. The drop was accounted for not by an increase in *is* following pronouns but by the increase in pronouns followed by Ø in the grade 7 data. The evidence seemed at first to indicate that *he's, she's,* and *it's* were formulas, developed through repetition drills and dialogues in grades 4, 5, and 6 and then broken down in grade 7. To investigate the possibility that pronoun plus 's was learned as an unanalyzed formula, we determined the frequency with which teacher and students used pronouns with and without 's in the grade 6 classroom data. The results, shown in Table 2, do not appear to support the hypothesis that learners never heard or used pronouns without 's. There were far more pronouns without than with 's in both the teacher's and the students' classroom speech. However, an examination of the content of the lessons which were presented in grades 4 and 5 shows that there was almost certainly a very high frequency of pronouns with 's in the teacher's and students' classroom language during pattern practice. *He's, she's, it's* may have been overlearned during that time. It is clear that by the time the students played the picture card game for the first time, they had had many opportunities to hear and practice pronouns both with and without 's. Nevertheless, the overlearned patterns of grades 4 and 5 had not yet broken down in grade 6, in spite of considerable exposure to *he, she,* and *it* without 's.

One thing which partly accounts for the increased frequency of pronouns without 's in grade 7 was the introduction of the verb *have.* In grade 6 *have* hardly ever occurred in the students' speech. It was one of the most frequent verbs in the teacher's speech, occurring an average of ten times per lesson, but it was never formally introduced in the textbook in grades 4, 5, and 6 and students never used it in the classroom data. In the picture card game data, only students with some exposure to English outside the classroom used the verb *have* in grade 6. Once they had been taught this verb (in grade 7), it replaced some of the sentence types used in grade 6. For example, instead of saying "she's holding three balloons" students might say "she has three balloons." In addition, they used a construction they had not used in grade 6: *have* as an introducer; for example, they would describe a picture saying "it has a boy"—probably by analogy with French "il y a."[13] However, even though there were still many cases of inappropriately used -*s* morphemes in grade 7, these rarely occurred with *have* (see Table 3). Thus, the addition of this verb which rarely occurs in

Table 2.   Pronouns with and without 's in 15
            Class Sessions (Grade 6)

	Teacher Percent	Students[a] Percent	
he/she/it	70	62	
he's/she's/it's	30	38	
Total number		640	639

[a]N = 26

Table 3.   *He/She/It* Followed by *Have* or *Has* in Students' Speech in Picture Card Game

Intervening Morpheme	Grade 6	Grade 7[a]
's (inappropriate)	15	2
is (inappropriate)	2	0
Ø (correct)	5	44
Total	22	46

[a]December

the progressive was partly responsible for the decrease in -*s* marked initial noun phrases, which is shown in Table 1.

The most striking change from grade 6 to grade 7 was the increase in the frequency of uninflected verbs accompanying a dramatic decrease in frequency and accuracy of -*ing* (see Figures 3 and 4). Thus, whereas a student might have described a picture in grade 6 with something like "he's taking a cake," in grade 7 there was an increase in the frequency of utterances such as "he take a cake." In grade 6, 56% of the full verbs produced in the picture card game (whether contextually appropriate or not) were inflected with -*ing*; in grade 7, the percentage was less than half that (see Figure 4). It is not, as one might first assume, a matter of different contexts requiring different forms. In grade 7, when the learners were engaged in the same picture card game, far more of their verbs occurred in the uninflected form—including many that had occurred with -*ing* in grade 6.

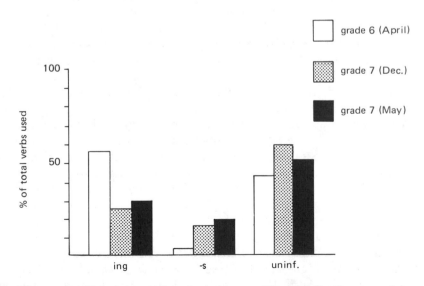

Figure 4.   Frequency of verbs with or without inflections used in picture card game. Results for 36 longitudinal subjects

Early accuracy and frequent use of -*ing* are consistent with most studies of morpheme acquisition. However, the results of this study differ from those of other studies in that both our cross-sectional and longitudinal results showed a dramatic decline in both frequency and accuracy in the use of this inflection. In order to determine whether early frequency and subsequent decline of -*ing* could be accounted for by classroom language, we examined the forms of verbs which appeared in the textbook and in the teacher's speech.

At the end of grade 5 and early in grade 6, the -*ing* was introduced and practiced extensively in class. Furthermore, it was virtually the only verb inflection students had been taught prior to their participation in the picture card game in grade 6. There had been a few occurrences of the 3rd singular form in a dialogue (specifically, *asks, answers,* and *says*) and one lesson in which the verbs *live* and *speak* were presented in the 3rd singular. The only verb which had been introduced for practice in more than a few sentences with the 3rd singular inflection was *want.* Even so, in fifteen classroom sessions, *want* was far more frequently uninflected than -*s* inflected (teacher's speech—135 to 37; students' speech—125 to 13).

The fact that no other verb inflections had been extensively practiced, and the high frequency of use of -*ing* in the grade 6 learners' speech in the picture card game, led us to wonder whether, in grade 6, students were using -*ing* because they had encountered some verbs only in this form and had learned them as lexical items rather than as a base verb form plus inflection. Analysis of the text materials and the teacher's speech made it clear that this could not be true. Of the thirty-two verbs used by more than one student in the grade 6 administration of the picture card game, ten had never appeared in their textbook (see Table 4). Some of these had occurred in the context of regular classroom activities outside the text; others appear to have been learned outside of school.

Of the twenty-two verbs that had been presented and practiced through the text materials, seventeen (75%) had appeared in both the -*ing* and uninflected forms. In all but three cases (*go, take, wear*), the uninflected form was presented first. Only one verb (*fight*) had been presented in the -*ing* form exclusively. Of the four that had been taught only in the uninflected form, the students used three (*pull, leave, read*) with -*ing*.[14]

We examined the grade 6 teacher's use of various verb inflections in her classroom speech, because it was possible that, even though -*ing* was rare in the textbook outside the lessons where it was taught explicitly, the teacher herself might use -*ing* inflected verbs more than any others. High frequency of -*ing* in the teacher's speech would probably override the low frequency of -*ing* in the text since the subjects' exposure to English would be largely determined by what their teacher chose to present.

The overall frequency of -*ing* inflected verbs in the teacher's speech was far lower than that of uninflected verbs—about 1:4. Other verb inflections were about half as frequent as -*ing* overall (see Table 5). In the sample of the teacher's speech collected in April, 1978, two weeks before the interviews, the teacher used sixty-three full verbs. Of these, 89% were uninflected,[15] 5% were -*ing*

Table 4. Forms of Full Verbs Used by Students in Picture Card Game Compared to Forms Presented in Textbook (Grade 6, N = 75)

Group I. *Verbs Used by Students in Uninflected Form Only*

	Textbook Uninflected	-Ing		
have	NT	NT	+	verb presented in this form in textbook
hit	NT	NT	−	verb not presented in this form in textbook
want	+	−	NT	not taught at all in textbook

Group II. *Verbs Used by Students in -ing Form Only*

	Textbook Uninflected	-Ing		Textbook Uninflected	-Ing
argue	NT	NT	laugh	+	+
blow[a]	+	+	leave	+	−
bump	NT	NT	look	+	+
carry	NT	NT	make	+	+
catch	NT	NT	open	+	+
come	+	+	rain[a]	NT	NT
dance	NT	NT	read	+	−
eat	+	+	talk	NT	NT
fight	−	+	teach	NT	NT
hold	+	+	wear	+	+
			write	+	+

Group III. *Verbs Used by Students in Both Uninflected and -ing Forms*

	Textbook Uninflected	-Ing	Number of students who used uninflected	Number of students who used -ing inflected
go	+	+	7	25
play	+	+	2	9
pull	+	−	7	9
run	+	+	2	20
sit	+	+	17	23
stand	+	+	2	11
take	+	+	14	13
touch	+	+	3	6

Note: Any verb used by only one student has been eliminated.
[a]Used once by one student in uninflected form.

Table 5. Forms of Full Verbs in Grade 6 Teacher's Speech

Date of Recording	Total Number of verbs	Percent uninflected	Percent inflected -ing	Other
Oct. 5, '77	86	71	17	12
Nov. 2, '77	132	81	4	16
Nov. 30, '77	95	60	33	7
Feb. 15, '78	161	72	24	3
Mar. 1, '78	259	74	15	11
Apr. 11, '78	63	89	5	6

inflected, and the remaining 6% had 3rd person singular or past tense inflections. In an earlier sample, collected in October, 1977, just a few days after students had completed eleven lessons in which the -*ing* was taught explicitly, uninflected verbs made up 71% of the total verbs used by the teacher.

When we further analyzed the teacher's speech, separating "textbook-based" from "spontaneous" verbs, that is, those that were included as part of the content of the day's lesson as opposed to those that were used for giving instructions or asking non-textbook-based questions, we found that -*ing* verbs were much more likely to be textbook-based than were uninflected verbs or verbs with other inflections. As shown in Table 6, half of the -*ing* verbs used by the teacher came from the text. This contrasts with 27% of the uninflected verbs and 19% of the verbs with other inflections.

In Larsen-Freeman's (1976b) ESL classroom data, -*ing* was the fourth most frequent of nine morphemes, following *article, copula, plural.* Larsen-Freeman did not report actual frequency of occurrence, but it seems quite likely that the frequency of -*ing* was considerably lower than the frequency of article and copula. In our data, copula (counting only *'s, is* forms) occurred about twice as frequently as -*ing* (see Table 7).

As shown in Table 8, our classroom data with elementary school children at a low level of proficiency and Larsen-Freeman's data from university ESL classes are very similar. Indeed, the rank order correlation is nearly perfect. Nevertheless, the frequency of plural and -*ing* are quite low when one takes into account the size of the language sample. The frequency of auxiliary -*s* is lower still and yet it is one of the morphemes students usually supply correctly. Frequency does not satisfactorily account for acquisition sequences when differences between ranks are so great, and when even high ranks represent fairly low frequency.

Finally, we examined in the grade 6 teacher's speech, in all fifteen sessions, the forms of those verbs that students had used in the picture card game. The tapes covered virtually the full year of grade 6, from early October to late May. Here again, frequency of use by the teacher would have been a poor predictor of the students' use of particular verb forms (see Table 9). The results for *have* and

Table 6.   Source of Different Verb Forms in Grade 6 Teacher's Speech in 4 Class Sessions*

	Total number of verbs	Percent text-based
Uninflected	471	27
-ing	114	51
Other inflections	62	19

*This table combines data from the recordings of Nov. 2 and Nov. 30, 1977, and Feb. 15 and May 1, 1978. (See Table 5.)

Table 7. Frequency of 7 Morphemes in Grade 6
Teacher's Speech (fifteen 30-minute
sessions)

article	1280	plural	323
copula -s		3rd singular	80
auxiliary -s	894[a]	possessive	33
-ing	324		

Note: These frequencies are based on the total sample of the
teacher's speech, 27,855 running words, approximately 23,000
of which were English. The remainder were French.

[a]Figures for copula -s and auxiliary -s (both contracted and
uncontracted forms) are combined because counts are based on
computer-generated word lists which do not distinguish, for
example, *"she's* happy" from *"she's* holding three balloons."
Judging from the frequency of -ing, one may infer that auxiliary -s
was far less frequent than copula -s, especially when it is recalled
that the -ing verbs also occurred with auxiliary forms other than -s
(I'*m,* they'*re,* etc.).

Table 8. Rank Order of Fre-
quency of 7
Morphemes in Larsen-
Freeman's University
Classes and Grade 6
Class

	University[a]		*Grade 6*
1	article	1	article
2	copula	2	copula
3	plural	3.5	plural
4	-ing	3.5	-ing
5	3rd singular	5	(auxiliary)
6	auxiliary	6	3rd singular
7	possessive	7	possessive

[a]My summary of 6 classes reported
separately by Larsen-Freeman (1976b).

want (Group I) are predictable since they would occur in relatively few contexts
with -*ing* in any language sample. In the classroom speech of the grade 6 teacher
and the students, they never occurred with -*ing*. However, the teacher's
frequency of use of verbs in the other groups was not directly related to the
students' performance. Although there appeared to be a relationship in the
teacher-student distribution of inflected and uninflected verbs in Group III (that
is, both the teacher and the students used both inflected and uninflected forms of
the verbs in this group), in Group II, the verbs that the students used only in the
-*ing* inflected form occurred far more often in the teacher's speech in the
uninflected form.

Table 9. Forms in Teacher's Speech of Verbs Used by Students in Picture Card Game (Grade 6) (Data from 15 Class Sessions)

	Uninflected Percent	Inflected -ing Percent	-s, other Percent
Group I. Verbs used by students in uninflected form only	87	—	13
Number in teacher's speech = 298			
Group II. Verbs used by students in -ing form only	71	25	4
Number in teacher's speech = 425			
Group III. Verbs used by students in both uninflected and -ing forms	52	37	11
Number in teacher's speech = 200			

Note: For list of verbs in each group, see Table 4.

The overall frequency of -*ing* relative to uninflected forms in the text materials and the teacher's speech does not correspond to students' frequent use of -*ing* in grade 6. Students had ample opportunity to hear uninflected verbs in grade 6, and it seems quite unlikely that they thought -*ing* was a part of the base form of the verbs. On the other hand, in grade 5 and in the month before we began recording in grade 6, students had had eleven lessons on the progressive form. The frequency of -*ing* verbs in those lessons was undoubtedly much higher and students no doubt practiced, repeated, and memorized sentences using -*ing* forms of verbs. In eight months of English instruction prior to the first picture card game, -*ing* was very infrequent in classroom speech. Yet it was the preferred form at grade 6—used almost exclusively by some students. Their preference for this form appears to be related to the period of overlearning which preceded the period of our observation.

In grade 7, when -*ing* had become both less frequent and less accurate in students' speech, we again examined the students' exposure to English in their ESL classes. Analysis of the students' textbook showed that, at the time of the grade 7 administration of the picture card game, the students had not had any formal instruction in using the -*ing* inflection for over a year. Indeed, the progressive does not appear at all in the 1971 Canadian edition of the *Lado English Series,* Book I. If we assume that the use of -*ing* was as rare in their teachers' non-textbook-based speech in grade 7 as it was in grade 6, we can conclude that it had virtually disappeared from the English they heard.

Verb forms that were practiced in the ESL materials in grade 7 were limited to copular BE and the 3rd person singular. The latter had been introduced shortly before the picture card game was played in grade 7. Accuracy on the 3rd person singular rose in grade 7 (see Figure 3), but the rise is accounted for almost entirely by the verb *has.* Separate analysis of the data elicited by questions about "the little boy who does the same thing every day" revealed an accuracy rate of 10% in December, 15% in May.

One plausible hypothesis is that, in grade 6, the learners equated the -*ing* form with the French simple present, using -*ing* in contexts where the simple present would be appropriate in French. This seems particularly likely since every context in which they practiced -*ing* in English corresponds to a simple present context in French. Since the progressive had been taught alone and with no specific contrast to any other form, there had been no opportunity to discover the limits of its appropriateness. This also led, as noted above, to overuse of -*ing* in contexts requiring simple present. If students had equated English progressive with French simple present, one can understand the confusion they seem to have experienced subsequently when the simple present—with its uninflected forms for all persons except the 3rd singular—was introduced. Evidence of this confusion lies in the dramatic decline in -*ing* frequency and accuracy. Our cross-sectional data suggest that the confusion will get worse before it gets better. Students in our grade 8, grade 9, and even grade 10 groups used -*ing* even less accurately and less frequently than these students in grade 7.

Noun morphemes: Plural and possessive. Overall accuracy on the plural was almost identical in grades 6 and 7 (just over 50% in both cases). As noted above, plural accuracy for our subjects is somewhat lower, relative to the other morphemes, than the relative accuracy observed in other morpheme acquisition research. Once again, we looked for an explanation in the classroom language. The plural was introduced about mid-way through *Look, Listen, and Learn,* Book I (thus near the end of grade 4). It occurred in the exercise drills in almost every lesson through the remainder of Book I (throughout grade 5). In Book II as well, there were practice sentences including plural nouns in almost every lesson. Furthermore, a few weeks before the grade 6 administration of the picture card game, there had been a series of lessons on forms such as *some, a lot of,* etc. with plural nouns. In grade 7, the noun plural was introduced in Unit 4 and practiced further in subsequent units of the *Lado English Series,* Book 1.

Even though the noun plural was a major grammatical point in the learner's ESL classes, its frequency was not high overall (see Table 7). The frequency varied widely in different class sessions—from as few as twelve occurrences (all in the teacher's speech) to as many as ninety-six (thirty-six of which were in the teacher's speech) when the focus of a lesson was on the plural.

Perhaps the best explanation for the fact that these learners had such low overall accuracy on noun plurals and appeared to be acquiring the plural more slowly—relative to other -*s* morphemes—than learners in other studies, lies in the learners' native language. The fact that one does not pronounce the final -*s,* which signals the plural in written French, may interfere with the learners' acquisition of a rule to pronounce the plural -*s* inflection in English. The majority of the subjects in previous morpheme accuracy studies are Spanish-speakers whose native language pluralizes nouns in a way that is similar to the English system. Thus, Spanish-speakers' accuracy on the plural is aided by the similarity to their native language. In some of the morpheme accuracy studies with subjects who are not Spanish-speakers, there are exceptions to the early accuracy of the plural, for example, Dulay and Burt's (1974) Chinese subjects.

As noted in the presentation of the procedures used in data collection, obligatory contexts for the possessive were very rare in the grade 6 data from the picture card game. When students did refer to a possessive relationship, they tended to use the *of* construction (e.g., the hat of the boy) rather than create an obligatory context for the -s inflection (e.g., the boy hat). In the grade 7 data, obligatory contexts for the -s inflection were created by two questions which the interviewer asked every student ("Whose present is it?" and "Whose birthday is it?"). With one exception, the only students whose responses included the possessive -s inflection (e.g., Linda's or it's Linda's or it's Linda's present) were bilingual students whose protocols were eliminated from the data analyzed in the present study. The one non-bilingual student who used the possessive -s was clearly more fluent than his peers and claimed to have learned English by watching English television programs.

The extremely poor performance on the possessive -s inflection is consistent with findings of other studies of morpheme accuracy. The fact that French forms the possessive by a prepositional phrase (le chapeau du garçon) rather than by inflection, together with the minimal salience of the -s morpheme between two nouns, may be sufficient to explain our subjects' low accuracy. The extremely low frequency of use of the possessive probably contributes to low accuracy as well.[16] Brown (1973) reported that in the speech the parents of his young subjects addressed to their children, the use of possessive inflection ranked very low in frequency compared with other inflections. Larsen-Freeman (1976b) found it the least frequent of the nine morphemes she analyzed in her ESL classroom data.

The possessive -s form was quite rare in the classroom data in grade 6 (see Table 7). It was first taught in Book I of *Look, Listen and Learn,* when our learners were in grade 4 ESL classes. It was formally introduced in Lesson 1 and was extensively practiced throughout the first eight lessons (thus, in grade 4). Although the possessive -s appeared in a few subsequent dialogues, it was not the focus of explicit instruction again until the last lessons of Book I, which the students would have had in grade 5.

In grade 6, when the learners were using Book II of the *Look, Listen and Learn* series, the possessive -s appeared in a few dialogues throughout the text, but it was not explicitly taught or practiced in mechanical exercise drills as it was in Book I. In nearly 45,000 running words in the fifteen classroom recordings, possessive nouns occurred only sixty-seven times—thirty-three times in the teacher's speech, thirty-four in the students'. It was always used as part of a dialogue or brief grammatical explanation.

An examination of the learners' grade 7 textbook (*Lado English Series,* Book I) revealed that the possessive -s was not formally re-introduced in their ESL instruction until Unit 14, that is, after they had participated in the picture card game for the second time. Thus, these learners had had almost two years of ESL instruction in which the possessive -*s* form had not been explicitly presented and practiced and during which it occurred very rarely in classroom language. They had practiced it extensively for several weeks at the very beginning of their ESL instruction, only to have it virtually disappear from their English language input.

Summary and Conclusions

The results of this study—of the use of grammatical morphemes by young French-speakers receiving formal ESL instruction and aspects of the language they heard in the classroom—suggest that there is no direct relationship between the frequency with which certain forms appear in the classroom and the frequency or accuracy of use of these forms in the learners' language at the same point in time. However, there is some evidence that frequency has a "delayed" effect. For example, the grade 6 students had practiced -*ing* and copula and auxiliary -*s* to the point of overlearning. Even though the -*ing* was relatively infrequent in grade 6 classroom language, their overlearning of the form may have caused it to remain in their speech throughout that year. Subsequently, the decline in frequency of -*ing* and the corresponding rise in frequency of uninflected verbs may have led to their later preference for uninflected verbs in their speech. Outside this kind of highly structured classroom setting one would expect learners to use uninflected verbs in the earliest stages of language acquisition, adding grammatical markers gradually, as their meaning became apparent in various contexts. This build-up from the simplest forms to the more complex ones may be a necessary part of development. By forcing learners to repeat and overlearn forms which have no associated meaning to contrast them with any other form(s), we may be setting up barriers which have to be broken down before the learners can begin to build up their own interlanguage systems. Interlanguage systems developed in communicative language use probably reflect a number of factors in addition to frequency in the environment— salience, usefulness for communication, uniqueness of form, etc. Our subjects' accuracy on -*ing* was not based on such factors. It appears, rather, to have been based on overlearning in an environment where the form occurred in isolation from others. Such rote learning may have to be overcome before a real system can be built.

There was a similar tendency to use overlearned patterns of -*s* morphemes on clause-initial noun phrases. The learners' use of clause-initial noun phrases with an inappropriate -*s* decreased over time. Unlike the -*ing* morpheme, however, appropriate use of -*s* in obligatory contexts for copula and auxiliary did not decrease at the same time.

Learners in natural environments also use memorized formulas which are grammatically complex (Wong-Fillmore, 1976; Hakuta, 1974a). These formulas or routines differ from the overlearned forms of the classroom environment in at least two ways. First, the phrases and sentences are heard and subsequently used in environments where their meaning is the important consideration. Second, they represent only a part of the learner's total output—the remainder being based on a simplified version of the target language. The role of memorized routines in language acquisition in natural environments is currently being debated. Some researchers consider that the routines themselves provide linguistic input which can be held in reserve for subsequent analysis (Wong-Fillmore, 1976). Others see the major role of routines in permitting interaction with speakers of the target language, thus providing the learner with new input from the environment (Krashen and Scarcella, 1978). Some researchers (e.g., Lamendella, 1979) have suggested that pattern practice involving memorized dialogues or "mechanical" drills is actually processed by the brain in a way different from the way in which language for communication is processed, and that only the latter processing actually leads to real language acquisition.

While we are convinced that there are predictable sequences in the acquisition of English as a second language, this paper is not meant to support the "natural sequence" hypothesis in any strict sense of a specific order of acquisition of six grammatical morphemes or even groups of morphemes (Krashen, 1977; Dulay and Burt, 1978). Indeed, we are skeptical of whether certain predictions of the "natural sequence" hypothesis (especially the early acquisition of the plural) would hold for French-speakers, even if they were learning English outside the classroom. On the other hand, we cannot argue that our results disconfirm the "natural sequence" hypothesis. The fact that our learners' accuracy orders differ from those observed in previous studies may be due to the exposure they had to a distorted version of the English language and to the fact that they were required to repeat and practice sentences whose grammatical complexities were far beyond what they would have included in their speech if they had been acquiring English through communicative interaction involving more varied natural language.

One important observation of this study is that there was relatively little improvement over time in the accuracy of learners' use of the six grammatical morphemes in obligatory contexts even though grammatical accuracy was always the focus of their ESL classes. Opportunities for real communicative interaction or discussion of student-selected topics were virtually nonexistent. It seems certain that greater developments in fluency and vocabulary could have been possible if more activities involving communicative language use had been available. Classroom experience with communicative language might have encouraged learners to seek opportunities to hear and use English outside the classroom. For learners whose exposure to English totals less than seventy-five hours per year, such expansion of the learning environment is essential.

Appendix

Notes

1. This research has been funded by grants from the Language Programs Branch of the Department of the Secretary of State of Canada and the Social Sciences and Humanities Research Council of Canada. Bruce Barkman is the other principal investigator whose research is funded by these grants. Research assistants whose aid has been indispensable in the preparation of this paper are Diane Malcom, Nina Spada, and Robert Wallace. Computer programs used for analysis of the classroom data were written by Anne Barkman. Special thanks are due to Catherine Faure.

2. It is important to note that in most morpheme accuracy studies, subjects had both formal instruction and fairly intensive exposure to English outside the ESL classroom; for example, as foreign students studying in American universities or as participants in bilingual education programs with an ESL component.

3. See Lightbown and Barkman (1978) for a detailed description of the project.

4. The study was based on transcripts of speech recorded while students played a "communication game" with a member of the research team. The game is described in more detail later on.

5. "Plural before auxiliary" is a relationship which Krashen (1977) lists among the "less clear cases" (p. 148). It is by no means true in all morpheme accuracy studies, even those that generally support the "natural sequence" hypothesis.

6. The relatively high accuracy on 3rd singular which is shown in Figure 1 is due largely to the fact that *has* was included as a 3rd singular verb. When *has* is eliminated, accuracy falls below 15%.

7. The pictures were drawn for us by Richard Yorkey. The game is similar to one described by Upshur (1971) and to "screen" tasks often used in Piagetian research (e.g., Glucksberg, Krauss, & Weisberg, 1976).

8. The older students were less widely scattered and we were to continue the collection of classroom data for them over two or even three years.

9. Note that Dulay and Burt's (1974) scoring method excludes *does* and *has*. In the present study, there were virtually no occurrences of *does*.

10. The analysis of the verb forms used in *Look, Listen and Learn* was done by Joyce Garavito.

11. No other verb inflections occur in the *Look, Listen and Learn* series.

12. The *'s* category refers to both [s] and [z] allomorphs.

13. An interesting footnote to this is that grade 6 students never made the "he *has* seven years" error made by the older students. As soon as the verb *have* was introduced in grade 7, however, they too began making this almost stereotypic interference error, a direct translation of "il *a* sept ans."

14. The only exception was *want*, which would not occur with -ing in native speakers' speech in the contexts in which it was used in the picture card game. It never appeared with -ing in the classroom recordings.

15. Uninflected verbs used by the grade 6 teacher included imperatives (sit down, take out your books), simple present, first or second persons (we want. . . ; you say. . .), or catenative verbs (let's do another one; I would like; I don't want, etc.).

16. Craig Chaudron (personal communication) has commented on the importance of L1 influence in pointing out that Danish learners of English have little trouble with the possessive due to its similarity to Danish possessive.

References

Alexander, L. G., & Dugas, A. *Look, Listen and Learn,* Books I and II. Centre Educatif et Culturel and Longman Canada Ltd., 1972–3.

Andersen, R. The impoverished state of cross-sectional morpheme acquisition/accuracy methodology (or: The leftovers are more nourishing than the main course). *Working Papers on Bilingualism,* 1977, 47–82.

Bailey, N., Madden, C., & Krashen, S. D. Is there a "natural sequence" on adult second language learning? *Language Learning,* 1974, *24,* 235–244.

Brown, R. *A First Language.* Cambridge, Mass.: Harvard University Press, 1973.

Burt, M., Dulay, H., & Hernandez, E. *Bilingual Syntax Measure.* New York: Harcourt Brace Jovanovich, 1975.

Chaudron, C. A descriptive model of discourse in the corrective treatment of learners' errors. *Language Learning,* 1977a, *27,* 29–46.

Chaudron, C. Teachers' priorities in correcting learners' errors in French immersion classes. *Working Papers on Bilingualism,* 1977b, *12,* 21–44.

Cross, T. Mothers' speech adjustments: The contribution of selected child listener variables. In C. Snow & C. A. Ferguson (Eds.), *Talking to Children,* Cambridge: Cambridge University Press, 1977.

Dulay, H., & Burt, M. K. Natural sequences in child second language acquisition. *Language Learning,* 1974, *24,* 37–53.

Dulay, K., & Burt, M. K. Some remarks on creativity in language acquisition. In W. C. Ritchie (Ed.), *Second Language Acquisition Research,* New York: Academic Press, 1978.

Gaies, S. J. The nature of linguistic input in formal second language learning: Linguistic and communicative strategies in ESL teacher's classroom language. In H. D. Brown, C. A. Yorio, & R. H. Crymes (Eds.), *On TESOL '77.* Washington D.C.: TESOL, 1977.

Glucksberg, S., Krauss, R., & Weisberg, R. Referential communication in nursery school children: Method and some preliminary findings. *Journal of Experimental Child Psychology,* 1966, *3,* 333–342.

Hakuta, K. Prefabricated patterns and the emergence of structure in second language acquisition. *Language Learning,* 1974a, *24,* 287–297.

Hakuta, K. A preliminary report on the development of grammatical morphemes in a Japanese girl learning English as a second language. *Working Papers on Bilingualism,* 1974b, *3,* 18–43.

Hatch, E. Second language learning—universals? *Working Papers on Bilingualism,* 1974, *3,* 1–17.

Hatch, E. Discourse analysis and second language acquisition. In E. Hatch (Ed.), *Second Language Acquisition.* Rowley, Mass.: Newbury House, 1978.

Krashen, S. Formal and informal linguistic environments in language acquisition and language learning. *TESOL Quarterly,* 1976, *10,* 157–168.

Krashen, S. Some issues relating to the monitor model. In H. D. Brown, C. A. Yorio, & R. H. Crymes (Eds.), *On TESOL '77.* Washington, D.C.: TESOL, 1977.

Krashen, S., & Scarcella, R. On routines and patterns in language acquisition and performance. *Language Learning,* 1978, *28,* 283–300.

Lado, R., & Tremblay, R. *Lado English Series,* 4 vols. (Canadian Edition). Centre Educatif et Culturel, 1971.

Lamendella, J. The neurofunctional basis of pattern practice. *TESOL Quarterly,* 1979, *13,* 5–19.

Larsen-Freeman, D. The acquisition of grammatical morphemes by adult ESL students. Doctoral dissertation, University of Michigan, 1975.

Larsen-Freeman, D. An explanation for the morpheme acquisition order of second language learners. *Language Learning,* 1976a, *26,* 125–134.

Larson-Freeman, D. ESL teacher speech as input to the ESL learner. *Workpapers in Teaching English as a Second Language,* 1976b, *X,* 45–50.

Lightbown, P. M. The acquisition and use of questions by French L2 learners. In S. W. Felix (Ed.), *Second Language Development: Trends and Issues.* Tübingen, Germany: Gunter Narr Verlag Tübingen, 1980.

Lightbown, P. M., & Barkman, B. Interactions among learners, teachers, texts, and methods of English as a second language. Report to the Department of the Secretary of State of Canada, 1978. ED 166 981.

Lightbown, P. M., & Spada, N. Performance on an oral communication task by francophone ESL learners. Paper presented at the SPEAQ convention, Montreal, May, 1979. Also in *SPEAQ Journal,* 1978, *2,* 4, 34–54.

Lightbown, P. M., Spada, N., & Wallace, R. Some effects of instruction on child and adolescent ESL learners. Paper presented at the Second Los Angeles Second Language Acquisition Research Forum, October, 1978. Also in R. Scarcella & S. Krashen (Eds.), *Research in Second Language Acquisition,* Rowley, Mass.: Newbury House, 1980.

Long, M. Inside the "black box": Methodological issues in classroom research on language learning. *Language Learning,* 1980, *30,* 1–42.

Moerk, E. L. *Pragmatic and Semantic Aspects of Early Language Development.* Baltimore: University Park Press, 1977.

Newport, E., Gleitman, H., & Gleitman, L. Mother, I'd rather do it myself: Some effects and non-effects of maternal speech style. In C. Snow & C. Ferguson (Eds.), *Talking to Children.* Cambridge: Cambridge University Press, 1977.

Porter, J. H. A cross-sectional study of morpheme acquisition in first language learners. *Language Learning,* 1977, *27,* 47–61.

Rosansky, E. J. Second language acquisition research: A question of methods. Doctoral dissertation, Harvard University, 1976.

Upshur, J. A. Objective evaluation of oral proficiency in the ESOL classroom. *TESOL Quarterly,* 1971, 5, 47–59.

Wagner-Gough, J., & Hatch, E. The importance of input data in second language acquisition studies. *Language Learning,* 1975, *25,* 297–308.

Wong-Fillmore, L. The second time around: Cognitive and social strategies in second language acquisition. Doctoral dissertation, Stanford University, 1976.

Questions for Discussion and Activities

1. Describe some differences between English as a second language and English as a foreign language. Do you think the results of this study might have also been obtained in an ESL environment? Under what conditions?

2. Why is it important to discover a natural order in the acquisition of language units (morphemes, syntactic rules, etc.)? What implications does this have for the language teacher or the textbook writer?

3. In what way might this study help resolve the distinction made by Krashen between learning and acquisition?

4. In what ways can language forms used by the teacher in the classroom affect acquisition order? What other sources of input is the learner exposed to? How might you investigate these other sources of input to find the effect on the learner's acquisition?

5. What is the problem regarding accuracy orders in relation to frequency orders? How is this problem as discussed by Lightbown related to the problem investigated by Larsen-Freeman in Chapter 13 of this volume?

6. What is meant by an "obligatory context" in this study?

7. Select several grammatical forms not discussed in this study and construct a simple communication task which you feel provides obligatory contexts for the use of these forms. Test out your task with a group of learners and report your findings to the class.

8. If you have access to a whole class of learners, administer your revised task after doing number 7 above. Analyze your findings in terms of order of accuracy for the ESL class.

9. Select a beginning level ESL textbook and analyze it for the grammatical morphemes it presents. In what sequence are these morphemes presented? How does this order correspond to the order found in the various morpheme ordering studies including Lightbown's? What is the rationale for such ordering in the ESL textbook?

10. How might you explain the high accuracy and frequency of the contracted copula forms such as *it's* and *there's*? Might it be explained on the basis of what teachers do or textbooks present? How does your explanation relate to the errors also produced by the learners in Lightbown's study such as *she's have three balloons*?

11. This study found that, while grade 6 learners used the contracted copula with the third person singular pronoun correctly 87% of the time, the same learners dropped to 68% in grade 7. What hypotheses does Lightbown suggest for this retrogression? What did she find?

12. What does the author conclude about the frequency of occurrence of a form in a textbook or in the teacher's speech in class and the sequence of acquisition? Can you think of some explanation for her conclusion?

13. What role does the learner's first language play in his or her sequence of acquisition and frequency of use? How might the explanations offered here affect the cross-sectional results obtained in other studies? Based on the author's conclusion, would you expect a different order of acquisition for Spanish-speakers learning ESL?

11

Learner Interaction in the Classroom and Its Effect on Language Acquisition[1]

Herbert W. Seliger

The language classroom may be viewed as a complex drama of social interaction. The agreed-upon purpose for this drama is the facilitation of language acquisition. That is, it is assumed that the language classroom somehow provides advantages for learners over a naturalistic setting.

There are two types of roles in this drama: the role of the learner or group of learners and the teacher's role. The role of the learner is defined by the biologically given abilities and potential capacities available to the learner, by the set of psychological factors which make the learner the individual he or she is and which determine the learner's preferred ways of learning, and by the learner's attitudes toward the language, the teacher, and the classroom. The learner's role may be described as dichotomous, because the learner not only practices the language in the formal sense by performing in drill exercises and other activities that are an expected part of the classroom language-learning context, but also switches into a role which requires the use of the target language for real communicative objectives such as asking for explanations, making small talk, and commenting.

The other role in this drama is filled by the teacher. The teacher's role may also be described as dichotomous, since the teacher both formally instructs, explains, and drills in the target language, and also acts as an interlocutor who communicates with the learner as any other interlocutor would outside the classroom. In the latter role, the teacher and the learner use language outside the structured, programmed, and nonspontaneous framework of the language lesson; that is, they switch to language interaction in which exchanges are spontaneous and represent real communicative intent. In this latter situation, language is used as a tool for social intercourse rather than as a tool to play the language-learning game. It may be surmised that both types of language interaction—the formal, nonspontaneous and the spontaneous, truly communicative—serve a purpose in the language acquisition process.

Adjunctive to the teacher's role is the role played by other learners in the drama of second language acquisition. While we don't normally view the other learners as playing a learner-teacher role, it is a truism that learners provide feedback and input to each other in various ways. While the quality of this learner input may be relatively poor in comparison to teacher input, there is no doubt that learners do interact with each other and do use each other as a source of input for the construction of learner grammars. As we shall see below, some learners do, in fact, "feed" on the input of other learners almost as much as or more than they feed on the input of the teacher. Still other learners appear to be dependent on the teacher for whatever input they receive.

We do not really know enough about the qualitative differences between the various sources of language input available to learners, or how learners really utilize these sources in order to construct or test hypotheses about the second language. What we do know, based on the studies summarized here, is that *quantity* of input appears to have a definite effect no matter what the source, and that good language learners do things that help increase the volume of the input to which they are exposed. Whether learners who do not carry on effective input-getting tactics in the classroom can be taught them is something that must be studied further. That is, an empirical research question is: To what extent can learners be taught behaviors that result in increased amounts of input being directed to them?

With the advent of innatist views of language acquisition and cognitive approaches to the explanation of language acquisition and processing, the role of practice has often been misunderstood, especially with regard to the use of various practice formats in the language classroom. What kind of practice is effective for acquiring communicative ability? Does practice serve to reinforce a habit or make it stronger, or does it serve some other role? Should formal practice be eliminated from the language classroom, since many of its more mechanical forms are often associated with more behavioristic methods of language teaching?

Under behaviorist methods of language teaching, the role of practice is essentially to shape a response to a given stimulus or set of stimuli. For this reason, methods emanating from this approach emphasize the isolation of linguistic units of form from content so that the item being practiced will not be confounded with semantic associations, translation, and so on. Practice under this approach is thought to develop what Osgood (1956) referred to as habit strength. Under the principle of habit strength, the more a particular association is practiced, the more likely that response will be called forth in a situation where the stimulus with which it is paired is presented. Under the behaviorist approach practice makes perfect, but only if the conditions for developing the association are adhered to. That is, the stimulus is carefully identified with a particular response, and care is taken from the beginning that only the correct response will be given to the stimulus. For this reason, from the very beginning, behaviorist methods are careful to correct all errors related to the association. Under this approach, errors are looked upon as being detrimental to language acquisition.

A cognitive approach to language acquisition and processing does not see language as being comprised of a set of habits. Rather, language is seen as a set of abstract concepts or rules which enable the speaker to construct an infinite variety of sentences in a language without having to accomplish the impossible task of memorizing all the possible sentences that a speaker will ever have to speak. The grammar of a language is viewed as a generative device for producing all the possible sentences of a language. The question before us, of course, is how someone acquires that set of rules or abstract language concepts that will enable that person to produce and comprehend all the many sentences he or she will ever hear which he or she has never before heard.

A main problem for the cognitive approach is explaining how the process of acquisition takes place. While the behaviorist explains learning as the result of habit formation, the cognitivist must explain it on the basis of some internal device which enables the learner to develop a concept or rule for the grammar or the meaning of a word. The model followed by second language acquisition is that of hypothesis formation. According to this explanation, the acquisition process consists of the formation of hypotheses about the nature of the second language. The learner tests an hypothesis by forming an utterance based on the hypothesized form. The response to his or her hypothesized utterance by either the native speaker interlocutor or the teacher is a form of feedback which indicates to the learner whether the hypothesis is confirmed or whether it must be rejected or adjusted in some way and a new hypothesis formed based on the feedback obtained. It is recognized, of course, that feedback to hypotheses relating to the formal aspects of the target language may be ignored by learners when their focus is on communication or content. That is, learners form hypotheses both about the structure of language as well as its ideational content.

As we well know, however, hypotheses must be formed on the basis of some form of previous knowledge. Because new hypotheses are formed on the basis of previous knowledge, they are often prematurely related to this previous knowledge in incorrect ways. That is, the learner often does not initially notice the distinctive differences between the old knowledge and the new hypothesis which is based upon it. For example, when a learner produces a sentence such as

*I don't know how is he going to do it.

we realize that the sentence is formed on the basis of the hypothesis that embedded questions are the same as nonembedded questions with regard to both content and word order. Only later, we hope, does the learner realize that word order for the embedded question is the same as normal sentence order.

Ausubel (1971) has explained this process on the basis of the principle of *obliterative subsumption*. Basically, what this means is that new concepts are attached to already established conceptual networks. New concepts are subsumed under already existing categories or conceptual networks because they are the most familiar to the learner and aid in retaining new information. However, while subsumption as a process aids in remembering, it also obliterates or erases the distinctive features of the new concept. The characteristics that distinguish the new concept become subsumed, or in a sense overwhelmed, by the features of the old, already established one.

In the example above, the learner who produces embedded questions without distinguishing embedded questions from regular WH-questions indicates that his or her hypothesis for embedded questions is subsumed under regular question-formation rules. The expected development for a situation such as this would be that the learner would eventually obtain enough feedback to realize that different rules are necessary for embedded questions.

In the case mentioned above, the false hypothesis which leads to the formation of embedded questions with inverted word order is the result of subsuming a new rule in English under a rule that the learner has already established for the formation of English sentences. That is, the learner is said to overgeneralize the English rule for regular questions to extend to embedded questions. Ausubel's explanation would be that the new rule is subsumed under the old rule.

A similar situation adheres with regard to the transfer of rules from the first language to the new language. Thus, it may be claimed that one of the first intuitive resources for the learner for knowledge about the new language is his or her first or native language. That is, again, already acquired knowledge acts as the basis upon which to form new hypotheses. In this case we are referring to the construction of hypotheses about the new language based on abstract rules which the learner has acquired in his or her first language. The learner may be said to be subsuming hypotheses about the new language under rules for the old language. This may express itself in word order, pronunciation, and so on. Gradually, it is expected that the learner will realized that rules in the first language cannot be a reliable source for hypotheses about the second language. While the second language and the first may share some rules, many rules are different.

A measure of development in the second language may be the degree to which the learner either still relies on the first language as a source of hypotheses or has begun the process of developing a separate conceptual network of second language rules and hypotheses. To what extent may hypotheses about the target language be categorized under the set of first language concepts or under an evolving set of second language hypotheses? That is, do the learner's hypotheses indicate a tactic of L1 transfer, or the overgeneralization of L2 rules?

Interaction—The Social Use of Language for Communication

Language, first or second, does not develop in a vacuum. The most extreme of innatist views about language development ascribe an important role to environmental factors. While it is assumed that children have an innate capacity to acquire a language (Lenneberg, 1967), it is also assumed that there exist at least two basic factors which contribute to the success or failure of language acquisition, first or second. The first factor is that the learner must have access to a social environment in which language is used as a tool for communication. The second factor is that the second language learner, whether child or adult, has the *need* to use the language as a tool for communicating with others.

The social environment for language use can exist in the classroom or outside. That is, any social environment in which language is used as a tool for communication is a potential environment for the acquisition of language. The classroom differs from the world outside the classroom in several ways, but the essential contributions of the classroom seem to be that it provides the language learner with isolated units of language upon which one can focus, and also provides, in addition to the feedback one regularly receives outside the classroom, feedback that is focused on particular errors in grammar, pronunciation, or semantics (Krashen and Seliger, 1975).

In language contact situations outside the classroom, feedback to language acquirers is rarely corrective unless the relationship between the learner and the other speaker is such that corrective feedback will not be viewed as a breach of social convention. In informal, naturalistic situations we do not normally correct the *form* of what others say. We may, however, ask for clarification or paraphrase or indicate in other ways that the message was not received clearly, thus leading the speaker to repair his or her utterance in some way. These communication strategies (Tarone, 1980) may serve as mechanisms for providing indirect input for the construction of hypotheses about the form of the second language.

Environments differ in the opportunities they provide for the communicative use of language. Indeed, if we examine the use of language in the classroom compared to language used outside the classroom, it is evident that there are important differences between the two. These differences are the necesssary result of the organization of contexts for the formal teaching of language that takes place inside the classroom. Outside the classroom, however, in naturalistic environments, language is a means to an end. That is, it is used to communicate content or meaning and usually takes place between only a few interlocutors. One may assume that in naturalistic environments where language is used as a tool for communication rather than as an object of learning, language interactions most often take place between two people. Such interactions are motivated by a need on the part of the interlocutors to say something to each other that may be considered important, necessary, or new.

Language use in the classroom is quite different. The language classroom is, by definition, a contrived context for the use of language as a tool of communication. The bulk of time in a language class is devoted to practicing language for its own sake because the participants in this activity realize that that is the expressed purpose of their gathering together in a room with a blackboard and a language expert, the teacher. The language class is not a natural social group which has come together for the normal reasons that social groups form. The people in the class may share little with each other in terms of real interests, friendship networks, and so on. Their common bond is the desire to learn the language being taught in the class.

Because of the *raison d'être* of language classes, few opportunities exist for the use of language as a social tool for communication. While modern language classes have developed many and varied techniques for learning what has been called communicative competence, these activities are again not naturally evolving ones but controlled and organized by the instructor.

Two general categories of language interaction may be identified: First, there are the opportunities for interaction that are determined by the teacher in the formal part of the language lesson. These opportunities consist of turns being determined by the teacher as part of the formal practice normally found in the language class. Turns in such situations are determined by the teacher either by specifically nominating or calling on a particular student, or by eliciting a response from the class as if it were a single interlocutor comprised of many parts. In the former case, when the teacher determines who will answer or respond, other learners are in a sense shut out of the interaction; they have the options of making believe the cue was directed at them and responding in some way, *sotto voce,* or of responding aloud, or, as often happens, of tuning out and awaiting their own turn. In the last case, when the teacher elicitation is directed at the class as a whole, again the learner has a choice—to respond or not. Since the response was not elicited from the learner in a personalized way, he or she may feel no need or motivation to respond. In fact, in such situations many learners are often found to be busy doing other things and not involved in this general kind of interaction. The other choice open to the learner is to take advantage of these generally directed elicitations and regard them as being directed at him or her personally. In such cases some learners respond aloud.

The second category of language interaction which can be identified in the language class consists of the opportunities for language use that learners create for themselves. In this case, the learner is essentially creating the type of language interaction that takes place outside the classroom between a single speaker and an interlocutor. By creating his or her own language use opportunities, the learner accomplishes two important objectives: the learner gets (1) the language interaction directed at him or her as an individual and (2) more language directed at him or her than if he or she were to wait passively for a turn in a class of fifteen to twenty students all competing for the attention of the same instructor. As we shall see in the studies summarized below, some students are good at creating these opportunities and do so in a consistent or patterned manner while other students play a relatively more passive role in the language class.

At the beginning of this section, it was suggested that two factors appear to be essential to successful language acquisition. The first, a conducive environment for language use, has been discussed above. The second of these factors is the presence of a need to use language for communication with others in the social environment. It is not the intent of this chapter to deal with the possibility of acquiring language in nonsocial situations, such as learning a language alone in a prison cell with only a dictionary as an interlocutor, but rather the more universal context, the one in which the language acquirer, as in the case of the child, interacts with other language users and through this interaction develops a grammar of the target language.

It was found through the studies reported below that some learners adopt a learning style in which they not only react to the language input of others but initiate interactions in the target language. This initiated interaction takes place with the teacher and with fellow language learners in the language class. The same learners who initiate interactions in the classroom were also found to seek out interaction in the target language with L2 speakers in naturalistic language environments.

Considering the patterns of interaction available to the second language learner—passivity and reaction to others or actively seeking out and initiating interactions—it might be supposed that the latter contributes more to acquiring competency in a second language. Given all that has been stated above regarding the role of hypothesis-testing as a central process for second language acquisition, it may be assumed that an active learning style would lead to acquisition at a faster rate, since its function would be to get more input directed at the learner and allow for more sustained and intensive opportunities for hypothesis testing.

Personalized Input: Input into Intake

It was pointed out above that input in the classroom can be directed or nondirected. In directed input, the teacher can nominate a particular student for response before a cue or question is presented. In such a case, the nominated student will respond to the cue or question differently from a student whose name was not called. By the same token, in the case of nondirected input, when the cue or question is directed at the class as a whole, it may be assumed that some students will attend to this input and respond while others, having the option, will not respond and perhaps not even listen carefully to the input. The same may be said about all utterances produced in the class by the teacher or some other speaker but having no particular addressee.

On the other hand, directed input requires that the addressee attend to the interlocutor's utterance closely because a response of some kind will be expected. In the case of a practice or drill context, the learner realizes that a correct response, mechanical or meaningful, will be expected. That is, it may be said that the learner, in the case of directed—as opposed to nondirected—input, changes the input into intake. The nomination or specification of a particular addressee *personalizes* the exchange and requires a higher level of attentiveness on the part of the receiver.

The same situation may be said to exist when one *initiates* an interaction. In this case, the initiator obligates himself or herself to attend to the response of the addressee of the initiated interaction. Initiated interactions may take the form of questions, requests, or statements directed at another speaker but which require a response. Note that in the case of the initiated interaction, the initiator must attend carefully to his or her own output in order to make the intent of the utterance clear, as well as attending to the response of the interlocutor. In the case of both output and input/intake, the level of involvement is greater than when the response results from a mechanical drill context where a correct response may be produced without a high level of mental involvement.

Initiated interactions, therefore, provide the learner with additional directed or personalized input which he or she must attend to differently from group-directed input. In addition to committing the learner to attend closely to the input engendered by his or her initiated interaction and converting this input into intake, the initiator of the interaction can exploit these exchanges for the formulation and testing of hypotheses about the target language. That is, language input derived from personalized or initiated language interactions may be a better source of material with which the learner can form or modify internal hypotheses about the target language.

Two Studies on the Effects of Interaction in the Language Classroom

Two studies will now be described in which the relationship between various types of interaction patterns in the language classroom were related to (1) achievement in the target language and (2) the error pattern exhibited by different learner interactor types. The two studies were done separately with different sets of subjects but following the same methodology described below. (For a fuller account of both studies, see Seliger, 1977, 1978.) All subjects were adult foreign students at the Queens College English Language Institute.

These studies tested the hypothesis that there would be a relationship between both learner achievement as measured on standardized language proficiency tests and the type of errors made by learners in a naturalistic interview situation on the one hand, and the type of interaction-practice pattern exhibited by the learner in the language classroom on the other. The studies classified learners into two categories at the two extremes of a continuum of learner behavior. At one extreme were those learners who practiced language by initiating interactions with the teacher and fellow learners, thereby generating more personalized input to themselves. They were called *High Input Generators* (HIG). At the other extreme were learners who played a passive role in the language classroom and did little to get input directed at them. Such learners were called *Low Input Generators* (LIG). Low Input Generators mostly limited their interactions to responses to the teacher during drill sessions and demonstrated little language interaction in the target language outside of this. In language classes such learners sometimes sit on the fringes of the group and prefer to be left alone. In a pilot study on interaction patterns LIGs had as much as 98% of their interactions with the teacher while HIGs had as little as 35% of their interactions with the teacher and 65% of their interactions with their classmates *in the target language.*

Design and methodology for the study of language interaction

In both studies to be reported here, the methodology used to determine which learners were HIGs and which were LIGs was the same. Two observers observed language interaction in the classroom during four hours of classes. Two observers were used to control for observer reliability. In these studies, interobserver reliability was found to correlate between .917 and .984. The exact number of language interactions differed for each observer but rankings of learners in the class showed the above levels of agreement. Observers sat on opposite sides of the classroom in order to have the entire group within the field of vision of the observers. It should also be remembered that the larger the group, the more difficult it is to observe levels of interaction accurately.

Each observer worked from a tabulation sheet on which the students' names were listed down the left-hand column in order of seating in the classroom. There were additional columns headed *Teacher, Students,* and *Group.* These columns were used to indicate whether the observed interaction took place between the student named in the first column and a teacher, another single student, or was addressed to the whole group. (See Appendix A.)

Any and all speech acts from a single word to complete sentences were recorded as interactions. However, no nonverbal behavior or gestures were recorded. All speech acts were considered interactions for two reasons: (1) Most utterances in normal conversation are not complete sentences; and (2) responses to questions may take the form of a sentence, a phrase, or simply *yes* or *no.* Such responses indicate that the input question which initiated the response has been processed in some way. That is, an attempt has been made by the respondent to process the question. For this reason, it may not be absolutely essential that the question be understood fully. Even partial comprehension of the input question indicates some level of linguistic processing and thus internal practicing of some form.

Using a code, the following information about each interaction was recorded on the tabulation sheet:

  a. Which student spoke? Did he/she address another student, the teacher, or the whole group?
  b. Did the student initiate the interaction (shown by +) or was he or she responding (shown by /)?
  c. Was the student using English or his or her L1 in the interaction? (Shown by (+) for initiated interaction but in L1 and (/) for responding but in L1.)

The number of these interactions was tabulated for each student in the observed class at the end of each observation session. At the conclusion of the four hours of observation, the students were ranked according to the total number of interactions and the type of interactions in L2. Three of the highest interactors (HIG) and three of the lowest interactors (LIG) were selected for further study. In each of the two studies to be reported below, six subjects were selected.

The behavior of High and Low Input Generators in the classroom was observed; in addition, all subjects were administered the Language Contact Profile (LCP) (see Appendix B) in order that the individual's use of the target language and motivation to use it outside the language class could be measured. The LCP is a self-report questionnaire administered by the experimenter to the subject. While numerical values are obtained in response to the variously weighted questions, the LCP admittedly provides only approximate measures of language contact.

Study #1: The relationship between interaction/practice and other criterion measures

In the first study, the relationship between interaction patterns of learners and their performance on standardized tests and field sensitivity tests was examined. (See Table 1.)

The standardized tests consisted of sub-tests of the English Language Institute Language Proficiency Test. The sub-parts of this test are an integrative test of aural comprehension, a discrete point structure test, and a cloze test with every fifth word deleted. On these tests subjects were compared for their performance at the beginning of the semester and their performance at the end of the semester.

Subjects were also administered the Group Embedded Figures Test. In this test, the subject is asked to find a designated figure which is embedded in another figure. The task is similar to those found in children's magazines in which the child is asked to find an object embedded in a larger shape of picture. In the Embedded Figures Test, all shapes are geometric.

A large body of literature exists with regard to the abilities demonstrated on the Embedded Figures Test and their relationship to other cognitive functions. Two general psychological types that relate to other affective and cognitive variables have been identified from these studies. Individuals are thought to be on a continuum of what is termed field independence to field dependence. The relative ability to perceive figures within a context is called field independence, while the relative inability to perform this task is termed field dependence. For a fuller discussion, see Witkin et al., 1954.

A study by Lefever and Ehri (1976) found a positive correlation between field independence and sentence disambiguation ability. DeFazio (1973) found that field independents performed better on cloze tests. Because of these and similar findings it was hypothesized that HIGs might be able to induce more in terms of implicit grammatical patterns from any language context, formal or informal, while LIGs were more dependent on structured drill and organized language learning environments. In addition, the fact that HIGs might be more intensely interacting with L2 outside the language classroom might be taken as an indication of their success in dealing with perceptually embedded language data. This success would in turn encourage further interaction. LIGs, on the other hand, if they are also field dependent, would be likely to experience difficulty in functioning in natural language environments and tend to avoid interaction.

Suzman (1973) states that field independent types use inner guides for action rather than relying on such external cues as authority. Suzman also found that field independents were more willing to take risks than field dependents. All of this tends to predict that HIGs would be field independent, less fearful of experimenting with langauge, less afraid to make mistakes, and less afraid to speak out. Field dependent subjects, on the other hand, would be more likely to speak only when asked to in the language class and more fearful of disapproval because of mistakes.

In summary, because of the affective and cognitive variables associated with field sensitivity, it was hypothesized that HIGs would also tend to be field independent while LIGs would tend toward field dependence. Table 1 shows the raw score results of both HIG and LIG subjects on the various criterion measures. What is interesting to note here is the comparison in performance on placement and final examinations for the same learner.

Table 1. Raw Scores on Criterion Measures and Percent Change for Pre-test and Post-test*

| Student | I | | | II | III | | | IV | | | V | VI |
	A	B	C		A	B	C	A	B	C		
(HIG) M	39	77	51%	45	84	92	8%	30	74	147%	43	60
(HIG) A	40	71.5	56	46	63	89	41	62	90	31	44	48
(HIG) N	62	92.5	67	52	64	91	42	64	86	34	41	48
(LIG) D	12	31.5	38	30	71	89	25	36	56	56	39	36
(LIG) Z	8	24.4	32	20	75	83	11	44	52	18	29	44
(LIG) G	0	11	0	20	80	74	−8	46	56	21	32	28

*I. Interactions = IA; initiated interactions = IB; total interactions = IC (percentage of total initiated).
II. Language Contact Profile Score (LCP).
III. Structure test = IIIA; placement = IIIB; final = IIIC (percentage of change between placement and final).
IV. Aural comprehension = IVA; placement = IVB; final = IVC (percentage of change between placement and final).
V. Cloze
VI. Group Embedded Figures Test (% of 25).

Results of Study Number 1. The hypothesis that HIGs outperformed LIGs both in terms of levels of interaction and performance of the final examinations was supported. It will be noted in Table 2 that negative or low correlations were found for initiated and total interactions when these were correlated with

Table 2.   Correlations of Interaction Measures with Measures of Achievement, Language Contact, and Field Sensitivity*

	Total interaction	Percent of initiated interaction
Total interaction		.942
Structure placement	−.314	−.600
Structure final	.929	.728
Percent change	.943	1.000
Aural comprehension placement	.200	.429
Aural comprehension final	.829	.886
Percent change	.657	.486
Cloze	.714	.771
Language contact profile	.936	.971
Embedded figures	.843	.757

*For all of the above, p is significant at .829 for a one-tailed test. (See G. A. Ferguson, *Statistical Analysis in Psychology and Education.* New York: McGraw-Hill, 1959.)

structure placement and aural comprehension placement. Based on these initial comparisons, it would not have been possible to predict the performance of these subjects on the final tests. However, as will be noted from Table 2, level of interaction correlated highly with final test results both in structure and aural comprehension. That is, interaction level was a good predictor of final test performance, while placement tests were not a good predictor of final test performance.

The results of Study #1 indicate that learners who initiate interaction are better able to turn input into intake. This increased intake has an effect on the *rate* of second language development as shown by the learners' improvement of their test scores relative to their own performance on the test at the beginning of the semester.

Study #2: The relationship between interaction/practice and error type

As stated in the first part of this chapter, language acquisition progresses when the learner forms hypotheses about the second language. An examination of the kinds of hypotheses formed by the learner may provide an indication of not only *how* the learner views second language data but also may provide information about the developmental stage of the learner's grammar.

As stated previously, all learning may be viewed as an attempt at relating new material to already acquired concepts. In the case of language learning, the second language learner has available three sources of knowledge upon which to base his hypotheses: (1) linguistic universals or abstract grammatical ideas about the nature of language which are true for all languages; (2) the set of concepts or rules represented by the first language grammar; and (3) developing set of concepts or rules acquired in the second language.

We would expect to find these three types of language knowledge represented in the error production of the second language learner, since this output is the product of the learner's internal grammar of L2. In the beginning stages, however, it is not logical to expect errors derived from source (3) that are the result of having learned a rule or form in L2 and overextending or overgeneralizing that rule. Rather it is more reasonable to expect that most of the error production will be of the first two types; i.e., errors resulting from some universal grammar and errors resulting from inappropriate transfer of first language rules. As the learner is exposed to increasing amounts of L2 data and has increased opportunities to form and test hypotheses about the nature of the target language, we would expect to find increasing amounts of errors from source (3). That is, the further along the learner is in testing second language hypotheses, the more errors of overgeneralization of target language rules will be found, and fewer errors of interference from L1 will appear in his or her output.

In short, the error profile of the learner—that is, the distribution of errors according to type or source from a random sample of the learner's output—should give us an indication of how far along the learner is in the process of second language acquisition. Error type should be an indication of the level of linguistic maturity for the adult language learner if we assume that hypotheses formed on the basis of knowledge from source (3) indicate an advanced stage in second language development.

Feedback. The most important ingredient in aiding the learner in evaluating hypotheses about the new language is feedback. Feedback allows the learner to correct, confirm, or reject hypotheses. The availability of and the ability to utilize feedback are important in moving the learner along the continuum from a grammar consisting of a high proportion of rules transferred from the first language to a grammar consisting of more rules deriving from L2.

Feedback refers to language-related responses to the learner's utterances, upon which the learner is focused and which can be used by the learner to validate or invalidate concepts he or she has about the target language. Feedback can take any of the following forms:

1. Teacher correction where the focus is on an isolated form.
2. Adjusted foreigner talk where native speaker interlocutors gear down the complexity of their utterances to accord with their perceptions of the learner's ability (Gaies, 1980).
3. Normal conversational responses that one gives in face-to-face situations. Such responses as *uh huh* or head nodding, to convey agreement or that the message has been received and is understood, can be seen as forms of feedback.

In a study of L2 speakers in interview situations (Seliger, 1980), responses from interlocutors that indicated that the L2 speaker's message had not been clear, resulted in the speaker's repeating or paraphrasing his or her original utterance. Second language learners in this study were found to repeat the utterances of their interlocutors as a kind of confirmation device. That is, the learner was confirming a hypothesis about comprehension. Mischler (1978) has shown that children use question-response-confirmation chains in their own communication and concludes that such strategies apparently lead to the expansion of the child's grammar.

As has been pointed out in the first part of this chapter, not all language in the classroom environment can be useful to the learner as feedback. It is possible that the least effective form of feedback is that supplied by the teacher during drill, because it is group directed and not personalized in the sense that it is directed at a particular learner, thus committing the learner to the exchange. Language that is not personalized, or that the learner does not perceive as directed at him or her as an individual, is probably of little use for construction or repair of learners' hypotheses.

If we combine the ideas expressed above that (1) increased availability of feedback should lead to a change in the source of error—that is, from errors stemming from L1 sources of knowledge to a greater proportion of errors stemming from other sources such as L2,—with (2) the concepts of High and Low Input Generators, we arrive at the primary research hypothesis for the second study. Since HIGs by nature generate greater amounts of language data to be directed at them, either in the form of modeling or in the form of adjusted foreigner talk outside the classroom, they have greater opportunity to test and modify hypotheses about the developing L2 grammar. LIGs, on the other hand, are almost exclusively limited to teacher responses in the classroom for feedback, and because of the necessary limitations on time that this amount of intake versus input can amount to, the LIGs' grammar would be predicted to be at a more "primitive" or immature stage of development.

For the purposes of this second study, linguistic maturity is defined, not according to particular instances of error *per se* (because even advanced bilinguals have been found to produce residual errors which may be traced back to L1), but rather as the relative amount of errors produced or derived from L1 sources compared to other sources such as L2 in a random sample of free discourse produced by the learner. Based on this view, HIGs were predicted to produce a smaller percentage of total errors that could be traced to an L1 source.

Data Collection and Analysis for Study #2. The null hypothesis for this study was that there would be no significant difference in the percentage of errors identified as interference among LIGs and HIGs. The research hypothesis was that LIGs would produce a significantly greater percentage of L1 errors when learners were matched for language background and proficiency level.

Data were collected from taped interviews in which individual subjects were asked the same set of questions. The taped interviews were conducted by an assistant to the researcher who conducted the interviews in a relaxed and natural manner. The interviews were conducted with the entire population from which the matched pairs were later drawn (an intermediate-level class in the English Language Institute) before subjects were classified according to interactor type and selected for closer study.

From the HIG and LIG groups studied, only HIGs and LIGs who could be matched for L1 were selected for further study. This resulted in three matched pairs of learners: one pair of female Persian-speakers, one pair of male Cypriot Greek-speakers, and one pair of male Spanish-speakers. The taped interviews of these six subjects were then transcribed for further analysis for error type.

Since it is often difficult to distinguish between errors of interference and errors of overgeneralization (in fact errors can often be judged to be either), it was decided to identify as L1 transfer only those errors that could easily be classified as coming from the learner's source language. In many cases, these errors could be traced to direct translations from L1.

The judging of errors was performed for the Persian-speakers by an Iranian-born Persian English bilingual, Ph.D. in linguistics. The Spanish-speaker data were analyzed by a high level English-Spanish bilingual ESL teacher who had lived and taught for several years in a Spanish-speaking country. The Greek-speaker errors were judged independently by two Greek-English bilinguals who were linguistics majors at Queens College. One of two Greek judges spoke the Greek dialect of the subjects.

The judges were given tapescripts of the taped interviews but were not told either the purpose of the analysis or how the learners whose scripts they were analyzing were classified. Instructions were to classify errors on the basis of "clearly from L1," and give a possible explanation, or "not from L1." Any errors of questionable source were to be classified as not from L1. Since the tapescripts noted everything including hesitations, pauses, retracings, and self-corrections, judges were instructed to analyze only the final form of the utterance. While hesitation and correction behavior is considered important in looking at the processing features of learners' grammars (Seliger, 1980), such behavior was not considered in this study, which was concerned with the learner's error profile rather than a description of processing.

Once the judges had classified the errors, the researcher tabulated the different categories which included L1 errors or other. For this study, only a percentage was computed for each learner consisting of the ratio of transfer errors to total error output of the individual learner. Note that the figures found in Table 3 are percentages for an individual learner's production in the taped interviews.

Looking at Table 3, we see that a higher percentage of transfer errors occurs with LIGs. What is surprising is the narrow range of percentages found for these subjects. Both LIGs and HIGs appear to produce error profiles whose range extends across languages. It would, of course, be necessary to examine many matched pairs of learners in order to see if such a pattern were common. That is, would we find that the error profiles of HIGs were limited to such a narrow range of four percentage points while LIGs were limited to the narrow range of about six points? What is also interesting is the discreteness of the parameters. There does not seem to be any overlapping of scores for the two types of populations. This, of course, may be a function of the fact that subjects were chosen on the

Table 3. Percentage of
Errors Traceable
to L1 According
to Interactor Type
and First Lan-
guage*

Language	HIG	LIG
Persian	36.17	52.38
Greek	38.46	55.88
Spanish	40.0	50.0

*Pooled differences for interactor
type significant for that .01 level.

basis of the extremes that they demonstrated with regard to interactive behavior. Such a finding of discreteness, it would seem, further proves the existence of these two quite distinct types of language learners, not only in terms of overt behavior but also in terms of qualitative differences in their language output. Further study would be necessary to see if overlapping or continuous error percentages would be obtained by examining the data from subjects who ranked between the two extremes examined here.

Table 4 shows the raw numbers of errors from each category produced by each of the subjects. It must be remembered that LIGs as a group usually produce less total output, and while HIGs produce many more errors than LIGs they also produce more language. Seliger (1980) found that HIGs produced many more overt errors requiring repair and retracing or self-correction than did LIGs. It was concluded in that study that the greater willingness of HIGs to make errors while interacting also allowed them to test more hypotheses about L2 than the more cautious LIGs. In short, more errors do not mean that the learner is learning less. It may mean just the opposite as seen by the data here.

Table 4. Number of Errors According to Type
from the Total Discourse Samples

Language	HIG			LIG		
	L1	Other	Total	L1	Other	Total
Persian	17	30	47	11	10	21
Greek	10	16	26	19	15	34
Spanish	10	15	25	8	8	16

Table 5 shows what was termed the *mean discourse length* (MDL) for the three matched pairs of subjects in this study. The MDL was computed as the average number of words produced by the subjects in answer to the two questions noted in the table. Such discourse segments were not necessarily continued without break. They were often interrupted by signals from the interviewer either that showed she was following the discourse and understood or that contained clarifying questions based on the utterances of the subject. Discourse was defined as that segment of the interview that began with one of the predetermined interview questions and ended with the onset of the next predetermined interview question.

Table 5. Mean Discourse Length for Subjects in Answer to the Questions:

1. What does it feel like to be a foreign student at Queens College?
2. If you were the director of the English Language Institute, what would you do to improve the program?

Language	HIG	LIG
Persian	119	64
Greek	152	49.5
Spanish	146.5	29.5

In summary, study #2 tested the hypothesis that the errors of high inter-actors would contain a lower ratio of interference-based errors, while the errors of learners exhibiting low levels of interaction would contain much higher ratios of interference-type errors. This hypothesis was confirmed for the three matched pairs of subjects studied. These findings are interpreted to mean that more intensive interaction leads to the evolution of a more linguistically mature error profile—that is, an error profile containing a lower ratio of interference errors and a greater ratio of errors from other sources such as L2 over-generalization.

Conclusions

The studies reported here tested the hypotheses that using the target language as a tool for social interaction affects the rate of second language acquisition and the quality of second language acquisition. These studies found that learners who maintained high levels of interaction in the second language, both in the classroom and outside, progressed at a faster rate than learners who interacted little in the classroom.

The language output of High Input Generators (HIGs) was found to differ significantly both *qualitatively* and *quantitatively* from the language produced by Low Input Generators (LIGs). An analysis of the L2 production of HIGs showed a lower percentage of errors that could be traced to transfer from the learner's first language. On the other hand, an analysis of the language output of LIGs showed a higher percentage of errors traceable to L1 transfer. These results were explained on the basis of higher levels of language interaction carried on by HIGs. The more the HIG interacts, in the second language, the more opportunities he or she has to form and test hypotheses about L2 by comparing his or her output with the feedback generated by his or her language interaction. On the basis of this increased amount of feedback, HIGs have more opportunities to reject false hypotheses about the second language being derived from the first and begin to develop a set of L2 hypotheses independent of L1 influence.

Appendix A.   Sample Observation Worksheet for Observing Learner Interaction

Code: / = non-initiated in L2, (/) = non-initiated in L1
+ = initiated in L2, (+) = initiated in L1

Observer _____

Class _____

Date _____

Lesson was very loosely controlled <u>1</u>   <u>5</u>   <u>10</u> highly controlled
Lesson concerned with reading _____ , writing _____ , oral skills _____ , other _____
Seating arrangement: Frontal _____ , circular _____ , other _____ .
Other comments may be made on the back of the worksheet.

Student (name or number)	Interactions with Other Students	Interactions with Teacher	Group-Directed Interactions
1.			
2.			
3.			
4.			
5.			
6.			
7.			
8.			
9.			
10.			
11.			
12.			

Appendix B

Language Contact Profile   E. _____

                                 Date _____

                                 Program _____ Level _____

Score   1. Student's name _____ Sex   M/F

              2. Country of origin _____ How long in U.S.? _____

              3. Educational level (grade school, h.s., college, etc.) _____

              4. Native language _____

              5. Age _____

_____   6. About how much time do you spend speaking English outside of class every
                  day? (circle one)
                  a. none = 0
                  b. very little (directions, shopping, etc.) = 1
                  c. occasionally (with friends) = 2
                  d. most of the time = 3

              7. How well do you think you speak English now?
                  a. poorly   b. fair   c. good   d. very good   e. excellent

                  (E, do you agree or disagree with S's evaluation? _____)

              8. How many years have you studied English? _____

                  Where? _____

_____   9. Do you live with anyone who speaks *only* English? _____

                  How much time do you spend with them on a daily basis?
                  a. less than one hour (2 points)
                  b. one to two hours (4 points)
                  c. more than two hours (6 points)

_____   10. Are newspapers and magazines available in your first language? Y/N
                  How often do you read them?
                  a. seldom = 4
                  b. once in a while = 3
                  c. weekly = 2
                  d. daily = 1

_____   11. When you have homework in English do you
                  a. do it as soon as you can = 4
                  b. do it if you find time = 3
                  c. do it at the last possible moment = 2
                  d. do it but turn it in late = 1
                  e. (none of these) _____

_____   12. During English classes do you
                  a. have a tendency to daydream about your country = 0
                  b. have to force yourself to listen to the lesson = 0
                  c. listen at all times, even when it's not your turn = 4
                  d. listen when it's your turn but do other things when it's not = 2

13. Do you watch television programs in English?
    a. as often as you can = 3
    b. once in awhile = 3
    c. not very often = 1
    d. never = 0
    e. prefer watching programs in your native language. Otherwise you do not watch television at all = 0

14. If you have a choice between listening to a radio program in your native language or in English you
    a. prefer English = 3
    b. sometimes listen to the English programs and sometimes to those in your language = 2
    c. would not listen to the English programs = 0

15. List your three closest friends in New York City.

               name of friend   language usually spoken with friend

    a. _____ _____

    b. _____ _____

    c. _____ _____

    (score: 3 points for each friend with whom English is used, 0 points for language other than English)

16. List the three *English speaking Americans* that you speak English with the most. In what capacity do you know them? (e.g., teacher, busdriver, friend, neighbor, landlord, storeclerk, boss, relative, etc.).

              name of American   relationship

    a. _____ _____

    b. _____ _____

    c. _____ _____

    (score: friend = 2 points, relative = 2 points, teacher = 1 point, other formal relationships such as busdriver, landlord, etc. = 1)

17. Do you spend time trying to improve your English outside of class? _____
    How? (list all activities, e.g., watching t.v., reading, writing, speaking with friends, going to movies, etc.)

    _____

    About how much time each day *for each activity*?
    a. one hour = 1
    b. two hours = 2
    c. three hours = 3, etc.
    (score: 4 points for each active or productive activity, 2 points for each passive or receptive activity. Multiply each of these by the amount of time spent in this activity per day; add up.)

Note

1. Portions of this chapter have been reprinted from Herbert W. Seliger, "Does Practice Make Perfect? A Study of Interaction Patterns and L2 Competence." (*Language Learning*, Vol. 27, No. 2, 1977.)

References

Ausubel, D. P. Some psychological aspects of the structure of knowledge. In P. E. Johnson (Ed.), *Learning: Theory and Practice.* New York: Thomas Y. Crowell, 1971.

Bales, R. F. *Personality and Interpersonal Behavior.* New York: Holt, Rinehart & Winston, 1970.

DeFazio, V. J. Field articulation differences in language abilities. *Journal of Personality and Social Psychology,* 1973, *25,* 351–356.

Gaies, S. J. Learner feedback: A taxonomy of intake control. *On TESOL '80.* Washington, D.C.: TESOL, 1980.

Krashen, S. D., & Seliger, H. W. The essential contributions of formal instruction in the adult second language classroom. *TESOL Quarterly,* 1975, *9,* 173–183.

Lefever, M. M., & Ehri, L. C. The relationship between field independence and sentence disambiguation ability. *Journal of Psycholinguistic Research,* 1976, *5,* 99–106.

Lenneberg, E. *The Biological Foundations of Language.* New York: Wiley, 1967.

Mishler, E. G. Studies in dialogue and discourse. *Journal of Psycholinguistic Research,* 1978, *7,* 4.

Osgood, C. F. Behavior theory and the social sciences. *Behavior Science,* 1956, *1,* 3, 167–185.

Seliger, H. W. Does practice make perfect?: A study of interaction patterns and L2 competence. *Language Learning,* 1977, *27,* 2, 263–278.

Seliger, H. W. On the evolution of error type in high and low interactors. *Indian Journal of Applied Linguistics,* 1978, *IV,* 1, 22–30.

Seliger, H. W. Data sources and the study of L2 speech performance: Some theoretical issues. *Interlanguage Studies Bulletin,* 1980, *5,* 1, 31–46.

Suzman, R. M. Psychological modernity. *International Journal of Comparative Sociology,* 1973, *14,* 273–287.

Tarone, E. Communication strategies, foreigner talk and repair in interlanguage. *Language Learning,* 1980, *30,* 2, 417–432.

Witkin, H. A., Lewis, H. B., Hetzman, M., Machover, K., Meissner, P. B., & Wagner, S. *Personality through Perception.* New York: Harper and Brothers, 1954.

Questions for Discussion and Activities

1. What alternative explanations can you think of to explain the findings that IIIGs and LIGs produce different kinds of errors in English?
2. In carrying out studies such as those described here, only small numbers of subjects may be used because of the problems of observing the interaction patterns in the classroom without changing the essential characteristics of classroom instruction. Can you think of a way of studying the same phenomenon but increasing the number of subjects?
3. What kinds of language classes seem to encourage HIG behavior? What kinds of classes seem to encourage LIG behavior? Compare an ESL classroom with a foreign language classroom.
4. Can you think of situations in which a learner might appear to be a LIG in the classroom but progress quickly in second language acquisition?
5. Make copies of the observation sheet and the Language Contact Profile in Appendices A and B. Observe ESL classes of children and adults. Can you replicate the results of Study #1?
6. What predictions might be made about the quality of the grammar of a learner who interacts primarily with other learners rather than with the teacher? How would you test these predictions?
7. If HIGs seem to be focused on communication, what hypotheses may be made about the nature of HIGs' grammar in terms of areas of development such as lexicon, syntax, and phonology? Would the rate of development in these areas be parallel or at different rates? How might these hypotheses be tested?
8. What happens to HIGs and LIGs when mixed together in small groups of three or four? Does the LIG participate more? What kinds of participation patterns emerge? Are they different from those observed for the same learners in the classroom?

12

Classroom Foreigner Talk Discourse: Forms and Functions of Teachers' Questions

Michael H. Long and Charlene J. Sato

Teachers' classroom questions have been the focus of a great deal of research in recent years, although to our knowledge none of this research has been conducted in ESL classrooms. Various perspectives have been adopted. In educational research, relationships have been sought and established between the form and cognitive level of questions and student achievement (see Winne, 1979, for review). From a sociological perspective, classroom questions have been examined in at least two ways. First, they have been shown to provide one means by which, in conversation between participants of unequal status, the dominant member exercises and maintains control of interaction (Mishler, 1975). Second, the ritual nature of teacher questioning behavior has been well documented (Hoetker and Ahlbrand, 1969), especially pervasive being those questions that oblige students to display knowledge rather than provide unknown information or express attitudes (Mehan, 1979). Finally, ethnographic studies comparing conversational patterns in the school with those in the wider community or in the home have highlighted the cultural specificity of much teacher questioning behavior (Boggs, 1972; Heath, 1979; Philips, 1972), thereby explaining some children's apparent "failure" to respond or "inappropriate" responses in the classroom.

Studies of these kinds are of great potential relevance to researchers and teachers working in second language (SL) classrooms. They offer insights into the dynamics of classroom conversation in general, and sometimes suggest variables of particular interest in SL teaching. For example, cultural differences in conversational style among students, and between teacher and students, are likely to be important factors in ESL classes. In the ESL classroom, multi-ethnic encounters are the norm, and ethnic differences have recently been found to relate to such issues as classroom speaking opportunities and patterns of turn-taking behavior (Sato, 1981). The importance of practice opportunities for second language acquisition (SLA) has in turn been suggested by Seliger (1977) through his concept of high/low input generators. In other words, teachers' questioning behavior is probably one of a subset of classroom *process* variables related to the phenomenon whose understanding is our ultimate goal, classroom SLA.

Despite their probable importance, to our knowledge there have been no studies of teachers' questions in SL classrooms to date. This is additionally surprising, given the important role questions have been found to play in native speaker/non-native speaker (NS-NNS) conversation *outside* the classroom. Research on "foreigner talk" (the speech of NSs addressing NNSs) by Freed (1978) and Long (1980a, 1981a), among others, suggests that the higher frequency and varied functions of questions are among the most significant and most consistent modifications made from NS-NS norms. In "foreigner talk discourse" (NS-NNS conversation in which the NS uses a modified register, foreigner talk, to address the NNS), questions are thought to facilitate and sustain participation by the NNS. For example, they can serve to signal speaking turns for the NNS, to make conversational topics salient, and generally to "compel" the NNS to participate, since in most cultures, questions require answers (Goody, 1978). In English, at least, they constitute the first part of a two-part "adjacency pair," question-answer (Sacks, Schegloff, and Jefferson, 1974). Further, certain *kinds* of questions, especially Yes/No and what Hatch (1978) has called "or-choice" questions, are particularly easy on the NNS. Long (1981a), for example, has noted that they require, respectively, only confirmation or denial of a fully encoded proposition:

NS: Are you Japanese?
NNS: Yes

or that the NNS select from a series of possible answers contained in the question itself:

NS: Do you like tea? Or coffee? Or . . .
NNS: Tea

Wh-questions, on the other hand, involve the NNS in supplying a missing element, or proposition:

NS: Where are you from?
NNS: I come from Japan

In various ways, therefore, questions can help make greater quantities of linguistic input comprehensible, and also offer a NNS interlocutor more speaking opportunities.

Access to comprehensible input and opportunities to use the target language for communicative purposes are probably the minimum requirements for successful classroom SLA. Conversation, after all, is the *only* SLA experience available to large numbers of people in many societies in the Third World where bi- or multi-lingualism is the norm. (In sharp contrast, the fluent bilingual is the exceptional, not normal, product of classroom instruction in many industrialized nations.) There is evidence consistent with the hypothesis that the necessary condition for such conversation to take place *outside* classrooms is modification, not of linguistic input *per se* (length and syntactic complexity of utterances, lexical diversity, etc.), but of the *interactional structure of* (NS-NS) *conversation* (Long, 1981b, 1981c). The latter type of modification is achieved through use of such devices as repetition, rephrasing, various forms of discourse repair, and questioning.

It follows that comparison of NS-NNS conversation inside and outside classrooms has the potential for revealing similarities and differences in their structure, one or more of which may eventually provide the key to making teacher-student conversation in the classroom a more useful experience for SL learners. The explicit comparison of NSs' questions, one feature of NS-NNS conversation in the two settings, was the focus of the study to be reported here. It is offered as a contribution to what, it is hoped, will become a growing field of inquiry in SLA research, NS-NNS conversation in and out of classrooms.

Purpose of the Study

The main purpose of the study reported here was to conduct an exploratory investigation of the forms and functions of teachers' questions in ESL classrooms, and to compare the findings with previously established patterns of questioning behavior in NS-NNS conversation outside classrooms. A second issue of interest was the relationship between the patterns established for teachers' questions and other characteristics of linguistic input to, and interaction with, NNSs during classroom SL instruction.

It was assumed that the classroom speech of SL teachers is affected by at least two kinds of constraints: those imposed by the classroom as the *setting* for the conversation, including the patterns of speech associated with the *role* of teacher, and those arising from the limited linguistic proficiency of the *interlocutor*. Previous research on other aspects of conversation in ESL classrooms, for example, has found several similar patterns of teacher feedback to those observed in content classrooms (see Long, 1977, for review). Similarly, there is evidence that ESL teachers and NSs addressing non-natives outside classrooms modify some features of their speech in similar ways (Gaies, 1977). Teacher speech during SL instruction, in other words, is probably a hybrid register characterized by features of both *teacher talk* (Cazden, 1979) and *foreigner talk* (Ferguson, 1975). Previous empirical work on both registers contributed to the formation of hypotheses for the present study.

Hypotheses

Reference has already been made to so-called "display," "test," or "known information" questions, e.g.

T: What's the capital of Peru?
S: Lima
T: Good

Experience suggests that such questions are pervasive in ESL instruction, too, where a focus on formal accuracy rather than communicative use of language is actually prescribed by most language teaching methods. Lower frequencies of display questions would be expected in non-instructional conversation, in which there is a two-way exchange of information. These ideas were expressed in three hypotheses:

H1: ESL teachers ask more display questions than information questions.
H2: ESL teachers ask more display questions than NSs in informal conversation with NNSs outside classrooms.
H3: ESL teachers ask fewer information questions than NSs in informal conversation with NNSs outside classrooms.

Hypothesis 3 was not a necessary corollary of hypothesis 2 since, as will become apparent, directions to display knowledge and requests for information are but two of several functions served by questions in both teacher-student and NS-NNS conversation.

As suggested above, the teaching/testing and information exchange functions, respectively, of much classroom conversation on the one hand, and of informal conversation outside classrooms on the other, should result in questions of different kinds (hypotheses 1, 2, and 3). These differences should also produce different relative frequencies of questions, statements, and imperatives in the NSs' speech. Here, however, competing forces may be at work. Both the role of the teacher and the status and power vested in that role should affect this issue. Management and disciplinary functions of teachers involve them in giving commands; their power and status *vis à vis* students mean that many of those commands will be encoded as imperatives, forms that would be marked (because unmitigated by politeness markers) in informal conversation among equals. Thus, teachers' speech should show more imperatives and so fewer questions and/or statements. On the other hand, if informal conversation involves the exchange of information (however, "phatic" that information may sometimes be), participating NSs will spend relatively more time responding to questions than teachers, and so use more statements.

This might take up the slack resulting from less use of imperatives, and leave the proportion of questions the same in each corpus. However, a third factor should offset this tendency, and so result overall in greater frequencies of questions by NSs in informal conversation. Approximately one-third of teachers' moves in classroom discourse involve the provision of feedback on student performance (cf. the initiation-response-*feedback* structure in Sinclair and Coulthard, 1975, or the structure-solicit-respond-*react* cycle in Bellack, Kliebard, Hyman, and Smith, 1966, confirmed for ESL lessons by Fanselow, 1977), and many of these feedback moves are statements. These expectations led to the fourth hypothesis:

H4: ESL teachers use different relative frequencies of questions, statements, and imperatives from NSs in conversation with NNSs outside classrooms.

Further hypotheses related to one aspect of what NSs talk *about* with NNSs, and to the impact this may have on temporal reference morphology. Two previous studies have shown that NS-NNS conversation tends to be more oriented to the "now" of the "here and now" of caretaker speech than conversation between adult NSs, at least when both types of dyads are engaged in performing the same tasks, and that *within* NS-NNS conversation, the proportion of talk with this orientation is also higher (Long, 1980a, 1981a). The measure of "nowness" used in that research was the relative frequency of verbs marked temporally for present and non-present. In the current study, it was believed that these tendencies would be accentuated in classroom SL instruction. First, the addressees were again NNSs. Second, SL teachers often contextualize classroom talk by reference to people, objects, and events within the immediate classroom environment. And third, many conversational topics that would lead naturally to non-present temporal reference, such as information about the students' own experiences and plans, are preempted by the frequent orientation of conversation toward what teachers tell students rather than the reverse. The power to determine conversational topic is, after all, another characteristic of the role of teacher (McHoul, 1978). Accordingly, it was hypothesized that:

H5: ESL teachers use more verbs marked temporally for present than non-present.

H6: ESL teachers use proportionately more verbs marked for present than do NSs in conversation with NNSs outside classrooms.

Finally, previous studies (Larsen-Freeman, 1976a; Long, 1980a, 1981a) have found positive correlations between the relative frequencies in linguistic input to NNSs of nine grammatical morphemes and the order in which those morphemes appear accurately supplied in the speech of SL acquirers. The Larsen-Freeman study involved the classroom speech of two ESL teachers (three lessons per teacher). Spearman rank order correlation coefficients between the input frequency orders for the six lessons and oral production orders ranged between .433 and .783, with most values significant beyond the .05 level. The studies by Long obtained values of .77 and .75 (p < .05 in both cases) for the relationship between input frequencies to NNSs during one-to-one conversation outside classrooms and Krashen's "average order" (Krashen, 1977).

On the basis of these findings, a significant positive correlation ($\alpha = .05$) might have been expected in this study between the input frequency orders in teachers' speech and Krashen's order. However, it had already been hypothesized that some morphemes in the order—specifically, regular past, irregular past, and third person *s,* which concern present and non-present temporal reference—would be affected by the anticipated relatively higher proportion of reference to present time in ESL instruction than in NS-NNS conversation outside classrooms. Therefore, a somewhat disturbed input frequency order was expected in the teachers' speech, with the result of a somewhat lower Spearman rank order correlation coefficient than had previously been obtained for input frequency orders in informal conversation. These considerations motivated the following hypotheses:

H7: The relative frequency order of nine grammatical morphemes in ESL teachers' speech correlates positively with their frequency in the speech of NSs in conversation with NNSs outside classrooms.

H8: The relative frequency order of nine grammatical morphemes in ESL teachers' speech correlates positively with the order of their appearance accurately supplied in the speech of ESL learners.

H9: The magnitude of the correlation coefficient between the relative frequency order of nine grammatical morphemes in ESL teachers' speech and Krashen's "average order" for ESL learners' production will be lower than that between the frequency order for the same morphemes in conversational input to NNSs and the "average order."

Method

The ESL classroom data.

Subjects. Subjects for the study comprised six ESL teachers and their students. There were three male and three female teachers, all with considerable TESL experience. Each was teaching his or her regular class at the elementary level in various adult ESL programs, two in Hawaii, three in Los Angeles, and one in Philadelphia. Class size ranged from fifteen to thirty–five, with students a mixture of beginners and false beginners and from a variety of first-language backgrounds. Most were fairly recent arrivals in the United States, and most needed English for academic, vocational, or professional purposes.

Data collection. Teachers were given a small cassette tape-recorder and asked to record a complete lesson with their regular class of students. They were told that any normal class activities were of interest to the researchers, and that they should not depart from their regular syllabus or lesson plan for the day because of the recording. The researchers did not observe the lessons involved in order not to make the data collection any more obtrusive than necessary. The tapes were later transcribed, and each verified by a second person.[1] Analyses were conducted using the sound tapes and/or transcripts, as needed.

The six lessons that made up the corpus seemed to the researchers to be typical of ESL instruction to students of the kind described. None of the teachers, for example, adhered to any of the recent "unconventional" language teaching methods, such as Silent Way, Total Physical Response, Natural Approach, Counseling-Learning, or Suggestopoedia. Rather, they could be described as using a variety of techniques and activities found in much audio-lingual, audio-visual, and structural-situational language teaching. They based most of their oral work on textbook exercises, prepared dialogues, and other teacher-made material.

The conversational data.   Subjects.   Subjects for this part of the study were thirty-six NSs and thirty-six NNSs, who met in dyads for the purpose of the research. The NSs comprised three groups, twelve experienced ESL teachers, twelve teachers of other subjects, and twelve people who were not teachers of any kind and who had had minimal prior contact with NNSs of English. All were adults with at least a bachelor's degree. There were six males and six females in each group. The NNSs were all Japanese young adults on a six-week visit to the USA, during part of which they were taking an ESL course for beginners and false beginners at UCLA. Dyads were formed by random assignment within each level of the variables (experience with foreigner talk discourse, sex of NS and sex of NNS) represented in the sample, such that there were an equal number of same-sex and cross-sex pairings. (See Long, 1981a, for further details.)

Data collection.   Subjects, who had no prior acquaintance with one another, were introduced by first name and asked to have a five-minute conversation in English about anything they liked. The investigator then left the room, leaving a cassette tape-recorder running. Subjects knew they were being recorded. Tapes were later transcribed by the first author. Analyses were conducted using the sound tapes and transcripts, as needed.

Analysis.   Kearsley (1976) conducted a cross-disciplinary review of questions and question-asking in verbal discourse. Part of that research resulted in a taxonomy of question functions, which is shown, with Kearsley's definitions, below.

1. *Echoic:* "those which ask for the repetition of an utterance or confirmation that an utterance has been interpreted as intended" (e.g., Pardon? What? Huh?).
2. *Epistemic:* those which "serve the purpose of acquiring information."
   a. *Referential:* "are intended to provide contextual information about situations, events, actions, purposes, relationships, or properties" (Wh-questions).
   b. *Evaluative:* "are asked to establish the addressee's knowledge of the answer" (cf. "display," "test," or "known information" questions).

3. *Expressive:* "convey attitudinal information to the addressee" (e.g., Are you coming or aren't you?).
4. *Social control:* "used to exert authority by maintaining control of the discourse."
   a. *Attentional:* "allow the questioner to take over the direction of the discourse" (metamessage is "listen to me" or "think about this").
   b. *Verbosity:* "asked only for the sake of politeness or to sustain conversation" (e.g., cocktail party questions).

This analytic framework was initially applied to the transcript of one lesson in the ESL corpus, whereupon certain modifications were made. The changes reflected (1) functions of questions found in the classroom data but not captured by Kearsley's categories (the subdivision of *echoic* and introduction of *rhetorical*), and (2) the elimination of categories found in Kearsley's scheme but not exemplified in the data (*attentional* and *verbosity* questions). As with the development of almost any set of categories for classifying functions of human behavior, it is possible to make ever finer distinctions (and more categories). This is a practice that can result in unwieldy coding systems whose increasingly subtle distinctions are accompanied by no parallel increase in understanding (predictive power) of the phenomenon under investigation (for discussion, see Long, 1980b, and Chapter 2, this volume). The additional distinctions introduced here, however, were motivated not just by the possibility of making them, but by previous research (Long, 1980a) showing that behavior in the new categories varies in frequency with the task upon which speakers are engaged. An explanation of the new categories follows.

A subdivision of Kearsley's category, *echoic,* into *comprehension checks, clarification requests,* and *confirmation checks* allowed distinctions to be made among acts whose function reflects (among other things) the direction of information-flow in preceding utterances and, indirectly, the degree to which conversation is negotiated through the modification of its interactional structure. Thus, *confirmation checks,* for example, will be more frequent in a teacher's speech if information is being conveyed by students. They involve exact or semantic, complete or partial repetition of the previous speaker's utterance, are encoded as either Yes/No or uninverted (rising intonation) questions (there is a presupposition of a "Yes" answer), and serve either to elicit confirmation that their user had heard and/or understood the previous speaker's previous utterance correctly or to dispel that belief.

Following Long (1980a, pp. 81–83), the following definitions were applied in the analysis of *comprehension checks* and *clarification requests,* the other two subcategories of Kearsley's *echoic. Comprehension checks* are any expressions by a NS designed to establish whether that speaker's preceding utterance has been understood *by the interlocutor.* They are typically formed by tag questions, by repetitions of all or part of the same speaker's preceding utterance spoken with rising intonation, or by utterances like *Do you understand?,* which explicitly check comprehension by the interlocutor. *Clarification requests* are any expressions by a NS designed to elicit clarification of the interlocutor's preceding utterance. Clarification requests are mostly formed by questions, but may consist of Yes/No *or* Wh-questions (unlike confirmation checks) as well as uninverted (rising intonation) and tag questions, for they require that the interlocutor either furnish new information or recode information previously given. Unlike confirmation checks, in other words, use of clarification requests implies no presupposition on the speaker's part that he or she has heard and understood the interlocutor's previous utterance. While clarification requests are frequently realized by questions, they are also encoded in statements like *I don't understand,* and through imperatives like *Try again.*

All questions in the ESL corpus were coded using the seven categories in the new taxonomy below, whether they occurred in T-units[2] or as conversational fragments:

1. *Echoic*
   a. *Comprehension checks* (e.g., Alright?; OK?; Does everyone understand "polite"?)
   b. *Clarification requests* (e.g., What do you mean?; I don't understand; What?)
   c. *Confirmation checks* (e.g., S: Carefully → T: Carefully?; Did you say "he"?)
2. *Epistemic*
   a. *Referential* (e.g., Why didn't you do your homework?)
   b. *Display* (e.g., What's the opposite of "up" in English?)
   c. *Expressive* (e.g., It's interesting the different pronunciations we have now, but isn't it?)
   d. *Rhetorical:* asked for effect only, no answer expected from listeners, answered by speaker (e.g., Why did I do that? Because I . . .)

Hypotheses 1, 2, and 3 were tested using totals referential and display questions derived from this analysis, together with data on these two question types in a random sample of 1,322 questions in the second, conversational corpus.

Hypothesis 4 was tested on a random sample of 2,029 questions, statements, and imperatives in T-units in the six ESL transcripts, and on all 1,434 questions, statements, and imperatives in T-units in the conversational data.

Hypotheses 5 and 6 were tested defining "present" and "non-present" temporal marking in the same way as had been used in earlier research on this variable. As before, all verbs marked for tense were included in the analysis. *Going to,* future and present progressive, and present simple verbal expressions with future time reference were coded as non-present.

The nine grammatical morphemes which form the basis of Krashen's "average order" are, in descending order of appearance accurately supplied in the speech of ESL acquirers: Progressive -*ing,* plural (combined long and short forms), copula, auxiliary, article (definite and indefinite), irregular past, regular past, 3rd person singular *s,* and possessive *'s.* The frequency of occurrence of these nine forms in the teachers' speech was determined using a random sample of 1,549 cases (derived from odd-numbered pages in the transcripts). The morphemes were then ranked by order of frequency, and Spearman rank order correlation coefficients calculated to ascertain the degree of association between this order and a NNS input order (Long, 1981a), and between the ESL teachers' order and Krashen's "average order." The Spearman statistics then served to test hypotheses 7, 8, and 9, with $\alpha = .05$ in all cases.

Results

Table 1 shows the distribution of questions of all types as they occurred in both the ESL and conversational corpora. Comparisons of subsets of these data served to test hypotheses 1, 2, and 3.

H 1: Display and referential questions in ESL teachers' speech. Of a total of 938 questions in the classroom corpus, 322 (34%) were echoic, and 604 (64%) epistemic. Within the epistemic category, 128 (21%) were referential and 476 (79%) display questions (Table 2). As predicted, there were significantly more display than referential questions in the teachers' speech ($x^2 = 199.35$, p < .0005).

H 2: Display questions in ESL teachers' speech and in the speech of NSs in informal NS-NNS conversation. Table 3 shows the frequencies of display questions in the six ESL lessons and in the thirty-six informal NS-NNS

Table 1.   Functions of Questions in 6 ESL Lessons and 36 Informal NS-NNS Conversations

| | Lesson | | | | | | Total | |
Function	1	2	3	4	5	6	TESL	NS-NNS
Echoic								
Comprehension checks	57	4	50	27	13	18	169	27
Clarification requests	11	4	8	10	1	7	41	50
Confirmation checks	32	20	21	14	3	22	112	206
Epistemic								
Referential	16	18	11	24	38	21	128	999
Display	73	15	52	143	85	108	476	2
Expressive	0	5	0	1	0	2	8	35
Rhetorical	0	4	0	0	0	0	4	3
Total	189	70	142	219	140	178	938	1322

Table 2.   Display and Referential Questions in 6 ESL Teachers' Speech

	Display questions	*Referential questions*	*Total*
ESL teachers (n = 6)	476	128	604
	$x^2 = 199.35$, df = 1, p < .0005		

conversations. Whereas the 476 display questions accounted for 51% of all questions asked by the six ESL teachers, there were only two display questions in a total of 1,567 in T-units and fragments in the conversation corpus. This difference was significant ($\chi^2 = 1,859,131.70$, p < .0005), using Yates's correction for a two-way χ^2 design with one degree of freedom.

H 3: Referential questions in ESL teachers' speech and in the speech of NSs in informal NS-NNS conversation. Table 4 shows the frequencies of referential questions in the six ESL lessons and in the random sample of 1,322 questions in the conversation corpus. 128 referential questions in the ESL corpus accounted for 14% of the total of 938. In the thirty-six NS-NNS conversations, there were 999 referential questions, 76% of the 1,322 total. This difference was significant ($\chi^2 = 844.01$, p < .0005), again using Yates's correction.

H 4: Questions, statements, and imperatives in T-units in ESL teachers' speech and in informal NS-NNS conversation. Table 5 shows the frequencies of questions, statements, and imperatives in 2,029 T-units in ESL teachers' speech and in the 1,434 T-units in the conversational data. Questions made up 35% of T-units in the teachers' speech, and 66% of those in the NSs' speech in informal conversations. Statements accounted for 54% of the teachers' other T-units, and imperatives for the remaining 11%. In the thirty-six informal conversations, statements comprised 33% and imperatives 1% of T-units by

Table 3.   Display Questions in 6 ESL Lessons and 36 Informal NS-NNS Conversations

	Display questions	Other questions	Total
ESL teachers (n = 6)	476	462	938
NSs (n = 36)	2	1320	1322
	$\chi^2 = 839.18$, df = 1, p < .0005		

Table 4.   Referential Questions in 6 ESL Lessons and 36 Informal NS-NNS Conversations

	Referential questions	Other questions	Total
ESL teachers (n = 6)	128	810	938
NSs (n = 36)	999	323	1322
	$\chi^2 = 844.01$, df = 1, p < .0005		

Table 5.   Questions, Statements, and Imperatives in T-units in 6 ESL Teachers' Speech and 36 Informal NS-NNS Conversations

	Questions	Statements	Imperatives	Total
ESL teachers (n = 6)	714	1091	224	2029
NSs (n = 36)	942	480	12	1434
	$\chi^2 = 308.10$, df = 2, p < .0005			

NSs. The difference between the distribution of questions, statements, and imperatives in the two corpora was significant ($\chi^2 = 308.10$, p < .0005).

H 5: Present and non-present temporal reference in ESL teachers' speech. Table 6 shows that, of a total of 620 verbs in the corpus, 441 (71%) were marked for present, and 179 (29%) for non-present time. This difference was significant ($\chi^2 = 109.87$, p < .0005).

H 6: Present time reference in ESL teachers' speech and in the speech of NSs in informal NS-NNS conversation. Table 7 shows that 441 (71%) of all verbs in ESL teachers' speech were marked for present time reference. In the corpus of informal NS-NNS conversation, 1,268 (60%) of the 2,119 total number of verbs were so marked. This difference was significant ($\chi^2 = 25.58$, p < .001).

H 7, H 8, and H 9: Morpheme frequencies in ESL teachers' speech and the speech of NSs in informal NS-NNS conversation, and the relationships between these frequencies and Krashen's "average order." Table 8 shows three morpheme frequency orders: Krashen's (1977) "average order," the six ESL teachers' frequency order, and the frequency order for the thirty-six NSs in the informal conversation corpus, together with raw scores for each item in the last two orders. As predicted (H7), the ESL teachers' order correlated positively with that for the thirty-six NSs in the informal conversations (rho = .77, p < .005). Contrary to expectations (H8), the ESL teachers' order did not correlate significantly with Krashen's "average order" for accurate appearance of the nine morphemes in the speech of ESL acquirers (rho = .46, p > .05, ns). As predicted (H9), the ESL teacher speech × "average order" Spearman coefficient (.46) was lower than the NS frequency order in informal conversations × "average order" (.77).

Discussion

The results reported above show that most predicted differences between the two corpora were borne out by this exploratory study, with eight of nine

Table 6.   Present and Non-present Temporal Reference in 6 ESL Teachers' Speech

	+present	−present	Total
ESL teachers (n = 6)	441	179	620

$\chi^2 = 109.87$, df = 1, p < .0005

Table 7.   Present Time Reference in 6 ESL Lessons and 36 Informal NS-NNS Conversations

	+present	Other	Total
ESL teachers (n = 6)	441	179	620
NSs (n = 36)	1268	851	2119

$\chi^2 = 25.58$, df = 1, p < .001

Table 8.   Nine Grammatical Morphemes in ESL Production, ESL Teacher Speech, and NS Speech in Informal NS-NNS Conversation

ESL accuracy order (Krashen's, 1977, "average order") ((A))	ESL teacher speech input frequency order ((B))		NS input frequency order to NNSs ((C))	
Rank	Rank	Frequency	Rank	Frequency
1. progressive -ing	1. article	579	1. article	511
2. plural	2. copula	436	2. copula	476
3. copula	3. plural	249	3. plural	319
4. aux.	4. 3rd person s	88	4.5. progressive -ing	146
5. article	5. progressive -ing	51	4.5. aux.	146
6. irregular past	6. regular past	49	6. irregular past	47
7. regular past	7. aux.	48	7. regular past	41
8. 3rd person s	8. irregular past	44	8. 3rd person s	23
9. possessive	9. possessive	5	9. possessive	12

$rho_{AB} = .46, p > .05$, ns. $rho_{BC} = .77, p < .05$ $rho_{AC} = .75, p < .05$ (Long, 1981a)

hypotheses being confirmed. In general, the speech of the six ESL teachers differed greatly from that of the NSs in informal conversation with NNSs *outside* the classroom. The most surprising aspect of the results, perhaps, was the *magnitude* of the differences observed.

The first major difference concerned the roles of display and referential questions (Hypotheses 1, 2, and 3). If the findings of this exploratory study prove to hold for a variety of ESL classrooms (including those with students of higher levels of ESL proficiency), it seems that whereas display questions predominate in ESL instruction (51% of all questions teachers posed), and are much more frequent than referential questions there (51% compared with 21%), they are virtually *unknown* in informal NS-NNS conversation (the target discourse for most ESL learners). In this study, there were only two display questions (0.12%) in a total of 1,567 in T-units in thirty-six NS-NNS conversations. (Both of those arose at the start of one encounter when a NS checked to see if her partner had heard her name when they were introduced.) Conversely, referential (information-seeking) questions, which predominate in NS-NNS conversation *outside* classrooms (76% of all questions asked), made up a mere 14% of questions asked by teachers. This result suggests that, contrary to the recommendations of many writers on SL teaching methodology, communicative use of the target language makes up only a minor part of typical classroom activities. "Is the clock on the wall?" and "Are you a student?" are still the staple diet, at least for beginners.

The difference in distribution of questions, statements, and imperatives in T-units in the two corpora (Hypothesis 4) was also marked. Inspection of the frequencies in each category (Table 5) reveals that questions were proportionately only half as frequent in classroom talk (35% of all T-units, compared with 66% in the informal NS-NNS conversations). Statements were more frequent (54%, compared with 33% in informal conversations), and so were imperatives

(11%, compared with less than 1%). The higher number of statements seemed to be due to their use in feedback moves, which often contain a model of the correct response to the teacher's previous question, e.g.,

T: What happened during the night?
S1: Somebody take it
S2: Remove different place (xx)
T: That's right   They didn't just move it   They took it   OK

The higher frequency of imperatives in the instructional talk could be attributed to their use in classroom management, e.g.,

T: Give me the present perfect
T: Let's hear it again

and

T: Now uh class, take a little piece of paper

Distressingly often, they were also needed to discipline students, e.g.,

T: Sit down, Maria

and

T: Don't write on the board in pencil

and to regain wandering attention, e.g.,

T: John, look in the book Now *look*!

In some classes, imperatives were also nearly the only communicative use of English to which students were exposed.

The findings of higher frequencies of present temporal reference in teacher speech (Hypothesis 5), and in teacher speech compared with NS speech to NNSs outside classrooms (Hypothesis 6), were as predicted. The "now" orientation was also reflected in the relatively high absolute frequency (88) and rank (4th) of 3rd person *s* in the teacher speech input frequency order, compared with its absolute frequency (23) and rank (8th) in input to NNSs outside classrooms, and its rank (also 8th) in Krashen's "average order" for accurate production. The irregular past morpheme is, correspondingly, depressed by two ranks in the ESL order. Although regular past actually *gained* a rank there, inspection of the absolute frequencies of progressive *-ing,* regular past, aux., and irregular past in the ESL order shows that this is because those four items were bunched close together, a difference of only seven occurrences covering the 5th, 6, 7th, and 8th ranked items.

The relative frequencies of the tense morphology in turn help to explain the last set of results, which concerns relationships between the three rank orders (Hypotheses 7, 8, and 9). Table 8 shows that four morphemes (article, copula, plural, and possessive) occupied identical positions in both input frequency orders. Four other items (progressive -*ing,* regular past, aux., and irregular past) differed only by between one half a rank and two-and-a-half ranks. Third person *s,* on the other hand, differed by four ranks. Thus, 21 out of 27.5, the d^2 value for calculating the Spearman statistic (rho = .77), was accounted for by the three VP tense morphemes, 3rd person *s,* regular and irregular past.

A similar pattern obtains when the input frequency orders and Krashen's "average order" are compared. Progressive -*ing* and article are badly out of place in both input orders. Of the remaining factors differentiating the ESL input order and the "average order," the higher rank of 3rd person *s* in the ESL order is the single item accounting for most of the d^2 value, which in turn produced the lower, nonsignificant correlation (rho = .46, p > .05), while the NS-NNS input frquency order and Krashen's order remain significantly correlated (rho = .75, p < .05, Long, 1981a).

While the weaker correlation between the ESL order and the "average order" was as predicted (Hypothesis 9), the *degree* of difference between the two was not, forcing rejection of Hypothesis 8. It is yet another indication of the amount of "distortion" both of the input and of the interactional structure of conversation to which beginning ESL students are exposed. It is also a result that poses two obvious questions. First, how can the nonsignificant correlation be reconciled with the findings by Larsen-Freeman (1976a), reported earlier, of mostly significant positive correlations between teachers' input frequency orders and a student accuracy order for ESL (Larsen-Freeman, 1975)? Second, if input frequency orders are related to accuracy orders for ESL, as has previously been claimed (Larsen-Freeman, 1976a, b; Long, 1980a, 1981a), why is the ESL input order here not significantly correlated with the "average order"?

The answer to the first question may lie in the fact that the six classes involved in this study were all at the beginner's level, where "distortion" of the kinds documented may be expected to be greatest, due to the students' low proficiency level. Some previous research on the speech addressed to classroom ESL learners (Gaies, 1977) has found various features of teachers' speech to be sensitive to this factor. Larsen-Freeman's classes, on the other hand, were all at the intermediate level.

The second question is more problematic. One possibility that must be considered is that previous findings of a positive relationship between input frequency orders and difficulty orders were based on spurious correlations. However, while this may yet turn out to be the case, it does not currently seem likely. Both Larsen-Freeman (1976b) and Long (1981a) considered other potentially causal factors—semantic and syntactic complexity, perceptual saliency, native language transfer, practice opportunities etc.—but while each seemed certain to play some role in the acquisition process, none seemed such a likely candidate as input frequency for determining accuracy orders. (Neither researcher, it should be noted, suggested either that correlational data of the kind available to them justified inferences of causal relationships or that input frequency was the only factor likely to be involved.)

Another potential explanation for the present result derives from the fact that the studies upon which Krashen (1977) based his "average order" dealt mostly with intermediate and advanced ESL speakers. On the basis of this study and that of Larsen-Freeman (1976a), it seems likely that classroom input frequencies change over time with the increasing SL proficiency of the NNSs, due to the general degree of distortion of classroom discourse at the beginner's level. Perhaps the relative frequency of various structures in the input is indeed related to accuracy orders for those structures, but becomes a salient factor for learners once they have enough of the SL to "tune in to the frequency" (see Long, 1981a, for further discussion), i.e., at something beyond the elementary level of learners in this study. This would mean that the previous finding (Long, 1981a) that even learners at this level display the "average order" in their speech may then be due partly to input frequency, but also to other to other factors yet to be determined.

Summary and conclusions

The research reported here was an exploratory study of the forms and functions of questions in ESL teacher speech and in the speech of NSs in informal NS-NNS conversation outside classrooms. Relationships were also sought between the questioning behavior and other characteristics of linguistic input to NNSs and of the interactional structure of NS-NNS conversation.

Six teachers were found to ask significantly more display than referential questions during ESL instruction. Verbal expressions in their speech also contained significantly more present than non-present temporal reference. Compared with NSs in informal NS-NNS conversations, the ESL teachers asked more display questions and fewer referential questions. The distribution of questions, statements, and imperatives in T-units in the instructional talk also differed significantly from that in the speech of the thirty-six NSs outside the classroom, with the teachers using fewer questions overall, and more statements and more imperatives. The teachers' speech contained significantly more verbal expressions marked for present time reference. The rank order of the relative frequencies of nine grammatical morphemes in the teachers' speech was significantly positively correlated with the frequency order for those items in the NSs' speech to NNSs outside classrooms, but nonsignificantly correlated with an accuracy order for those items. The correlation between the ESL teachers' input frequency order and the accuracy order was lower than that between the NS frequency order outside classrooms and the accuracy order.

While there is as yet no direct evidence that communicative use of the target language in the SL classroom is more beneficial to SLA than engagement of learners in discourse whose focus is the language itself, there is an increasing amount of indirect evidence that this is indeed the case (see Long, 1981b, for review). Certainly, many writers on language-teaching methodology in the last twenty years have encouraged teachers to focus more, or even exclusively, on communication. From the evidence here, however, ESL teachers continue to emphasize form over meaning, accuracy over communication. This is illustrated, for example, by the preference for display over referential questions, and results in classroom NS-NNS conversation which differs greatly from its counterpart outside classrooms, even when the NNSs there are of equally low SL proficiency. Indeed, on this evidence, NS-NNS conversation during SL instruction is a greatly distorted version of its equivalent in the real world. Further research is needed to determine whether, as one suspects, this difference is important, and if so, how the interactional structure of classroom NS-NNS conversation can be changed.

Notes

1. We would like to express our appreciation to Lisa Huber for her help with transcription and coding.
2. A T-unit (Hunt, 1970) was defined in this study as "a main clause plus all subordinate clauses and nonclausal structures attached to or embedded in it."

References

Bellack, A., Kliebard, H., Hyman, R., & Smith, F. *The Language of the Classroom.* New York: Teachers College Press, 1966.

Boggs, S. The meaning of questions and narratives to Hawaiian children. In C. Cazden, V. P. John, & D. Hymes (Eds.), *Functions of Language in the Classroom.* New York: Teachers College Press, 1972, 299–327.

Cazden, C. Language in education: Variation in the teacher-talk register. In J. Alatis & R. Tucker (Eds.), *Language in Public Life.* Washington, D.C.: Georgetown University Press, 1979, 144–162.

Cazden, C., John, V. P, & Hymes, D. (Eds.). *Functions of Language in the Classroom.* New York: Teachers College Press, 1972.

Fanselow, J. Beyond "Rashomon"—Conceptualizing and describing the teaching act. *TESOL Quarterly,* 1977, *11,* 1, 17–39.

Ferguson, C. A. Towards a characterization of English foreigner talk. *Anthropological Linguistics,* 1975, *17,* 1–14.

Freed, B. F. Foreigner talk: A study of speech adjustments made by native speakers of English in conversation with non-native speakers. Doctoral dissertation, University of Pennsylvania, 1978.

Gaies, S. The nature of linguistic input in formal second language learning: Linguistic and communicative strategies in teachers' classroom language. In H. D. Brown, C. A. Yorio, & R. Crymes (Eds.), *On TESOL '77. Teaching and Learning English as a Second Language: Trends in Research and Practice.* Washington, D.C.: TESOL, 1977.

Goody, E. N. Towards a theory of questions. In E. N. Goody (Ed.), *Questions and Politeness: Strategies in Social Interaction.* Cambridge: Cambridge University Press, 1978.

Hatch, E. M. Discourse analysis and second language acquisition. In E. M. Hatch (Ed.), *Second Language Acquisition: A book of readings.* Rowley, Mass.: Newbury House, 1978.

Heath, S.B. Questioning at home and at school: A comparative study. In G. Spindler (Ed.), *Doing the Ethnography of Schooling: Educational Anthropology in Action.* New York: Holt, Rinehart & Winston, 1979.

Hoetker, J., & Ahlbrand, W. P. The persistence of the recitation. *American Educational Research Journal,* 1969, *6,* 1, 145–167.

Hunt, K. W. Syntactic maturity in schoolchildren and adults. *Monographs of the Society for Research in Child Development,* 1970, *53,* 1 (Serial No. 134).

Kearsley, G. P. Questions and question-asking in verbal discourse: A cross-disciplinary review. *Journal of Psycholinguistic Research,* 1976, *5,* 4, 355–375.

Krashen, S. D. Some issues relating to the monitor model. In H. D. Brown, C. Yorio, & R. Crymes (Eds.), *On TESOL '77: Teaching and Learning English as a Second Language: Trends in Research and Practice.* Washington, D.C.: TESOL, 1977.

Larsen-Freeman, D. The acquisition of grammatical morphemes by adult learners of English as a second language. Ph.D. dissertation, University of Michigan, 1975.

Larsen-Freeman, D. ESL teacher speech as input to the ESL learner. *UCLA Workpapers in Teaching English as a Second Language,* 1976a, *10,* 45–49.

Larsen-Freeman, D. An explanation for the morpheme acquisition of second language learners. *Language Learning,* 1976b, *26,* 1, 125–134.

Long, M. H. Teacher feedback on learner error: Mapping cognitions. In H. D. Brown, C. A. Yorio, & R. Crymes (Eds.), *On TESOL '77. Teaching and Learning English as a Second Language: Trends in Research and Practice.* Washington, D.C.: TESOL, 1977.

Long, M. H. Input, interaction, and second language acquisition. Ph.D. dissertation, University of California, Los Angeles, 1980a.

Long, M. H. Inside the "black box": Methodological issues in classroom research on language learning. *Language Learning,* 1980b, *30,* 1, 1–42.

Long, M. H. Questions in foreigner talk discourse. *Language Learning,* and Chapter 2, this volume. 1981a, *31,* 1, 135–157.

Long, M. H. Input, interaction, and second language acquisition. Paper presented at the New York Academy of Sciences Conference on Native Language and Foreign Language Acquisition, New York, January 15–16, 1981b. To appear in *Annals of the New York Academy of Sciences.*

Long, M. H. Native speaker/non-native speaker conversation and the negotiation of comprehensible input. Paper to appear (in German translation) in special issue on second language acquisition of W. Klein & J. Weissenborn (Eds.), *Zeitschrift für Literaturwissenchaft und Linguistik,* 1981c.

McHoul, A. The organization of turns at formal talk in the classroom. *Language in Society,* 1978, *7,* 183–213.

Mehan, H. "What time is it, Denise?": Asking known information questions in classroom discourse. *Theory into Practice,* 1979, *18,* 4.

Mishler, E. Studies in dialogue and discourse: II. Types of discourse initiated by and sustained through questioning. *Journal of Psycholinguistic Research,* 1975, *4,* 2, 99–121.

Philips, S. U. Participant structures and communicative competence: Warm Springs children in community and classroom. In C. Cazden, V. P. John, & D. Hymes (Eds.), *Functions of Language in the Classroom.* New York: Teachers College Press, 1972, 370–394.

Sacks, H., Schegloff, E., & Jefferson, G. A simplest systematics for the organization of turn-taking for conversation. *Language,* 1974, *50,* 696–735.

Sato, C. J. Ethnic styles in classroom discourse. In M. Hines & W. Rutherford (Eds.), *On TESOL '81.* Washington, D.C.: TESOL, 1981.

Seliger, H. W. Does practice make perfect?: A study of interaction patterns and L2 competence. *Language Learning,* 1977, *27,* 2, 263–278.

Sinclair, J. McH., & Coulthard, R. M. *Towards an Analysis of Discourse. The English Used by Teachers and Pupils.* London: Oxford University Press, 1975.

Winne, P. H. Experiments relating teachers' use of higher cognitive questions to student achievement. *Review of Educational Research,* 1979, *49,* 1, 13–50.

Questions for Discussion and Activities

1. In Table 1, Long and Sato provide data of the functions of questions in the six individual lessons. Are the patterns they find *across* the six teachers borne out in each of the six classrooms, or is there a significant amount of variability?

2. Data in Table 1 suggest that the interactional structure in NS-NNS conversation in and out of classrooms differs in additional ways to those the researchers focus upon. Conduct separate chi-square tests to determine whether the numbers of comprehension checks, clarification requests, and confirmation checks in the two corpora differ significantly ($\alpha = .05$). How do you interpret your results?

3. Along what other dimensions might teachers' questions be classified? What would be the potential of such classifications for explaining some aspect of second language acquisition or use in classrooms?

4. Tape-record a lesson in a content classroom and transcribe the data. Quantify the question data in your corpus using Long and Sato's categories, and then compare your findings with theirs for ESL lessons. What hypotheses about the functions of questions in the two types of instruction seem justified on the basis of your pilot study?

5. What gains (if any) can you foresee in combining, as Long and Sato have done, the study of linguistic input to second language acquirers with study of the interactional structure of NS-NNS conversation?

6. What variables would you hypothesize are related to the interactional structure of NS-NNS conversation in and out of classrooms? Why should they be related? Consider, for example, speaker and interlocutor variables, such as age, sex, and language proficiency, as well as task and setting.

7. Design a study to test one of the predicted relationships you identified in answer to question 6.

8. Conduct a pilot version of the study you designed in Number 7. Revise your research design in light of your results and any problems identified by the pilot study.

13

Assessing Global Second Language Proficiency[1]

Diane Larsen-Freeman

The purpose of this chapter is to present some of the recent studies we have conducted in our attempt to establish a second language index of development. This index would be a developmental yardstick against which global (i.e., not skill nor item specific) second language proficiency could be gauged.

With the aid of an index, second language acquisition researchers could report a much more precise, objective description of their subjects' L2 proficiency than what the labels "beginning," "intermediate," and "advanced" currently allow. I have advanced several arguments (Larsen-Freeman, 1976) to demonstrate the need for precision in this area, not the least of which is acknowledging the fact that different factors influence the L2 acquisition process depending upon the level of the learners' proficiency. This index would also be of use to language program adminstrators who would obtain a reliable means of placing L2 learners in classes appropriate to the learners' level of proficiency. Second language teachers, too, stand to gain if such an index could be constructed, since they might then possess a way of measuring any change in overall proficiency of their students over the course of a term.

What we have been attempting to do in order to derive these benefits is to find an objective, easily applied measure with which to assess English as a second language proficiency. Our hope was that if we could define an ESL index that was not based upon the structure of English itself, we might be able to apply the same developmental index to other target languages.

The two studies we have published (Larsen-Freeman and Strom, 1977; Larsen-Freeman, 1978) were based on analyses of ESL learners' writing. In the 1977 pilot study we examined forty-eight compositions written by UCLA ESL students representing different L1 backgrounds and English proficiencies. We independently and impressionistically divided the forty-eight compositions into five quality categories: poor, fair, average, good, and excellent. Because we essentially agreed on the quality of each composition, we next tried to identify the features that made each group of compositions unique, i.e., distinct from the others.

We analyzed the compositions for organizational features, control of grammatical structures and vocabulary, and many other characteristics; however, in order to satisfy our criteria of objectivity, reliability, ease of application, and universality, we found that the best discrimination measures were the average number of words written per T-unit and the total number of error-free T-units written per composition.

Kellogg Hunt (1965), a first language acquisition researcher, first devised the construct of a T-unit. "Very simply, T-units slice a passage up into the shortest possible units which are grammatically allowable to be punctuated as sentences. The T-unit can be described as one main clause plus whatever clauses, phrases and words happen to be attached to or embedded within it." (Street, 1971, p. 13) So, for example, the sentence "I've got a dog and his name is Blue," would be segmented into two T-units because it is a compound sentence with two independent clauses (*and* is counted with the second main clause); whereas "I've got a dog named Blue," would constitute a single T-unit.

Encouraged by the fact that we had found two objective measures which appeared to discriminate among compositions of various qualities, we next undertook a large-scale study of compositions written by ESL students (Larsen-Freeman, 1978). We performed an extensive quantitative and qualitative analysis of each of 212 compositions. From these analyses we found that the measures that best discriminated among different proficiency levels and that increased linearly with proficiency levels were the average number of words per T-unit, the percentage of error-free T-units, the average number of words per error-free T-unit, and the total number of error-free T-units.

The reader will note that two new performance variables, both involving the notion of "error-free," were found to work in this study. We had discovered (like Monroe for French, 1975, Gaies for ESL, 1976, and Cooper for German, 1976) that T-unit length served to discriminate among ESL learners of varying proficiencies. However, we also found that more powerful measures (i.e., ones giving us both higher correlations with another measure of proficiency and giving us greater variance or dispersion of scores among proficiency levels) were measures acknowledging that L2 learners (unlike older L1 learners) regularly commit lexical, syntactic, and morphological errors.

We concurred with Gaies who contended that subjects' length of T-units alone might not be sufficient evidence for ascertaining their proficiency level. Gaies observed that "some account must be taken of structural errors which occur in L2 learners' writing, for they, too, are an indication of incomplete syntactic control, just as much perhaps as is oversimplified (i.e., short) sentence structure." (1976, p. 7)

Thus, our performance variable of average number of words per error-free T-unit which measured learners' success at both syntactic elaboration and error elimination seemed intuitively and empirically to have a great deal of appeal as a basis for an index of development. We decided at this point to determine if performance variables based on T-units would be applicable to oral data. What follows is a discussion of our next study which involved analyses of the speech of ESL learners.

Study of Speech Data

Subjects

For this study twenty-five subjects were used: five each from each of five different ESL proficiency levels. The subjects were each assigned to one of these levels according to their performance on the UCLA English as a Second Language Placement Examination (ESLPE)—a statistically well-established instrument, having a high internal consistency reliability of .97.[2] Those subjects who placed in Level 1 had scored the lowest on the exam, thus indicating they required a great deal of ESL instruction before being permitted to freely join the academic mainstream, those who placed in Level 5 were those subjects who scored sufficiently highly on the placement exam to have all ESL requirements waived.

These subjects, both graduate and undergraduate students at UCLA, represented eleven different L1 backgrounds as follows: seven Chinese-speakers, five Farsi-speakers, three Spanish-speakers, two French-speakers, two Russian-speakers, one speaker each from Arabic, Greek, Indonesian, Japanese, Korean and Tagalog native languages.

Procedure

Each subject was given four oral tasks to perform. They were administered individually in the following order:

I. Interview

Each subject was asked his/her name, native country, how long s/he had been in the United States, what his/her major was, how s/he had been studying English, and what his/her future plans were. These were the basic questions asked of all subjects. Subjects were also asked follow-up questions embroidering on their responses to these basic questions.

II. Picture Composition Task

Using four picture series from Donn Byrne's book, *Progressive Picture Compositions*, each subject was asked to relate the chain of events in each of the four picture series. Prior to each subject's beginning the task, the experimenter provided a model using different picture series.

III. Conversation

Using anything the experimenter picked up of interest from the student's comments during the interview, the experimenter initiated a conversation with each student. The other topics brought in and discussed at this time were:
- the subject's impressions of Los Angeles
- any travel the subject had done while in the United States
- an elaboration of the composition topic each subject had written about earlier which was "Should a person live in a large city or a small town?"

IV. Story Retelling

The experimenter read a story to each subject once (a slightly modified version of "The Brahman and His Two Wives"—from *International Folktales I* by Binner) and each subject was asked to retell the story using his/her own words.

These four tasks were performed by each subject with one of two experimenters doing the administration. Each subject's responses were tape-recorded and later transcribed for analysis. The analysis was in part performed based upon the O'Donnell, Griffin, and Norris (1967) procedure for analyzing speech samples.

Results

Interview. For the first task, the interview, we conducted an error analysis of the transcripts to see if the total number of errors or different error types were useful in discriminating among proficiency levels. We were not optimistic about these since we had used this same tack when we analyzed writing samples (Larsen-Freeman and Strom, 1977) and found little of significance, but we didn't want to overlook any possibility.

We devised a classification schema consisting of twenty-nine categories of errors. Each error we found in the transcripts was placed into one of these categories. We discovered that the different groups of subjects essentially committed the same types of errors. Errors involving prepositions, articles, and verb tense were most prevalent. The other categories were not as consistently ranked after these, but errors in the top ten error types for each level did account for approximately 80% of the total number of errors. The other 20% of the errors were accounted for by the remaining nineteen error types.

Curiously enough, as far as the interview was concerned, even the sheer number of errors committed by the different groups did not distinguish among proficiency levels. While Level 1 committed 94 errors and Level 2, 42, Level 3 committed 67, Level 4, 78, and Level 5, 76. Thus, there was no reduction in the number of errors made as proficiency level increased. One explanation for this surprising finding is that, although we asked the same questions of each subject, and each interview lasted approximately the same length of time, the more advanced subjects elaborated each answer more. In fact, they produced more utterances,[3] thus creating more occasions for errors to be made.

Picture Composition. For Task II, the picture composition task, we also conducted an error analysis. This time, perhaps due to this being a more structured task, the number of errors did decline as the proficiency level increased. Level 1 committed 207 errors, Level 2, 168, Level 3, 134, Level 4, 130, and Level 5, 88.

It is also interesting to note that while errors involving prepositions and articles were still among the most prevalent error types, the error types of verb tense, subject-verb agreement, and lexical choice surpassed them in frequency of occurrence. Apparently when given a picture composition to relate, a more structured task than an interview, avoidance is more difficult and error types of a different kind surface. Of course, it is also possible that it is easier to discern errors of a certain type when the context is clearly defined.

Let us now turn to the quantitative analyses we conducted. We first examined the transcripts of the subjects' description of each of the picture series and calculated the following: the total number of error-free T-units, the average number of words per T-unit, the average number of words per error-free T-unit, and the percentage of error-free T-units. To establish the concurrent validity[4] of any or all of these measures, we next correlated these four performance variables (for each picture series and for the combined picture series) with our subjects' level of proficiency as defined by their score on the ESLPE. (See Table 1.)

As can be seen in Table 1, we obtained significant correlations[5] for all four of our performance variables. We chose to probe the average number of words per error-free T-unit variable further since there were more significant correlations for it (and a much higher correlation for the combined picture score) than for the average number of words per T-unit variable. The other variable we chose to explore further was the percentage of error-free T-units, since it correlated the highest of all the performance variables with the ESL levels. The total number of error-free T-units variable also correlated significantly with the ESL levels for most of the picture series, but since an individual's total would be task dependent

Table 1. Correlations between ESL levels and Performance Variables from Picture Composition Task

	Picture Series A	Picture Series B	Picture Series C	Picture Series D	Combined pictures
Total number of error-free T-units	.2426 S = .121	.5673** S = .002	.2411 S = .123	.4108* S = .021	.4811** S = .007
Average number of words/ T-unit	.5209** S = .004	.0914 S = .332	.0402 S = .424	.3288 S = .054	.3570* S = .040
Average number of words/ error-free T-unit	.4093* S = .021	.4988** S = .006	.4213* S = .018	.3302 S = .053	.5725** S = .001
Percent of error-free T-units	.4316* S = .016	.5916** S = .001	.5432** S = .003	.5271** S = .003	.6745** S = .000

*p < .05   **p < .01

(i.e., it would vary with the length of his or her output), we decided it wasn't worthwhile to examine this variable further. We wanted a measure which could be applied to most any output, independent of length or task.

Focusing on average length of error-free T-unit and the percentage of error-free T-units, we next conducted analyses of variance.[6] (See Tables 2 and 3.)

From Table 2, it can be seen that an n of 5 per group was too small to produce a significant analysis of variance. Curious as to what size n one would need to obtain significant results, we next divided our twenty-five subjects into two groups—those above the mean ESLPE score and those below it. When we reduced the groups to two, we did indeed discover that significant differences resulted. Heartened by this finding, we next conducted an ANOVA with three groups, each having an n of 8. A significant F ratio was obtained.

Table 2. ANOVA—Average Number of Words/Error-free T-unit (Combined Pictures)

5 groups				3 groups				2 groups			
level	n	mean	SD	level	n	mean	SD	level	n	mean	SD
1	5	5.76	2.20	1	8	6.69	.97	1	14	6.62	1.80
2	5	7.07	1.11	2	8	7.10	1.45	2	11	8.34	2.02
3	5	6.94	1.79	3	8	8.97	2.03				
4	5	8.18	2.48								
5	5	8.93	1.57								

F ratio = 2.07 F ratio = 4.93 F ratio = 5.07
F prob. = .123 F prob. = .0176* F prob. = .034*

Post hoc analysis:	t obs
L1 vs. L2 NS	.93
L2 vs. L3 SIG	4.32
L1 vs. L3 SIG	5.11
	t crit = 2.61

*$p < .05$

Table 3. ANOVA—Percentage of Error-free T-units (Combined Pictures)

level	n	mean	SD	Post hoc analysis	
1	5	28.52	14.5	L1 vs. L2	NS
2	5	40.51	9.4	L1 vs. L3	NS
3	5	40.26	12.9	L1 vs. L4	SIG
4	5	51.80	15.9	L1 vs. L5	SIG
5	5	63.34	14.5	L2 vs. L3	NS
				L2 vs. L4	NS
				L2 vs. L5	SIG
	F ratio = 2.07			L3 vs. L4	NS
	F prob. = .007**			L3 vs. L5	SIG
				L4 vs. L5	NS

**$p < .01$

Next we applied the Sheffe method of post-hoc analysis to see whether each group was significantly different from the others. This analysis revealed that groups 2 and 3 and groups 1 and 3 were significantly different from each other.

We were able to obtain a significant F ratio with five groups for the percentage of error-free T-unit variable. Applying the Sheffe method of post-hoc analysis, we discovered that four out of a possible ten pair combinations were significantly different, all involving nonadjacent pairs.

Conversation. We had discovered in our earlier study of ESL students' compositions that sheer length of output was distinctive. In general, more advanced learners tended to produce longer compositions than less proficient learners. However, at a certain developmental point, there was a leveling off and the most proficient learners did not necessarily produce the longest compositions. We applied a measure of length (total number of words) to the conversation task to see if this characterization would hold true for the oral modality as well. (See Table 4.)

Although we didn't achieve significance with any of our ANOVA's, it is interesting to note that the general pattern regarding length is the same as it was for the composition, i.e., the length of speaking increases gradually for the first four groups (although there is some backsliding between the first and second groups), and then length drops off with the fifth group. We speculated with regards to writing that the top group perhaps didn't feel the need to demonstrate their competence by sheer volume of output, and instead confined their energies more to refining the final product. Perhaps this is the case here as well.

Table 4.   ANOVA—Total Number of Words

5 groups				3 groups				2 groups			
level	n	mean	SD	level	n	mean	SD	level	n	mean	SD
1	5	293.79	108.93	1	8	252.37	112.19	1	14	285.50	151.00
2	5	234.20	121.02	2	8	370.12	172.70	2	11	381.81	162.70
3	5	327.20	205.21	3	8	376.25	180.73				
4	5	424.59	152.72								
5	5	359.59	193.31								
	F ratio = .981				F ratio = 1.558				F ratio = 2.340		
	F. prob. = .44				F prob. = .23				F prob. = .13		

Story Retelling. We conducted basically the same quantitative analysis that we did for the picture composition task for the story-retelling task, beginning by correlating the four performance variables with the subjects' ESL level as determined by their score on the ESLPE. (See Table 5.)

Taking the average number of words per error-free T-unit as one of the measures with the highest correlation and as the measure that best satisfies the criteria mentioned earlier, we again performed an analysis of variance. (See Table 6.) Although none of the analyses were significant, the analysis with two groups was not too far off. Furthermore, we can see from each analysis that the mean length of error-free T-unit did increase in length with each increase in proficiency level.

Table 5.   Correlation Between ESL Levels and
Performance Variables from Story Retelling
Task

Total # of error-free T-units	.5031	S = .005**
Average # of words/T-unit	.2710	S = .095
Average # of words/error-free T-unit	.5057	S = .005**
% of error-free T-units	.5295	S = .003**

**p < .01

Table 6.   ANOVA—Average Number of Words/Error-free T-unit

5 groups				3 groups				2 groups			
level	n	mean	SD	level	n	mean	SD	level	n	mean	SD
1	5	7.39	2.06	1	8	7.83	1.68	1	14	7.77	1.67
2	5	7.56	1.84	2	8	8.28	0.84	2	11	9.29	2.98
3	5	8.21	1.04	3	8	9.73	3.41				
4	5	8.44	1.03								
5	5	10.61	4.10								

F ratio = 1.552	F ratio = 1.565	F ratio = 2.608
F prob. = .2257	F prob. = .2326	F prob. = .1200

Table 7.   ANOVA—
Percentage of Error-
free T-units

5 groups			
level	n	mean	SD
1	5	29.13	14.5
2	5	37.08	10.6
3	5	33.92	9.7
4	5	51.34	16.1
5	5	55.72	76.3

F ratio = 2.42
F prob. = .0822

When we calculated the ANOVA for five groups for the percentage of error-free T-units variable, the F ratio was close to being significant at the .05 level. Unfortunately there was an exception to the linear progression we had observed earlier with level 2 having a higher percentage of error-free T-units than level 3.

Discussion

From all available evidence, it appears that the average length of T-units is a satisfactory index of syntactic maturity for L1 acquisition. Yet we have learned from our own research that a more powerful measure of L2 proficiency is the length of *error-free* T-units.[7] L2 learners are conceivably capable of producing T-units of some length before they can be said to have truly acquired the L2. By assessing a learner's proficiency through a quantitative analysis of a learner's *error-free* T-units, a learner's score cannot be artificially inflated by his or her simply stringing words together. Even this measure, however, seems to work well to discriminate only among groups of subjects having an n of a certain size. There seemed to be some hope that the percentage of error-free T-units would serve as the basis for an index of development. Of course, as we have seen, this variable does not discriminate among ESL proficiency levels equally well in all cases either. We felt we had made some progress in our search for an index of development, but wanted to further refine our procedures so that we were left with an index that worked for groups of even a small n.

We therefore decided next to turn once again to written data to see if an analysis of a controlled writing sample (elicited through a set task) would yield better proficiency discrimination results than analysis of a "free" composition. Concurrently, we conducted another study of written data to see if our performance variables applied to samples of writing obtained from the same learners at different points of time would reveal a gain presumed to reflect the learners' overall gain in ESL proficiency.

Study of Controlled versus Free Writing Samples

Up until this study, all of the written data that we analyzed were generated from students writing freely on an assigned composition topic. Holding the thought in mind that a more structured task might be even more discriminating among proficiency levels for small n groups, we decided to administer a rewrite exercise. In this exercise, the subjects are given a passage comprised of single clause sentences and asked to rewrite the passage in a better way. Our reason for believing that this might be a superior method for assessing proficiency is due to the fact that all subjects would be writing about the same thing, thus eliminating variations in writing because one subject had greater knowledge about a particular topic than another when both subjects were at the same general proficiency level.

Subjects and procedure

We decided to employ the rewrite passage that O'Donnell developed (as discussed in Hunt, 1970) to investigate the development of syntactic maturity in the writing of school children and adults. The exercise, known as the "Aluminum Passage," consists of thirty-two single-clause sentences of connected discourse. For example, the first three sentences in the passage are: "Aluminum is a metal. It is abundant. It has many uses." Subjects are instructed to rewrite the passage in a better way. For instance, a better way of writing these first three sentences might be "Aluminum, an abundant metal, has many uses." A subject responding thusly would have produced a T-unit seven words long rather than three T-units three to four words long.

We administered the aluminum rewrite passage to UCLA students studying ESL. A total of 109 students, heterogeneous with regards to language background, field of study, and academic status, took part in this study.

Soon after we administered the rewrite passage to these subjects, we also collected a sample of their "free" writing in order to have a basis of comparison with the rewrite passage.[8] All the subjects wrote on the same topic for this free-writing exercise.[9] We next analyzed both samples of writing for four perform-ance variables: the total number of words produced, the average number of words per T-unit, the percentage of error-free T-units, and the average number of words per error-free T-unit.

The levels listed in Table 8 each represent a different ESL proficiency adhering to the same definitions used in the speech data study.

Results

In Table 8, looking first at the sheer average length of the sample given the controlled writing task, we notice an obvious clustering at the upper levels. Nevertheless, the number of words produced does increase with proficiency level, and an analysis of variance proved to be significant at the .01 level. Turning next to the free-writing analysis, we note that for the same feature, total number of words, the ANOVA again proved significant at the .01 level. Also, happily we note, there is no obvious clustering under this condition as there was with the controlled writing. This, of course, is in part due to the fact that the word limit was less restricted with the free composition.

When we turn to the average number of words per T-unit (the measure Hunt and others reported as being effective in the L1 literature), we find for both samples the measures operated in the predicted fashion, i.e., they increased with

Table 8. Four Performance Variables for Controlled and Free Writing Samples

		Controlled Writing							
		Total # of words		Average # of words/T-unit		% of error-free T-units		Average # of words/error-free T-unit	
level	n	mean	SD	mean	SD	mean	SD	mean	SD
1	8	88.38	29.87	6.22	.90	74.1	17.1	5.64	1.04
2	13	111.31	31.68	7.45	1.72	85.2	13.7	7.55	2.84
3	30	115.33	17.34	9.34	2.31	78.2	13.4	8.43	2.33
4	59	115.65	20.79	9.95	1.76	76.3	16.5	9.34	1.96
		Free Writing							
		Total # of words		Average # of words/T-unit		% of error-free T-units		Average # of words/error-free T-unit	
level	n	mean	SD	mean	SD	mean	SD	mean	SD
2	13	51.08	26.43	13.73	4.57	41.7	37.8	8.36	9.67
3	30	84.73	24.42	17.11	3.72	42.7	30.3	12.61	7.35
4	59	110.12	36.77	17.21	4.86	38.4	24.9	11.36	7.18

each level of proficiency. Furthermore, there were significant differences between levels 1 and 2 and 3 under the controlled condition and between levels 1 and 2 in the free. However, neither task discriminates significantly between the top two groups. It is also interesting to note the disparity in length of T-units which the two tasks produced. The free composition resulted in T-units almost twice as long as the controlled. On the other hand, the T-units produced under the controlled condition were twice as accurate as those produced in the free compositions as can be seen in the next column, an accuracy measure, the average percentage of error-free T-units in each sample.

Although we had found this measure useful in the past for discriminating among proficiency levels in writing samples, this time for the controlled writing samples the percentages do not increase with proficiency, level 2 having the highest percentage. The groups under the free-writing condition exhibited little variance with regard to the percentage of error-free T-units.

With regard to our final measure, the average number of words per error-free T-unit, we again found, as you would expect from the previous measure, that subjects produced longer T-units when given a topic on which to write freely. The length difference was significant between levels 2 and 3 for the free-writing task; however, level 4 subjects produced shorter error-free T-units than level 3. With the controlled task, the length increases again in the desired direction, but only levels 1 and 2 were found to be significantly different.

Discussion

What we are left with after all this is the realization that both conditions elicit some significant difference among proficiency levels—but not in all cases. The controlled writing task did not seem particularly superior to the free composition in discriminating among proficiency levels. This is not really disappointing since we would prefer to have an index task independent—something one can apply to any sample of writing, not just that generated by a particular rewrite passage.

With the exception of the percentage of error-free T-units variable, the other variables operated by and large according to the pattern we had come to expect: as the proficiency level of the subjects increased, so did the total number of words they wrote, the average length of their T-units, and the average length of their error-free T-units. The only disconcerting contradiction to these general trends occurred with the reversal between levels 3 and 4 for the average number of words per error-free T-unit under the free-writing condition. This was particularly disappointing because it was this variable, readers will recall, that we had earlier decided (and which the research of others had confirmed) was the most promising measure on which to base an index of development.

Another thing we had hoped for, but failed to find, was a greater dispersion among the scores for different levels for each of the performance variables. We pointed out above that for some of the variables only minimal or nonsignificant differences were disclosed between adjacent levels.

Simultaneous with the study just discussed, we conducted another study we wish to report on here. This final study dealt with the effect of time on these variables when the subjects were receiving ESL instruction.

Study of Writing Over Time

What we had hoped to find from this study, of course, was that each variable increased relative to the increasing proficiency of the subjects during their course of instruction.

Procedure and subjects

In order to determine if the expected increase did occur, we collected writing samples from a level 4 ESL class periodically over the duration of a ten-week term. We collected five compositions[10] from each of twenty-three ESL students, each composition written at an interval of approximately two weeks. We next calculated the same four performance variables as in the earlier study for these 115 samples of writing. We then performed repeated measure ANOVA's for each of these variables.

Results

For the variable, the total number of words written in each composition, the ANOVA proved to be significant. There were significant differences in length among these five compositions. However, from Table 9 we see that the total number of words measured failed to accurately portray what was hopefully an increase in proficiency over time. If we were to plot this variable on a graph with words on the ordinate and time the abscissa, we would see a line with peaks and valleys, not the upward slope that we sought.

The average number of words per T-unit, on the other hand, does meet our criterion of increasing length over time, and using a repeated measure ANOVA was determined to be significant. It can be noted the peak here was reached with level 4—the length dropping off once again with level 5. This was initially troubling because we didn't want to discover that our measures fluctuated depending on the topic of the composition. Fortunately, this was not apparently

Table 9.   Four Performance Variables for Study of Writing Over Time

Time	n	Total # of words		Average # of words/T-unit		% of error-free T-units		Average # of words/error-free T-unit	
		mean	SD	mean	SD	mean	SD	mean	SD
1	23	329.96	108.10	13.77	3.02	59.7	23.1	12.08	2.60
2	23	372.00	179.66	13.92	1.97	55.9	20.7	12.17	3.02
3	23	317.22	120.01	14.82	3.39	56.9	26.5	11.94	2.35
4	23	407.13	209.26	16.99	3.49	70.3	18.7	16.15	4.69
5	23	353.00	179.13	15.37	3.39	60.7	21.7	12.58	3.47

the case here, since of the five compositions, number 4 was a take-home assignment in which the students were to write about an invention. They were permitted to use outside references and many did as evidenced by the sources listed following the compositions. With the aid of references, subjects were apparently able to produce longer T-units—longer than their ability permitted on an in-class composition.

Turning to the next column, we see that the accuracy measure of percentage of error-free T-units was somewhat erratic, i.e., variable over time. The percentages were relatively homogeneous, and were not correlated with the increasing proficiency of the groups.

As for the average number of words per error-free T-unit variable, this measure once again generally conformed to the expected pattern; the exception here was where there was a slight decline in length with level 3. This slackening off might be explained by looking at subject 7's performance. For some inexplicable reason, subject 7 did not conform to the general pattern at all, writing uncharacteristically short T-units on the third composition. If for the sake of illustration we omit subject 7's performance from our calculations, we get a smoother, more regular linear increase in the average number of words per T-unit and the average number of words per error-free T-unit for the remaining 22 subjects. This can be seen in Table 10. In both cases (with and without subject 7), the ANOVA's were statistically significant.

Discussion

For two of the four performance variables we calculated, the average number of words per T-unit and the average number of words per error-free T-unit, the means did increase over time. If the take-home composition (number 4) is discounted, we note that a linear progression did occur. It is somewhat disturbing, however, that subject 7 did not conform to the general pattern since it would be highly desirable to have each individual in the study exhibit the same behavior as the group as a whole. Perhaps such a goal, to have a measure

Table 10.   Four Performance Variables
for Study of Writing over Time
(without subject 7)

Time	n	Average # of words/T-unit		Average # of words/error-free T-unit	
		mean	SD	mean	SD
1	22	13.66	3.06	11.86	2.48
2	22	13.85	1.99	12.03	3.04
3	22	15.16	3.12	12.14	2.23
4	22	16.45	2.58	15.58	4.09
5	22	15.74	3.02	12.92	3.21

sensitive to all individuals, is too lofty to be attained. Nevertheless, we were pleased that two of our measures did seem to reflect an improving proficiency on the part of the subjects who took part in this study.

Conclusion

The studies reported on here were meant to exemplify the process we have followed in our pursuit of an L2 index of development. We have used these studies to address three different questions:

1. Would the measures we had found earlier to be successful for discrim-inating among writing abilities of ESL learners be equally applicable to oral data?
2. Do written data elicited through a controlled task give us a more accurate portrayal of ESL proficiency than data elicited through "free" composi-tions?
3. Do the performance variables or measures we have identified increase over time when the subjects are receiving ESL instruction?

As is usually the case with L2 acquisition studies, the results we obtained from our studies were mixed. We discovered that sometimes a performance variable, like the percentage of error-free T-units, worked well in one study (e.g., the study we had conducted earlier in which we analyzed 212 compositions written by ESL learners), but not in another (e.g., in the controlled versus the free writing study, the percentage of error-free T-units did not increase linearly with proficiency level). Sometimes a performance variable discriminated significantly between adjacent proficiency levels and sometimes it did not. For instance, in the oral data study when the subjects were divided into three groups, the average number of words per error-free T-unit variable discriminated between level 1 and level 3, but not between level 1 and level 2. Sometimes a performance variable did not distinguish between levels with small n's (e.g., in the oral data study on the story-retelling task, for the average number of words per error-free T-unit for three levels with n's of eight) and sometimes it did (e.g., within the same study on the picture composition task for three levels with n's of eight). We also noted that even when our performance variables appeared to work well for a group of learners (i.e., the average number of words per error-free T-unit in the writing over time study), there was an exception with subject 7 deviating from the norm. Thus, this measure is apparently not always sensitive to individual differences.

With regard to the failure of our measures to discriminate between adjacent levels, however, it should be remembered that we were dealing with a fairly homogeneous population—UCLA students studying ESL. Perhaps given the whole spectrum of ESL learners, the ability of our measures to discriminate between proficiency levels would be more apparent.

Perhaps we will find that the assessment of proficiency of any group of L2 learners requires a two-step procedure. The first step will be to use one performance variable to make a gross estimate of a learner's overall L2 proficiency. Once an individual learner has been categorized as "beginning," for example, a second step might invove the use of another performance variable to more precisely identify his or her proficiency. The performance variable used in the second step of this procedure might differ depending upon the initial category into which a learner was placed.

It is possible that T-unit length is not immune to influence from the L1 as much as we had hoped. It might be the case that a person's tendency to write long T-units in his or her L1 can be positively transferred to an L2.

Perhaps it is also the case that performance variables involving T-units will be found to work well only for English as a second language but not for Spanish, French, Chinese. etc., as second languages.

Perhaps we will learn that measures involving errors only—like the total number of errors in a composition, or the total number of error-free T-units in a composition—work well if we set a limit on the length of a composition to which we will apply these measures. For example, we might calculate the total number of error-free T-units in the first 200 words of a composition.

Perhaps it will be the case that learners can be taught to "beat the system" and learn to produce longer T-units than their level of proficiency would lead us to expect. However, if we use the length of error-free T-units as our measure, this is not likely to occur since a learner probably would not be able to produce longer error-free T-units than his or her ability permits.

While only the third study discussed in this chapter was carried out directly with data collected in the classroom, the implications for classroom research should be obvious. The classroom setting provides an ideal environment in which to collect data that will address many of the concerns cited above. After all, it is they who are most intimately involved with the classroom, i.e., teachers, program administrators, and classroom researchers who would realize the benefits if an index of development could be constructed.

The questions involved in the construction of an index are formidable. Nevertheless, one should bear in mind the thought that these questions are empirical. Given enough time, patience, or researchers willing to invest in this project, each issue in turn should be able to be resolved. The rewards for the investment could be significant for the construction of an index of development would have enormous value for teachers, administrators, researchers, and learners in our field.

Notes

1. I wish to thank Virginia Strom, Meredith Pike, Diane Holdich, Hossein Farhady, and Kathy Maston for their help with the studies reported on in this chapter.

2. The reliability of a test refers to its dependability. For example, we might want to know if it is likely that we will obtain similar results with the same test when administered at two different times. Internal consistency reliability indicates the degree to which subjects score comparably on different parts of a test taken at one time.

3. Such a finding brings to mind the work of a group of researchers at Saint Louis University (Kowal, O'Connell, O'Brien, and Bryant, 1975) who found an inverse relationship between pause length/frequency during an oral reading task and the subjects' linguistic proficiency. Apparently our subjects of higher proficiency paused less often and for shorter spans of time since they were able to generate more utterances in the same amount of interview time than the less proficient subjects. Pause length and frequency deserve further attention as possible measures of proficiency upon which to base an index of development. It should be noted, however, that these same researchers did not find that these two variables had the same inverse relationship with proficiency when the subjects were asked to retell a story. Furthermore, the instrumentation necessary to measure pause length would probably prohibit this variable from satisfying our criterion of ease of applicability. I am grateful to Teresa de Johnson for bringing the work of these researchers to my attention.

4. Validity in general refers to the degree to which a test measures what it purports to measure. We attempted to validate our measures by comparing the scores they yielded with those obtained from the ESLPE.

5. John Oller (personal communication) has pointed out that even though many of the correlations are *significant,* they are not *substantial.* For example, the correlation of the ESLPE with the average number of words per error-free T-unit for the combined pictures (.5725) is statistically significant at the .01 level. Nevertheless, this correlation only shows a variance overlap between these two measures of .33, discouragingly low. While Oller's point is well-taken, what he offers in place of length of T-units as measures of proficiency (cloze tests, dictations, oral interviews) are not acceptable for our purposes since we want to establish an index of development which is instrument-free. This is essential for several reasons:

1. While individual cloze tests have been proven to be useful for discriminating among different proficiency levels of a given group of L2 learners, the numerical score that any one learner receives varies from cloze test to cloze test depending upon the passage chosen. We note along this regard, Alderson's (1969) admonition that "individual cloze tests vary greatly as measures of ESL proficiency." (p. 225) We would like to discover a measure that results in roughly the same score for a learner of a certain proficiency level regardless of the writing sample or speech sample that is used. This is not to say that a subject's score based on an analysis of his or her composition and his or her speech sample will be equivalent (because they won't be), but within any given modality, a subject's scores should be consistent. If we find that a subject's T-units vary in length depending upon the topic of a composition, then, of course, this will prove troublesome. We await the results of a study currently being conducted by Mehlia and Schrek for some evidence as to how topic-independent T-unit length is.

2. We would like to establish an L2 index of development that works equally well with populations of differing L1 backgrounds, ages, educational backgrounds, etc. A cloze test probably would not be useful for ascertaining the proficiency level of very young L2 learners, for example. A sample of their speech, however, might well be suitable for calculating their proficiency level with our measures.

3. We do not want to create an index that is based upon a standardized test which is not readily accessible. What we hope to do is design a simple technique that is available for use by classroom teachers, second language acquisition researchers, etc.

4. Quantitative assessments of the type we are proposing are totally reliable. There is little judgment to be made on the part of the researcher. A simple count of words after T-unit or error-free T-unit boundaries are established is something which requires a little practice, but then becomes rather routine.

5. T-unit analysis is something which can be applied post hoc. All one would need would be a sample of the writing (or speech) of the subjects which had been studied.

6. This type of measure could also be applied by one researcher to another researcher's data if the former were interested in comparing his/her findings with those of the latter.

All this is not to say that some performance variable based on T-units will prove to be the best contender for an index of development. All we can say for the moment is that for the qualities we are seeking, it holds the most promise at this time.

6. In this case, analysis of variance is simply a method for determining if the differences found between levels is due to chance or due to one of our performance variables. If the ANOVA is said to be significant, we conclude that the differences among the levels could not be due to chance alone.

7. Subsequent to our study, Perkins (1979) conducted a study in which he examined a number of objective measures of compositions that have been claimed to discriminate among various levels of writing proficiency. He, too, found that those variables which took the elimination of error production into account (total error-free T-units per composition, number of words in error-free T-units, errors per T-unit, and total number of errors) discriminated best among levels of writing ability established by holistic evaluation. This same finding is underscored in a study by Vann who reported, "Thus for written data, the error-free T-unit, especially its mean length, appears to be the best indicator of adult foreign language proficiency." (1979, p. 8)

8. Unfortunately, we were unable to obtain a sample of the "free" writing from the eight subjects in level 1 proximate enough in time to when the controlled writing sample was elicited.

9. The topic of the composition was: Should ESL students receive letter grades in their ESL courses or be evaluated by a pass/not pass system?

10. The titles of the five compositions in chronological order were: Three Wishes, The Rights of Non-Smokers, The Advantages and Disadvantages of _____, An Invention, Advice You Would Give an American Who Wanted to Visit Your Country.

References

Alderson, J. C. The cloze procedure and proficiency in English as a foreign language. *TESOL Quarterly,* 1979, *13,* 2, 219—227.

Binner, V. O. *International Folktales I.* New York: Thomas Y. Crowell, 1967.

Byrne, D. *Progressive Picture Compositions.* London: Longman, 1967.

Celce-Murcia, M., Santos, T. On the interlanguage of a native user of American sign language. An expanded version of a paper presented at the Los Angeles Second Language Research Forum, USC, October 6–8, 1978.

Cooper, T. C. Measuring written syntactic patterns of second language learners of German. *Journal of Educational Research,* 1976, *69,* 5, 176–183.

Gaies, S. J. Sentence-combining: A technique for assessing proficiency in a second language. Paper presented at the Conference on Perspectives on Language, University of Louisville, Louisville, Kentucky, May 6–8, 1976.

Hunt, K. W. *Grammatical Structures Written at Three Grade Levels.* NCTE Research Report No. 3. Champaign, Ill.: National Council of Teachers of English, 1965.

Hunt, K. W. Syntactic maturity in school children and adults. *Monographs of the Society for Research in Child Development, 35,* 1 (serial no. 134), 1970.

Kowal, S., O'Connell, D.C., O'Brien, E., & Bryant, E. Temporal aspects of reading aloud and speaking: Three experiments. *American Journal of Psychology,* 1975, *88,* 4; 549–569.

Larsen-Freeman, D. Evidence of the need for a second language acquisition index of development. Paper presented at the Linguistic Society of America Meeting, Oswego, New York, 1976. Later published in W. C. Ritchie (Ed.), *Principles of Second Language Learning and Teaching.* New York: Academic Press, 1978.

Larsen-Freeman, D. An ESL index of development. *TESOL Quarterly,* 1978, *12,* 4, 439–448.

Larsen-Freeman, D., & Strom, V. The construction of a second language acquisition index of development. *Language Learning,* 1977, *27,* 1, 123–134.

Mendelsohn, D. J. The case for considering syntactic maturity in ESL and EFL. To appear in *International Review of Applied Linguistics,* 1982.

Monroe, J. H. 1975. Measuring and enhancing syntactic fluency in French. *The French Review,* 1975, *XLVIII,* 6, 1023–1031.

O'Donnell, R. C., Griffin, W. J., & Norris, R. C. *Syntax of kindergarten and elementary school children: A transformational analysis.* NCTE Research Report No. 8. Champaign, Ill.: National Council of Teachers of English, 1967.

Perkins, K. Using objective measures of attained writing proficiency to discriminate among holistic evaluations. Unpublished manuscript, 1979.

Street, J. H. Readability of UCLA materials used for foreign students. Master's thesis, University of California, Los Angeles, 1971.

Vann, R. J. Oral and written syntactic relationships in second language learning. Paper presented at the TESOL Convention, Boston, Mass., February 27–March 4, 1979.

Questions for Discussion and Activities

1. Think about the factors that contribute to global proficiency in second language. Are there any that come to mind which could be considered as the basis for an index of development? Do they satisfy the criteria discussed in this chapter? If so, how would you go about testing their suitability for measuring global proficiency?

2. Look at samples of student writing at different levels of proficiency. Rank them separately according to the different criteria discussed by the author: (1) organization; (2) control of grammar; (3) richness of vocabulary, and others you might want to consider. How do your rankings compare for the different criteria? What problems do you encounter?

3. Rank the same compositions according to T-units. What do your findings suggest? Do you find a different ranking for the number of T-units *per se* versus the number of error-free T-units? Do you find any difference for first language background in your rankings?

4. In what way are adult L2 learners different from younger L1 learners when considering T-unit length as a criteria for language development?

5. How might you explain Larsen-Freeman's findings regarding sheer number of errors according to level of proficiency?

6. Explain why the number of errors differed for the Picture Composition task and the interview.

7. Discuss Oller's criticism (note 5) of the significance levels described in Table 1 and Larsen-Freeman's response. Why is the T-unit measure more attractive to her than some other criterion for assessing general language proficiency?

8. Why is ANOVA useful for looking at group differences? Consult a statistics book to determine what ANOVA consists of and what assumptions underlie its use.

9. Apply ANOVA to the compositions you graded according to T-units in exercise 2 above. What did you find?

10. What reasons might be hypothesized for the author's findings regarding error-free T-units in the oral sample?

11. Larsen-Freeman's measures did not lead to a device for discriminating between levels of proficiency according to some developmental measure as she had hoped. In spite of this, why do you think such a study is important? What is the relationship between a failure to prove the hypothesis established by the researcher and the discovery of penicillin by Sir Alexander Fleming?